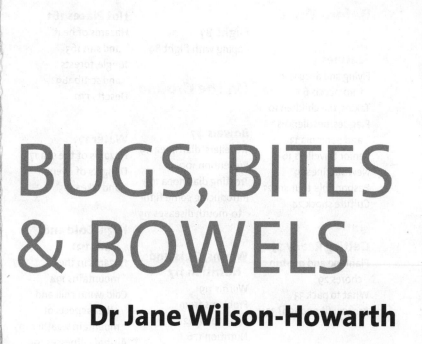

BUGS, BITES & BOWELS

Dr Jane Wilson-Howarth

CONTENTS

Maps

Tables

About the author

Jane Wilson-Howarth trained first in zoology (BSc from Plymouth) and then medicine (BM Southampton), and through her work overseas has maintained a strong interest in parasitology and vector ecology and control. She worked in Asia for 11 years on various health and hygiene education and child-survival programmes for numerous agencies, including in Lombok for the Australian government, in Pakistan for the European Union and World Bank, in Nepal, Bangladesh and India with WaterAid, and in Nepal for USAID. In each location she has acted as GP to her expatriate neighbours and has been involved in various free clinics as a volunteer including in Ladakh, Sri Lanka and Nepal. Since qualifying as a physician, Dr Jane has trained in General Practice, Family Planning and Child Health (DFFP, DCH and DCCH). Her fascination for natural history led to her first expedition to the Himalayas, a six-month trip which provided her with her first intimate experience of histoplasmosis and intestinal worms, and provoked a particular loathing of leeches, ticks and parasites, stimulating a desire to work towards their control. Research in Oxford (MSc Parasitology) has given her a sound academic training, but fieldwork abroad (including leading three expeditions to Peru and Madagascar) has also allowed her to develop practical approaches to research and other work in remote regions where proper resources are wanting; her first book *Lemurs of the Lost World* describes some of these experiences. She has served as a cave rescue warden and is a trained SCUBA diver, cave diver and lifesaver (ASA Award of Merit) and an experienced expedition doctor. She lived with three children under five in a remote village in lowland west Nepal, alongside four species of highly venomous snake, as well as scorpions, malaria mosquitoes and mugger crocodiles. During more than five years in Nepal she did a dozen high-altitude treks with her children aged three months upwards and in between gave medical briefings to British VSOs, US Peace Corps volunteers and others.

Dr Wilson-Howarth is a fellow of the Royal Society of Tropical Medicine and Hygiene, has published a range of papers in academic medical journals, and lectures widely, including at the Royal Geographical Society, for the Register of Engineers for Disaster Relief, the London School of Hygiene & Tropical Medicine and at the University of Cambridge. She has written a regular medical feature for *Wanderlust* magazine since it was first published in 1993 and writes occasionally for the *Independent* newspaper, *Condé Nast Traveller* and *BBC Wildlife* magazines. She now also works as a General Practitioner in England.

To three compassionate and inspiring physicians: Dr Hugh Dawson, Dr Julie Draper and Dr Jim Waddell.

Acknowledgements

Jane Wilson-Howarth

Laura Fleminger first pointed out the need for this book and then convinced me I could write it; Hilary Bradt also encouraged me to write about travel health and gave wise advice on early versions of the text. Another great motivator was Shane Winser, who gave lots of useful advice when I was first naïvely planning various expeditions; more recently, she also commented on the book.

I did most of the work on the first edition whilst living in west Nepal, many hours from even the most basic library. My already too-busy, long-suffering friends and relations, particularly Drs Mary Styles, Mark Howarth and Jill Sutcliffe, were generous in helping ensure I received information I needed and also commented on the manuscript. Sally Crook, Dr Hugh Dawson, Louise Hatton, Lorna and John Howell, Andy Robinson, Dr Jim Waddell and Dr David Wilks read drafts of the book and contributed greatly by freely sharing their experience and wisdom. Professor David Bradley, Dr Anne Denning, Dr Angus McCrae, Dr Andy Pollard, Dr John Scott and Dr Paul Stewart made invaluable comments on particular chapters.

Thanks to others for promptly answering specific enquiries or for making helpful suggestions: Prof. Charles Bangham (London), Dr Mauro Bodio (Basel), Hilary Bradt, Dr Jo (AR) Bradwell (Birmingham Medical School), Philip Briggs (Johannesburg), Dr Peter Brock (of Lederle), Julian Bruce (Blood Care Foundation), Alex Budden (sometime Vice Consul, British Embassy, Kathmandu), Dr Glen Chandler (Melbourne), Kate Cooper (La Paz), Dr Christopher Ellis (Birmingham Heartlands Hospital), Dr Matthew Ellis (Bristol), Dr Marjory Foyle (London), Dr Catherine Howarth (Aberystwyth), Rupert Howes (Brighton), Dr Helen Hutchinson (Cambridge), Dr Grant Hutchison (Dundee), Barbara Ikin (Mozambique), Mary Kenny (Kathmandu), Dr Marianne Janosi (sometime of VSO), Dr Thomas Junghanss (Basel), Dr Gil Lea (London), Dr Deborah Mills (TMVC Brisbane), Dr John Richens (London), Alex Robinson (Kununurra), Karen Shimada (Kathmandu and Tokyo), Dr David Shlim (Kathmandu and Jackson Hole), Jean Sinclair RGN, Dr Vaughan Southgate (London), Debbie Waldron (Rome), Joseph Wilson (my ever-encouraging Dad) and Dr Jane Zuckerman (Royal Free Travel Health Centre, London). Thanks also to Baxter Vaccine Aktiengesellschaft, Vienna and Chiron Behring GmbH for information on European tick-borne encephalitis risk areas. Despite all the expert advice I have received, though, I am to blame for any errors or omissions. At Cadogan's office in London I owe thanks to Rachel Fielding for taking the risk in first publishing this book, and for the hard work and support given by Vicki Ingle and my editors Dominique Shead, Linda McQueen, Nick Rider, Kate Paice and especially Justine Montgomery, who did so much work on this new, enlarged and updated edition.

Many others have unwittingly contributed during the processes of my zoological, parasitological and medical education; I have gleaned snippets from many sources including letters from *Wanderlust* readers, from meetings and literature of the British Travel Health Association and the International Society of Travel Medicine, from *Bandolier* and, most of all, from my patients and fellow travellers who continue to educate me.

Without the quiet but unstinting support of my best friend, mentor and husband, Simon Howarth, who has read various versions of the text *ad nauseam* and protected me from our children at critical points, the book would never have been finished and certainly would not have appeared in three editions.

Cadogan Guides

We would like to thank St. John Ambulance for permission to reproduce the image of the Recovery Position shown in the Accidents chapter on p.301. Copyright 2002 St. John Ambulance. Recovery position illustration correct at time of going to press.

Cadogan Guides
Network House, 1 Ariel Way, London W12 7SL
cadoganguides@morrispub.co.uk
www.cadoganguides.com

The Globe Pequot Press
246 Goose Lane, PO Box 480, Guilford,
Connecticut 06437–0480

Series design: Andrew Barker
Series cover design: Sheridan Wall, adapted by Jodi Louw
Art Director: Jodi Louw
Front cover photograph © ImageState
Author photograph: Sarah Lyon
Cover illustrations: from drawings of a scorpion, spider and mosquito by Jodi Louw
Illustrations © Betty Levene
Map design (disease risk areas): Tracey Ridgewell
Contributors: Grant Hutchison, Barbara Ikin, John Richens, Jean Sinclair, Jane Zuckerman
Editorial Director: Vicki Ingle
Series Editor: Christine Stroyan
Editor: Justine Montgomery
Editorial Assistant: Tori Perrot
Proofreading: Joss Waterfall
Indexing: Isobel McLean
Production: Book Production Services
Printed in Great Britain by The Cromwell Press Ltd.
A catalogue record for this book is available from the British Library
ISBN 1860118682

Disease outbreak and surveillance information globally is imperfect and even expert sources vary in their assessments of which geographical regions harbour which diseases. The maps and tables in this book are offered as a guide and details should be double checked at a travel clinic before departure.

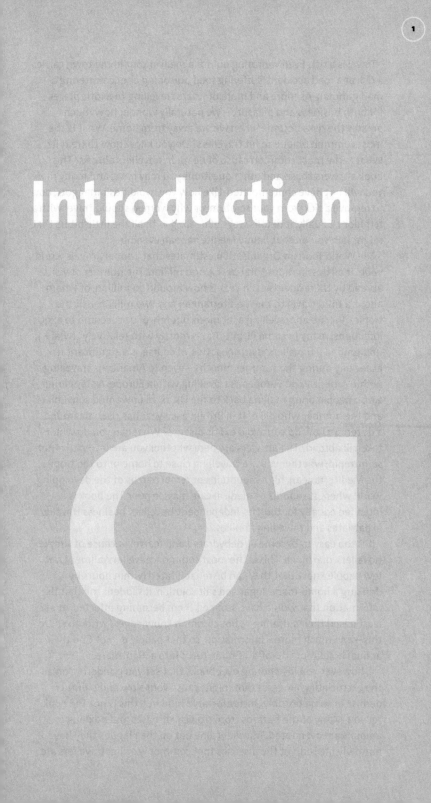

Introduction

01

Travel is a risk. Even venturing out for a meal in your home town carries a risk of a road accident, suffering food poisoning or encountering a mad gunman. As more and more of us are travelling to exotic places – for both business and pleasure – we naturally wonder how much greater the risks become when we are away from home. What is the most common plague to hit travellers? Do you know how to treat it? What is the most common cause of death in travellers abroad? This book answers these and other questions you may have, and many more you will not have contemplated. Like how you avoid flesh maggots, how to remove a tick from your scrotum, or why women should travel with a femidom. Equally, it details ways of dealing with all the little biters that might join you on that balmy Mediterranean evening.

The World Tourism Organisation estimates that annual arrivals worldwide at all destinations total over 4,000 million. The number of visits abroad by UK residents each year is now around 50 million, of whom about a third travel to the Mediterranean and two million visit the tropics. We are all travelling a lot more, but few of us succumb to exotic infections; many become ill, but that is mostly with relatively trivial – if undignified – travellers' diarrhoea. This, of course, is a significant risk, especially during the summer months – even to Americans travelling within America and Europeans travelling within Europe. A staggering 2,000 people bring malaria back to the UK as an unwanted souvenir – and the number who die of it in Britain each year has risen to around a dozen. So how do you avoid exotic disease? What can you do when taken ill abroad? The answers are here whether you are intrepid or not-so-intrepid; whether you are travelling close to home or to the tropics, the Mediterranean, high mountains or remote areas of the developing world where standards of medical care may be poor. The book is intended equally for tourists, independent travellers, business travellers, expatriates and travelling families.

It is too easy to become ill, dehydrated and fearful because of simple travellers' diarrhoea. This is the most common travellers' ailment, yet few people know that they can be rehabilitated within hours by drinking a home-made sugar and salt solution. It saddens me that the information that would have stopped them becoming infected, or at least eased their suffering, is not common knowledge. I write to share this – and much more – information, so that people do not find their annual holiday or trip-of-a-lifetime turns into a nightmare.

If, however, you love poring over books that set you pondering on all the excruciating illnesses that might cause your slow and painful demise in some horribly uncomfortable mud hut, this is not the book for you. Many of the hazards from tropical diseases and noxious animals are overstated. Travellers dine out on the plagues they have narrowly missed, yet the diseases that commonly afflict travellers are dull: diarrhoea, colds and sore throats. The most common killers are actually accidents and pre-existing disease: half of all deaths among travellers, tourists and expatriates are due to heart attacks and similar problems that would have occurred whether they had travelled or not. Malaria is the only 'tropical' disease you need worry about, and is largely avoidable with sensible precautions.

It is worth knowing which specific problems you are most likely to encounter at your destination. Until very recently nearly all malaria imported into Britain came from Africa, but today cases are also arriving from the Indian subcontinent, which is also the source of most British cases of hepatitis A, typhoid and other filth-to-mouth diseases among travellers. Americans tend to bring home their filth-to-mouth diseases from Peru and neighbouring countries. Read about the few problems that you do need to be aware of and how to avoid them, then go forth to enjoy your travels and explorations.

Tropical diseases are covered extensively in these pages because these are the ailments that often worry travellers. They are really not so much diseases of the tropics as diseases that are rife where sanitation and standards of housing and hygiene are poor. 'Tropical' is shorthand for somewhere warm with poor housing and infrastructure. In tropical Queensland, Singapore or Florida there is a small risk of encountering tropical disease: Florida spends millions annually on mosquito control, whereas poor (non-tropical) Nepal cannot and is thus an excellent place to meet vectors and tropical infections.

A book of this size cannot be comprehensive, nor is it intended to replace a consultation with a doctor (if you can find one). It is a simple guide to the health precautions and treatment necessary while you are away; the advice should work as well in Bencleuch or Benidorm as it does in Benares or Buenos Aires. The book offers information on the hazards of cold climates and all the problems a tourist, expeditionary or intrepid backpacker might encounter in any conditions, whether tropical or tundra. It should also serve as an anxiety-defuser for those who worry about exotic diseases. The first aid that the book contains is of the kind needed in situations where secondary aid might be poor or completely absent. It is intended to supplement, but not replace, proper first aid training.

Styles of medical practice abroad may be very different from those we are used to at home. We expect our doctors to offer a diagnosis and explain the purpose and possible side effects of prescribed treatment. Many doctors practising abroad may be unused to patients who know enough about their bodies to discuss medical conditions and their treatments. Uneducated patients commonly consult doctors to be given medicine that will make them feel better, and so their doctors may not volunteer the information you expect. Tactfully ask what you

Naming drugs and medicines

Around the world different tablets and medicines generally each have two names to identify them: the trade or brand name, which tends to vary a great deal from country to country, and the longer, less-easy-to-pronounce ***generic*** name, which should be similar everywhere, even in different languages. It is usually written in small print somewhere on the medicine's packaging, perhaps beneath the brand name. This generic name is what you should look for when buying medicines overseas. Throughout this book I give the generic names of all medicines I suggest; these are written in *italics*.

wish to know, and be aware that linguistic difficulties may make him (or you) seem rude. Then use this book to discuss alternatives, and check that the doctor's prescription makes sense.

Doctors in the developing world not only have to cope with diseases that are rife in insanitary conditions, they are also often hampered by lack of facilities (the budget to run a 150-bed hospital in Uganda is one-tenth of the salary of some US consultants). This means, though, that their pure clinical skills are often sharp and impressive. Unfortunately, however, due to the fact that medical students in some countries bribe their way through their final exams, doctors' skills can also be very poor. If you need a medical consultation, ask around first. Hotel staff, expatriates and embassy staff may know who is competent, and (perhaps almost as important) which doctors are used to dealing with foreigners.

This book is primarily preventative; it is not a do-it-yourself doctor kit. Some treatments are given, where this seems appropriate, but seek a medical opinion whenever possible. If you are going somewhere remote ensure that one member of your group has first aid or paramedical training.

My aim has been to tell you what to do, rather than to provide lists of long medical names. It has been a tough task condensing the essentials of several mighty medical tomes (the index alone of one source book ran to 114 pages), but I have selected the most useful nuggets, limiting suggested treatments to those for which there is good scientific evidence that they work. If, due to my simplifying the information, you feel that there are deficiencies or omissions, do write to tell me.

Take care, *bon voyage*, *salamat jalan* and *pheri betau la*!

J.M.W-H.
March 2002
Cambridge, UK

Before You Go

Features

02

FLYING AND DEEP VEIN THROMBOSIS

Although the association between long flights and life-threatening blood clots has recently come to public notice, it has long been recognized that being immobile is a predisposing factor for having a deep vein thrombosis or blood clot. While the heart pumps blood out under pressure in arteries, returning blood within the veins has to be massaged back by movement and muscle contractions, facilitated by non-return valves in the legs. So immobility tends to lead to slowing of circulation and pooling of fluids at the low points of the body. A stint in a hospital bed after a fracture or operation encourages stagnation of the blood and is well known to cause clots in a significant minority. Even during the Second World War Blitz, doctors noticed that people who slept all night in The Underground in deckchairs had a high rate of blood clots; their special risk factors included immobility in the sitting position and probably some inhibition of movement of the blood in the legs due to the chair frame pressing against the calves and/or thighs.

People especially prone to DVT

➜ Those who have had a DVT or pulmonary (lung) embolus previously.
➜ Anyone who has undergone a major operation or surgery for varicose veins in the previous three months.
➜ Anyone who has had a recent serious leg injury or leg fracture.
➜ Someone who has had a hip or knee replacement in the previous three months.
➜ Cancer sufferers or those treated for cancer in the previous six months.
➜ Those who have ever had a stroke.
➜ People with heart disease.
➜ Those with close blood relatives who have a clot – they may have an inherited tendancy to clot because of Leiden V factor.

People with a slightly increased risk (compared to others with no risk factors)

➜ Smokers.
➜ The very obese.
➜ Pregnant women or those who have recently had a baby.
➜ Women who are taking the combined oral contraceptive pill or HRT (*see also* pp.236–7).
➜ People over 40 years of age.
➜ Very tall people (over 6ft) or short people (under 5ft tall).
➜ People with very severe varicose veins.

Why DVT is known as 'Economy Class Syndrome'

→ **Cramped seating** discourages movement, while movement promotes normal circulation.
→ **Lack of leg room** can create pressure on the calf region; this impedes normal flow of the blood in veins of the legs.
→ **Dehydration**, caused by low humidity in the aircraft and by excessive alcohol or coffee consumption, increases the blood's tendency to clot.
→ **Reduced oxygen** in flight slightly increases the clotability of blood.

The association between long flights and deep vein thrombosis (DVT) was first recognized in 1946, when a doctor flying 14 hours non-stop between Boston and Venezuela himself suffered a DVT. The term 'Economy Class Syndrome' was coined in 1977 but not really rediscovered until the late 1990s when, because of the ever-increasing numbers of people flying, it was noticed that more people are being affected. Over 400 million international journeys by plane are made each year, yet the size of the DVT problem is difficult to estimate, not least because even a competent specialist doctor cannot diagnose the condition without an ultrasound scan. It is also a common condition in the general population, with about 1 in 2,000 people, on average, suffering a significant DVT annually. There are around 1,000 cases of flight-associated DVT in Britain each year amongst around 50 million arrivals in the UK, although those in the business of selling 'flight socks' suggest it is as high as 30,000. The most believable, unbiased estimate I could find was somewhere between 1–4 cases of DVT per 10,000 long-haul travellers.

Most DVTs are diagnosed and treated in hospital. A few are fatal; more than 98% survive. The symptoms are: swelling of a leg (although most often swelling is due to the pooling of normal tissue fluids that is common on long flights), a painful calf or thigh and/or a reddening or darkening of the leg making it feel hot. This classically comes on in susceptible people 10 days after a period of immobility but can (rarely) start on the flight itself, or weeks later. The danger is that a big clot in the leg can break off and travel to lodge in the lungs. A clot in the lung will usually cause a sudden onset of breathlessness, and often chest or shoulder pain. This needs emergency medical treatment. Whether the sufferer survives this or not largely depends on the size of the clot.

The idea of calling this 'Economy Class Syndrome' was that although DVT occurs in first class passengers and on any journey where people sit for more than five hours, conditions in the economy section of long-haul flights contribute to the problem. **Cramped seating** and a **lack of leg room** discourage movement, therefore impeding normal circulation of the blood. On top of this, the **reduced oxygen** during the flight and the fact that passengers are often **dehydrated** means that the blood has a greater tendency to clot (*see also* **Flight**, pp.90–91).

Certain people are especially prone to DVT, while others have a slightly increased risk compared to those with no risk factors (*see* box, p.6). People who have had a previous clot (and some others in the above categories) may have already been prescribed *warfarin*, which will protect them from a further clot. Otherwise, a shot of *heparin* may be suggested just for the flight. Moving around the cabin and also wearing prescribable, graduated support stockings or flight socks will also have a useful protective effect.

So long as they are not already taking *warfarin*, are not asthmatic and are not upset by *aspirin*, these higher risk travellers might consider taking a 75mg *aspirin* several hours before flying. There is good evidence that a meal of oily fish eaten in the 24 hours prior to a flight has similar protective properties to taking *aspirin* and increases its protective effect. It also has fewer side effects than *aspirin*. Moving

Protective actions for all travellers

➜ Consider eating some oily fish in the 24 hours before your flight.
➜ Take exercise (a run, brisk walk or a swim) before and after the flight.
➜ Get up and move around the aircraft every few hours.
➜ Do calf-tensing exercises every hour. Have a look in the in-flight magazine; it may detail special exercises. Some airlines (e.g. Emirates) even provide long-haul passengers – at cost – with an Airogym (*see* facing page) to encourage people to exercise on board.
➜ Pressing the balls of the feet down hard against the floor or footrest improves blood circulation in the legs.
➜ Breathe deeply several times every hour; this stimulates blood circulation and maintains a fresh oxygen supply to the brain.
➜ Avoid excessive tea and coffee; drink plenty of juices or still water.
➜ Avoid taking sleeping tablets, excessive quantities of alcohol or any other form of sedation.
➜ Consider breaking long journeys into shorter stages; flights of more than 12 hours are the most dangerous.
➜ Consider the advantages of upgrading to business class if space is going to be a problem for you.
➜ An aisle seat allows more mobility.
➜ Avoid carrying aboard large, bulky items of hand baggage that will cramp you in your seat.
➜ Avoid sitting with your calves pressed against the seat, or against a footrest. This inhibits blood flow.
➜ Try not to sit with your legs crossed.
➜ Avoid wearing tight ankle socks on long flights.
➜ Wear loose clothing.

around the cabin, simulating walking movements and avoiding dehydration are also protective. The risk of clotting is lowest in people with the O blood group.

The best (proven) 'gizmos' are properly fitting **support stockings** or **flight socks** (*see* **Contact information**, below). Be aware, however, that although properly fitting flight socks are universally protective, those passengers with significant varicose veins, especially if they are in the upper calf, may get some inflammation of the skin of the upper calf where the socks slightly inhibit superficial circulation of blood. This may lead to uncomfortable phlebitis but it is not dangerous. Wearing long support stockings will avoid this complication.

Alternatively, you could buy your own **Airogym** or a **Pocket Gym**. These are small, foldable, inflatable devices you can take on board the plane, used to stimulate the circulation. Note, though, that it is possible to 'cheat' when using an Airogym. For these devices to be really useful and protective, the calf muscles need to be tensed and relaxed as they would be during walking. Don't cheat by moving thighs up and down rather than flexing the calf muscles. Used properly, these gadgets do promote blood flow, but so does getting up out of your seat.

Contact information: DVT

Further information is available on ***www.doh.gov.uk/dvt*** and ***www.who.int/ncd/cvd/dvt.htm***, or visit the Aviation Health Institute website ***www.aviation-health.org***.

Activa Healthcare Ltd, Units 26–7 Imex Business Park, Shobnall Road, Burton on Trent, Staffordshire DE14 2AU, **UK t** (01283) 540 957, **f** (01283) 845 361, *information@activa.uk.com*, *sales@activa.uk.com*, *www.legshealth.com*. Produces flight socks; note that Activa socks need to be fitted by a pharmacist.

Airogym, 10 Crystal Business Centre, Ramsgate Rd, Sandwich, Kent CT13 9QX, **UK t** (01304) 614 650, *info@airogym.com*, *www.airogym.com*. Airogyms available for £11 including postage and packing.

Pocket Gym Ltd, Corbin Way, Gore Cross Business Park, Bradpole, Bridport, Dorset DT6 3UX, **UK t** (01308) 421 150 or **t** (**order hotline**) 0800 072 0898, *salespocketgym@btinternet.com*. Costs £17.95.

Scholl, **UK t** (0161) 654 3000, *www.schollflightsocks.co.uk*. Produces support stockings and flight socks.

TAKING THE CHILDREN

People sometimes look slightly disapproving when I talk of the trips I've done with my children. Whether a trip overseas with a child is sensible or reckless depends largely on your knowledge, temperament and experience. Parents planning a trip to a poorly resourced region who were experienced travellers in the developing world in the years BC – before child – will do best. Children cope with most things well and so misfortune tends to strike when parents are at the limits of their ability to cope. Many 'southern' countries are wonderfully child-centred and child-friendly but there are hazards, especially for the under-threes. Wherever you are it is important to remember that safety regulations are different from at home. Unsafe electrics can be accessible to a crawling child even in quite good hotels, so check around whenever you arrive in a new place and before you set your toddler loose.

The journey

Challenges start on any flight or long journey. Travel with children is relatively easy before they become independently mobile, at around the age of nine months. The easiest and safest age to travel – assuming parental confidence and that you have the energy – is when the baby is still at the sleeping and eating stage, from six weeks of age, during the first few months while the infant is exclusively breast-fed. As soon as anything other than breast-milk is taken, there is a risk of filth-to-mouth infection: diarrhoea is dangerous and difficult to manage in very small children who are yet to acquire much natural immunity.

With mobility comes the chance of the child wandering away. Some young children cling, but others are natural explorers so that when you are queuing to pay or ask a question, or even check in for a flight, they will go off to find something more interesting. It is worth labelling little explorers. At the airport, a note should state your destination, airline and flight and maybe a phone number if you have a mobile phone; this will avoid the angst of losing children for hours in busy airports – as does happen. Once you have arrived at your destination, collect the card of the hotel where you are staying, and either put it in a pocket or pin it to their clothes (out of reach and out of sight). Mothers travelling with sons, or fathers with daughters, may have problems when there is a need to go to the toilet. Usually boys are tolerated in the Ladies while they are small – up to the age of about five – although my youngest son has been reluctant to venture into female facilities since the age of four. However you solve this problem, be aware that standards vary throughout the world. In many 'southern' countries a child can go alone into the appropriate lavatory as soon as they can manage alone, but a New York city policewoman screamed at a friend of mine recently for waiting for her 11-year-old son outside the men's room rather than taking him into the Ladies, which he would have refused to do.

Diarrhoea risk increases when children start to crawl and put things into their mouths. This is the age when they are easily bored if restrained on long flights; they have little sense of danger, yet they cannot be distracted effectively. Between the age of about nine months and until the age they really start communicating properly, usually around the age of three years, when they can be effectively stalled through bribery, travel can be exhausting. A long flight with an unsympathetic aircrew can be nothing short of a waking nightmare.

At any unfamiliar destination, small children are at risk of mishaps and of accidentally swallowing something noxious. Medicines may not be in childproof containers; children mistake Granny's pills for sweets, or paraffin stored in drinks bottles as Coke (*see also* **Expatriates**, p.318).

Dealing with disease and infection

If your destination is the developing world or even southern Europe, **gastro-intestinal disease** may strike. Some doctors more cautious than I say children under the age of three should not visit high-risk, poorly resourced countries at all, given the risk of diarrhoea and dysentery; it certainly is important for parents/carers to be confident about oral rehydration treatment (*see* **Bowels**, pp.109–111). Toddlers who get bacillary dysentery can get really very ill with high fever and profuse diarrhoea and become dangerously dehydrated surprisingly quickly; it is also wise to know about safe, locally available drinks that will tempt.

Fussy children might have problems finding **foods** that they will eat. Most destinations offer lots of foods suitable for toddlers, but there will be quite a lot that is not available or only available in certain big supermarkets and at a price. Quality may not be the same as at home either. If there is any doubt, and certainly in less hygienic destinations, small children should not be allowed to eat ice cream, lettuce or strawberries: these items carry a high risk of gastroenteritis. If bringing disposable nappies/diapers from home, plan for diarrhoea and pack some washable nappies. In Asia and South America disposables are at least double the price they are at home and eco-responsible disposal is just not possible.

Infectious disease is potentially an issue for small children who travel. In the West even unimmunized children are partially protected because their peers are immunized (so-called 'herd immunity'); currently 88% of British children over the age of 13 months are vaccine-protected from measles, mumps and rubella whereas in Nepal coverage is around 40%. The success of Western immunization programmes may make it easy to forget that measles and mumps can kill even well-nourished, previously healthy children, and that both infections can leave children deaf or with other long-term problems. It is crucial that travelling children receive the usual childhood vaccines as well as specific travel jabs.

Travelling with kids: points to note

→ The most difficult age to travel with children is from the time when they begin to crawl until the age of about three years.

→ Involve the children with planning and reading before departure, and only allow them to take toys and books that they can carry themselves.

→ If using an antihistamine to prevent motion sickness, dose the children three hours before travel.

→ Check with a travel clinic to see if you are planning to visit a region with a high risk for malaria.

→ Travelling children are at much higher risk of infectious disease and so must be fully immunized against the usual childhood infections as well as any vaccines recommended for their destination.

→ Malaria or not, pack a good insect repellent, plus sunscreen and plenty of long, loose, 100% cotton clothes.

→ The best insect repellent is DEET and physicians recommend a 10% solution for children. Even at this dilution it stings if rubbed into the eyes, so other bite avoidance techniques are worth exploring, *see* p.144.

→ Travellers to the tropics or the less developed world run at least a 50:50 risk of each member of the family contracting travellers' diarrhoea; children under three have an even higher hit rate, so plan for it. Take extra nappies and bottom cream.

→ Accidents are the main killers of travellers in every age group; become safety conscious.

→ Keep emergency entertainment (e.g. paper, coloured pens, balloons), snacks and safe drinks to hand at all times. Penguin's children's 60s series are ideal mini books to counteract boredom on journeys.

Children are highly susceptible to **malaria**, and are more likely to die if they contract it. Travel to highly malarious regions (especially sub-Saharan Africa, *see* **map**, p.131) with young children could be seen as just reckless, so think seriously about whether a trip is necessary and take expert advice before travelling. **Sunburn** in childhood is associated with a risk of skin cancer in later life so take sunscreen and UV protective clothes (e.g. from Young Explorers, *see* below); repellents protect from insect-borne disease and avoid the misery of itchy hot skin.

Pack colourful sticking plasters and a good, drying antiseptic (e.g. Savlon Dry) for the inevitable **grazes**. Small people will sustain grazes and it is very important – especially in warm climates – to clean and cover the wound properly to prevent secondary infection. It might be wise to travel with this book, so you will know when to panic – or not.

Contact information: stockists of UV-protective clothes

Young Explorers, The Minories, Stratford-upon-Avon CV37 6NF, **UK t** (01789) 414 791, *www.youngexplorers.co.uk*.

PLAGUES, PESTILENCES AND PARANOIA

There's nothing better for catching the attention than a good gruesome plague or deadly epidemic. Yet they are few and, where they do break out, they are seldom a real risk to ordinary travellers. It is still the mundane things like accidents and muggings that are most likely to harm us. It was instructive to be living in the Indian sub-continent during the great outbreak of Plague Paranoia in 1994. The media had done a great job of scaring the pants off everyone and in Surat, where the first cases of plague were identified, there was a veritable stampede of at least 200,000 people out of the city. Doctors had been the first to run away. If the doctors were scared, no wonder the public panicked. Schools and movie halls were shut and the India-Nepal border was closed. Nepali newspapers told us that plague comes from rats via their fleas and that the treatment is *tetracycline*. Headlines announced 'Keep cool – there is enough tetracycline'. This precipitated panic-buying of the antibiotic. People walked the streets with surgical masks on to protect themselves. Sad stories appeared in the local press. The *Rising Nepal* reported that a man with a cough who had turned up at the hospital at Biratnagar, near the Indian border in Eastern Nepal, was refused admission. Doctors said it wasn't their fault. They had run out of surgical masks so the patient was placed under armed guard in a field. The *Kathmandu Post* told the story of an unhinged Gujarati who killed three plague suspects with an axe – including a seven-year-old girl. And an early October edition carried this: 'Traffic halted in the Indian city of Lucknow after a dead rat was spotted on a busy road. Students at a nearby polytechnic immediately gulped down antibiotics and the lifeless rodent was whisked away in an ambulance.'

We were a thousand miles from the outbreak, yet tourists fled Kathmandu and expatriate friends asked me if they should flee too. 'Surely you're not staying here – not with the children?'

Yet there was no real risk – not to us. They didn't seem reassured when I said that plague is a disease of extreme poverty and most unlikely to strike expatriates or ordinary travellers. Locals were scared, too, but they wouldn't stoop to clearing the rubbish which encouraged the rats that harboured plague in Kathmandu. Finally the Municipality started trucking it away and for a few months Kathmandu was relatively clean underfoot. There were never any confirmed cases of plague in Nepal, and after all the hysteria subsided the death toll was reported as 52 in India.

Bubonic plague has been with us for many thousands of years and continues to simmer in the USA, Bolivia, Brazil, Madagascar, Tanzania,

Uganda, China, Myanmar and Vietnam. So why was everyone so worried? Plague has struck fear into the hearts of people throughout history. It was the disease against which, in 1377, the first quarantine regulations were instituted. It probably killed nearly half of the population of Constantinople in the 6th century AD and, in the 14th century (when it was called the Black Death), it wiped out 20 million people. Perhaps it was deadly because it hit a debilitated, starving society. Certainly, bubonic plague hits the poor very hard, and in times of strife and war it breaks out to add to the death toll. Early in the twentieth century it killed six million people in India. That was the last great outbreak and I imagine that it was some memory of this that rekindled the terror in 1994; that, and irresponsible journalists.

There is nothing quite like a scary disease outbreak to sell newspapers. **Legionnaires' Disease** was another shocking, deadly pestilence until it was recognized, when doctors discovered that fewer than 5% of people who are exposed to the bacteria suffer any symptoms at all, and that these are all treatable with antibiotics. **Lassa Fever**, too, is rarely contracted by ordinary travellers; most cases are in health workers staffing in unsanitary, under-resourced hospitals. And most of the other few remaining, horrendously dangerous, incurable tropical infections will be side-stepped by the mosquito and tick bite-avoidance measures described in **Biters and Insect-borne Diseases**, pp.144–9.

But back to plague. It is harboured in wild animals and, from time to time (for reasons that are not well understood), it infects rats sharing the unsanitary accommodation of the very poor. As the rats die from plague they are deserted by their fleas, which then seek a new host to bite. People bitten by such homeless rat fleas thus acquire bubonic plague, which is treatable with antibiotics. Buboes are lymph glands that are painfully distended by the infection as the body tries to restrict the plague organisms to one area; the most common sites are the nodes in the groin, since rat fleas tend to bite the legs.

In the few unfortunates who do not receive treatment for their bubonic plague, the disease then worsens into septicaemia and often the highly infectious, usually fatal pneumonic plague. Even in a big epidemic, though, nearly all those infected acquire their disease from rat flea bites, so that there is little risk of catching plague during normal travel; those at risk are nurses caring for those dying of plague, laboratory technicians working with specimens from plague patients and zoologists handling infected animals. Those travelling into areas where a plague epidemic is going on could carry forty 500mg *tetracycline* tablets and see a doctor if they develop a fever, particularly if they notice painful swellings in the groin, armpits or neck. The incubation period is 2–8 days.

Tips for those travelling into an epidemic area

If you do wish to travel during an epidemic, check your facts from a reliable source before you go:

→ **Where is the outbreak now?** If it is restricted to the industrial area of Surat (which few travellers visit anyway) in the Gujarat state of India, it is likely that other parts of this huge country will be unaffected – except by panic.

→ **How is it caught?** Does it come from contaminated unhygienically prepared food (like cholera) or from flea bites in slum dwellings which you are never likely to enter? Transmission routes for most diseases are covered later in the book (*refer to the* **Index**, p.334).

→ **Am I at particular risk?** Does my work or lifestyle mean I am more likely to catch the disease than other travellers?

→ **What precautions can I take to avoid it?**

→ **Is there a vaccine?**

→ **If I catch the disease how will I recognize it?**

→ **What treatment is there?** Should I carry a suitable treatment course?

→ **Is it particularly dangerous if I catch it?** Do I have any medical problem which makes me more at risk than most?

→ **Do I now feel I have sufficient information** to be armed against mass panic all around?

Avoiding epidemic hysteria

There is quite a selection of epidemics raging in various corners of the globe, in addition to those reported in the refugee camps of Rwanda. Most of us know about the AIDS pandemic, but we now appreciate the precautions we can take to avoid it so few of us worry much about it. And it is knowledge, surely, which is the best vaccine against epidemic hysteria. Many travellers were totally unaware of the cholera epidemic in Peru, but then, why should they worry? Cholera is not a risk to ordinary travellers and the routine precautions that most travellers take to avoid diarrhoea will protect them from cholera. And who has heard of the epidemic of Kala-azar Fever in northeastern India or in southern Sudan? Few people, as outsiders are unlikely to contract this treatable disease and so it is hardly newsworthy. Nor do newspapers choose to focus on the five million or so children who die each year from diarrhoea.

How strange it seems that the media can fire our imaginations and play on our own ignorance and cause us to worry so much about a disease which can only harm the desperately poor.

SENIOR TRAVELLERS

Insurance

Providing that older travellers are fit for what they intend to do on their trip, the main challenge is finding insurance. Several companies that offer cover for senior travellers are listed below. Most have upper age limits. It is also worth checking with your household insurers. Travelling through a specialist company like **Saga** (*see* below) may carry the added bonus of included health insurance, but it is important to check exactly what you are buying. Get insurance arranged well ahead of departure so that if you are taken ill you won't feel pressured to travel anyway. Don't be tempted to mislead insurance companies (you may not be covered in case of illness), tour operators or anyone else about any medical condition or your capabilities.

Tips for senior travellers

→ People over the age of 75 may have problems finding travel insurance, particularly if they have ongoing medical problems or take regular treatment. It is wise to sort out insurance early in your travel plans.

→ Take expert advice on the vaccines you need for your journey. Tick-borne encephalitis (a risk to those walking and camping in parts of Eastern Europe) is more serious in older victims. Make sure, though, that you don't receive vaccines that you don't need: the risk of a serious allergic reaction to Yellow Fever immunization is greater in the elderly than in younger vaccinees.

→ Consider 'flu immunization and realize that the season for 'flu epidemics in the Southern Hemisphere is between April and November.

→ Get fit for your trip: older bodies need to train for unfamiliar activities. Successful older adventurers invest a lot of time in keeping in condition.

→ Anyone who can manage to walk 50m without becoming breathless should tolerate the reduced oxygen availabilty in flight and should be fit to fly (*see also* **Special Travellers**, pp.61, 65).

→ More than 10% of long-haul travellers over the age of 50 have small, silent thromboses, most of which resolve without causing problems.

→ When planning a long intercontinental journey that you expect to be tiring or stressful, consider buying a business class ticket. The check-in environment is less hostile and you will arrive feeling fresher.

→ If you are less-than-mobile or need help with luggage, notify the airline well before your flight so that assistance with transfers, help or a buggy can be provided.

→ Consider too whether cramped economy-class seating will suit you. Do stiff hips make it difficult for you to squeeze in?

Health preparations

Start fit and return fit. Over the age of about 40 it becomes more important to prepare properly for whatever you plan to do on your trip. Older bodies are less forgiving of abuse than younger ones and even a relatively trivial 'failure' – like a filling falling out of a tooth – can cause a lot of distress and inconvenience. Do as much as you can to get any potential problems sorted out well before travel and try to avoid dramatic changes in any medication that you take just before departure. People on regular medication often forget their supplies. This could cause considerable problems if, for example, the medication is for heart disorders and/or to control fluid overload in the lungs. It is wise to understand what treatment you are taking, for what purpose and what the consequences of stopping treatment might be. It is also sensible to travel with a note of the tablets you take, including the *generic* name and the exact dose in milligrams. Armed with that information, you

➜ People over the age of 80 have a high risk of dangerous deep vein thrombosis and on flights of more than five hours duration must be especially careful to move about (*see also* pp.6–9).

➜ Some car hire firms will not rent cars to drivers over the age of 75 or, if they do, the cost may be high. Enquire before you travel and don't just assume you can organize it on arrival at the airport.

➜ Know your medication. What is it for? What if you stop taking it? Carry extra supplies in different suitcases with a note of the *generic* name and doses. You may not be able to get more at your destination.

➜ Those taking tablets to control maturity-onset diabetes must be aware that they if they become even mildly ill – even with something as common as an attack of travellers' diarrhoea – they may need treatment with an insulin infusion in hospital.

➜ Anyone taking diuretic ('water') tablets who suffers a significant attack of diarrhoea should seek medical help promptly if they start to feel dizzy on rising out of a chair or from bed. This is a sign of dehydration (*see* **Bowels**, p.111) and probably indicates the loss of electrolytes as well as essential fluids.

➜ Those with ongoing medical conditions should ask their doctor to advise them on travel. Long car journeys and jarring bus rides will make even bad backs worse.

➜ If some illness strikes just before your departure, consider postponing the trip. Your insurance should cover any rebooking costs. It is no fun travelling while ill and unfamiliar doctors may not be very reassuring.

➜ Make a hard, rational assessment of your capabilities before any trip and ensure that you are up to it. Be honest about medical conditions and any disability.

should be able to procure a new supply of your medicines if you forget them or your luggage is lost or delayed. It is also worth packing extra supplies in different pieces of luggage.

There are plenty of over-70-year-olds who remain very active and adventurous, but as the years roll on it is important to think through the consequences of things going wrong if you have an accident in a remote place. If you fall you are more likely to fracture a bone, and a thrombosis is more likely if that fracture immobilizes you. Be aware, too, that those who take diuretic or 'water' tablets (to control blood pressure or swelling of the ankles) will suffer sooner from imbalance of the blood electrolytes in the case of diarrhoea and/or vomiting, so it is especially important to know about oral rehydration therapy (*see* **Bowels**, p.109–111) and replacement of lost potassium.

If you are going on any kind of activity trip, do a little fitness training beforehand. This doesn't need to be a full work-out, but something appropriate to what you will be doing: such as, perhaps, a brisk daily walk. This will make the trip itself more enjoyable and less exhausting.

Lavatories can be a challenge for less nimble travellers. In many public facilities with pedestal lavatories, there may be no seat. Consequently one needs to be able to hover over the pan, a trick that may be difficult for older travellers or those with hip joint disease. Some remote places or budget destinations may only offer squat toilets. If you can't squat to relieve yourself, limber up or re-book; alternatively, women might invest in a **Whizzy**, an ingenious foldable, disposable, gutter-like device that allows you to pee standing. These are also good for the squeamish who want to keep clear of less-than-salubrious lavatories. Another solution is the disposable **Mini Potti** urinal (*see* below for contact details).

Contact information: senior travellers

Age Concern Insurance Services, Lowthian House, Market St, Preston PR1 2ET, **UK t** 0845 601 2234. Covers most medically stable passengers with the exception of those travelling against medical advice. No age limit.

BCB, Freepost, Cardiff CF1 1YS, **UK t** 0808 100 2867. Produces the Mini Potti Urinal, costing £5 for three.

New Angle Products, Box 25641, Chicago, IL 60625, **US t** (773) 293 2655; *www.whizzy4you.com*. Produces the Whizzy, priced $6.50 for 10.

Saga, **UK t** 0800 056 5880, *www.sagaflights.co.uk*. Travel for over-50s.

www.everybody.co.uk/airline: has a directory of access arrangements on board major airlines.

Companies offering travel insurance for over-65s:

Club Direct, **UK t** 0800 074 4558, *www.clubdirect.co.uk*. Up to age 74.

Coventry, **UK t** (01243) 621 010. Up to age 75.

Options, **UK t** 0870 848 0870. Cover up to the age of 84.

Perry Gamble, **UK t** (020) 8542 1122. Up to age 79.

Travel Protection, **UK t** (02890) 320 797. Up to age 75.

NEW VACCINES

The 20th century saw the development of few new vaccines and all were aimed at mass protection from common diseases. Vaccines to protect minorities or to avoid rare or exotic diseases are unlikely to be commercially viable, despite the fact that the burden of disease is often much greater and the risks more substantial in the tropics. Modern medical developments rarely emerge to benefit the needy of the developing world, but aim to protect citizens of the developed world or soldiers. Many therapeutic advances have been stimulated by war. The first modern travel vaccine – a whole-cell typhoid vaccine – was developed during the Boer War and, despite causing quite unpleasant side effects, the original vaccine was only improved and superseded in the early 1990s. Things are changing fast though. With easier, cheaper air travel, the world is shrinking. UK residents alone make more than 50 million overseas visits annually. This means that markets for travel vaccines are increasing and there is now commercial capital to be made. There is now a lot of investment in this area, with, for example, a race underway between at least a dozen companies to produce a Dengue Fever vaccine. Let's hope too that there will be a spin-off in more vaccines becoming available to citizens of the tropics.

A whole new clutch of vaccines will appear within the next five to 10 years: one company alone, Peptide Therapeutics, plans within the next five years to launch new vaccines against Yellow Fever, Japanese B encephalitis, tick-borne encephalitis, Dengue, oral typhoid and ETEC. These 'cleaner' antigens will be good news for those who are allergic to components of products that are currently in use. The product that excites me most amongst the 'new boys' is the ETEC vaccine: enterotoxigenic *Escherichia coli* (*E-coli*) the deviant of our normal bowel flora that is responsible for most cases of travellers' diarrhoea. Generally the bug precipitates a desire, which lasts 36–48 hours, to be close to a WC. Medically the illness is usually trivial, but it often necessitates changes to travel plans that can seriously spoil your holiday and can precipitate undignified interruptions to business trips. The risk of this kind of inconvenience is high, especially in those travelling to a developing country, so many of us will welcome a vaccine that can be taken by mouth. The first ETEC vaccine has already been field-tested and should be available any time now. And, no doubt, the next five years will bring capsules to protect us against bacillary dysentery, *Campylobacter* and the various other causes of travellers' diarrhoea.

Soon, not only will there be more vaccines against more infections, but more choice of products and means of administration. Vaccines will also become 'cleaner' and less likely to provoke nasty allergic reactions which, though rare, are real, major concerns with the present Japanese B encephalitis and Yellow Fever antigens (*see* **Immunizations by Region**, pp.42–4). Vaccine combinations are also being launched to reduce the number of jabs taken before any trip, although travel clinic nurses complain that such combinations take up too much precious fridge space, and when the different components have different booster intervals (as with hepatitis A and B, and also the new hepatitis A and typhoid) immunization schedules become mind-bogglingly complex. So try to be patient with your clinic nurse and allow her plenty of time to work it all out.

There will be more and more vaccines developed, but the last two decades will be remembered perhaps amongst tropical physicians as the time of the first real glimmer of hope for eradication of malaria. When the World Health Organisation was set up in the 1940s, malaria, venereal diseases and tuberculosis were identified as the most devastating public health problems globally and the Malaria Eradication Division of the WHO was formed. By the mid-1970s though, it had become clear that 'eradication' was impossible and the word was removed from the divisional name. Then, in the late 1980s, an unknown Colombian scientist published an account of an effective vaccine. There was disbelief amongst the Western scientific community. How could an under-resourced scientist from a developing country succeed where high-tech labs continued to fail? Dr Manuel Patarroyo managed to persuade the sceptics and field trials were extended to Asia and Africa. The vaccine did give some protection, but in only about 30% of the population: insufficient for a control or eradication campaign. He is undaunted, however, continuing to work on that first vaccine, and remains hopeful of producing a more effective version within a few years. If he succeeds, he will save lives on a global scale. If he fails, other scientists predict that malaria immunization may not be a reality for another couple of decades. Dr Gil Lea (co-editor of *Health Information for Overseas Travel*, the standard manual for health professionals) commented, 'I have been working in travel medicine for 28 years and the malaria vaccine always seems to be five years off.'

'The next five years,' Dr Lea added, 'will bring a much wider selection of vaccines which should stimulate doctors to seek better information to advise travellers. At present countries where travellers face the greatest risks of infectious disease are those unable to provide good public health information: there may be an epidemic before the authorities are aware. I foresee a time though when we will give carefully tailored advice about the precise health risks of any particular journey based on good global surveillance information. Thus we will know how best to protect the traveller.'

RESPONSIBLE TOURISM

The realities of poor or non-existent medical care in the developing world can shock and appal. A man with neurofibromatosis (Elephant Man's disease) approached me in Hala, Sindh: a pendulous piece of flesh hung from his eyebrow down to his waist. A minor operation would have removed this horrendous growth. But, it would also have deprived him of the means of earning a living as a beggar.

For every case who would refuse surgery, though, there are 10,000 who would give anything to be helped, and it can be hard for visitors to cope with this. In the West – even with our health service's problems – we can generally get any treatment we need. Even the simplest surgery is denied, however, to most Third World citizens. Proper medical care with the right medicines is just not available. TB is a frequent killer, yet treatment is often impossible to arrange. We cannot do much about such injustices, except maybe give a little money to charities.

Because surgery, gross disability, handicap and chronic disease are so common and (to us) intrusive in the developing world, we may be seduced into interfering by trying to treat simpler conditions. Living surrounded by a disabled population, though, often makes local people noticeably comfortable with handicap. They do not need Westerners dabbling just to salve their own consciences.

Handing out medicines

If you want to 'patch up the locals' while travelling, think carefully what you are doing and why. Do a little research, and try to offer more than a 'quick fix'. If your Western 'quick fix' works, the recipient will lose any confidence he had in the few facilities available locally and, more important, is unlikely ever to learn how to avoid future attacks. If your treatment fails, he will lose confidence in local practitioners and you may wreck opportunities for health workers who follow. Few diseases respond to a single dose of a drug, and unless you stay to supervise treatment you can never be sure medicine has been taken properly.

In many situations there is a temptation to hand out antibiotics. Even educated Westerners have a bad record of taking medicines as they should, and villagers who have had little exposure to Western

Case History: Nepal

We walked into a village just after someone had handed out packets of oral rehydration solution. A toddler had opened his packet on to the ground and was licking it off his fingers, while a dog shared it. The donors, Nepali health workers, had failed to communicate the life-saving value of the packets; they had not given the villagers enough time.

treatment will be most unlikely to take a full course as required. In most places where I have worked, local practitioners, Western and traditional, prescribe a selection of medicines. One so-called Ayurvedic practitioner in Sri Lanka prescribed for a woman with fever: *amoxycillin* (antibiotic), *Valium* (tranquillizer), *paracetamol* (to reduce the fever), *propranolol* (heart medicine) and a vitamin capsule – one of each. Even qualified doctors sometimes prescribe part-courses of antibiotics. So, when villagers acquire a course they may well take one or two and save the rest for when they are ill again. This promotes resistance to antibiotics, so that when someone competent comes to treat a serious infection the antibiotic may well be useless. Giving out antibiotics is harmful in the long term unless you are prepared to stay for a week and supervise taking of the medicine; this is the kind of commitment you should be ready to make if you feel treatment is so necessary. This may sound hard, but then, so is treating people properly.

The big killer in the developing world is diarrhoea; people die of dehydration because they do not realize how much fluid is lost or how to replace it. A traveller interested in helping people he meets may save lives by teaching villagers how to make and use sugar and salt solution (*see* pp.110–11). It is easier perhaps to hand out packets of oral rehydration solution, but this on its own will not do much to make villagers self-sufficient in the next diarrhoea outbreak.

If you want to help, give it serious thought before plunging in, and allow lots of time (days perhaps) to teach people about what you are giving them. If you are desperate to hand out pills there are some that you can give away with relative impunity, and even do some good. Many women of child-bearing age in developing countries are anaemic, due to a combination of poor diet, constant pregnancies and hookworm infestation. Consequently they suffer chronic fatigue, are less efficient workers and breadwinners, and are more likely to die in childbirth or deliver small, weaker babies. Dishing out iron tablets (*ferrous sulphate*) to women and older girls is useful (but note that an overdose of iron is dangerous, especially to young children). Locally made tablets are usually very cheap.

Play it safe

→ Don't treat diseases you know nothing about. Consider your motives: will treatment be conscience-salving, but destructive for your patients?
→ Try to carry locally-bought medicines if you intend to treat people. *Paracetamol* or *aspirin*, ORS packets, iron tablets and *potassium permanganate* can do a lot of good.
→ If you have a full medical kit, donate it to a clinic/hospital at the end of your trip; it is unwise to give medicines to a non-medical local friend.
→ Resist practising on local people.

Case History: Nepal

A tourist had stopped at a house on a popular trekking route in West Nepal. He was attempting to treat a child with an area of oozing, infected skin on her face. He was applying *germoline* antiseptic ointment to the little girl's cheek. This is ineffective against impetigo, and by further moisturizing the infection may even encourage it to spread. No doubt the victim's family would have faith in the clever Western 'cure', and would then delay seeking assistance from a medical post with a paramedic with experience of treating impetigo. It is a common complaint in warm climates, and at this superficial stage is easy to treat with cheap, locally manufactured medicine.

The additional delay in seeking proper help has two consequences. The infection, which is highly contagious, could well spread to the rest of the family and playmates. Secondly, impetigo can spread into the eyes.

Also relatively harmless is *paracetamol* (Tylenol; also – if you're sure they have no stomach problems – *aspirin*). *Paracetamol* and *aspirin* are very effective in reducing fever and pain. Even so you must explain carefully what they are for and what they can and cannot do. Again, you will do your patients a service if you give them recognizably local tablets. They will be able to buy the next supply, and avoid being exploited by some unscrupulous practitioner. The poor spend too much of their tiny incomes on medicines, yet many are useless or actually dangerous.

Skin infections

Travellers are often asked to treat skin infections. This is one problem that is fairly safe to treat, and you can demonstrate how to deal with the next episode so that they learn to help themselves. Superficial impetigo (*see* **Skin**, p.222) is easy to treat, but you may see festering sores that need a week of supervised *flucloxacillin* treatment.

In India and Nepal little packets of *potassium permanganate* crystals (sufficient to treat maybe 100 people) cost a few rupees, and it's easy to carry a handful of them. Demonstrate dissolving a few crystals in water (*see* **Skin**, p.216), then rub the solution into the infected area with cotton wool or a scrap of clean cloth, and leave the packet with the family. Try to explain that wounds should be treated like this three times a day for a few days, and that future infections can be avoided by cleaning even the smallest wounds and sterilizing with *potassium permanganate*. Even this level of explanation takes time, and ideally you should devote some hours at least to keeping an eye on your patient to see they are following your advice. Remember that local paramedics will be experts in treating skin infections, so if there is an accessible clinic it may be best simply to refer your 'patient' there.

CULTURE SHOCK

Culture shock is a sense of unease and often anxiety that is commonly felt by travellers when they arrive at a new destination, or sometimes when they return home after a long absence. These feelings can range from disorientation and mild disquiet through to near panic, but they are compounded by factors such as lack of preparation, fatigue and illness, or even anxiety about tasks left undone at home.

New arrivals

Travel often brings experiences that are emotionally loaded. Often these are exciting and stimulating, and they can be one of the attractions of travel. The tingle-factor, though, comes partly from the fact that the sensations stress us a little. On top of the predictable excitements of your arrival in a new country, you have to deal with a lot of things – all at once. Yet you are fatigued and jet-lagged, bombarded with sights and sounds, bewildered by unfamiliar sign-posting, disorientated, bereft of familiar support systems and you may have experienced a painful separation. You may feel pursued by touts and beggars, or people seem to stand far too close and just won't leave you alone.

Accomplishing simple tasks, such as finding a decent room for the night, buying a bus ticket, extending a visa or finding out about onward flights, can take hours and life becomes exasperating. Yet you are here to enjoy yourself, and you ought to be having a good time. You resent feelings of homesickness. You may start to resent the people around you, if they seem to be putting up barriers for no apparent reason. However, if you listen to locals, you will start hearing jokes about how cumbersome systems are: there is talk of especially slow 'Peruvian time', of *mañana*, *insh'Allah*, or just, 'that's life'. It is important to slow down, and to accept that in some cultures, things just move a little more slowly and at a more relaxed pace than you may be used to.

Understandably, travellers – and especially expatriates – often go through a process of emotional responses. On newly arriving in an unfamiliar environment, there is frequently a sense of excitement, delight and even euphoria. Next comes a honeymoon period, when you don't see any problems, or when problems and disadvantages are minimized. Then there may be some pining – for Marmite, a decent cup of tea or a friend – and some of the ugliness and inconvenience starts to intrude. You may have periods of feeling angry, shocked or numb, in response to the injustice of poverty, the inequality of healthcare, or even just the levels of waste and inefficiency you see around you. Then you may feel guilty at having so much in comparison to the people you are travelling amongst. As the adjustment process continues, you might even become depressed and apathetic, or you may become adjusted and simply accept your surroundings as understanding evolves. However you respond to your destination, though, culture shock can hit unexpectedly and take you by surprise – again and again.

Control

At home we are used to exerting a great deal of control over our lives; that way, we can establish routines and life is safe and predictable. We know how to avoid undue hazards: we know which parts of the city are unsafe after dark; we wear seat-belts in cars, or a helmet when on a motorcycle. Many of us travel to take a break from such predictability, but this means surrendering to some loss of control. Again, this adds to the excitement, but when things go a little wrong, such as when there are seemingly avoidable delays or there is illness, travellers will cope better if they become fatalistic.

In comparison to the controlled environment we have been used to, travel often puts us into difficult situations and, during adventurous trips, we may find ourselves in a situation which is truly beyond our control. It is then good to be able to recognize your limits and work within the bounds of what you are able to do. Getting through such challenges is life-enhancing and often makes a person more capable back home, too. Most adventurers set themselves targets, such as circumnavigating Annapurna, reaching a certain altitude or a remote glacier, or seeing every listed site, and such goal-driven trips can lead to disappointments and frustrations. There may be unavoidable delays, or plans can be scuppered by bad weather, and yet, if the journey, rather than the goal, is the main objective, the trip will still be enjoyable. I have met many trekkers whose opening response on what they'd seen in Nepal was about the failed objective rather than the delights that they had seen. Those who loiter and are not driven by goals often see more, meet friends along the way and feel more satisfied.

People sometimes leave home so as to find meaning to life, perhaps after some relationship crisis or other loss. Inner journeys comprise a whole literary genre, in which travel is rather idealized as a healing experience. It can be, but it can be hurtful, too, if travel adds stress to unbearable stress. If you set out on your journey in a fragile state, try to ensure that your have set up some safety nets. Consider linking up with other travellers, ensure that you can get to somewhere that feels safe wherever you are, and go properly insured.

If the travel experience becomes a major stressor, it may be tempting to seek solace in alcohol or other recreational drugs; these not only hold dangers in themselves, but they can also lead to accidents and/or unsafe sexual behaviour. If you don't manage to unwind or de-stress, things might worsen. A well-recognized symptom of being stressed out is having panic attacks. These are associated with an overwhelming sense of dread, and they cause physical symptoms that often include

Symptoms that you are struggling to cope include:

- → Over-reaction to minor problems or inevitable delays.
- → Racism and angry, irrational outbursts.
- → Lack of interest in learning anything about your destination.
- → Withdrawal and negativism.
- → Excessive eating or drinking – or loss of appetite.
- → Feelings of uneasiness with strangers.
- → Fear of dirt and disease.
- → Great fatigue.
- → An overwhelming sense of doom.

breathlessness, weakness, dizziness, sometimes chest discomfort, often nausea, and cramps or tingling in the hands and feet. If stress levels have reached this pitch you need to find somewhere to chill out and, if a few days of doing nothing in a restful place doesn't help, you may need to find a doctor. Treatment of stress and panic attacks is straightforward, but it is best done by someone who speaks your language and has experience of Western lifestyles.

Culture shock and travel-induced stress seldom get this bad, however. Most people adjust and enjoy themselves, and are changed forever by their experiences. Then there is only the **reverse-culture shock** to cope with on returning home after a long trip away. Many people feel this is worse than the first culture shock. The period of adjustment once you get home is partially determined by the length of time you've been away but also depends on whether you have had any life-changing experiences. Those who have been moved deeply by seeing profound poverty or disfiguring disease may find it difficult to talk of this back home, and it's possible that friends and relations who have stayed at home may not understand and remain disinterested. This is isolating. The process of readjustment after years away may take as long as a year or eighteen months. During this time, it is especially important to develop links with others who have had parallel experiences; travel clubs are often good places to find kindred spirits. Long-term travellers often enrol on long or short academic or development courses. If you have been employed overseas long-term, some organizations offer debriefing and/or counselling. If you feel seriously down on your return, however, remember that your family doctor should be able to help.

Treating culture shock: natural approaches

St John's wort is effective in treating many of the symptoms common in culture shock, including low mood, panic or anxiety. It takes about a week to have any noticeable effect. Alternatively, it is often possible to develop **meditation** or relaxation techniques through courses on yoga or Buddhism, aimed particularly at foreign travellers.

Before You Go

Getting Ready

03

What needs to be done to ensure a healthy trip? There is more to arrange than immunizations and buying malaria tablets. Appropriate clothing protects from insects and sun, while thinking about road safety, knowing which foods are risky and practising only safe sex will do you far more good than having an armful of injections.

Seek impartial information about health and other risks. Travel agents can be ignorant or lax about warning of any hazards. It is not in their interests, for example, to detail the risk of catching malaria in Africa. General practitioners (GPs) are increasingly knowledgeable about travel health, and some have online access to expert information, but travel clinics are probably the best sources (*see* **Useful Addresses**, p.326).

Summary

→ Arrange a dental check before your trip to avoid, as far as possible, dental treatment abroad (and AIDS and hepatitis B infection risks).

→ Sort out any niggling health problems before departure, as any aggravation could make your trip miserable.

→ Arrange adequate health insurance; take it out when booking your trip to ensure cover even if you have an accident or illness before departure.

→ Pack a note of the *generic* name and dose of any medication you take regularly or for problems that you commonly experience, and travel with a copy of your spectacles prescription in case you need a replacement.

→ Of travellers who die abroad, about half succumb to accidents; become safety conscious when travelling.

→ For pre-departure preparation tips have a look at *www.fco.gov.uk/knowbeforeyougo*.

PLANNING AND PRE-TRIP CHORES

Is your destination safe?

Your first pre-trip chore should be to check that your destination is safe and right for you. Despite the speed with which news travels, a surprising number of travellers get caught up in riots and civil unrest; some are held by armed robbers or even terrorists. It can be difficult to sort out whether the particular area of the country you intend to visit is dangerous. Some travel clinic printouts include security warnings. The **UK Foreign and Commonwealth Office** or **US State Department** (both can be consulted on the Internet) will advise; diplomats are sometimes over-cautious, but that is because it is often they who have to bale out foolhardy adventurers. Another good source of information is returning expatriates, expeditionaries or travellers, although they may not always be up to date. Newspapers, consulates and embassies also provide information. Restrictions, like whether an HIV test is required before entry, will be detailed with visa application paperwork. Advice can also be obtained through the Royal Geographical Society's **Expedition Advisory Centre**, organizations like the **South American Explorers Club** and smaller bodies like the London-based Anglo-Malagasy, Anglo-Peruvian, Anglo-Indonesian or Britain-Nepal Societies.

Contact information: planning resources

Expedition Advisory Centre, Royal Geographical Society, 1 Kensington Gore, London SW7 2AR, **UK t** (020) 7581 2057, **f** (020) 758 4447.
South American Explorers Club, 126 Indian Creek Road, Ithaca, NY 14850, **US t** (607) 277 0488.
UK Foreign and Commonwealth Office, UK t (020) 7008 0232/3, *www.fco.gov.uk*.
US State Department, US t (202) 647 4000, *www.state.gov*.

Case History: Pakistan

Some keen Japanese expeditionaries set out to canoe down the Indus. They were kidnapped by *dacoits* (armed robbers). Had they troubled to enquire of almost anyone, they would have discovered that they were entering a lawless area where *dacoits* see foreigners as rich and vulnerable. They were released once a ransom was paid. In Pakistan kidnapping is common, although foreigners are less often involved than locals.

If 100,000 people visit a developing country for a month:

- → Half will develop some kind of illness.
- → 8,000 will visit a doctor.
- → 5,000 will be confined to bed.
- → 500 will require repatriation by air.
- → 300 will be admitted to hospital during their trip or on return.
- → 1 will die.

Source: International Society of Travel Medicine, 1999

What might kill you?

Of those who die on their travels more than half succumb to diseases that would have taken them wherever they were, while most of the other deaths are from accidents. Less than 4% of those who die succumb to communicable disease. Road accidents are common everywhere: an estimated 300 people are killed on the world's roads every day. In the developing world vehicles are often poorly maintained because spares are both expensive and difficult to obtain, safety has a low priority, legal controls may be lax and some people drive crazily. Inside buildings, electrical equipment may be dangerous, so burns and electrocution are not uncommon. Drowning takes many traveller's lives. Poisoning from stoves in tents or badly maintained gas/kerosene fires is another hazard. Even if you're not usually safety conscious, take care when travelling. Hazards will not be signposted in the way you are used to at home.

Accident prevention, then, is especially important on your travels. Jet lag, culture shock, not understanding local signs and signals, interesting distractions, unfamiliar vehicles and vehicles on the 'wrong' side of the road all contribute to the risk of mishap. In the less developed world accidents can be a double disaster because rescue services may not exist and emergency medical facilities are often poor or distant. Do not attempt a dangerous sport for the first time in a place where they do not seem geared up for beginners; if, for example, you plan to do a scuba diving course, check that the instructors are properly qualified. Travel with safety equipment as appropriate, such as safety helmets if you plan to cycle or hire motor bikes, life jackets if you will be trying any watersports, or a restraining car-seat for the baby.

Insurance

Arrange insurance to cover medical care and accidents, including air repatriation. Evacuation by 'air ambulance' costs the equivalent of at least three full-price seats, plus nursing care. You need to be quite well and medically stable to be medically evacuated, so if, for example, you have a bad car smash, you may stay in intensive care locally for a while before you are well enough to be evacuated. Your insurance must cover all these expenses. Make sure the worst case is covered: £2 million's worth of cover is a sensible target. Check, too, that the policy that you buy gives you what you need for your trip, such as a helicopter rescue from Everest Base Camp. Altitude is often a limiting factor in travel insurance; many companies put an upper limit of 2,000m, which is easily reached even in the Atlas or Tatra Mountains, for example. Insurance for mountain rescue is not usually included in standard policies, even if they do cover hill walking. The UK is unusual in having free mountain rescue from volunteer teams or RAF helicopters. Some insurance policies include emergency administration of screened blood which might be a comfort to some travellers (*see* **contacts**, p.32).

In addition to adequate insurance, try to have another back-up, like a credit card, in case of unforeseen and uncovered events such as an earthquake or terrorist attack. Travel insurance is available through

Case History: travel insurance

Joe, aged 81, keeps active and bicycles to the pool twice a week for a strenuous, fast-lane, quarter-mile swim. About six years previously he'd suffered some 'funny turns' due to night epilepsy. He was put on treatment and had no further problems. He had not needed even to see his own GP except for repeat prescriptions. He decided to visit his son in Washington DC and also do a bus tour to enjoy the fall colours of New England. Since his home was insured with **Saga**, he phoned for a travel insurance quote. Saga, who specialize in cover for the over-50s, say they have no upper age limit, yet they refused cover saying that with his epilepsy America was too risky for them. He phoned around and found that most insurance companies and building society insurers would not cover someone over 80, although several said that cover might be possible if he obtained a medical certificate confirming fitness to travel. Surprisingly, Joe's GP refused to provide such a certificate because of his slow pulse: 'heart block' that had been fully investigated seven years before and was causing Joe no symptoms. The GP referred Joe to a consultant cardiologist and for an echocardiogram. Reluctant to pay the fees for this, Joe tried **Age Concern**; once he could confirm that he had not been in hospital during the previous year, they offered cover for himself and his 75-year-old wife for £309; the policy was valid for up to 31 days' travel any time during the following 12 months. What insurance companies need to know is whether travellers are stable. The fact that Joe hadn't been in hospital for six years should have demonstrated that any problems that his epilepsy or heart might cause were stable, and he was not therefore a high-risk traveller. People with other medical conditions would be well advised to shop around for insurance or consult a patient support group for advice or special deals.

insurance companies, banks, travel agents and tour operators. Many household insurance policies can be extended to cover multiple trips abroad: domestic and standard travel policies often exclude extended or remote trips and adventurous activities (these may include skiing or diving), in which case you should call a specialist firm. Conventional insurers and travel agents often refuse even short-term cover if you have any long-standing medical problem or are pregnant. Travellers with specific health requirements are covered in **Special Travellers** (*see* p.59). The RGS Expedition Advisory Centre advises on companies that insure expeditions (*see* p.29).

Within the **European Community**, emergency treatment is provided free or at reduced cost to EC residents with an **E111 form**. These arrangements do not cover treatment of long-standing complaints or conditions. The free UK Department of Health booklet *Health Advice for Travellers* explains how to get medical treatment inside and outside the EC (*see* below). It is wise to have medical insurance as well. Reciprocal arrangements (where some non-British nationals receive free or subsidized treatment in certain countries) are now unusual except within the European Community. Countries without reciprocal agreements with the UK include Switzerland, Turkey, Cyprus, Canada, the USA, Mexico and all South American nations, most Caribbean islands, all Middle Eastern countries, all African countries, all of Asia including some republics of the former Soviet Union, and the whole Pacific region except Australia and New Zealand. Check how to arrange treatment at your intended destination. Your travel insurance hotline should be able to help.

Contact information: travel advice and insurance

To obtain the free UK Department of Health booklet *Health Advice for Travellers*, call **UK t** 0800 555 777, look on *www.doh.gov.uk/hat* or pick up a copy at a Post Office or your doctor's surgery. Take a look at ***www.bloodcare.org.uk*** for advice on obtaining properly screened blood.

Age Concern Insurance Services, **UK t** 0845 601 2234 (*lines open Mon–Fri 8am–8pm, Sat 9–5*), *www.ageconcern.org.uk*. Covers most medically stable passengers and has no age limits.

Columbus, **UK t** 0845 330 7076, *www.columbusdirect.com*.

Holiday Care Service, **UK t** (01293) 774 535, **f** (01293) 784 647, *holiday.care@virgin.net*. Offers information for travellers with health problems and a list of sympathetic insurance companies.

ITIS, **UK t** 0870 179 8081, **f** 0870 241 1683, *www.itis.dircon.co.uk*.

Saga Services, **UK t** 0800 056 5464, *www.saga.co.uk*.

Travel Insurance Club, **UK t** 0800 163 518, *www.ticdirect.co.uk*.

Worldwide, **UK t** (01892) 833 338, *www.worldwideinsure.com*.

See also **Special Travellers**, pp.59–74, for firms offering travel advice and insurance to those with particular health conditions; other insurance companies offering cover to over-65s are listed in **Features**, p.18.

WHAT TO PACK

A first-aid kit

Guidelines on medicines to take are given on pp.77–9. If you are planning a remote or long trip, try to attend a first aid course before you go; in Britain, possible choices are **Red Cross**, **St John's**, **Wilderness Medical Training** or **Life Support** (*see* contacts, below). It might also be worth investing time in gaining other skills that will be helpful if you are heading for remote places; reflexology, for example, relieves pain without medicines, and I have seen it used as a self-treatment to great effect in the mountains. Mobile phones are a useful item of safety equipment: as long as children or travelling companions carry a note of the number, they allow people to find each other or call for help. Two British tourists were left dangling 10m above the ground on a ski lift in Italy during 2002, when the lift was switched off for the night; they used their mobile phone to call rescuers.

If you ask your doctor to prescribe medicines to take abroad, British National Health Service rules say that a private prescription fee should be charged. A specialist service like **Nomad** might be cheaper. Sterile medical packs containing needles, etc., may be purchased from Nomad, Interhealth and MASTA clinics, Homeway Medical, BCB (*see* **Useful Addresses**, pp.329–30), and there are many others.

If you are going somewhere hot, pack one or two large (one-litre) water bottles. Thermos flasks are also useful, even in the tropics (*see* p.104).

Contact information: first-aid courses and supplies

Life Support, **UK t** (01229) 772 708.
St John's, **UK t** (01438) 740 044.
Wilderness Medical Training, **UK t** (01926) 882 763.
See also **Useful Addresses**, pp.329–30.

Clothes

Think about what you will wear. If you are going somewhere hot, ensure that you have at least one long-sleeved, 100% cotton shirt and long, loose trousers; these will help protect you from biting beasts, barbed vegetation and the sun. Dark clothes attract insects and absorb sunlight, so light colours keep you coolest. Jeans are unsuitable travel wear: they're heavy, dry slowly, are hot and clingy in hot weather and yet not warm enough in cold climates. T-shirts are not particularly comfortable tropical wear either; they are hotter than ordinary cotton shirts and do not protect the back of the neck from sunburn. They are, however, very useful as additional layers if the weather is cold or you ascend to cooler conditions from a hot, low area. Layers are warmer than one thick garment, and more adaptable if travelling through several climatic zones. *Weather to Travel* by E. Rowlands (Tomorrows Guides, Hungerford, 2001) is a useful resouce if you want to know how hot it will be at your destination or you are deciding which is the kindest season climatically.

Even in tourist destinations, dressing modestly seems to be appreciated and those who do so are treated with more respect. Ask people who have travelled to your intended destination about local dressing customs. Even men can offend by stripping off, and if women dress as they would at home they may encourage problems and even sexual assault. In many cultures it is unacceptable to be scantily clad, while figure-hugging clothes and leggings may not be appreciated (or, on women, may be appreciated too much). In some Muslim countries and many Asian cities it would be considered almost obscene for men to go out in public bare-chested or wearing shorts. Men and women wear loose-fitting garments that cover all but the head, hands and feet. In many places where outsiders are a rarity, stripping down to a bathing costume is never done and, if women bathe at all, they bathe fully clothed. Until recently, women in Malawi were not allowed to wear trousers at all. In warm climates my favourite outfits include long wide skirts. These are especially good when on long bus rides since – by spreading the skirt wide and squatting – it is possible to take a discreet pee. The long tails of the sub-continental *shalwar-kameez* are also good for this purpose. Loose skirts allow healthy circulation of air, reducing the problems of thrush commonly experienced by women travelling in hot, humid climates. Note that a drawstring skirt can be pulled up under the armpits for a complete bath at the village tap. A tube of cloth sold as a sarong in the Far East or lungi in South Asia is also good for bathing in public.

It is common for the girth to shrink dramatically on tropical trips: women's waists seem particularly variable. Heat tends to reduce the appetite, there may be fewer tempting snacks, there may be a bout or two of diarrhoea and there is often more exercise. Pack a belt.

ARE YOU FIT ENOUGH?

A pre-trip check-up?

A routine medical check-up is rarely useful in people who feel fit and well, even if your proposed trip is to somewhere very remote. However, when planning any journey, consider whether you are fit enough for what you plan to do. For example, a surprising number of people who take little exercise book trekking holidays in high mountains. At best they are in pain from aching muscles for much of their holiday; at worst they put themselves at serious risk.

Inexperienced travellers and **smokers** are more likely to become ill abroad, and so should be particularly cautious. Smokers, for example, are the group most likely to contract Legionnaires' Disease. And there are many countries now where smoking in public places is illegal. Smokers travelling to Singapore, India or intending to use city public transport systems would be wise to pack nicotine replacement patches. **Overweight people** are at higher risk of heat exhaustion and may find that heat alone makes them feel miserable. **Backpackers** and **independent travellers** also seem to have more than their fair share of problems. A survey commissioned by the UK Foreign Office recently showed that one third of British independent travellers experienced some kind of 'major problem' for which they sought help from an embassy: 13% fell ill; 9% missed flights; 6% were robbed; 20% had no travel health insurance.

Try to sort out any recurrent medical problems that have been bothering you; an exotic trip can make them a lot worse. Even athlete's foot can become a misery.

Teeth

Have a dental check-up before you go. Dentists may not charge very much abroad but the standard of treatment is sometimes poor, and if equipment sterilization is also deficient there is a risk of hepatitis B or HIV. Stones in rice and lentils often cause dental trouble, so consider taking temporary fillings or a dental 'first aid kit'; travel clinics often sell them. Meat in the developing world is often very stringy, so pack some dental floss too (it can also be used as a washing line when travelling); you should floss daily wherever you are in any case.

Ear and sinus problems

Those with active middle ear or sinus congestion or infection, or severe hay fever, may suffer from a great deal of pain if they fly. Anyone suffering from a middle ear infection (otitis media) should delay flying until they have taken at least 36 hours (several doses) of a course of an appropriate antibiotic. Anyone who has had an operation on the inner ear should avoid flying for two months. Wait 10–14 days before flying after tonsillectomy or any operation on the middle ear.

Eyes

Conjunctivitis is common on tropical trips and contact-lens wearers should travel with a pair of glasses so that they can manage without lenses in case of infection, or in case they have to contend with a long, dusty bus ride. Those with a cataract should pack a peaked cap to cut down glare; this is a particular problem in northern latitudes where the sun is low and when the cataract scatters sunlight and thus dazzles. During surgery for a retinal detachment, a gas bubble is often injected into the eye and it is necessary to wait for this to be reabsorbed before flying; the wait is two weeks if sulphahexafluoride or six weeks if perfluoropropane gas was used. Surgery for cataracts or corneal laser surgery are not influenced by air travel but wait a week after any penetrating injury to the eye. Check all this with your eye doctor. Travel with a spare pair of glasses and/or your prescription.

Before You Go

Immunizations by Region

04

Accidents take many travellers' lives, others succumb to malaria and many suffer from travellers' diarrhoea or dysentery, and yet there are no vaccines against these health risks. It is necessary, therefore, to think 'prevention', not just 'what jabs do I need?' Furthermore, although vaccines that are currently available give good protection against many serious infectious diseases, not all infections are vaccine-preventable. With expert advice, though, you can receive appropriate injections which will enhance your immune defences and help you side-step serious disease. As new vaccines are developed, it will become more and more important to receive immunizations that are tailored carefully to your needs and your journey.

Summary

→ Start to organize immunizations at least a couple of months before travel; last-minute immunization may leave you inadequately protected, and – in the case of Yellow Fever – may prevent entry at your destination.

→ Wise travellers keep up to date with routine immunization against tetanus, and travelling children should have received their routine childhood injections.

→ Some travellers with ongoing illnesses or other considerations may not be able to have **live vaccines**; these are oral polio, oral typhoid (though the injections for both these are alright), BCG, MMR and Yellow Fever. *See* your individual condition and **Special Travellers**, pp.59–74.

→ Although trips to northern Europe may require few extra immunizations, summer visitors who intend to go walking in the forests or rural areas should check whether **TBE** is a risk (*see* p.45).

→ Find out if your destination is malarious, and take tablets and bite-prevention precautions as necessary.

IMMUNIZATIONS

Go to a travel clinic at least two months before departure. Immunization schedules are becoming more complex and experts now recognize that requirements vary within regions of countries and by season. Schedules also vary with the nationality of the vaccinator. Furthermore, situations change, so these notes provide information on the immunizations available and who should have them. Further up-to-date advice can be obtained from a specialist travel clinic. Clinics linked to a computer database can give you a print-out specific to the area of the country that you are visiting during different seasons. Information on any recent outbreaks will also be available (*see* **Useful Addresses**, p.326).

Once you know what immunization you need, British readers should be able to organize immunization free from their GP against hepatitis A, polio, tetanus and typhoid; others may also be administered but at a charge. Special vaccines such as Japanese B encephalitis are not usually available, and even BCG is only available from the NHS at special hospital clinics. Travel clinics can provide everything, but charge the full rate for all that they give; you pay for convenience. Where you choose to have your vaccines will depend on whether you are more limited by time or money, or perhaps the access facilities offered by the clinic: if you are less mobile or travelling with more than one small child, some clinics may not offer easy wheelchair or buggie access. Several new vaccines should soon be available against travellers' diarrhoea, bacillary dysentery and *Campylobacter* diarrhoea. Travel clinics will usually hear about them first.

In North America, check locally with the public health department for travel clinics in your town. Australians can arrange pre-trip immunizations through local doctors. Many local doctors carry or can prescribe vaccines and antimalarial tablets, but some don't, so check that they are available when you make an appointment. Travel clinics will probably prove more convenient because they keep more vaccines, so that you can avoid getting scripts, then going to the chemist and then coming back to the doctor to get the vaccine administered. It may be wise to contact a travel clinic if your destination is off-beat, very long, covering multiple countries or if you have medical problems that could complicate your situation. The cost of a consultation with a local doctor and in a travel clinic is comparable and Australians can claim these on Medicare. Travel clinic charges vary depending on how long you spend with the doctor but would be about AUS$39 for an average trip, although it may be much less if the person is just coming to top up some shots. For a second hepatitis A immunization, for example, the charge would be about AUS$10 for the visit, plus the vaccine cost.

Immunizations for trips abroad

The vaccine against malaria promised a few years ago has proved ineffective. Antimalarial tablets need to be taken in a great many regions; travel clinics will say what is best for which area. For details of tablets and other precautions, *see* pp.133–8.

Tetanus

You will probably have been immunized against tetanus, polio and diphtheria as a child, but check if you need a booster to protect you from these very serious diseases. Tetanus is acquired from deep, dirty skin wounds, and also from puncture wounds contaminated by cow or horse droppings. It is safe to be immunized against tetanus during pregnancy. It is a **killed vaccine** and needs boosting every 10 years.

Polio

Poliomyelitis is still a danger to travellers; it is a filth-to-mouth disease so is a risk in countries where standards of enviromental hygiene are poor. The Western hemisphere had been declared free from polio during the closing years of the 20th century, and for a time polio vaccination was not required for travel to the Americas. Unfortunately, however, there was an outbreak in the Dominican Republic in 2001, so it is probably wise still to keep polio immunity up to date for travel to any third world destination. You do not have to go very far afield to contract polio; an unimmunized British tourist on a short trip to Morocco suffered from paralytic polio. Polio immunization is usually by drops in the mouth, but the usual **live oral polio vaccine** is unsafe in pregnancy and in those with compromised immunity; there is, however, a safe, **killed, injectable form**. It needs boosting every 10 years.

Diphtheria

Diphtheria is spread by droplets in the air; it still prevalent in Africa, Asia and Central and South America, and is a risk in Russia and the Ukraine. If you already have immunity from previous diphtheria immunization, it can be unpleasant to have the full-strength jab; a special, low-dose vaccine is given as the booster. There is now also a low-dose diphtheria vaccine combined in a single injection with tetanus toxoid, so both can be boosted at once. Immunity needs boosting every 10 years; it is a **killed vaccine**.

Tuberculosis and BCG (*Bacille Calmette-Guérin*)

Tuberculosis (TB) is on the increase worldwide. For notes on the disease, *see* p.277. Most British adults will have been immunized against TB with BCG at about the age of 13. Check whether this was done; it leaves a little scar on the upper arm. It is unlikely to need boosting again. British children under the age of 13 should be given BCG if they are living abroad in high-risk areas. This can be done from the first day of life, and for expatriate families this is the most convenient time to arrange it. Get it done well before travel if you can, since occasionally BCG causes an ulcer that takes over a month to heal and may need to be shown to the vaccinating doctor. People who have reduced immunity (those with cancer, HIV) or are pregnant should avoid this **live vaccine**. There is a debate about the efficacy of BCG, but European doctors favour it since it protects against two fatal forms of TB (TB meningitis and miliary TB). American physicians do not give BCG because it makes diagnosis of TB more difficult; if you see an American doctor about symptoms that might possibly be due to a TB infection, be sure to mention whether you have had BCG.

Hepatitis A

Viral hepatitis is common, affecting 5% of unimmunized travellers to the developing world. The most common form is hepatitis A. Amongst British travellers there has been an eight-fold fall in imported cases of hepatitis A since 1989 and this is probably due to the availability of a good vaccine with few side-effects. Gamma globulin, being derived from human blood, carries some theoretical risk and has been superseded; it gave only partial, rapidly waning protection. There are several effective **killed vaccines** (Havrix and Avaxim) and a version for children (Havrix junior) which can be given from the age of one year. Two injections give 10 years' protection. There have been some recent problems with the vaccine, though. Unfortunately, during 2001 Aventis Pasteur announced that people previously immunized with VAQTA or VAQTA paediatric hepatitis A vaccines were not protected and that these people need to be reimmunized with the SmithKline Beecham vaccine (e.g. Havrix). Travel clinics and GPs are aware of this problem and should be able to tell their patients whether reimmunization is necessary before their next trip.

If you have had jaundice due to hepatitis A (this can be checked with a blood test), you will have life-long immunity to A and further immunization against it will be unnecessary. Immunization does not protect against hepatitis E or the other causes of hepatitis.

Typhoid

The first typhoid vaccine was given in 1896. Typhoid is rare in travellers, and some would argue that immunization against it is not strictly necessary for travel to sub-Saharan Africa or Southeast Asia, since the likelihood of contracting the disease there is small (similar to that in southern Europe). An overall figure of risk in travellers (from the USA) is six cases per million journeys. The risk is higher among travellers to the Indian subcontinent (around 100 cases per million travellers) and some areas of tropical South America, notably Peru (174 per million). It is also quite common in Central Asia, particularly Tajikistan.

Typhoid immunization is notorious for causing a sore arm, but the new typhoid vaccines cause fewer side effects and now if you are one of the unfortunate 7% to experience pain, swelling and/or redness at the injection site after one product, you can try the other. Or you can even take capsules – as long as you are prepared to pay six times as much in order to avoid the needle: £25 compared to about £4 for intra-muscular Typhim Vi. The **live oral vaccine** consists of capsules swallowed over five days. These require refrigeration and are not recommended for children under six or for the immuno-compromised. Immunity is boosted with capsules after a year, while injections with the **killed vaccines** need boosting every three years. People over 35 who have had four or more typhoid courses do not need further immunization. The vaccine gives only 70–80% protection so it is important for all travellers in risk regions to avoid raw or partly cooked food and dubious water (*see* pp.100–104).

Immunizations required for some areas

Yellow Fever

This is a very serious, untreatable mosquito-borne disease endemic in much of sub-Saharan Africa, Central America and parts of South America (*see* map, below). The **live vaccine** protects for 10 years. Many countries require an international vaccination certificate if you are travelling from an endemic area, because there are mosquitoes capable of spreading the disease in many warm regions, and no one wants to see it spread into new areas. Anyone with a severe allergy to eggs, infants under nine

Risk areas: Yellow Fever

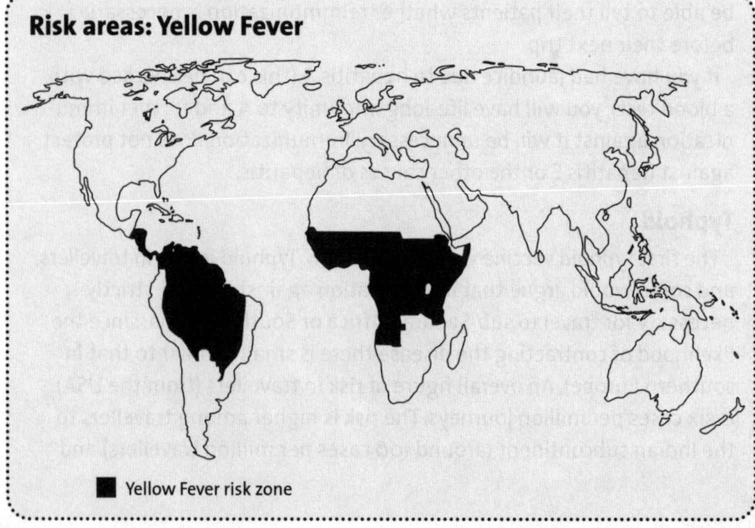

months, pregnant women or people who are immunosuppressed (such as cancer sufferers, or people on high-dose steroids) should avoid this live vaccine. There is a higher risk of severe and life-threatening side effects from Yellow Fever immunization in the elderly, so it is important to ensure that immunization is actually needed, especially in the over-60s. Discuss this with your doctor before travelling. You cannot enter a Yellow Fever area without being vaccinated unless you have a medical exemption certificate.

Japanese B encephalitis

This is a problem in Sri Lanka, India, Nepal and as far north as Pacific Russia; it also occurs sporadically in Southeast and East Asia, particularly where pigs are kept. It usually only infects villagers living near pigs and rice fields, but the vector has been known to bite 20km from its breeding grounds. It was said to be rare in Muslim countries, but has been reported in Pakistan, where egrets may be the intermediate hosts. Transmission in seasonal climates is mainly April–October (peaking at the onset of the monsoon); closer to the Equator this is less predictable.

This is another serious mosquito-borne disease (so bite prevention is again important), but it is unusual for travellers to acquire it. There were only three proven cases among all the Australians travelling in South and Southeast Asia from 1970 to 1991. The risk in tourists and business travellers is estimated to be one case per million travellers, because in more than 99% of people bitten by an infective mosquito there are no symptoms and no illness. However, in those who develop symptoms, the death rate can be as high as 30% and half of the survivors are left with long-term neurological disability. It is a nasty, incurable disease, and those travelling or working in rural Asia may

Risk areas: Japanese B encephalitis

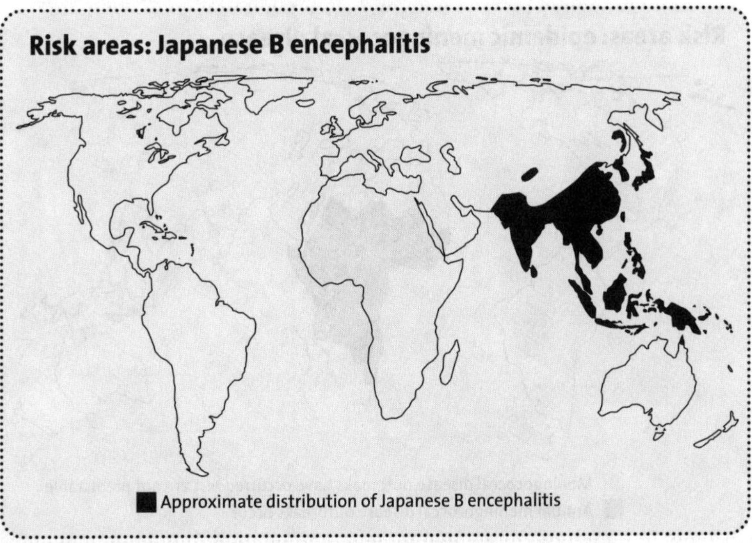

■ Approximate distribution of Japanese B encephalitis

wish to take the precaution of the vaccine. It is an unpleasant disease, but current (**killed**) vaccines may cause severe allergic reactions, which can occur within minutes and up to two weeks after the second dose (most commonly two days later). The course consists of two injections one week apart (one dose gives no protection). Discuss with your doctor whether you are at particular risk; if you decide to be vaccinated have the last dose at least two weeks before departure. The vaccine protects for at least two years; boosters are required after three.

Meningococcus

There are several **killed vaccines**, but the one that is usually given as a travel immunization protects against meningococcus A and C; these are two strains of the bacteria responsible for the most devastating forms of meningitis and meningococcal septacaemia, and it is the latter which is actually more of a killer than meningitis. This vaccine is needed for travel to India, Nepal and the 'meningitis belt' of Africa (mainly in latitudes 15°N to 5°N, but extending to the Equator in Kenya and Uganda). This includes sub-Saharan Senegal, Mali, Chad and Sudan; all of Gambia, Guinea, Togo and Benin; southwest Ethiopia, northern Sierra Leone, Liberia, Ivory Coast, Nigeria, Cameroon and the Central African Republic. In the 'belt', epidemics commonly occur at the onset of the dry season (December–February) and usually stop with the first rains (May–June); cases occur from November to April. For all pilgrims to Mecca, Saudi Arabia requires proof of immunization with the quadrivalent meningococcus ACWY vaccine, issued not more than three years and not less than 10 days before arrival in the country. Meningococcus vaccine can be given to anyone aged over 18 months and is a single injection. It is entirely different to the routine Hib vaccine, which

Risk areas: epidemic meningococcal disease

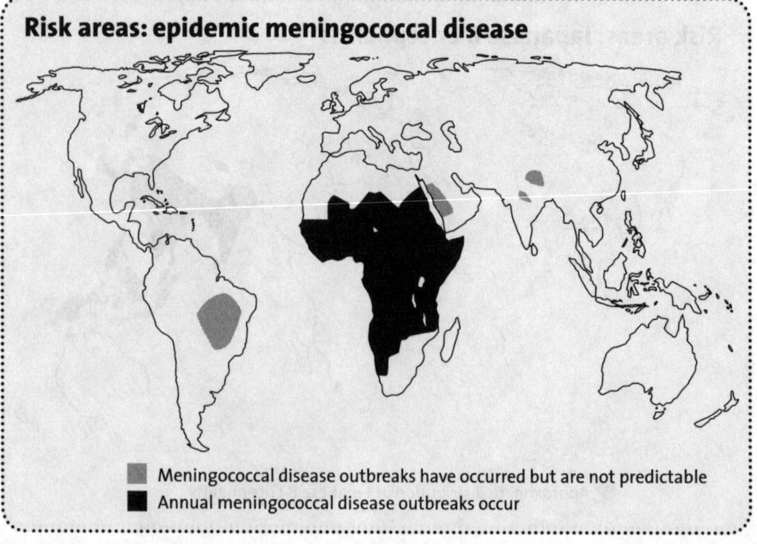

protects children under four from a different kind of meningitis. Neither vaccine protects against all forms of meningitis. Boosters are given after 3–5 years.

Pneumococcus immunization is required for those who have lost their spleen or have sickle cell disease. Originally such people were told that they needed immunization once in a lifetime but for asplenic travellers the experts now recommend boosting every five years. Pneumococcal immunization is also now recommended in the UK once in a lifetime for people with long-standing illnesses that put them at risk if they contract pneumonia, including those with asthma and diabetes. The incidence of pneumococcal infection in travellers is hard to research, but it does seem unusually common in otherwise healthy people who would not be expected to be at special risk while at home. A few doctors advise it for all travellers. Your doctor or travel clinic can arrange this. It is a **killed vaccine**.

'European' tick-borne encephalitis (TBE)

This is a risk for people walking or camping in lowland forest areas in parts of Scandinavia, former Soviet countries and central Europe (the Czech and Slovak Republics, Austria, Germany, ex-Yugoslavia; *see* inside back cover); April to August are high-risk months. The virus can also be transmitted through unpasteurized dairy products from cows, sheep or goats. Unimmunized people who have received a tick bite within the previous four days can be given a protective immunoglobulin injection. The vaccines are not available in the USA, and do not protect against tick-borne diseases other than 'European' tick-borne encephalitis. 'European' TBE occurs in Asia (*see* map below) where it is known under a variety of names, listed overleaf under 'TBE subtypes'.

Risk areas: 'European' tick-borne encephalitis (TBE)

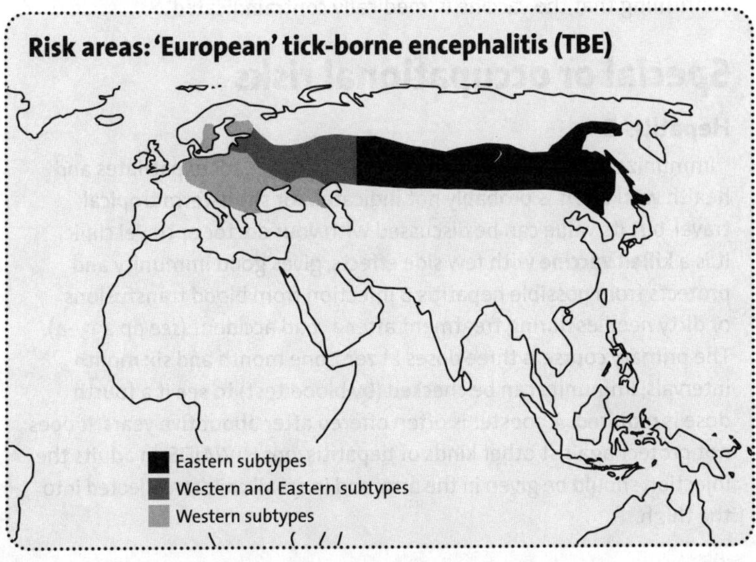

TBE subtypes

TBE comes in western and eastern subtypes but the vaccine protects against both. 'European' TBE occurs in Asia and is also variously called:

- → **Central European encephalitis.**
- → **Taiga encephalitis.**
- → **Far East Russian encephalitis.**
- → **Biundulating meningoencephalitis.**
- → **Diphasic milk fever.**
- → **Kumlinge disease.**
- → **Schneider's disease.**

Cholera

Cholera is now very rare in travellers, even in epidemic areas. The best way to remain cholera-free is to avoid contaminated food and water (*see* pp.100–104). Travellers are no longer vaccinated against cholera, even for travel to endemic and epidemic areas, and this policy has not led to an increase in travellers contracting the disease. The injectable vaccine is no longer available in the UK. There is an **oral vaccine** available in mainland Europe but it is thought that at present, because the risk of disease in normal travellers is so low, immunization is unnecessary. This situation may change when more effective vaccines are developed: at least one vaccine that is currently being developed against microbes causing travellers' diarrhoea includes cholera antigen. It is now internationally agreed that immunizing travellers does not prevent introduction of cholera infection into a country, but unofficial demands occur. This is rare and seems to be confined to a few remote land borders. Travel clinics should be able to supply a certificate confirming that the vaccine is 'medically contraindicated'.

Special or occupational risks

Hepatitis B

Immunization against hepatitis B is worthwhile for expatriates and health workers; it is probably not indicated for short-term tropical travel, but its value can be discussed with your doctor or travel clinic. It is a **killed vaccine** with few side effects, gives good immunity and protects from possible hepatitis B infection from blood transfusions or dirty needles during treatment after a road accident (*see* pp.293–4). The primary course is three doses at zero, one month and six month intervals; immunity can be checked (by blood test) to see if a fourth dose is required. A booster is often offered after about five years. It does not protect against other kinds of hepatitis, nor HIV/AIDS. In adults the injection should be given in the arm, and in small children injected into the thigh.

Influenza

'Flu vaccination does not protect against the common cold. It safeguards people at special risk from some strains of influenza: those with diabetes, long-standing heart or respiratory problems (including asthma), those taking steroid tablets and other ongoing illnesses. Your doctor or practice nurse can arrange it. It is offered each winter to everyone over 65 years of age and would be a sensible immunization for many travellers, including the elderly going into the southern hemisphere winter. It is a **killed vaccine**.

Rabies

Rabies is a risk in most countries. The only continents to be free of it are Australasia and Antarctica. In addition, the UK, Ireland, Cyprus, Faroes and some parts of Scandinavia are safe; in much of southern Europe the risk is low and post-exposure vaccination available. Travellers to all other destinations should consider immunization and it is advisable for those on long trips and to remote regions. It is a **killed vaccine**; an innocuous immunization and a sensible precaution for people living in the Indian subcontinent (including Pakistan and Sri Lanka) or wherever there are a lot of stray dogs; it is also wise for those intending to enter caves in the Americas. Rabies is especially prevalent in Thailand (though not in major cities), with 200–300 human deaths a year. Rabies vaccine is a must for veterinarians or zoologists doing field work in the developing world. The incubation period (the amount of time you have to get treatment after a bite) depends on the distance of the bite site from the brain and the severity of the bite. Small children often get bitten on the face, so that there is very little time to get medical help. It is important that young children visiting endemic areas should be vaccinated.

Risk areas: Rabies

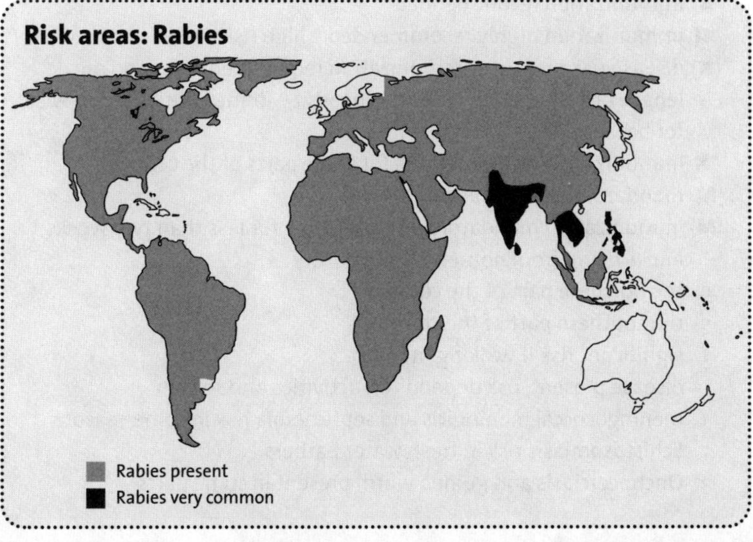

Two injections are given a month apart, with a reinforcing dose after 6–12 months, then boosters every three years. The cheapest way to be immunized is with a part dose (8–9 people can be injected intradermally from a 1ml vial) and travel clinics often arrange this. The vaccine's efficacy is reduced if you are taking *chloroquine* antimalaria tablets at the same time, so get immunized well before you start your tablets or, if this is impossible, have an intramuscular (larger) dose of rabies vaccine.

Plague

Few travellers need immunization against plague even during an epidemic (*see also* 'Plagues, pestilences and paranoia', pp.13–15). Rodent ecologists or medical staff are sometimes immunized if working during an outbreak. There have been recent outbreaks of plague in Bolivia, Brazil, Madagascar, Tanzania, Uganda, Mozambique, China, Myanmar, Vietnam and India, and there are sporadic cases in the USA. It is not a particularly effective vaccine.

Key to regional health risk tables on pp.50–58

- O malaria risk patchy or seasonal; prophylaxis may vary across the country. Check with the malaria reference laboratory
- ● (white) small risk of contracting malaria: no tablets are necessary so bite prevention still important
- ● malaria risk, recommended prophylaxis is indicated
- Mf *Mefloquine* (Larium)
- Dx *Doxycycline* (Vibramycin)
- Ml Malarone (*Proguanil with atovaquone*)
- C+P *Chloroquine and proguanil* (Paludrine)
- C *Chloroquine* alone
- **✖** immunization recommended
- **✖!** immunization highly recommended – high risk
- (**✖**) disease risk present – immunization requirements depend on length of stay and activities during visit – immunization often wise for backpackers
- ***✖** immunization recommended for some parts of the country
- **M** mandatory immunization
- (**M**) immunization mandatory unless staying for less than two weeks and arriving from non-endemic country
- n the northern part of the country
- s the southern part of the country
- **!** significant risk if walking in forest
- ! (white) disease present; risk depends on activities and season
- 1 meningococcal meningitis and septicaemia risk in some seasons
- 2 Schistosomiasis risk in fresh water bathers
- 3 Onchocerciasis and guinea worm present in some parts

REGIONAL HEALTH RISKS

Travel anywhere involves health risks. This section and the accompanying tables highlight special risks in different geographical regions: the immunization tables (*see* pp.50–58) mention vaccines that will be required for travellers. These are not comprehensive and are intended to aid a traveller to focus on whether a particular destination might be sensible for them and what preventative strategies might be wise. Things change with new disease outbreaks so it is wise to double check with a travel clinic before you travel. Everyone should keep up to date with routine immunizations, especially tetanus, and those going on extended trips to rural regions or to less well resourced regions should – in addition – consider immunization against hepatitis B, rabies and perhaps TB (BCG). Those working overseas long term should probably arrange cover against diphtheria. People passing through countries where Yellow Fever is recorded – even if they are not visiting a region where the disease is transmitted – may find border crossings easier if they are immunized and are carrying an international vaccination certificate.

USA and Canada

The risk of **gastro-intestinal disease** is present although small. **Tick-borne infections** are a concern to those enjoying outdoor activities and so bite avoidance is wise (*see* p.157) and symptoms after a tick bite should be properly treated. **Rabies** is a risk after any animal bite. Although there are no immunizations required for entry into the USA or Canada, children and some university students must show documentary evidence of immunization status against diphtheria, measles, polio, rubella, and usually also against tetanus, pertussis, mumps and hepatitis B. Chickenpox immunization is also required by some institutions. Health insurance may be expensive but adequate cover is crucial. **Scorpions** in Arizona and New Mexico are dangerous but antivenom is available; venomous **snakes** rarely cause harm because of the availability of medical services and antivenom.

Australia and New Zealand

The risk of **gastro-intestinal disease** exists although it is low. There are several unpleasant **mosquito-borne infections** on offer to those bitten in the northeast of Australia; **Japanese B encephalitis** immunization might be worth considering for anyone going to live or work in the Torres Strait Islands. The continent boasts a range of venomous **spiders** and **snakes**, so it is best to treat even small wildlife with respect.

Europe

As with all destinations, there is a risk of gastro-intestinal infection, and this risk is greatest in the south and east of the region during the summer and autumn. **Hepatitis A** is more common in eastern European countries. **Legionnaires' Disease** occurs amongst hotel holiday-makers throughout the region but it seldom causes symptoms even amongst the people exposed to the bacteria (*see* p.226). Those travellers who venture into woods or who camp or orienteer may expose themselves to tick-borne infections: both **Lyme Disease** and **tick-borne encephalitis (TBE)** exist in much of the area and TBE immunization is wise in summer hikers in the countries indicated (*see* **table** below for risks; key on p.48).

Europe
(*see* **key**, p.48)

	Malaria	Polio	Hepatitis A	Typhoid	Diphtheria	TBE	Rabies
Albania		✖	✖			!	(✖)
Andorra		(✖)					(✖)
Austria		(✖)				!	
Azores		(✖)	(✖)				(✖)
Belarus		(✖)	✖		✖	!	(✖)
Bosnia		(✖)	✖				(✖)
Bulgaria		(✖)	✖			!	(✖)
Canary Islands		(✖)					(✖)
Croatia		(✖)	✖			!	(✖)
Cyprus		(✖)					(✖)
Czech Republic		(✖)	✖			!	(✖)
Denmark		(✖)				!	
Estonia		(✖)			✖	!	(✖)
Finland		(✖)			✖	!	
France	O	(✖)				!	
Georgia	C: Ju–Oct	(✖)	✖				(✖)
Germany		(✖)				!	
Gibraltar		(✖)					(✖)
Greece		(✖)	(✖)			!	(✖)
Herzegovina		(✖)	✖			!	(✖)
Hungary		(✖)				!	
Iceland		(✖)					
Ireland		(✖)					
Italy		(✖)				!!	(✖)
Kosovo		(✖)				!	(✖)
Latvia		(✖)			✖	!	(✖)

There is **rabies** in the region although post-bite treatment is usually within reach of any victim. In southern Europe insect bites can be a nuisance and there is a slight risk of **insect-borne infection**, including Leishmania and some other rarities. There has been a rash of reports of holiday-makers returning from the Mediterranean suffering from a nasty fever, muscle aches and severe headache. They had viral sand-fly fever (*see* pp.154–5 for bite avoidance). All victims recovered without specific treatment, but these cases highlight the good sense in avoiding insect bites even when as close to home as the Mediterranean. There is no longer any **malaria** in Europe, although it does occur in Georgia and in Asian Turkey.

	Malaria	Polio	Hepatitis A	Typhoid	Diphtheria	TBE	Rabies
Liechtenstein		(✖)					(✖)
Lithuania		(✖)			✖	!	(✖)
Luxembourg		(✖)					
Macedonia		(✖)	✖			!	(✖)
Madeira		(✖)	(✖)				(✖)
Malta		(✖)					
Moldova		(✖)	✖		✖	!	(✖)
Monaco		(✖)					
Montenegro		(✖)				!	(✖)
Netherlands		(✖)					
Norway		(✖)				!	
Poland		(✖)			✖	!	(✖)
Portugal		(✖)	(✖)				(✖)
Romania		(✖)	✖			!	(✖)
Russia (European)		✖	✖	✖	✖	!	(✖)
San Marino		(✖)					
Serbia		(✖)				!	(✖)
Slovakia		(✖)	✖			!	(✖)
Slovenia		(✖)	✖			!	(✖)
Spain		(✖)					(✖)
Sweden		(✖)				!	
Switzerland		(✖)				!	
Turkey (European)		(✖)	✖	(✖)			(✖)
Ukraine		(✖)	✖		✖	!	(✖)
ex-Yugoslavia		(✖)	✖			!	(✖)

Central America and the Caribbean

This is a high-risk region for **food-borne gastroenteritis**, **hepatitis A** and **E, worms** and **typhoid**. **Rabies** is a significant risk after animal bites. There are plenty of **insect**- and **tick-borne infections**, so bite precautions are important. **Dengue** (and some Dengue Haemorrhagic) **Fever** has been on the increase in the region, and there are unpredictable outbreaks.

Central America and the Caribbean
(*see* **key**, p.48)

	Malaria	Polio	Hepatitis A	Typhoid	Diphtheria	Rabies	Yellow Fever	Other
Anguilla		(✖)	✖	(✖)	(✖)			
Antigua & Barbuda		(✖)	✖	(✖)	(✖)			
Aruba		(✖)	✖	(✖)	(✖)			
Bahamas		(✖)	✖	(✖)	(✖)			
Barbados		(✖)	✖	(✖)	(✖)			
Belize	● C	(✖)	✖	✖	(✖)	(✖)	(✖)	
British Virgin Is.		(✖)	✖	(✖)	(✖)			
Cayman Is.		(✖)	✖	(✖)	(✖)			
Costa Rica	○ C	(✖)	✖	✖	(✖)	(✖)	(✖)	
Cuba		(✖)	✖	(✖)	(✖)			
Dominica		(✖)	✖	(✖)	(✖)			
Dominican Rep.	● C	✖	✖	(✖)	(✖)			2
El Salvador	○ C	(✖)	✖	✖	(✖)	(✖)		
Genadines		(✖)	✖	(✖)	(✖)			
Granada		(✖)	✖	(✖)	(✖)			
Guadeloupe		(✖)	✖	(✖)	(✖)			2
Guatemala	● C	(✖)	✖	✖	(✖)	(✖)		3
Haiti	● C	✖	✖	(✖)	(✖)			
Honduras	● C	(✖)	✖	✖	(✖)	(✖)		
Jamaica		(✖)	✖	(✖)	(✖)			
Martinique	○	(✖)	✖	(✖)	(✖)			2
Mexico	C	(✖)	✖	✖	(✖)	(✖)		3
Montserrat		(✖)	✖	(✖)	(✖)			
Neth. Antilles		(✖)	✖	(✖)	(✖)			
Nicaragua	● C	(✖)	✖	✖	(✖)	(✖)		
Panama	○ C	(✖)	✖	✖	(✖)	(✖)	*✖	
Puerto Rico		(✖)	✖	(✖)	(✖)			2
Saint Kitts & Nevis		(✖)	✖	(✖)	(✖)			
Saint Lucia		(✖)	✖	(✖)	(✖)			2
Saint Vincent		(✖)	✖	(✖)	(✖)			
Trinidad & Tobago		(✖)	✖	(✖)	(✖)		*✖	
Turks & Caicos Is.		(✖)	✖	(✖)	(✖)			
Virgin Is. (US)		(✖)	✖	(✖)	(✖)			

Schistosomiasis is present in the Dominican Republic, Guadeloupe, Martinique, Puerto Rico, St Lucia and may occur sporadically in other islands (*see* p.187). **Elephantiasis** has been recorded in Haiti and some other islands. The Americas had been declared free from **polio** in 1994 but in 2000 there was an outbreak in the Caribbean region, so polio immunization requirements are under constant review.

Pacific islands

There are many underwater hazards amongst the **sea creatures** of the region and there have been reports of **shellfish poisoning** (*see* pp.123–4). **Malaria** is a big problem in Papua New Guinea, Irian Jaya, Vanuatu and the Solomons but other islands are currently malaria-free. There are frequent but unpredictable outbreaks of **Dengue Fever** in most of the islands as well as some cases of **Elephantiasis** and **Ross River Fever** (*see* 'Arboviruses', p.152), so it is important to avoid insect bites. **Rabies** is not a great problem and immunization against it not usually recommended.

Pacific islands
(*see* **key**, p.48)

	Malaria	Polio	Hepatitis A	Typhoid	Diphtheria	Jap. Encephalitis
American Samoa		✖	✖	✖	(✖)	
Cook Is.		✖	✖	✖	(✖)	
Easter Is.		✖	✖	✖	(✖)	
Fiji		✖	✖	✖	(✖)	
Fr. Polynesia (Tahiti)		✖	✖	✖	(✖)	
Guam		✖	✖	✖	(✖)	(✖)
Kiribati		✖	✖	✖	(✖)	
Marshall Is.		✖	✖	✖	(✖)	
Micronesia, Fed.		✖	✖	✖	(✖)	
Nauru		✖	✖	✖	(✖)	
New Caledonia		✖	✖	✖	(✖)	
Niue		✖	✖	✖	(✖)	
Palau		✖	✖	✖	(✖)	
Papua New Guinea	● Mf, Dx, Ml	✖	✖	✖	(✖)	(✖)
Saipan					(✖)	(✖)
Samoa		✖	✖	✖	(✖)	
Solomon Is	● Mf, Dx, Ml	✖	✖	✖	(✖)	
Tokelau		✖	✖	✖	(✖)	
Tonga		✖	✖	✖	(✖)	
Trust Terr. Pacific Is.		✖	✖	✖	(✖)	
Tuvalu		✖	✖	✖	(✖)	
Vanuatu	● Mf, Dx, Ml	✖	✖	✖	(✖)	
Wallis & Futuna Is.		✖	✖	✖	(✖)	

Africa

The two big threats to health in much of sub-Saharan Africa are **road accidents** – from the crazy driving styles – and **malaria**. Bite prevention and correct antimalarial tablets are essential throughout, although most of South Africa is malaria-free. Northeastern South Africa including the Kruger National Park carries a risk of severe *falciparum* malaria. The region of risk expands sometimes after heavy rains. There have been some cases of **sleeping sickness** in visitors to Tanzania's game parks. Dangerous **snakes** exist but rarely attack or cause problems.

Africa
(*see* **key**, p.48)

	Malaria	Polio	Hepatitis A	Typhoid	Diphtheria	Rabies	Yellow Fever	Meningitis
Algeria	○	✖	✖	(✖)	(✖)	(✖)		
Angola	● Mf, Dx, Ml	✖	✖	✖	(✖)	(✖)	✖	(✖)
Benin	● Mf, Dx, Ml	✖	✖	✖	(✖)	(✖)	M	(✖)
Botswana	O C+P	✖	✖	✖	(✖)	(✖)		
Burkina Faso	● Mf, Dx, Ml	✖	✖	✖	(✖)	(✖)	M	(✖)
Burundi	● Mf, Dx, Ml	✖	✖	✖	(✖)	(✖)	✖	(✖)
Cameroon	● Mf, Dx, Ml	✖	✖	✖	(✖)	(✖)	M	(✖)
Cape Verde	○	(✖)	✖	✖	(✖)	(✖)	✖	
Cent. African Rep.	● Mf, Dx, Ml	✖	✖	✖	(✖)	(✖)	M	(✖)
Chad	● Mf, Dx, Ml	✖	✖	✖	(✖)	(✖)	✖	(✖)
Comoros	● Mf, Dx, Ml	(✖)	✖	✖	(✖)	(✖)		
Congo	● Mf, Dx, Ml	✖	✖	✖	(✖)	(✖)	M	
D. R. Congo (Zaire)	● Mf, Dx, Ml	✖	✖	✖	(✖)	(✖)	✖	
Djibouti	● Mf, Dx, Ml	✖	✖	✖	(✖)	(✖)	✖	(✖)
Egypt	O C	✖	✖	(✖)	(✖)	(✖)		
Equatorial Guinea	● Mf, Dx, Ml	✖	✖	✖	(✖)	(✖)	✖	
Eritrea	O Mf, Dx, Ml	✖	✖	✖	(✖)	(✖)	M	(✖)
Ethopia	● Mf, Dx, Ml	✖	✖	✖	(✖)	(✖)	✖	(✖)
Gabon	● Mf, Dx, Ml	✖	✖	✖	(✖)	(✖)	M	
Gambia	● Mf, Dx, Ml	✖	✖	✖	(✖)	(✖)	✖	(✖)
Ghana	● Mf, Dx, Ml	✖	✖	✖	(✖)	(✖)	✖	(✖)
Guinea	● Mf, Dx, Ml	✖	✖	✖	(✖)	(✖)	✖	(✖)
Guinea-Bissau	● Mf, Dx, Ml	✖	✖	✖	(✖)	(✖)	✖	(✖)
Ivory Coast	● Mf, Dx, Ml	✖	✖	✖	(✖)	(✖)	M	(✖)
Kenya	O Mf, Dx, Ml	✖	✖	✖	(✖)	(✖)	✖	(✖)
Lesotho		✖	✖	✖	(✖)	(✖)		
Liberia	● Mf, Dx, Ml	✖	✖	✖	(✖)	(✖)	M	
Libya	○	✖	✖	✖	(✖)	(✖)		
Madagascar	● Mf, Dx, Ml	✖	✖	✖	(✖)	(✖)		

The region is fairly risky for **food-borne infections**, and travel to Mediterranean Africa, including Egypt, carries a substantial risk of contracting significant **diarrhoea** or **dysentery** and the other filth-to-mouth infections. **Meningococcal infection** is a considerable risk to those living and working, and probably to those back-packing, in much of Africa (*see* p.44); the risk is seasonal.

Schistosomiasis (or **Bilharzia**) is a problem in some of Africa (*see* p.187), particularly in the Rift Valley area. Most cases imported into Britain are currently coming from Malawi but it occurs in patchy distribution over much of the continent and also in parts of Madagascar.

	Malaria	Polio	Hepatitis A	Typhoid	Diphtheria	Rabies	Yellow Fever	Meningitis
Malawi	● Mf, Dx, Ml	✖	✖	✖	(✖)	(✖)		(✖)
Mali	● Mf, Dx, Ml	✖	✖	✖	(✖)	(✖)	M	(✖)
Mauritania	○ C+P	✖	✖	✖	(✖)	(✖)	(M)	
Mauritius	○ C	(✖)	✖	✖	(✖)	(✖)		
Morocco	○	✖	(✖)	(✖)	(✖)	(✖)		
Mayotte	● Mf, Dx, Ml	✖	✖	✖	(✖)	(✖)		
Mozambique	● Mf, Dx, Ml	✖	✖	✖	(✖)	(✖)	M	(✖)
Namibia	○ C+P	✖	✖	✖	(✖)	(✖)		(✖)
Niger	● Mf, Dx, Ml	✖	✖	✖	(✖)	(✖)	M	(✖)
Nigeria	● Mf, Dx, Ml	✖	✖	✖	(✖)	(✖)	✖	(✖)
Reunion		(✖)	✖	✖	(✖)	(✖)		
Rwanda	● Mf, Dx, Ml	✖	✖	✖	(✖)	(✖)	M	(✖)
Saint Helena		✖	✖	✖	(✖)	(✖)		
Sao Tome & Principe	● Mf, Dx, Ml	✖	✖	✖	(✖)	(✖)	M	
Senegal	● Mf, Dx, Ml	✖	✖	✖	(✖)	(✖)	✖	(✖)
Seychelles		(✖)	✖	✖	(✖)	(✖)		
Sierra Leone	● Mf, Dx, Ml	✖	✖	✖	(✖)	(✖)	✖	
Somalia	● Mf, Dx, Ml	✖	✖	✖	(✖)	(✖)	✖	(✖)
South Africa	○ Mf, Dx, Ml	✖	✖	✖	(✖)	(✖)		
Sudan	● Mf, Dx, Ml	✖	✖	✖	(✖)	(✖)	✖	(✖)
Swaziland	● Mf, Dx, Ml	✖	✖	✖	(✖)	(✖)	✖	
Tanzania	● Mf, Dx, Ml	✖	✖	✖	(✖)	(✖)	✖	(✖)
Togo	● Mf, Dx, Ml	✖	✖	✖	(✖)	(✖)	M	(✖)
Tunisia		✖	(✖)	(✖)	(✖)	(✖)		
Uganda	● Mf, Dx, Ml	✖	✖	✖	(✖)	(✖)	✖	(✖)
Zambia	● Mf, Dx, Ml	✖	✖	✖	(✖)	(✖)	✖	(✖)
Zimbabwe	○ Mf, Dx, Ml	✖	✖	✖	(✖)	(✖)	M	(✖)
Zanzibar (Tanzania)	● Mf, Dx, Ml	✖	✖	✖	(✖)	(✖)	✖	(✖)

Asia

Middle East

Food-related **gastro-intestinal infections** including tapeworm are moderately common throughout the region and there is a significant risk of **hepatitis A, dysentery**, etc. There is some transmission of **vector-borne disease** and **rabies** in dogs and wild animals. **Scorpions** are quite dangerous. **Summer temperatures** are fierce and, if driving across desert regions, arrange contingency in case of breakdown.

Far and South East

The risk of **food-borne diarrhoeal disease**, etc. is less than for South Asia and tropical Latin America but, nevertheless, those new to tropical travel would be wise to follow the rules of safe eating found on pp.100–104. Insect-bite avoidance protects against **malaria, Dengue**,

Asia
(*see* **key**, p.48)

	Malaria	Polio	Hepatitis A	Typhoid	Diphtheria	TBE	Rabies	Jap. Encephalitis	Other
Afghanistan	O C+P	✖	✖	✖	(✖)		(✖)		
Armenia	O C: Ju–Oct	(✖)	✖	✖	✖		(✖)		
Azerbaijan	O C: Ju–Oct	(✖)	✖	✖	✖		(✖)		
Bahrain		(✖)	(✖)	(✖)	(✖)		(✖)		
Bangladesh	O Mf, Dx, Ml	(✖)	✖	✖	(✖)		(✖)	(✖)	
Bhutan	O C+P	(✖)	✖	✖	(✖)		(✖)	(✖)s	1
Brunei Darussalem	O	(✖)	✖	(✖)	(✖)		(✖)	(✖)	
Cambodia	O Mf, Dx, Ml	✖	✖	(✖)	(✖)		(✖)	(✖)s	
China	mostly O C	(✖)	✖	(✖)	(✖)		(✖)	(✖)s	
East Timor	● Mf, Dx, Ml	(✖)	✖	(✖)	(✖)		(✖)		
Georgia	O C: Ju–Oct	(✖)	✖	(✖)	(✖)		(✖)		
Hong Kong	○	(✖)	✖	(✖)	(✖)		(✖)		
India	O C+P	(✖)	✖	✖	(✖)		✖!	(✖)	
Indonesia	● Mf, Dx, Ml	(✖)	✖	✖	(✖)		(✖)	(✖)	
Iran	O C+P	(✖)	✖	(✖)	(✖)		(✖)		2
Iraq	O C	✖	✖	(✖)	(✖)		(✖)		2
Israel		(✖)	✖	(✖)	(✖)		(✖)		
Japan		(✖)	✖	✖	(✖)		(✖)		
Jordan		(✖)	✖	(✖)	(✖)		(✖)		
Kazakhstan		✖	✖	✖	(✖)	*✖n	(✖)	(✖)	
Korea	O	(✖)	✖	✖	(✖)		(✖)	(✖)	
Kuwait		(✖)	✖	(✖)	(✖)		(✖)		
Kyrgyzstan		✖	✖	✖	(✖)		(✖)		
Laos	● Mf, Dx, Ml	(✖)	✖	✖	(✖)		(✖)	(✖)	
Lebanon		(✖)	✖	(✖)	(✖)		(✖)		

Elephantiasis, **Leishmania** and **Japanese B encephalitis**. There are some highly venomous **snakes** in the region although it is unusual for travellers to encounter them. **Leeches** are an inconvenience in wet forest areas. Immunization against **hepatitis A** and especially **typhoid** is less important for short stays in business or tourist hotels.

India, Pakistan, Nepal, Sri Lanka, Bhutan, Bangladesh

Transmission of disease (**diarrhoea**, **dysentery**, **hepatitis A** and **E**, **worms** and **typhoid**) via contaminated food is very common in this region and the highest risk season is in the two months before the onset of the monsoon in June. This is also a time of very **high temperatures** and risk of heat stroke in lowland areas. Venomous **snakes** occur but they are usually very shy and rarely seen. **Leeches** are a nuisance during the monsoon in rural regions.

	Malaria	Polio	Hepatitis A	Typhoid	Diphtheria	TBE	Rabies	Jap. Encephalitis	Other
Macao		(✖)	✖	✖	(✖)		(✖)		
Malaysia	O Mf, Dx, Ml	(✖)	✖	✖	(✖)		(✖)	(✖)	
Maldives		(✖)					(✖)		
Mongolia		(✖)	✖	✖	(✖)	*✖n	(✖)		(1)
Myanmar (Burma)	O Mf, Dx, Ml	(✖)	✖	✖	(✖)		(✖)	(✖)s	
Nepal	O C+P	(✖)	✖	✖	(✖)		(✖)	(✖)s	1
Oman	O C+P	(✖)	✖	(✖)	(✖)		(✖)		
Pakistan	O C+P	(✖)	✖	✖	(✖)		(✖)	(✖)s	
Philippines	O C+P	(✖)	✖	✖	(✖)		(✖)		
Qatar		(✖)	✖	(✖)	(✖)		(✖)		
Russia (Asian)		✖	✖	✖	✖	*✖s	(✖)	(✖)s	
Saudi Arabia	O C+P	(✖)	✖	(✖)	(✖)		(✖)		1, 2
Singapore		(✖)	✖	✖	(✖)		(✖)		
Sri Lanka	O C+P	(✖)	✖	✖	(✖)		(✖)	(✖)	
Syria	O C	(✖)	✖	(✖)	(✖)		(✖)		2
Tajikistan	O C: Ju–Oct	✖	✖	✖	(✖)		(✖)		
Taiwan		(✖)	✖	✖	(✖)		(✖)	(✖)s	
Thailand	O Dx, Ml	(✖)	✖	✖	(✖)		✖!	(✖)s	
Tibet		(✖)	✖	✖	(✖)		(✖)		
Turkey	O C	(✖)	✖	✖			(✖)		
Turkmenistan	O C: Ju–Oct	✖	✖	✖	(✖)		(✖)		
U. A. E.	O C+P	(✖)	✖	(✖)	(✖)		(✖)		
Uzbekistan		✖	✖	✖	(✖)		(✖)		
Vietnam	● Mf, Dx, Ml	✖	✖	✖	(✖)		(✖)	(✖)s	
Yemen	● C+P	✖	✖	✖	(✖)		(✖)		2, 3

South America

Food-borne diseases, including **diarrhoea**, **hepatitis A** and **worms**, are common. There is a great range of **insect-** and **tick-borne** disease in the jungle and tropical parts of the region and bite-prevention is crucial. Sand-fly-borne **Leishmania** is a significant risk in many of the moist, tropical forests of South America (*see* pp.154–5), while **Schistosomiasis** exists in a few areas in the east (*see* p.187). **Leeches** also occur. There are dangerous **snakes** but envenomation is rare in travellers. Immunization against **rabies** would be wise for backpackers or anyone going far from medical facilities.

South America

(*see* **key**, p.48)

	Malaria	Polio	Hepatitis A	Typhoid	Diphtheria	Rabies	Yellow Fever	Other
Argentina	O C	(✖)	(✖)	(✖)	(✖)	(✖)		
Bolivia	O Mf, Dx, Ml	(✖)	✖	✖	(✖)	(✖)	(✖)	
Brazil	O Mf, Dx, Ml	(✖)	✖	✖	(✖)	(✖)	(✖)	(1), 3
Chile		(✖)	(✖)	(✖)	(✖)	(✖)		(1)
Columbia	O Mf, Dx, Ml	(✖)	✖	✖	(✖)	(✖)	(✖)	
Ecuador	O Mf, Dx, Ml	(✖)	✖	(✖)	(✖)	(✖)	✖	4
Falkland Is.		(✖)			(✖)	(✖)		
French Guiana	● Mf, Dx, Ml	(✖)	✖	✖	(✖)	(✖)	M	
Galapagos		(✖)	✖	✖	(✖)	(✖)		
Guyana	● Mf, Dx, Ml	(✖)	✖	✖	(✖)	(✖)	✖	
Marguerita Is.	O Mf, Dx, Ml	(✖)	✖	✖	(✖)	(✖)	✖	
Paraguay	O C	(✖)	✖	✖	(✖)	(✖)		
Peru	O Mf, Dx, Ml	(✖)	✖	✖	(✖)	(✖)	(✖)	
Surinam	O Mf, Dx, Ml	(✖)	✖	✖	(✖)	(✖)	✖	2
Uruguay		(✖)		(✖)	(✖)	(✖)		
Venezuela	O Mf, Dx, Ml	(✖)	✖	✖	(✖)	(✖)	✖	2, 3

Before You Go

Special Travellers

05

It is impossible to give comprehensive guidelines on who is and is not fit to travel. Given two people in an identical physical condition, it is quite possible that one may manage travelling rough for months, while the other may get into trouble on a short package tour.

Discuss any concerns or problems with your own doctor. Medical clearance is sometimes required from the airline in cases where there has been recent illness, admission to hospital, injury or instability of a medical condition. A medical information form (MEDIF) is available from airlines and travel agents, part of which needs to be completed by the passenger's doctor. Inform the airline ahead of time if you will need help getting aboard or with your baggage, if you need to travel with a wheelchair or have special seating or dietary requirements.

Summary

→ There are no medical conditions that absolutely preclude travel, but some travellers will need to prepare more carefully, and may need medical clearance.

→ Travellers with long-standing medical conditions may be refused insurance, but it is essential to find a company willing to provide cover, including for complications of the known medical condition.

→ Don't be tempted to conceal any medical conditions from insurers, or you may pay a premium but still not be covered.

→ Get expert advice on particular risks and challenges relating to your travel. This advice may come from your usual medical advisor and/or a specialist travel clinic.

→ Pack a full list of any regular medicines that you take, along with exact doses and the *generic* name of the drug.

→ A clinical summary written by your regular doctor should be carried on your travels.

SPECIAL RISKS AND HEALTH CHALLENGES

Pre-existing medical conditions

Those with ongoing medical problems, such as diabetes, asthma, epilepsy and heart conditions, need to **declare these to the insurer**. For stable, well-controlled conditions, policies need not cost more than for other people, if you search around. Specialist insurers, as recommended by patients' organizations, can help, but many regular insurers are also suitable. Self-help medical groups (which your doctor should know about) have often negotiated special deals; *see* p.330. Residents of the European Union who have an E111 form are entitled to subsidised emergency medical treatment. However, this arrangement does not cover treatment of existing conditions.

It is probably wise to travel with a **written doctor's summary**; a physician's letter of explanation may be useful if you need to travel with syringes and needles. Make your own careful **note of your medicines** with their *generic* (medical) names. Carry plenty to last the trip,

Fit to fly?

The following usually make air travel too hazardous and medical advice/clearance should be sought before boarding:

→ **Anaemia** – haemoglobin below 7.5g.
→ **Breathlessness** at rest or making the traveller unable to walk 50m.
→ **Contagious** or **communicable disease** in its infectious period – including chickenpox.
→ **DVT** – recent, unstable and untreated.
→ **Ear infection** or severe congestion – it will hurt if you fly.
→ **Epileptic fit** in the previous 24 hours.
→ **Haemorrage** from stomach or duodenum that has happened recently – you could bleed again.
→ **Heart attack** within the last seven days.
→ **Heart failure** – uncontrolled.
→ **Fracture** of leg and full plaster applied within previous 48 hours.
→ **Jaw wired** – unless you can release or cut it.
→ **Operations** within the last five to 10 days.
→ **Pneumothorax** (collapsed lung) that has not been treated.
→ **Sinusitis** – severe; it will hurt if you fly.
→ **Stroke** within the last three days.
→ **Unstable medical conditions** of any sort.

For further information visit *www.britishairways.com/health*.

Notes for sufferers of longstanding medical conditions

Those with longstanding medical conditions including **diabetes mellitus**, **liver** or **kidney failure**, those **without a spleen**, and those with **immune disorders** (*see* box, p.68) should be aware that:

→ Malaria may be more severe although the risk of infection is no greater than for any other traveller.
→ Levels of protection given by vaccines may be diminished.
→ Live vaccines (oral polio, oral typhoid, BCG, MMR and Yellow Fever) may be unsuitable, however immunization against pneumococcus, haemophilus influenzae (Hib), and influenza vaccine are beneficial.
→ Some antimalarials don't mix with some prescribed regular medicines.
→ Travellers' diarrhoea may be more severe.
→ A MedicAlert bracelet is a useful precaution.

The following precautions are also recommended:

→ Carry a card and/or written clinical summary, so that an overseas doctor can understand your condition and the medicines you take.
→ Ask your doctor whether it is necessary to travel with an emergency course of antibiotics or other specific medicines.
→ Don't even think about travelling without adequate insurance and always declare your condition to your insurers.

allowing for changes of plans or delays, and do not pack them all in one place (luggage gets delayed or lost). If possible, avoid making changes to any medication just before travel. If you are unsure whether you're fit to travel, ask your doctor. If you don't like what you're told, get another opinion from a travel clinic. Be well informed and assess your particular risks with the help of your usual doctor.

General resources for travellers with special requirements

Age Concern Insurance Services, UK t 0845 601 2235. Covers almost anyone with very few exclusions; like many insurers they would not cover those travelling against medical advice. They have no age limits.

Blood Care Foundation, *www.bloodcare.org.uk*.

Holiday Care Service, Holiday Care Information Unit, 2nd Floor Imperial Buildings, Victoria Road, Horley, Surrey RH6 7PZ, **UK t** (01293) 774 535, **f** (01293) 784 647, *holiday.care@virgin.net*. Has information on holidays for those with health problems and a list of sympathetic travel insurers.

Medic Alert Foundation, Freepost, 1 Bridge Warf, 156 Caledonian Road, London N1 9BR, **UK t** 0800 581 420; or **Medic Alert Foundation Intl**, Turlock, CA 95380-1009, **US t** (209) 668 3333 or **t** (toll-free) 1 800 344 3226. Supplies bracelets alerting medics to medical conditions; allow 28 days for delivery.

The Stroke Association, Stroke House, Whitecross Street, London EC1Y 8JJ, **UK t** (020) 7566 0300, **f** (020) 7490 2686, **t** (**helpline**) 0845 303 3100.

Diabetes

Diabetics may need help or advice from their doctor on rescheduling medicines, and they should be aware of special problems they face when they start vomiting or get travellers' diarrhoea. Diabetics can safely take oral rehydration solutions containing glucose, and it would be wise to travel with several packets. Diarrhoeal illness can upset normal diabetic control – even in those taking tablets – and it is important to be aware that you can become particularly ill, and may need treatment with an insulin infusion in hospital if you suffer some other infection, including travellers' diarrhoea. It is wise to discuss danger signs with your doctor. Hot climates tend to reduce the amount of insulin needed, making low blood sugars, a 'hypo' or hypoglycaemia more likely. Careful monitoring is therefore necessary initally, as well as on the journey. Some people with diabetes are relatively unaware of the warning signs of a 'hypo'; these travellers would be wise to travel with a companion and carry

Diabetes

Travellers with diabetes are not more prone to infections. However, insulin requirements often increase during even mild illness and even in those taking tablets to control blood sugar; gastroenteritis is therefore best avoided (*see* pp.100–108). Medical professionals can advise on precautions, danger signs, adjusting doses and food intake when ill.

For insulin users, a basal bolus regime is very flexible. A long acting (basal) dose is taken around bedtime and a short acting (bolus) dose before or after each meal (usually three). When flying west across time zones, extra meals can easily be managed with extra shots. It helps to have a dual time watch, set on both home and local time. Insulin is quite robust (manufacturers are helpful in providing storage information), but it should be protected from heat or freezing in an unbreakable vacuum flask or in a plastic container that can be stored in a hotel fridge. Plenty of spare injection pens or syringes should be carried. A back-up to a blood glucose meter is advisable: BM sticks, for example, are good, since they can be read by eye.

Diabetics who know enough of the local language to be able to read menus and labels will enjoy their trip more, while vegetarians and fussy eaters may have difficulties. Liking all local carbohydrates helps. Carry emergency food: biscuits, cereal bars and wrapped sweets are good; sometimes fruit, vegetables, meat, or dairy products may not be carried across certain state or international borders. Diet soft drinks may not be widely available, yet bottled water gets boring. Low sugar drink powder or citrus juice covers the taste of chemically treated water, or you can add vitamin C after iodine treatment (*see* pp.104–5).

Jean Sinclair RGN MSc

dextrose sweets or injectable medication to raise blood sugar. It is worth finding out (from the manufacturer) about the insulin you use. Insulin should remain stable at room temperature for up to a month. Generally, clear, fast-acting insulins are more robust and can survive freezing, while cloudy, medium- to long-acting and bimodal insulins are more delicate and are best kept cool. An advantage of a basal bolus regime (medium-acting insulin at night and short-acting before meals) is that in an emergency, if cloudy insulin is damaged or becomes discoloured, control can be achieved with short-acting insulin alone. Sun-sensitive rashes can occur – albeit rarely – in those taking *chlorpropamide* and *glipizide* tablets to control diabetes (*see* p.167).

Contact information: Diabetes

Diabetes UK, 10 Queen Anne Street, London W1G 9HL, **UK t** (020) 7636 6112, *www.diabetes.org.uk*. Issues fact sheets about individual countries, including which insulins are available; they also offer travel insurance, but compare their rates to other deals.

Frio Cooling Products, Freepost SWC 0667, Haverfordwest, SA62 5ZZ, **UK t** (01437) 741 700, *www.friouk.com*. Sells a range of wallets that, after immersion in water, keep contents cool for several days.

The American Diabetes Association, *lcann@diabetes.org*.

Epilepsy

Stable epilepsy should not inhibit travel, although it may take some searching to find an adequate insurer. Airlines say that someone who has had a grand mal seizure in the previous 24 hours should delay their flight. People who have epilepsy are limited in the **antimalarial tablets** that they may take. Those with epilepsy or a past history of epilepsy should avoid taking *mefloquine* (Larium) and also *chloroquine* as these two medicines can cause seizures in those prone to them. Find out which other prophylactics will protect you for your particular journey and then choose between the other tablets. Malarone and *proguanil* (Paludrine) may be taken safely. If *doxycycline* is suggested and you take *carbamazepine* (Tegretol), *phenytoin* (Epanutin) or *phenobarbital* (*phenobarbitone*), you need to take 100mg capsules twice daily, which is twice the normal dose. If Maloprim is suggested and you take *phenytoin* or *phenobarbitone*, it should be taken with *folic acid* 5mg daily.

Contact information: Epilepsy

British Epilepsy Association, **UK t** (0113) 210 8800; **t** (**helpline**) 0808 800 5050. For 50p, the helpline will issue an 'epilepsy passport', which can be personalized, containing first-aid information about epilepsy (translated into six European languages).

Epilepsy Research Foundation, PO Box 3004, London W4 1XT, **UK t** (020) 8995 4781, *www.erf.org.uk*. Publishes a helpful leaflet entitled *Epilepsy and Antimalarial Medication*.

Tyser, UK t (01268) 284 361, *www.tyseruk.co.uk*. Insurance brokers who are sympathetic to epileptics; they realize that well-controlled epilepsy is not risky and will often offer cover with no extra loading.

Asthma

Anyone who has ever had an inhaler prescribed or who has been told they are asthmatic should be aware that travel might precipitate an asthma attack, so it is best to be prepared. Asthma can emerge as a new problem – or a childhood tendency that returns – in travellers to congested big cities. Polluted Mexico City, at an altitude of 9,500ft, is probably not a good destination for asthmatics or people with respiratory problems. In well-chosen destinations, though, many asthmatics improve, having escaped the pollen of temperate plants and the house dust mites of dingy student garrets. Asthma can be unpredictable, as can travel; it is a serious disease that kills about 1,500 Britons annually. If you have ever been admitted to hospital with asthma you should discuss your travel plans with your doctor who may suggest that you carry a course of steroid tablets. In case of needing to buy more inhalers while abroad, it is important to know exactly what medicines you are taking. Many of the newer inhalers or devices will not be available overseas. Carry plenty, including a *salbutamol* (Ventolin) inhaler in your carry-on bag in case the stuffiness of the aircraft climate makes you breathless. Although *salbutamol* (Ventolin) and *beclomethasone* (Becotide) inhalers are available in many countries, propriatory names will be different and doses may vary, so be careful. (*See also* **allergic reactions** below, p.66).

Contact information: Asthma

National Asthma Campaign, Providence House, Providence Place, London N1 0NT, **UK t** (020) 7226 2260; **t** (**helpline**) 08457 010 203, *www.asthma.org.uk*. Has information on travel insurance for asthmatics.

Lungs and breathlessness

Anyone who has had symptoms of breathlessness should get a diagnosis and adequate treatment before flying. Being breathless at rest, or breathlessness that prevents walking 50m, will mean you are not fit enough to fly, although oxygen may be provided by the airline if a request is made in advance; there is a charge for this and the traveller needs to make their own arrangements during transfers. An untreated **pneumothorax** (partially 'collapsed' lung), for example, might get considerably worse during a flight. Those with **cystic fibrosis** may also have problems due to decreased oxygen and, since they lose lots of salt in sweat, may also have problems acclimatizing to heat if the destination is steamy.

Allergic reactions

Anyone who has had a severe allergic reaction (difficulty breathing, facial swelling or collapse) to insect stings or other substances should carry an *adrenaline* (*epinephrine* in the USA) injection or Epipen that they can administer themselves in case of a repeat reaction. Otherwise, for those who don't like injections, the Medihaler EPI (made by Riker) also dispenses *adrenaline/epinephrine*; it works like an asthma inhaler and is rapidly effective but is not available in the UK. A Medicalert bracelet or pendant is also a sensible precaution (*see* **General resources for travellers with special requirements**, p.62). Desensitization treatment is not without risk and requires commitment. This involves 2–3 years of monthly injections at a specialist allergy clinic.

Those who suffer – or have ever suffered and/or have lots of close family members who suffer – from **hay fever** and/or **eczema** and/or **asthma** are more likely to get an 'out of the blue' allergic reaction to something exotic. These travellers would be well advised to travel with some antihistamine tablets (e.g. *cetirazine* Zirtek or *loratidine* Clarityn or *desloratidine* Neoclarytin). These are also useful in relief of itching from insect bites. True pollen-induced hay fever often gets better overseas.

Contact information: allergies

British Allergy Foundation, Deepdene House, 30 Bellegrove Rd, Welling, Kent DA16 3PY, **UK t** (020) 8303 8525, **t** (**helpline**) (020) 8303 8583, **f** (020) 8303 8792, *allergybaf@compuserve.com*, *www.allergyfoundation.com*.
British Society for Allergy and Clinical Immunology, 66 Weston Park, Thames Ditton, Surrey KT7 0HL, **UK t** (020) 8398 9240, **f** (020) 8398 2766.

Heart conditions and pacemakers

Most aircraft are pressurized to the equivalent of about 2,000m; people with long-standing heart disease may suffer from the 10% reduction in oxygen supply and could become unwell during a flight. Many people with heart conditions are at increased risk of **deep vein thrombosis** or a blood clot (*see* pp.6–9). Doctors may advise taking a 75mg *aspirin* before the flight, though most heart patients will already be taking daily *aspirin* or an equivalent such as *clopidogrel* (Plavix).

It is inadvisable to fly within 10 days of having suffered a heart attack. After a severe attack it would be wise to wait a month. Wait at least two weeks after major surgery to the heart or chest before flying. The 'high altitude' conditions on board the aircraft stress the heart, so those with breathlessness after suffering from any kind of heart problem may need to check with their doctor whether they are fit to fly. Generally, though, if you are able to walk 50m without resting, you are probably fit enough. If in doubt, your doctor can discuss particular medical conditions with the airline's medics. Airlines can often provide supplementary oxygen but it must be arranged well in advance and there is a charge. Oxygen needed in transit must be arranged by the passenger.

Pacemakers can be affected by the metal-detecting loops used in security checks at airports. Ask to be hand searched, and carry a doctor's letter explaining that you have a pacemaker.

Contact information: heart conditions

British Heart Foundation, 14 Fitzhardinge St, London W1H 4DH, **UK t** (020) 7935 0185. Has information on insurance for people with heart problems including angina and high blood pressure.

Hypertension

As with many conditions, well-controlled blood pressure should impinge little on travel, although it is crucial to travel with enough medication. Running out, and the consequent rebound rise in blood pressure, is dangerous and it may be difficult to find or identify your particular medicines overseas. Those taking **diuretics** (e.g. *furosemide/frusemide*, *bendrofluazide*) must not stop them for convenience when travelling. They must also be wary and seek medical advice early in case of profuse diarrhoea, since it is easier for such people to develop problems due to an imbalance of body salts, especially lack of potassium.

Takers of anticoagulants

People who are taking anticoagulants (usually *warfarin*) to 'thin the blood', should avoid intramuscular immunization, because it is likely to cause bleeding into the injected muscle. Many immunizations can be given subcutaneously instead. Those on anticoagulants must also consider their special risks when travelling. Taking an anticoagulant makes disastrous bleeding after any kind of accident more likely, or there could be bleeding into the brain after a fall, and such dangerous complications are a significant risk where emergency services are not of a high standard: supplies of fresh frozen plasma and other treatments are not readily available. People who are taking anticoagulants are also more likely to need **blood transfusions** in emergencies; the risks are described on pp.293–4. Anticoagulant control is affected by changes in diet, by alcohol consumption and by illness; necessary blood tests may be difficult to organize in less developed countries.

Contact information: anticoagulants

Blood Care Foundation, *www.bloodcare.org.uk*.

Cancer and HIV

Those who have had treatment for cancer will have lost immunity gained from previous immunizations. Travel and routine childhood vaccinations may therefore need to be repeated after cancer treatment

Travelling with immunosuppression

There are some issues for people whose immune system has been suppressed by disease or medical treatment. Immunosuppression commonly occurs in HIV, cancer (*see* above, p.67, and facing page), after transplants and in those taking long-term steroid (and certain other) tablets. Your prescribing doctor will be able to tell you, and your usual doctor or a specialist travel clinic will be an important first port of call in the planning stage of your trip. Organizing adequate insurance is crucial, and be aware of the information highlighted on pp.30–32.

Human Immunodeficiency Virus (HIV)

Infection with HIV does not and should not prevent individuals from travelling. The CD4 count suggests the degree of suppression of the immune system and correlates well with the potential risk of infections. A CD4 count below 400/mm³ precludes the administration of live vaccines – especially Yellow Fever vaccine – and advice should be sought from an experienced travel medicine practitioner. There are potential mismatches between antimalarial tablets and some anti-HIV agents, and consideration must be given to this. *Ciprofloxacin* (often prescribed for travellers' diarrhoea) and *doxycycline* (for malaria prophylaxis), may also interfere with anti-HIV agents and must be given either several hours before or after these other medicines.

Travellers with HIV infection should find out about any current political restrictions prior to travel (*see* Immunosuppression contacts, listed on the facing page).

Other immune disorders

Travellers with immune systems that are suppressed by medicines should seek advice from both their regular hospital consultant, and also a travel medicine specialist. The administration of vaccines in particular, as well as other medicines, will depend upon the dose and duration of immunosuppressive treatment being received. Live vaccines (oral polio, oral typhoid, BCG, MMR and Yellow Fever) cannot be given, and inactivated vaccines may provide limited protection. Live vaccines may be administered six months after completion of chemotherapy.

Transplant recipients are also immunosuppressed and must not receive live vaccines. These travellers are at increased risk of skin cancer and must avoid exposure to strong sun. Travellers with challenged immune systems must pay particular attention to bite prevention (pp.144–9) and avoidance of travellers' diarrhoea (pp.100–108).

Dr Jane N Zuckerman, Royal Free Travel Health Centre, London

is completed and once the immune system has recovered. **Live vaccines** should be avoided in people who are immunosuppressed, such as those who have active cancer. Those who have contracted human immunodeficiency virus and who are HIV-positive should avoid BCG and also immunization by mouth with typhoid capsules (although injected typhoid vaccine is safe). Yellow Fever immunization is also unsafe. **Killed vaccines** and also the live polio and MMR vaccines are safe.

Patients who have been treated with **radiotherapy** or **chemotherapy** should avoid live vaccines until six months after the end of treatment. Those with cancer who are stable are often fit to travel although the condition must be declared to insurers. Sufferers from certain cancers may have an increased tendency to blood clots, so ask your oncologist whether you should take an *aspirin* before any long flight.

Contact information: immunosuppression

Aidsnet, *www.aidsnet.ch*. Lists entry restrictions for individual countries.
Blood Care Foundation, *www.bloodcare.org.uk*.
HIVinfoweb, *www.infoweb.org* (click on Travel-Related). HIV and AIDS-related information for travellers.
The Body, *www.thebody.com*. In-depth HIV/AIDS-related information.

People without a spleen

Anyone who has had their spleen removed after an accident or suffers from a **red bloodcell disorder**, including thalacaemia or sickle disease (not the trait), is more likely to become severely ill if they develop a pneumococcal or meningococcal infection. The risk of serious infections is highest in the first two years after the loss of the spleen. Previous advice had been to receive pneumococcal immunization once in a lifetime; recently though, it has been realized that asplenic people may not maintain enough protective antibodies to pneumococcus, so five-yearly boosters are recommended. Asplenic people also need regular boosters against meningococcus. All vaccines – including live ones – are safe for them. Asplenic people need to be aware that they have lost one component of their immune system and in case of any sign of infection they should not hesitate to seek medical help. They should travel with a course of *amoxycillin* antibiotics to treat any chest infections that arise while overseas. Should such people contract malaria they are likely to become rapidly ill and die. As a result, travel to a high-risk malarious area (including much of lowland sub-Saharan Africa, *see* map, p.131) is probably not worth the risk. There are, however, large areas within the Republic of South Africa that are malaria-free, where it would be possible to travel safely.

Kidney stones

People who have had kidney stones in the past are likely to get them again when in hot climates; they must make a special effort to drink plenty of liquids (*see* p.164). For advice for those with troublesome and recurrent kidney or bladder infections *see* **cystitis** on pp.233–4.

The disabled

Whether the disability is temporary – because of a fracture – or permanent, the biggest challenge is likely to be transferring to a toilet; airline facilities can be very difficult and travellers usually need to be able to manage independently.

Useful contact information: disabled access

www.everybody.co.uk/airline: a directory of access arrangements on board major airlines.

www.justmobility.co.uk: a good site for links to other helpful sites.

www.dmoz.org/Society/Disabled/Travel: good for US travellers.

The Society for Advancement of Travel for the Handicapped, 347 Fifth Ave, Suite 610, New York NY 10016, **US t** (212) 447 0027. Useful resources.

Recent surgery, serious illness and fractures

If you have just had an operation, ask your surgeon when it is all right for you to travel. Most doctors would say you should wait at least a week before flying. If you fly soon after **laparoscopy** you may feel very uncomfortable, as gas left in the abdomen expands by about 30% in low cabin pressures; this expansion can also stretch a surgical scar if you fly within 10 days of an **abdominal operation**. After an **operation in the chest**, wait at least three weeks before flying. Air travel should also be delayed for three weeks after significant bleeding from a **stomach** or **duodenal ulcer**, since pressure changes can stimulate another bleed, which could be a medical emergency. **People with colostomies** may find that they produce more waste during a flight so should use a large bag and also travel with extra in the carry-on luggage. After a **leg fracture**, flying is not advised for 48 hours because of the risk of swelling within the cast; back-slabs and casts that are split in two should avoid harmful swelling. If there is a full-length or above-knee plaster, or if the leg needs to be kept raised up, it may be necessary to travel first class or to buy two seats, because the plastered leg is not allowed to stick out into the aisle or obstruct emergency exits. Fractures or other significant injuries or operations on the leg, including to varicose veins, carry an increased risk of blood clots if you fly too soon, and anyone with their **jaw wired** after a fracture should either be accompanied by an escort with wire cutters, or with some self-activating quick release in case of vomiting. Some kinds of **surgery** will also increase your risk of a clot (*see* p.6).

THERAPEUTIC TRAVEL

Some conditions may be helped by a trip to warmer climates. Aches and pains in joints and muscles, fibrositis and arthritis often get better. Acne and severe eczema (but *see also* **allergic reactions** above, p.66) can worsen in strong sunshine, although eczema may also diminish in the heat, especially with plenty of moisturizers. Psoriasis improves with plenty of exposure to sunlight, but can be aggravated by taking *chloroquine*.

Travelling abroad for medical treatment

People sometimes travel abroad specifically for specialist or pioneering treatments, or for quick or cheap operations. This should be done with caution and after seeking as much advice as you can find from medical professionals and patient advisory groups, since – just as at home – the quality of medical care is variable, and the advantage of treatment at home is that your usual doctor should know or can find out how good your treatment will be. It is likely that it will become more commonplace for Europeans to be treated in other European countries; however, it is also worth considering the non-medical/technical aspects of opting for this. Travel itself causes stress, and undergoing medical treatment or an operation is also stressful. Even assuming that language and communication are not a problem, most people would probably feel most comfortable undergoing treatment by people of their own cultural background: different assumptions and senses of humour are common and can make for misunderstanding and upset. There are, too, the practicalities of knowing what a hospital in-patient is expected to provide on admission. And finally, note that travelling for treatment will probably isolate you from the support of family and friends.

TRAVELLING WHILE PREGNANT

If you feel well during pregnancy, and feel like travelling, do it! The late Alison Hargreaves managed a successful ascent of the north face of the Eiger when six months pregnant. There are, though, some special considerations to be borne in mind if your trip is long or the destination is without reasonable medical facilities.

Ideally a travelling woman should arrange as many travel immunizations as she can before conception, since **all live vaccines** are thought to be unsafe in pregancy and **most killed vaccines** are best avoided, especially during the first three months. If immunization is being considered after the first 12 weeks of pregnancy, an assessment of the actual risk of the disease to the woman and her unborn child must be balanced against the risk to the foetus of the immunization itself. Some women will delay or reschedule travel plans accordingly. Immunization against polio may be required since there is an increased risk of disease and paralysis in the pregnant woman and also of foetal death. Ideally, the pregnant traveller will already be immune from previous immunizations. If immunization is necessary during pregnancy, the injection is safer than the oral live version.

The safest time to travel when pregnant is during the middle three months, from the 12th week of pregnancy (when the risk of miscarriage and ectopic pregnancy has largely passed) until about the 26th week (when the risk of early delivery starts to increase). Organize as many of the routine antenatal checks as your travel plans will allow; there is no harm in having some done overseas. Keeping in touch with doctors will make it easier for them to certify that flying is not an undue hazard. Flying when very anaemic (haemoglobin lower than 7.5g) would be dangerous. Pregnancy must be declared to insurers. It is important to make sure that the policy covers any complications of pregnancy and also covers all eventualities, including care of a premature newborn! Some insurers or the airline may ask for a doctor's letter and this is a common request after the 28th week; GPs will charge a fee for this. Even if such a letter is not a requirement, carry a document confirming the estimated date of delivery and the number of foetuses.

Any health problems that arise overseas for a pregnant woman will need to be dealt with, at least initially, within the local health set-up, and yet facilities may be less favourable than at home: blood for transfusion may be unscreened (*see* pp.293–4) and it may be difficult to find an English-speaking doctor. These may or may not be issues for the travelling pregnant woman.

Flying during pregnancy

Airlines discourage flying in late pregnancy not because it is unsafe, but because cabin crews do not want women delivering babies in the cramped conditions of a plane. Having attended to people who had merely fainted in a jumbo jet, while people climbed over us to get to the toilets, I find it hard to imagine a more unpleasant place to give birth. Airlines vary in their rules and requirements (and insurance companies are the most stringent). For most long-haul airlines the deadline for flights is before the 36th week of pregnancy, but it can be as early as 28 weeks, and varies with the length of flight. Multiple pregnancies are usually delivered well before the normal 40th week and airlines do not like carrying women with twin pregnancies beyond the 32nd week. Sometimes a pre-flight medical examination is required. Long-haul flights take passengers to an altitude where there is increased exposure to radiation. Ideally, unborn babies – especially during the first three months of the pregnancy – should have minimal exposure to unnecessary radiation, so frequent fliers may wish to reschedule overseas meetings or use the phone.

Pregnancy increases the clotability of the blood and so increases the risk of **deep vein thrombosis**, especially on long flights. It is crucial that long-haul travellers exercise during the flight and follow other advice detailed on pp.6–9.

Miscarriages

Miscarriages are very common: even in normal circumstances, perhaps one-fifth of pregnancies miscarry. Having a miscarriage in a remote place could be a horrendous experience. In addition, women sometimes also need a surgical dilatation and curettage under general anaesthetic to remove retained products of conception after a miscarriage. There are many developing countries where I would be reluctant to undergo such a procedure. If you are planning a shortish trip (less than four months) you should be able to delay your departure until after the 12th week, when the risk of miscarriage is largely passed.

Disease and dietary risks

Malaria is a very real risk throughout pregnancy. If you contract the disease when pregnant it will affect you much more severely than at other times. Pregnant women are highly susceptible to the parasite and more likely to die if they contract it. Malaria is also a common cause of miscarriage and premature labour. Most doctors (myself included) therefore counsel against travel to high-risk malarious regions (especially sub-Saharan Africa, the Pacific Islands and Indo-China) when

Case History: East Africa

A Canadian woman living in Uganda stopped taking antimalarials because she was pregnant and feared the tablets might harm the baby. She contracted cerebral malaria, and both she and the baby died, despite receiving emergency treatment in a hospital with a great deal of expertise in treating severe malaria. If she had discussed her worries with a medical expert before she stopped taking the tablets, she could have selected antimalarials that are known to be safe in pregnancy.

pregnant unless there are very good reasons for going. Those travelling overseas to live are better able to protect themselves from bites, so they might consider the risks acceptable. Measures to avoid mosquito bites from dusk to dawn are essential.

Antimalarial tablets must be taken rigorously (*see* **Malaria**, pp.133–8, for a discussion of the antimalarial options). Taking nothing is not the 'safe option' as some people believe. It is probably best to discuss malaria prophylaxis with an expert (*see* **Sources of advice on malaria**, p.128). *Chloroquine* can be taken in pregnancy; this is often taken with *proguanil* and, if this or Paludrine is taken, it must be accompanied by *folic acid*. A common regime is Paludrine and *folic acid* 5mg daily, and *chloroquine* weekly. *Mefloquine* (Larium) is also relatively safe to take from the fourth month of pregnancy. Those planning a pregnancy should avoid conceiving for three months after stopping *mefloquine*.

Hepatitis E can make pregnant women desperately ill; it may be wise to avoid the highest risk regions (the Indian sub-continent and tropical Latin America), and tight precautions must be followed against filth-to-mouth diseases (*see* pp.100–108).

Chickenpox and **'Slapped Cheek' Disease** (*see* **Ailments**, p.273) can be dangerous in pregnant women who have not already become immune to these viral infections; blood tests may be necessary, so if there is any doubt medical advice should be sought.

Whether they're travelling or not, there are **dietary precautions** that all pregnant women should take, and travellers need to be extra careful. Ensure that milk and dairy products are pasteurized or boiled, and avoid unpasteurized soft cheeses, meat pâté and raw eggs; dried egg is safe. Avoid shark, marlin and swordfish.

Taking medicine while pregnant

You should be very careful about taking any medicines in pregnancy, especially in the first three months and when trying to conceive. *Amoxycillin* and *erythromycin* are safe to take while pregnant or breast-feeding. Avoid *doxycycline* (e.g. Vibramycin) and other *tetracyclines*, and do not take *co-trimoxazole* or *trimethoprim*.

Before You Go

Medicines

06

Most medicines that you are likely to need while travelling will be available over the counter in developing countries, although capitals and big cities are obviously likely to be better stocked than small towns. New drugs and some contraceptive pills may be hard to find in some countries. Palatable preparations for children are also surprisingly difficult to come by, so parents must plan carefully and take professional advice if travelling to remote places with small children. And don't forget the Calpol or soluble Tylenol.

Summary

→ In many overseas destinations it is possible to buy preparations which at home would be available only on a doctor's prescription.

→ Only self-prescribe if you understand what you are taking and are aware of the potential side effects and disadvantages of the drug.

→ Check that what you are taking contains only one medicine. In many regions, combinations are the norm and you may be in for more than you bargained for.

→ Try to understand which medicines upset you, and find out the *generic* names of these preparations and their chemical relatives.

→ Take medical advice wherever you can.

WHAT TO TAKE

The more I travel the less I carry, as increasingly I realize that almost anything I really need is either available, or there is a reasonable substitute. The exception to this is perhaps dressings. A list of what I consider a fairly comprehensive kit can be found on p.78, although of course some destinations will have better products on offer than at home.

If you wish to take a comprehensive medical kit because you are going on a major expedition, get professional advice. **The Royal Geographical Society** (RGS; *see* below) runs seminars in London on expedition planning, expedition medicine and independent travel. You can also buy custom-made medical kits from many travel stores. Many organized tours and treks carry a comprehensive medical kit, which means you need to carry less medical clutter of your own.

Note that if you are carrying any sharp objects in your hand luggage they may be confiscated at the airport (*see also* **Flight**, p.91). Such objects include tweezers, nail files and razorblades, which may form part of your first-aid kit.

Dressings and bandages

If you plan to do anything remotely athletic, adventurous or dangerous on your travels, it would be worth shopping around for good dressings and support bandages. In particular, those with recurrent tendencies to injure a particular body part need to pack supports for their weak joint; these are available in pharmacies. I always pack a knee support now when walking in the mountains. They take up very little room.

For most wrenches and sprains a simple crêpe, ace or rayon/elastic bandage (like the Elset by Seton) is excellent and is also perfect for first aid after a snake bite (*see* **Animals**, pp.260–62). Hydrocoloid dressings are expensive (about £3 for a pack of 5), but excellent for healing blisters; they stay on until the dressing falls off. A condom filled with ice makes an excellent soothing emergency cool-pack to be placed on swollen, painful joints or piles.

Carrying hypodermic syringes

If you take an 'AIDS' kit and/or your own needles (*see* pp.293–4), remember that some countries, notably Malaysia, will assume you are a drug addict unless the syringes are obviously part of a medical kit and/or you have a medical certificate. Diabetics and other legitimate syringe- and needle-users should carry an official-looking doctor's letter, ideally in English and the relevant local language(s), and with lots of rubber stamps if travelling to a country where bureacracy is complex.

Contents of a first-aid kit

→ ***Antimalarial tablets** – Paludrine is never available abroad.
→ ***Insect repellent**, DEET-based; sticks or roll-ons are least messy.
→ ***Sunscreen** and **lip screen**.
→ **Soluble *aspirin*** or ***paracetamol*** (*acetaminophen*, Tylenol)[1].
→ A strongish **painkiller** containing *codeine*[2].
→ Sore-throat **pastilles**.
→ Heavy **moisturizer** (e.g. white soft paraffin, petroleum jelly, Vaseline or Sudocrem).
→ **Oral rehydration sachets** or a ***measuring spoon** to make sugar and salt rehydration solution.
→ **Anusol** – especially if prone to piles.
→ Drying **antiseptic** of your choice (*see* pp.215–16).
→ ***Calamine lotion** or After Bite.
→ **Crêpe bandage** and **safety pins**.
→ ***Plasters/Band-Aids** (which stick and stay stuck when you sweat).
→ ***Non-stick dressings** (e.g. Melonin).
→ ***Micropore tape** to stick on dressings or to tape sore eyes closed.
→ ***Steri-Strips** or **butterfly closures**.
→ **Injection swabs**.
→ **Cotton buds** (10 is plenty).
→ ***Dental first-aid kit**/temporary fillings.
→ **Antihistamine tablets** such as *chlorpheniramine* (e.g. Piriton) or *diphenhydramine* (e.g. Benadryl).
→ Fine-pointed **tweezers** for removing splinters and coral[3].
→ **Scissors**[3].
→ **Artery forceps**[4].
→ **Paperclip** for releasing blood under a nail (*see* p.304).
→ ***Condoms** and **contraceptive pills**.
→ A **torch/flashlight**.

Footnotes

* Asterisked items are those that are scarce or difficult to come by abroad, or may be of poor quality. Some destinations will, of course, have better products on offer than at home.

1. Soluble tablets allow gargling when the throat is sore.

2. Painkillers like DF118, Distalgesic or *codeine phosphate* also calm abdominal cramps in severe diarrhoea. Mixes of *paracetamol* (*acetaminophen*/Tylenol) and *codeine* are also good. All cause constipation.

3. Sharp objects (e.g. tweezers/scissors) must be packed in hold luggage; they may not be carried on board as hand luggage.

4. Useful for pulling out thorns, clamping off spurting arteries, repairing tents and removing fish hooks from people – and fish.

Extra first-aid items for some particular conditions

→ **Thermometer**: if travelling with medicines for self-treatment of malaria.

→ **Mouth ulcer gel** (*Bonjela or Teejel): for travellers taking Paludrine or Malarone in case of mouth ulcers.

→ Low-reading **thermometer** and **space blanket**: if going to cold places.

→ ****Aciclovir*** (*acyclovir*, Zovirax) **cream**: if a cold sore sufferer.

→ ***Adrenaline*** (*epinephrine* in the USA) injection (0.5% or 0.1% or 1:1,000): if allergic to stings, nuts, etc. (*see* p.66).

→ Two different courses of **antibiotics**: if going somewhere remote.

→ ***Paracetamol/acetaminophen*** or ***ibuprofen*** syrup: if travelling with children.

→ A fine-toothed **louse comb**: if travelling with children.

Thermometers

Mercury-filled thermometers haven't been allowed on aeroplanes for some years and now European regulations are forbidding their use on the ground, too. Alternatives are the inaccurate and unreliable forehead strips or various electronic devices. The in-the-ear versions seem very good, although they are pricey and heavy; they are now used by many British doctors. Another alternative is a single-use clinical thermometer; it can be used several times or for several people if cleaned adequately, but they are so cheap, small and light, that each person could carry their own (they are made by Zeal and sold by **TALC** for 15 pence). They read from 35.5°C to 40.5°C in 60 seconds when placed under the tongue or in three minutes when under the arm.

Contact information: what to take

Expedition Advisory Centre, Royal Geographical Society, 1 Kensington Gore, London SW7 2AR, **UK t** (020) 7581 2057, **f** (020) 758 4447.

TALC (**Teaching Aids at Low Cost**), PO Box 49, St Albans, Herts, AL1 5TX, **UK t** (01727) 853 869, **f** (01727) 846 852, *talc@talcuk.org*, *www.talcuk.org*.

BUYING AND CONSUMING MEDICINES ABROAD

Few Third World countries have adequate policies to control the use of medicines. This means it is possible to buy unsuitable or even dangerous medicines over the counter. Buying medicines abroad is also confusing, as many trade names are very different to those you will be used to at home. Stick to ***generic*** names (in italics throughout this book). Most drugs have at least two names: the trade name, snappy and memorable but often different in different countries; and the generic name, usually in much smaller print on the packet, which should be similar in all countries.

Once you have sorted out the name the next challenge is finding out what is available. Pharmacists may say that a drug does not exist, when what they mean is that they simply don't have it and would rather sell you something they do have. Some medicines, even common and very useful ones, are just not available in some countries. Asian pharmaceutical companies are very fond of manufacturing combinations of drugs, which are also best avoided. When buying, you should check three main things: that the generic name is correct; that the preparation contains only one medicine; that the expiry date hasn't been and gone.

Very few out-of-date tablets are dangerous (an exception is *tetracycline*, which degrades into toxic products), but out-of-date medicines, even *aspirin*, are likely to be ineffective. Syrups and liquids have a shorter shelf life than dry medicines, especially in hot climates, so opt for tablets if you can. When taking medicines, take a full course. Do not be intimidated by suggestions from pharmacists that you are buying too many antibiotic tablets. They will be used to dispensing three or four at a time.

Most medicines you buy abroad are of acceptable quality, but some drugs are made to very poor standards. Try to buy drugs made by local branches of international drug companies, or, in Nepal, by the national drug company, Royal Drugs. Swindles or mistakes make a minority of drugs unsafe or ineffective in some countries.

Buying medicines abroad: checklist

Before you buy, check that:

→ The ***generic*** name is correct.

→ The preparation contains only **one medicine**.

→ The **expiry date** is still in the future.

What to avoid

➜ Never take *chloramphenicol* (called Chloromycetin, Catilan, Enteromycetin) except as eye or ear drops. It should only be used for hospital treatment.

➜ Enterovioform was banned as a dangerous cure for diarrhoea. Avoid it.

➜ Do not take steroids or corticosteroids unless prescribed by a doctor you trust.

➜ 'Mexican aspirin' or *dipyrone*, which is sold as a 'stronger' variety of *aspirin*, is dangerous; avoid it.

➜ Avoid all injections if possible. If an injection is necessary in a developing country, provide or buy your own syringe.

➜ Do not buy or use out-of-date medicines.

➜ Women trying to conceive should be wary of taking medicines. Some drugs are dangerous in pregnancy, especially in the first three months; take advice.

Beware of injections and drips

In all Asian countries where I have worked, people who consult a doctor are very often offered an injection. Hypodermics have a powerful placebo effect, but it can be dangerous to have unnecessary injections. You are more likely to suffer an allergic reaction, and there is a risk of abscesses or major infections from dirty needles. Before accepting the proffered injection, ask if the medicine is available in tablet form. Dirty needles, including those for acupuncture, and unsterilized body-piercing and tattooing needles can give you hepatitis B or HIV. Beware.

I have seen Afghan and Nepali medics giving intravenous saline infusions to treat 'weakness', but in such small quantities (20ml or so) that even if 'weakness' was due to dehydration it would not have had any effect. The patients thought this treatment was marvellous, though, a very 'strong' medicine, earning paramedics high prestige.

COMMON MEDICINES, ANTIBIOTICS AND THEIR ALTERNATIVES

Painkillers

Aspirin (*acetylsalicylic acid*) is an underrated and underused medicine. It is a good painkiller, reduces inflammation and swelling and is a good, cheap drug for lowering fevers. Those with stomach ulcers or a lot of indigestion should not take it (nor should they take other non-steroidal anti-inflammatory medicine). Nor should it be given to children under 12. The alternatives are *paracetamol* (*acetaminophen* or Tylenol in the USA) or *ibuprofen*. The non-steroidal anti-inflammatory medicines are excellent for treating aches and pains, sprains, strains, wrenches and breaks, though people with asthma will probably be unable to take them. Start with *ibuprofen* (e.g. Nurofen, Brufen in the UK; Motrin, Nuprin, Advil in the USA); if it is not strong enough move on to *naproxen* (e.g. Naprosyn in the UK and the USA; Anaprox in the USA) or *diclofenac* (e.g. Voltarol). If you get indigestion or nausea while taking these, stop and use a combination of *paracetamol* and *codeine* instead. The prime side effect of *paracetamol*, *codeine*, DF118, Distalgesic and other painkillers is constipation. Avoid 'Mexican aspirin', *dipyrone*. It is

Emergency treatment for HIV exposure

The risk of being infected with HIV may be reduced by 80% by giving emergency treatment with AZT. A one-month course is normally undertaken only with expert assessment and counselling, often hard to find in developing countries. Travellers heading for environments with a high risk of occupational or sexual exposure to HIV should check to see what help is available in the event of accidents. If anti-HIV drugs are unlikely to be available, ask a knowledgeable specialist (such as a GU consultant, *see* below) to give you a private prescription for an emergency starter pack before departure. The **treatment** recommended by the UK Department of Health is one month of triple therapy with AZT 250mg twice daily, *lamivudine* (3TC) 150mg twice daily and a protease inhibitor such as *nelfinavir* 1250mg twice daily. Common **side effects** are nausea, vomiting and diarrhoea. Current information suggests AZT is mostly safe in pregnancy but there is less information about other drugs. The cost of a 5-day starter pack is approximately £50 for AZT, £40 for 3TC and £80 for *nelfinavir*. The added benefit of three drugs over AZT alone is unknown, but three drugs might be important if the source has developed drug resistance. Treatment is best started within two hours,

sold as a 'stronger' variety of *aspirin*, but can cause agranulocytosis: a fatal AIDS-like condition.

Pain lasting over a day is best controlled by regular painkillers. Letting pain return before taking another painkiller makes pain control harder.

Antibiotics

Antibiotics have no effect on viral infections (including common colds). **Penicillin** in its various forms is probably the most useful antibiotic for travellers. However, allergy to it is common, and allergic people should not take *penicillin*, *amoxycillin*, *ampicillin*, *flucloxacillin*, *cloxacillin* or *co-amoxiclav* (Augmentin). The generic names of most but not all the penicillins end in *–icillin*. The common alternative for allergic people is *erythromycin*. All these antibiotics are safe to take in pregnancy.

Flucloxacillin (250mg four times a day) is excellent for clearing skin infections, but is not available in much of Asia; ***cloxacillin*** (500mg four times a day) is the alternative. The ***tetracyclines*** (including *doxycycline*) are good, broad spectrum antibiotics for respiratory and other infections; it should not be taken in pregnancy, while breast-feeding nor given to children under 12. *Trimethoprim* is excellent for respiratory and urinary tract infections; this should be avoided in pregnancy (*see also* **Special Travellers**, p.74). Uses and cautions regarding ***ciprofloxacin*** (which can be taken by those allergic to penicillins) are given on p.113.

Metronidazole (e.g. Flagyl) is a good, safe antibiotic for treatment of *giardia*, amoebae as well as some dental and gynaecological problems.

following first aid (allowing any wound to bleed freely, then thoroughly washing or irrigating the area). You should seek expert advice about the next step as soon as possible.

If you have special occupational risk of HIV, you may be able to negotiate a special package which includes repatriation in case of a needle stick accident. **Club Direct** or the **British Medical Association** may be able to help.

Dr John Richens, University College Medical School, London

Sources of information: exposure to HIV

www.doh.gov.uk/eaga/pepgu20fin.pdf: Advice on HIV post-exposure prophylaxis from the UK Chief Medical Officers' Expert Advisory Group on AIDS.

BMA, BMA House, Tavistock Square, London WC1H 9JP, **UK t** (020) 7387 4499, **f** (020) 7383 6400, *info.web@bma.org.uk*.

Club Direct, UK t 0800 018 6638, *www.clubdirect.com*.

UK & Republic of Ireland Directory of Genito Urinary Medicine Clinics, *www.agum.org.uk/directory.htm*. GU clinics should be able to provide advice as to how to obtain a private prescription for a starter pack.

Reasons for not taking antibiotics or other medicines

A wise physician once said, 'Show me a drug without side effects and I will show you a drug that does not work.' There are costs to any treatment, and a doctor's job is to weigh up the costs and benefits of any treatment he prescribes. There are some antibiotics (such as *chloramphenicol*) that treat travellers' diarrhoea very effectively, but in a minority of patients they shut down the body's immune system and kill. Be wary of taking drugs that you do not know, particularly steroids.

The side effects of most medicines are trivial and short lived, but they are still better avoided unless genuinely necessary. If prescribing for yourself, consider the length and severity of your illness and compare them to the possible side effects of any drug. Simple travellers' diarrhoea, for example, usually lasts less than 48 hours, so is a course of antibiotics justified?

Antibiotics tend to deplete body's protective and useful bacteria; losing them can have a variety of effects, from mild loosening of the bowels to serious diarrhoea needing hospital treatment. Absence of these friendly bacteria can allow troublesome bugs to establish themselves, such as thrush, which causes soreness and white plaques in the tongue, mouth or vagina. Profligate use of antibiotics also promotes resistance to all antibiotics, so that when there is a real need for effective antibiotic therapy it will not work. This is the most powerful argument against taking antibiotics too readily. Antibiotic resistance is much less likely to develop if antibiotic courses are properly completed, so do not change your mind after a few days and certainly do not stop the course part-completed just because you feel better. Most courses run for five to seven days. In general, avoid using medicines as your first resort in dealing with any symptoms.

Some medicines (including *doxycycline* and other antibiotics, anti-inflammatories and many others) can render the skin super-sensitive to the sun, so if you notice that sun-exposed areas become unexpectedly sunburned, and you are taking a medicine that can be safely discontinued, try stopping it; the symptoms should improve within days. Meanwhile, avoid further sun exposure (*see also* **Hot Places**, p.167). Certain drugs are unsuitable for some people. Some have a drug allergy, which usually causes an itchy red rash or, less often, breathing problems, swelling of the face and collapse. Mild diarrhoea or slight stomach ache (common in takers of antibiotics) are not signs of allergy. Many medicines are unsuitable for pregnant women (*see* p.74).

Herbal remedies

Many essential medicines have been developed from herbs and natural sources: *aspirin* comes from willow bark and *digoxin* from foxgloves, for example. There are undoubtedly many more effective cures amongst the remedies offered by herbalists and alternative practitioners, but how are we to judge which are effective and which might even be dangerous? Amongst conventional doctors of medicine we always try to consider the evidence when prescribing any treatment, balancing the risk of possible side effects against the expected benefits from the treatment. It is harder to do this with herbal remedies, because good, controlled studies are rarely done. Recently, though, there was a Cochrane Review of the benefits of echinacea in preventing and treating the common cold. Given the number of colds that are apparently acquired on board international aircraft, I was particularly interested in the conclusions.

Echinacea is a popular remedy in Europe and the USA, with millions of people taking it in the belief that it stimulates the immune system in some non-specific way. There are over 200 preparations containing extract of echinacea available in Germany alone, and these are made from either the roots or the leaves or the whole plant of one of three different species of echinacea. The review looked at 40 clinical trials and concluded, 'Preparations containing extract of echinacea probably can be effective in the prevention and treatment of common colds.' They point out, however, that if any trials that showed little effect were left unpublished, this would result in a bias in favour of the remedy.

The big problem concerning herbal remedies is quality control and variability of effective doses. You may not know what dose you are taking and – worse – unusual components that can have harmful effects may be added. A dramatic if very unusual example of this was reported in 2001, when a 58-year-old woman went into a coma after taking Chinese 'herbal' Xiaoke Wan tablets. These contain *glibenclamide*, which in Britain is a prescription-only medicine used to lower blood sugar in maturity-onset diabetes. This incident illustrates that if you feel unwell after taking any unprescribed remedy – even if it is 'natural' or 'herbal' – it is best to stop taking it and see if you feel better.

Herbal remedies contact information

Further information on herbal medicines can be found on ***www.herbs.org*** and ***www.herbmed.org***.

www.24DrTravel.com can supply some forms of echinacea and other supplements and remedies by mail order.

Medicines, alcohol and contraception

If you drink alcohol while taking *metronidazole* (Flagyl) you will vomit. It is also unwise to drink alcohol when taking drugs with sedative effects such as antihistamines (especially Piriton). Avoid combining alcohol, medicines and driving. This is an especially important precaution when driving in unfamiliar conditions, such as on the 'wrong' side of the road. Many antibiotics make contraceptive pills less effective (*see* p.235).

Before You Go

Flight

07

Airlines and travel agents try to sell us an image of jet-setting glamour, but the realities of busy airports and cramped seating on-board, where we share other peoples' exhaled gases, are rather a long way from that image. Lowering expectations a little will help reduce some of the stresses of flying and make it a more tolerable experience. Drinking plenty of non-alcoholic, non-fizzy drinks will make you feel better too. Some wise travellers bring drinks aboard with them.

Summary

→ Eat a portion of oily fish before a long flight to help protect against flight-induced thrombosis (*see also* p.8).

→ Thrombosis or DVT is unlikely in a flight of less than five hours and more of a risk on uninterrupted journeys of more than 12 hours (*see* pp.7–8). For further information on DVT, look at *www.who.int/ncd/dvt.htm*.

→ Allow yourself time to adapt to the pace of the country you are visiting.

→ For more details on the health effects of flying, check the Aviation Health Institute website *www.aviation-health.org* or look at *www.britishairways.com/health*; see *www.boeing.com/commercial/cabinair* if you want to know about air quality on board.

COPING WITH FLIGHT

Exercising both before and after any long flight will make you feel better. Think about what you will and won't check in; don't weigh yourself down with excessive hand-baggage. You may end up having to pack it around your legs, which will make you uncomfortable, restrict movement and thus contribute to the risk of a blood clot (*see* pp.6–9). Don't check in essential regular medication, especially if it is temperature sensitive. Contents of aircraft holds get frozen in the aeroplane hold, or it could get lost, delayed or stolen.

Most people find at least some aspects of flying unpleasant and it is worth giving some consideration to what your special wind-up triggers are. Quite a lot of the experience of international air travel involves submitting to the control of another, and this loss of control can be stressful. This in itself adds stress to other stressors: anxiety about being on time, queues, delays, service failures, separations from loved ones, unfinished business, health concerns, a bewildering environment where the senses are assaulted with incomprehensible announcements, etc. You can do a little to insulate yourself from all this: take some light reading, use a personal stereo to play an audio book or relaxation tapes, take something to help you sleep, wear ear plugs or learn to meditate. Knowing what to do in case of emergency does improve your chances if there is a disaster and helps contribute to feeling more under control. Pay attention to the safety briefings and to in-flight announcements. Finally, if the level of service has been poor, use your flying time to write a letter of complaint. Such letters will help diffuse any frustration and anger.

Over three-quarters of people who fly admit to feeling **anxiety** about it; as many as one in five have felt severely incapacitated by the fear of flying and some people are so scared they cannot fly at all. There is an excellent little book that will help: *Stress-free Flying*, by R. Bor, J. Josse & S. Palmer (Quay Books, Wiltshire). Or there are courses. In the UK, both **Britannia Airways** and **British Airways** run one-day schemes to help people cope with flying phobia and which end in a flight with a specially trained crew (*see* below). Alternatively you could try treatment by a team of psychologists; one example of a treatment service is that offered at the **Royal Free Travel Health Clinic** in London.

Flying phobia courses: contact information

Britannia Airways, UK t (01582) 424 155. A one-day course costs £130.

British Airways, UK t (0161) 832 7972. BA charges £169 for a course in Manchester, or £189 in London.

Royal Free Travel Health Clinic, Pond St, London NW3 2QG, **UK t** (020) 7830 2885, *www.travel-health.co.uk*. Offers treatment by psychologists.

Pressure effects and reduced oxygen

Pressure changes (most rapid on take-off and landing) bother some adults and many children. They are more noticeable if you have a cold or ear or sinus problems, in which case it may be worth taking a one-off dose of a decongestant such as *pseudoephedrine* (e.g. Sudafed in the UK and the USA, Actifed in the UK, Drixoral in the USA) a couple of hours before take-off (athletes note: this is a banned drug). Sucking a sweet, chewing gum, yawning or swallowing equalizes the pressure either side of the eardrum. Airwaves menthol gum by Wrigley might be worth a try if flying when you are congested. If you experience earache on or after take-off, grasp the nose, close the mouth and suck in to reduce pressure in the ears as it drops in the aircraft; if the pain is on descent, grasp the nose, close the mouth and gently blow to increase pressure in the ears. Giving babies a drink during ascents and descents will stop them suffering earache. Tooth pain in flight suggests a loose filling, so this is one of several justifications for a pre-travel dental check, especially if you are overdue for one.

Food, drink and exercise on long flights

The cabin environment is drying and low in oxygen and tends to lead to feelings of irritability and discomfort, which are compounded by sleep deprivation. You will feel better during long flights if you move around every hour or so and do some exercises. Keeping hand baggage to a minimum will allow you more space to move. Loose-fitting clothes (abandon that corset), moving about, support tights, ankle-flexing and calf-tensing exercises all help avoid ankle-swelling. These measures – especially movement – also protect against the rarer but serious risk of thrombosis (blood clot); any car or plane journey that involves sitting for more than five hours carries a risk of thrombosis.

Dehydration is common on long flights, and adds to the effects of jet lag. Use a skin moisturizer. Abstain from alcohol (one drink on the ground is worth two in the air). Go easy on tea and coffee. Drink plenty of non-fizzy fruit juices or water. The gas bubbles in carbonated drinks expand at reduced pressures on board the aircraft and will contribute to bloating, abdominal cramps and flatus. Take only light food. Alcohol and smoking also aggravate jet lag and flight fatigue. These days, few flights allow smoking on board. If addicted to nicotine, get some patches or gum to get you through the flight without air rage, or get help by phoning the **Quitline** (*see* below). Prescribed sleeping tablets can be very useful if you are poor at sleeping naturally, although getting heavily sedated will probably increase your risk of a blood clot on a long-haul flight (*see* pp.6–9). Sleeping pills take about half an hour to work and are effective for six to eight hours. Some are good mind-body

Case History: swollen ankles

Sid, a sprightly 81-year-old, turned up at a morning clinic complaining that his legs were swollen and that the left one had become quite sore. He'd travelled from Scotland to the south of England by bus three days before to spend time with his daughter and grandchildren. He was on seven different prescribed tablets, didn't know what they were or what they were for and had forgotten to pack any of them. His legs were indeed very swollen and the left one was hot and red. I was concerned that he had a deep vein thrombosis after his 10-hour bus trip. Even without travel, his risk was already high. It is about 1 in 500 annually for over-80-year-olds, compared to about 1 in 3,000 in people under 40. Luckily, the hospital was able to reassure me that he didn't have a clot. I phoned Sid's GP to find out which tablets he should have been taking; some diuretics ('water tablets') soon cured the ankle-swelling.

relaxants too, so they are helpful if you are tense about flying. Don't try any new medicine for the very first time on a flight in case it doesn't suit you; Phenergan (*promethazine hydrochloride*), for example, an antihistamine that is also often used to sedate children, can make some individuals hyperactive.

Frequent fliers are exposed to greater doses of radiation than those of us who keep our feet on the ground; taking vitamins C and E after a long flight is said to help mop up the free radicals produced by irradiation. Another consequence of long flights can be that they stimulate what is effectively a moult: hair loss about three months after the flight. This is an alarming but temporary phenomenon. Hair loss is sometimes unjustly blamed on antimalarial tablets.

Contact information: air travel

For further information on the health effects of flying, check the Aviation Health Institute website ***www.aviation-health.org*** or look at ***www.britishairways.com/health***. If you want to know about air quality on board, look at: ***www.boeing.com/commercial/cabinair***. For further information on DVT, see the WHO website: ***www.who.int/ncd/dvt.htm***.
Quitline, **UK t** 0800 002 200. Offers help and advice for smokers.

Packing sharp objects

Sharp objects are not permitted in hand luggage on board the plane and may be confiscated at the airport. They should be packed in the luggage you are checking in to the hold. Such objects include: scissors, corkscrews, tweezers, pen-knives, Swisscards, nail files and cutlery (remember to check your first-aid kit). Toy guns, catapults, razorblades, knitting needles and darts are also banned from carry-on baggage.

Motion Sickness

Motion sickness is the response of a confused brain trying to unscramble conflicting messages coming from the eyes and the balance organs in the inner ear. It is thus possible to be motion sick when you are not moving but watching a film or simulator. Your position in any vehicle or vessel affects the amount of motion sickness you experience: choose the place that rolls and pitches least. In a plane this is between the wings; in ships it's in the middle, amidships, and it is best to look at the horizon rather than close to. Alternatively, try lying down with your eyes shut, if possible. In a car or bus, sit in the front

Commonly used preparations to counteract motion sickness

***Generic* name**	**common names**	**adult dose**
cinnarizine	Stugeron (UK, India) Vertigon (India)	15–30mg
cyclizine	Valoid (UK), Marezine (USA)	50mg
dimenhydrinate	Dramamine	50–100mg
diphenhydramine hydrochloride	Dreemon, Medinex, Nytol (UK) Benadryl (USA)	10–50mg
hyoscine	Joy-rides, Kwells (UK); scopolamine (USA, Canada)	0.15–0.6mg
hyoscine	Scopoderm (UK) Transdermscop (USA)	1.5mg
hyoscine		0.2mg
meclozine	Sea-legs (UK) Antivert, Bonine (USA)	12.5mg
promethazine hydrochloride	Phenergan (UK, USA)	10–25mg
promethazine hydrochloride	Phenergan	50mg
promethazine teoclate (theoclate)	Avomine (UK, India); Anergan Prorex (USA)	25mg
ginger		500–2,000mg

seat, look forwards (not sideways) and do not read or try to navigate. Back seats on buses 'roll' the most. Travel sickness is aggravated by eating heavy meals and drinking large volumes of fluids.

Cures for travel sickness

You may find that unfamiliar means of travel will provoke travel sickness where it is no problem at home. The table below lists the preparations you can buy while travelling.

With the exception of *hyoscine* and ginger, the medicines in the table below are all antihistamines and so they are also useful for treating stings, allergies and itchy rashes. They all cause drowsiness to a greater

preparation type	onset of effect	duration	notes
tablet	4hrs	8hrs	less sedating; not available in the USA
tablet	2hrs	8–12hrs	less sedating
tablet	2hrs	8hrs	very sedating
tablet or syrup			very sedating
melt in the mouth or chewable tablets	30mins	4hrs	very sedating; dry mouth; most rapidly effective
patch	6–8hrs	72hrs	fewer side effects than tablets; prescription in UK only
injection	15mins	4hrs	
tablet	2hrs	8hrs	less sedating
tablet or elixir	2hrs	18hrs	usually very sedating
injection	15mins	18hrs	
tablet	2hrs	24hrs	sedating; take at bedtime the night before or 3–4hrs before; also used in vomiting of pregnancy
by mouth	30mins	4hrs	

or lesser extent. Responses vary; if one preparation doesn't work, try another. Many of the antihistamines are best taken three to four hours before travel, or if you are setting out early, take them at bedtime. Tablets and syrups are useless once motion-induced nausea or vomiting has started. *Metoclopramide* (Maxolon) is not effective against travel-induced nausea, but can be used in gastroenteritis. It is also safe and effective in the nausea of pregnancy.

Natural remedies

Elasticated wrist bands called Sea Bands or Travel Bands press on acupuncture points and work well for some people in preventing travel sickness, even in children; they have no side effects. Trials by the Royal Air Force, however, concluded that the effect wasn't enough for their own stringent conditions (but if it works for ordinary travel, who cares?). Ginger is of proven benefit in preventing nausea of any kind, whether it is due to motion sickness, cancer treatment or pregnancy. An effective dose is one gram of ginger extract taken as a tablet; this is equivalent to a handful of fresh root ginger. In two studies this was found to be as effective as *metoclopramide*, a commonly prescribed anti-emetic. It might also be worth a try in the queasiness of travellers' diarrhoea.

Sneezes and colds on board

The dryness experienced during long flights can cause itching, discomfort and bouts of sneezing. A bland grease like white, soft paraffin (petroleum jelly, Vaseline), anointed inside the nose, should help. Taking any decongestants (e.g. Sudafed *pseudoephedrine* tablets or *ephedrine* nasal spray) just before or during a flight will make any symptoms of dry nose, mouth and throat worse.

There is a real risk of picking up minor air-borne infections during a long flight. There is also evidence that TB transmission may occur on flights of longer than eight hours – if someone with the disease is on board – although no cases of active TB have been identified as a result of exposure on a commercial airline. WHO state that risk is no greater than to those travelling by train or bus. Airlines are aware of these infection risks (although they would rather this wasn't publicized) and they occur despite that fact that modern planes are now fitted with High Efficiency Particulate Air (HEPA) filters that remove viruses. I think that if there was a realistic solution, the airlines would already have solved the problem. If you are sitting close to someone with a cold or other infection the chances are that you will catch it. I have family members who on two separate occasions caught chickenpox during a flight. Even in the best-filtered planes, infection transmission happens because there isn't a dedicated filter for each passenger, filters cannot remove all microbes, and air is usually drawn to the sides of the aircraft.

The air circulation and filtration systems in older aircraft used to 'cost' fuel and aircrews were said to reduce the amount of air that was moved around the cabin, particularly at night. In modern aircraft this is no longer the practice. If, though, you are in some ancient airliner and the air seems stale, you might ask the cabin crew to increase flows, or purchase a mask.

Jet lag

Long-haul flights – either East or West – may be accompanied by a horrible set of symptoms including insomnia, dullness of mind and a general feeling of awfulness. There are no scientifically proven, effective 'treatments' for jet lag, so if you have crossed more than five time zones, don't expect to be at your best for some days. It is said to take one day to adjust to each hour of time difference, and your bowels may need more. It seems to take longer to adjust flying east than flying west.

The timing of flights makes some difference to jet lag and flight fatigue, and it may be worth paying more to avoid inconvenient times. If there is a choice – this applies especially to inexperienced, lone travellers arriving in an unfamiliar country – aim to avoid arriving in the dark, and beware of who offers you a lift; ask advice from locals and team up with other travellers. On eastward flights an evening departure means that you arrive the next afternoon, in time for a meal and relaxation before bed. You will adjust faster if you try to slot into local times immediately. If you are tired or tense before your flight, expect jet lag to hit harder. There are routines that are said to limit the effects of jet lag, but they are probably little better than adequate rest and pacing yourself.

Two other approaches may work for you. The first affects **melatonin**, a hormone normally produced by the body in the evening, the secretion of which is inhibited by sunlight. Getting outside in sunlight should help improve the quality of sleep after a long flight (but don't get burned). The other approach is dietary. Protein-rich meals help the body produce the hormones needed for a full day, and a light evening meal with plenty of carbohydrate helps provide those necessary for sleep. Some experts also recommend artificial tyrosine and tryptophan supplements, while the homeopathic remedy **arnica** seems to help some people get over their jet lag and might be worth a try.

More on melatonin

Melatonin is said to resynchronize the internal body clock; the substance does seem to shift circadian rhythms and thus, it was hoped, it would reduce the symptoms of jet lag. Melatonin tablets were available from herbalists in Britain until it was realized that this product had some important physiological effects: it interferes, for example, with human ovulation. It is still on sale in the USA and is probably quite safe to take. However, although it does seem to have some effect on sleep patterns, it may not be effective. Recently, a carefully designed double-blind trial compared the symptoms of jet lag in 339 Norwegian physicians, who flew to New York, spent at least five days there and then returned to Oslo. On their return home they either took 5mg melatonin at bedtime on the day of travel and then daily for five days, or 0.5mg with the same schedule, or 0.5mg taken progressively one hour earlier each day, or placebo. The participants did not know whether they took melatonin or placebo. The symptoms of jet lag (fatigue, daytime sleepiness, impaired concentration, decreased alertness, trouble with memory, physical clumsiness, weakness, lethargy and light-headedness) were scored and a record was kept of sleep times. There was no difference between the symptom scores between those taking melatonin and those taking an inactive placebo. This seems pretty good evidence against this being a useful remedy, and indeed, one participant taking low-dose melatonin suffered a significant reaction to it: it caused difficulty in breathing and swallowing. The symptoms settled, but then returned when he tried another dose.

Many doctors and other travellers, however, feel that melatonin does them some good. It is possible that the form of melatonin tested by the Norwegian doctors contained inadequate amounts of active ingredient. A common problem with herbal treatments or supplements is that tablet components may be non-standard, and the variability in responses to melatonin that different travellers report may be because some preparations are more potent than others. Quality analysis of 19 commercial melatonin products revealed problems of pharmacautical quality and consistency. Melatonin has not needed approval by the Food and Drug Administration as it is sold over the counter in the USA as a 'dietary supplement'; in the UK or elsewhere it can be obtained by mail order from **PharmWest** or from **Worldwide Health**.

Contact information: stockists of melatonin

PharmWest, 520 Washington Blvd No. 401, Marina Del Rey, CA 90292, **US t** (310) 301 4015, **Ireland t** 463 7317, **UK t** (freephone) 800 8923 8923, **US f** (310) 577 0296, **Ireland f** 463 7310, *www.pharmwest.com*.
Worldwide Health, Freepost, Alderney GY1 5SS, **UK t** 08700 760 750.

On The Ground
Bowels

08

Diarrhoea is a common affliction in travellers, but for most it is inconvenient rather than dangerous. And yet it also kills about three and a half million children every year, mostly among the poor and malnourished, who die from dehydration. Even this deadly complication, though, is easily corrected by drinking clear fluids or home-made sugar and salt solution. Travellers, fortunately, seldom become very ill, and if they do the treatment is accessible and simple.

Summary

→ Eat piping hot, thoroughly cooked food. Avoid salads and other raw foods; do not take ice or ice cream.

→ It is dehydration that makes you feel bad when you have diarrhoea; in this case you should drink at least three litres of clear fluids a day.

→ Drink in sips if you are vomiting or nauseated.

→ Headache and dizziness are symptoms of dehydration.

→ Three good-volume passings of light yellow-coloured urine is normal; less implies dehydration, so drink more.

→ A very light, plain diet will usually cure the abdominal cramps of travellers' diarrhoea, and also reduce nausea.

→ Avoid fatty and oily foods and dairy products if your stomach is upset.

→ Taking very hot or very cold drinks or food often stimulates a reflex bowel action (the gastro-colic reflex), accompanied by abdominal pain.

→ In the absence of medical advice, the only safe remedy for childhood diarrhoea is oral rehydration solution.

→ Babies who travel abroad should be breast-fed. This protects against diarrhoea.

→ If you use iodine crystals to sterilize water, you need to pack one 20ml screw-top non-plastic bottle, a 10ml measure (e.g. a syringe) and a one-litre water bottle.

TRAVELLERS' DIARRHOEA

Diarrhoea, gastroenteritis, food poisoning, the squits, Montezuma's Revenge, gippy tummy, Delhi Belly, the Kathmandu Quickstep, Tandoori Trots, the Aztec Two-step, *turista*, the runs, or whatever you call it, is the most common medical problem for travellers. The symptoms depend upon the microbe. Some gastroenteritis, which has a short incubation period, provokes a prompt puke. Those microbes that travel further down the 9m (30ft) of tubing that is the adult human alimentary canal, take longer to cause mischief and cause more diarrhoea than vomiting.

Travelling anywhere carries a risk of travellers' diarrhoea, and the chances of it are greater when visiting warmer climates (because food preservation is more difficult) and places where unreliable electricity can lead to refrigeration breakdowns. Cracked or seldom-cleaned water filters also harbour microbes. On average, half of those travelling to the developing world will suffer from travellers' diarrhoea. About 30% of British visitors to southern Europe (including Spain) are also hit, with the risk being highest during the warmest months. The common cause of travellers' diarrhoea is ETEC (*enterotoxigenic Escherichia coli*), which are nasty forms of normally friendly intestinal bacteria. There are many other causes (*see* below), but do not be put off by the long list of diseases, because identical precautions will protect you from them all.

Why do you get travellers' diarrhoea?

Travellers' diarrhoea comes from getting other people's faeces into your mouth, usually via other people's dirty hands or via food. It is a bad hygiene disease. Dirty water can be a source, but is much less risky than eating contaminated food. The risk of developing disease is related to the number of 'germs' consumed, and bad food contains large numbers of microbes. As you travel more, you develop some immunity to some kinds of diarrhoea (notably ETEC). Only the foolish do not continue to take precautions, though, as the transmission route for ETEC diarrhoea is the same as for many other diseases. In a survey of visitors to East Africa, only 2% were taking adequate protective dietary precautions.

Diarrhoea and other filth-to-mouth diseases are a problem anywhere that environmental sanitation is poor. Although more common in warm, humid climates, they are not restricted to tropical countries. Cholera was a problem in Victorian cities in Britain until there were improvements in housing and sanitation. The highest-risk regions are the Indian subcontinent (including Nepal) and tropical Latin America.

PREVENTION

There is not yet any vaccine against travellers' diarrhoea (although it's coming soon); it is avoided by eating sensibly. Although there are many causes of diarrhoea, the avoidance strategies are essentially the same for each type. Ensure that your food is prepared and stored in a hygienic manner, that you always wash your hands with soap before eating anything, and that your drinking water is safe. Food is the main problem: expatriates who cook for themselves, or employ reliable servants, are able to ensure that it is hygienically prepared. Travellers staying in hotels have less control over the way their food is prepared, so they are at much greater risk. Ordering cooked-to-order hot meals in restaurants is safer than eating ready-made dishes. Be at your most cautious when you are staying in large centres of population, since the more people that there are around you the more faeces there will be. The star ratings of hotels are no guide to hygiene. You can, however, reduce the risks by taking some simple precautions (*see* box, 'How to reduce the risks', p.103.)

On expeditions or while camping do not allow anyone to do the cooking if they are ill. It is especially tempting to expect an ailing travelling companion to cook while he or she is recuperating in camp, but this is the best way to ensure that the whole team goes down with the same tummy-bug. If you employ a cook when trekking, for example, make sure that he understands the basic principles of hygiene, and check that he washes his hands with soap after defecating and before preparing food. Short fingernails are easier to keep clean than long ones.

If you find yourself consuming something that you suspect is unsafe, take as little of it as possible. The less you eat the less likely you are to become ill: the severity of diarrhoea usually depends upon the number of microbes that get inside your insides. Never assume that you are immune. The body is never able to build up an immunity to *Shigella*, which causes bacillary dysentery, for example, so it is possible to suffer from dysentery several times a year and in some unhygienic environments people do.

Which foods are unsafe?

In unhygienic environments, uncooked foods are unsafe. Food can be contaminated with human faeces while it is growing, during transport, preparation, cooking, storage or serving. 'Nightsoil' is a traditional fertilizer in Nepal and China, and in some parts of Peru and Bolivia irrigation water is at such a premium that farmers break into sewage mains to water their crops with untreated effluent. Even with all this contamination, thorough cooking will sterilize food.

Salads are always a likely source of diarrhoea, and lettuce can only be rendered safe by being vigorously boiled. Stick to tomatoes and smooth-skinned items that can be washed and, preferably, soaked in dilute chlorine ('Milton' or bleach) or iodine (12 drops per litre) for 30 minutes. **Fried rice** is a high risk; it is often made with 'bits' lying around in the kitchen, and flash frying may not sterilize everything. **Ice** is often made with contaminated water. It may then have travelled from an ice factory on the back of someone's bike and have been deposited at the roadside on the way to your drink. Then it may be handled by unwashed fingers when it is put into your drink. It is safer to pack ice around the outside of the glass or bottle to keep it cool. **Ice cream** is usually very risky, though the acidity of sorbets kills many bacteria (including *Salmonella*), so they are fairly safe. **Strawberries** are uncleanable and grow close to unpleasant brown deposits on the ground; they are high risk unless grown in a hygienic environment. The maxim that will protect you is:

peel it,
boil it,
cook it,
shell it, or...
... forget it.

Diseases avoided by eating safe foods

A host of filth-to-mouth microbes cause diarrhoea in careless travellers and stay-at-homes alike, but the precautions for avoiding all of them are similar and straightforward (*see* box, p.103).

→ *Enterotoxigenic Escherichia coli* (ETEC).
→ *Enteroadherent*, *enteroaggregative* and other strains of *Escherichia coli*.
→ *Campylobacter*, which causes a lot of griping pains with the diarrhoea.
→ *Shigella* causes severe bloody diarrhoea (*see* p.115).
→ Other bacterial causes of diarrhoea, like *Salmonella* food poisoning.
→ *Giardia* (*see* p.116).
→ A variety of other parasites (*see* pp.115–16) and worms (*see* pp.119–20).
→ Amoebic dysentery (*see* p.115).
→ *Cryptosporidium*; causes 14-day diarrhoea with cramps (*see* p.115).
→ *Cyclospora*, a 'new' illness; similarities to blue-green algae (*see* p.115).
→ Rotaviruses, which cause winter epidemics of diarrhoea in Britain and are also a common cause of diarrhoea in the tropics.
→ A catalogue of rarer diarrhoea-causing viruses.
→ Cholera (*see* p.115).
→ Typhoid (*see* p.282).
→ Paratyphoid A, B and C (*see* p.282).
→ Hepatitis A and E (*see* p.278).
→ Polio.
→ *Cystocercosis* (worm cysts in the brain) (*see* p.121).

Eggs

Raw or lightly cooked eggs carry a risk of *Salmonella* poisoning; pregnant women and anyone frail should eat eggs cooked. Fresh mayonnaise is made with raw eggs.

Milk

Make sure that any milk you drink has been boiled, even if it claims to be pasteurized. I have found wood shavings and buffalo hair in 'pasteurized' milk. Unboiled pasteurized milk (and/or the water used to adulterate it) can give you TB, Brucellosis, Q-Fever, typhoid and polio, as well as dysentery and diarrhoea. Powdered or tinned milks are as safe as the water used for reconstitution. Yoghurt is usually safe. Goat's milk is not much safer than cow or buffalo milk; it can carry **Brucellosis** and other organisms. Cheese is only as safe as the milk it was made from, while drinks containing yoghurt and ice (e.g. lassi in Nepal) are risky because ingredients are handled during preparation. In the Indian subcontinent milk is usually safe because it has been boiled, but always check. Finally, be aware that milk should probably be avoided when you have diarrhoea or a stomach upset. A temporary (six-week-long) milk allergy can be the consequence of continuing to take dairy products during profuse diarrhoea; this will make the diarrhoea go on longer.

Case History: Nepal

We went into a restaurant in Kathmandu. It was stark but pretentiously laid out. Was there a good reason for its lack of customers? Should we eat somewhere else? No, it was getting late, so we ordered. I chose a Mexican dish described as being served on a bed of lettuce and covered in sour cream. It sounded delicious, but I said that I did not like lettuce. It arrived topped with chopped raw tomatoes, and accompanied by a little dish of cold sour cream. I had expected the cream to be cooked in some kind of sauce. Sadly, I rejected the cream but ate the rest, including the tomatoes, thinking that if they had been thoroughly washed and had not been cut up in the same place as the raw meat, they would be reasonably harmless (in fact, I was hungry, and thus justified eating what otherwise I might not have).

It was not long before I realized I had to pay for ignoring my own rules. I awoke in the small hours knowing I was going to be very ill, and lay awake all night, waiting. I spent the morning emptying my stomach, and by lunchtime had drunk six glasses of cooled hot lemon (with a pinch of salt and plenty of sugar) and a cola (with another pinch of salt). I felt a lot better. That evening I nibbled a few crackers with my hot lemons, and was fine again by the next morning, although I stuck to a light, plain diet for the rest of the day.

How to reduce the risks

→ Avoid salads, especially lettuce and watercress.
→ Vegetables are usually safer than meat dishes.
→ A la carte is safer than food from a buffet.
→ Any meat that you eat must be thoroughly cooked and steaming hot.
→ Piping hot foods that are freshly cooked or thoroughly reheated are safe; sizzling hot street snacks are usually safe.
→ Fried rice may be risky where reliable electricity is lacking (*see* p.101).
→ Avoid ice and ice cream when in less hygienic places.
→ Refuse soft fruits that cannot be peeled, like strawberries.
→ Be wary of seafood; make sure it is properly cooked (*see* p.123).
→ Avoid obviously soiled cutlery, plates, cups and glasses and plates that have been licked by dogs.
→ Only drink safe water (*see* pp.104–7).

Flies

It is unaesthetic to see these six-legged filth-mongers running around uninvited on your food, but it seems that flies do not spread much disease – except trachoma and other eye infections. You can estimate the length of time an expatriate has lived in the tropics by his response to a fly dive-bombing his beer. A recent arrival will discard the beer and pour himself another. A settled expat will fish out the fly and finish his pint. But a truly aculturated expatriate will drink the beer, eat the fly and extol the virtues of this ready source of protein: 'The chicken is so stringy, you see.'

Safe drinks

The vast majority of diarrhoea episodes come from contaminated food and poor food hygiene, but water can also make you ill. The greatest risk of this is in towns with intermittent piped water supplies; water is often cleaner at source than it is after it has been treated and delivered to the taps, because there is suction into the pipe when water starts flowing along it, and any slight leaks will allow material in the soil to enter the water supply. This is quite a common problem in congested third world cities. Tap water in North America, Northern Europe, the European Union, Australasia and other destinations with good infrastructure should be of drinkable quality. In francophone Europe ordering a *carafe* or *pichet de l'eau* will get you tap water and will avoid you getting charged for bottled drinks; empty mineral water bottles have become a new concern producing a problem of litter in many areas. Bottled water, which may just be treated (or untreated) tap water, is less safe than boiled water, even if the seal is intact. Studies in

India, Nepal and Pakistan have found faecal bacteria in sealed bottles of mineral water, and it is likely that bottled water in other developing countries can be contaminated too. That said, this is the source I use when I'm thirsty and unprepared.

As alternatives to water there are other safe drinks: hot lemon, fresh lime soda, tea and coffee; in Indonesia *air putih* (boiled water served warm, but beware of added ice); in Madagascar *ranovola*; in Latin America camomile tea (*manzanilla*). Starting a meal with hot soup also provides tasty and safe liquid.

Treating water to make it safe

Boiling

Boiling is the most effective means of sterilizing water; it kills amoebae and other cyst-formers that are resistant to iodine and chlorine. Purists say that to sterilize water it should be brought to a rolling boil and kept there for a full minute, and that at high altitude (e.g. 5,800m/19,000ft, where water boils at 81°C/178°F) water should be boiled for five minutes. Pressure cookers reduce boiling times and save on fuel. However, merely bringing water to the boil makes it safe enough for most purposes. The flat taste of boiled water disappears if it is left standing for several hours in a partly-filled, covered container, or if it is shaken vigorously for a minute in a container with an air gap.

Boiled water is much safer than water treated with iodine. Iodine is safer than using water sterilization tablets, bleach or other forms of chlorine. *Cryptosporidium* and amoebae survive in chlorine, and *Cyclospora* is resistant to iodine and chlorine, but all of these microbes are killed by boiling. If you need water to be completely sterile (e.g. for feeding to babies) ask the restaurant or hotel for some boiling water and fill a thermos flask with it; it will soon be sterile even if it was not absolutely boiling.

Clearly, obtaining boiling or boiled water is not always easy and so most travellers will carry tablets to chemically purify water; note, though, that purification takes time, and that this time is longer if the water is cold. It is best to crush tablets into your water bottle to speed up dissolution and in cold conditions allow an hour for the chemical to work – leave it overnight if possible.

Iodine

Iodine comes in several forms but produces drinkable water in 20–30 minutes. Add four drops of **tincture of iodine** (usually 2% iodine) to a litre of water, shake and leave to stand for at least 20 minutes. If the water is very cloudy or cold, double the iodine concentration or leave the water to stand for longer (a few hours if possible).

Case History: Indonesia

An expatriate family living in a smart suburb of Jakarta were meticulous about sterilizing food: they soaked all fruit, tomatoes and cucumbers in soap powder then in dilute bleach, rinsed them in boiled water, then dried them and stored them in the refrigerator. They also boiled their water for a full 20 minutes before filtering it. All their food came from a very plush ultra-clean supermarket used almost entirely by expatriates. The family came down with typhoid. Their disease came from locally manufactured ice cream bought at the supermarket.

The family's health precautions were mostly sound, even verging on the obsessional, yet they had not realized that ice cream – even from an apparently hygienic supermarket – is very risky stuff. There are frequent power cuts in Indonesia. Frozen foods may have been allowed to thaw and then been refrozen. Many Jakarta residents say that they avoid buying frozen foods for a week or so after any long power cut; this may reduce the risk – so long as other shoppers are not all doing the same.

Iodine crystals may be better for longer-term travellers. Make a saturated solution of iodine by roughly quarter-filling a 20ml screw-topped bottle with crystals (but note that this form of iodine eats through plastic). Top up with any water. Shake for a few seconds (the crystals settle and nothing appears to dissolve) and leave for at least half an hour. Shake again. Pour about 10ml of the solution (not the crystals) into a one-litre bottle and dilute with water; shake and leave for at least 20 minutes. Top up the 20ml bottle ready for the next time it's needed. This should make up to 1,000 litres. A 20ml bottle with volume marks on the side makes it easy to estimate the 10ml volume.

The somewhat unpleasant taste of iodine is improved by adding vitamin C (*ascorbic acid*) **after** the 20–30 minute period of sterilization. Alternatively, you can add enough drink powder to cover the taste without making the water sweet, or add a squirt of citrus juice. In Latin America, limes are cheap, available in most markets and travel fairly well; they are also easy to find in much of Asia and parts of Africa.

Toxicity of iodine

It is safe to use iodine – including iodine in iodine-resin water filters – for months at a stretch, but be cautious about using it very long term, especially if you have a thyroid problem, are pregnant or are treating water for young children. It is best to take a variety of safe drinks, including hot or bottled drinks, and boiled and cooled water; thus it will not be necessary to swallow much iodine. Travellers' folklore warns that swallowing concentrated iodine or iodine crystals is dangerous. Nothing dramatic will happen to you; seek medical advice if you feel unwell in the following couple of weeks. Doctors looking after Peace Corps Volunteers recently reported reversible thyroid enlargement (goitre) and other mild symptoms, which were attributed to absorbing at least 330 times the recommended daily intake of 0.15mg iodine. These volunteers were working in Niger, where extremely hot desert conditions required them to drink 5–9 litres of water a day, and the volunteers with symptoms treated their water with a two-stage iodine matrix filter. It was felt that use of a three-stage filter, including a carbon-based third stage to remove iodine, would have reduced or avoided the problem. A cheaper option, and one already adopted by most expatriates, would be to use more boiled water, soups and other safe fluids, and rely less on chemical sterilization, which in any case doesn't taste as good.

Filters and water purification units

Ceramic water filters designed for use in the kitchen are readily available in the Indian subcontinent (but not Indonesia), and they allow expatriates to organize a ready supply of safe water. The filter removes sediment and the largest microbes. Check the filter candles for cracks and clean the filter by scrubbing, then boil the candles for 20 minutes once every couple of weeks; otherwise you may introduce more bugs than were in the original water supply. Ideally, you should filter the tap water first, boil it in a large covered saucepan, and allow it to cool a little, then pour it into bottles for refrigeration. Most expatriates boil and then filter; the danger here is that if the filter is contaminated, microbes may be introduced during filtering.

Filtered water is not necessarily safe. When hotels or restaurants say their drinking water is filtered, this usually means it has been passed through a large-pore porcelain filter. Even if these are cleaned regularly and are not cracked they do not remove all microbes. Portable filters and purification devices are available for travellers. The newer, pump-action models are a huge improvement on the heavy, slow gravity versions, but they are expensive. Many of the bacteriological filters work well, but check that they remove viruses as well as bacteria: in some places viruses cause over half of diarrhoea cases, and filters that do not remove hepatitis viruses do not render water completely safe unless they also include a form of chemical sterilization. An example is the **PUR filters** with iodine matrixes; these give safe water, but cost up to £180. If you envisage very remote and difficult travel conditions, you may like to look at the Millbank bag; this is a canvas bag developed by the British Army and designed to remove sediment before boiling or treating with chemicals. It can produce drinkable water from liquid mud. Many travel shops now stock a range of filters.

What's swimming about in your glass of water

There is a huge range of sizes amongst the mischievous microbes that may contaminate drinking water. Few filters will take out viruses like hepatitis A and even if the filter is fine enough to exclude this virus, it will clog up easily and is impractical for travel use. **Boiling** kills all these microbes. *See* the **table** below for a list of microbes and their sizes.

Devices

Knowing the pore sizing of your water filtration device will help you judge what it can do. The Aqua Pure Traveller, for example, has a 0.2 micron filter, which means it will exclude all the above organisms except hepatitis and other viruses. Iodine or boiling kills viruses.

Contact information: stockists of water filters

The following offer a wide choice of water filters:
Cotswold, UK t (01285) 860 612, **f** (01285) 860 483.
Nomad, UK t (020) 8889 7014, **f** (020) 889 9529. Also sells Millbank bags; *see* **Useful Addresses**, p.327, for more details about Nomad stores.

Size and treatment of water microbes

Sizes in microns (smallest diameter given for ovoid cysts/eggs)

Microbe	size	treatment
Ascaris roundworm eggs	35	readily filtered
Cryptosporidium	4	chlorine resistant
Cyclospora	8	chlorine and iodine resistant
Entomoeba histolytica (amoebic dysentery)	10	chlorine 'less effective'; iodine kills
Giardia lamblia	7	iodine kills if plenty added; chlorine resistant
Guinea worm	500 -700 long	readily filtered even with only a cloth
Hepatitis A virus	0.03	susceptible to iodine treatment
Hookworm eggs	36	readily filtered
Schistosoma (Bilharzia)	70+	susceptible to most chemical treatments
Tapeworms (*Taenia* spp.)	31	readily filtered

Prevention with medicines

Taking medicines to prevent diarrhoea can create more problems than it solves. The US Navy is particularly active in researching ways to avoid travellers' diarrhoea. Interestingly, even they (perhaps less interested in the long-term health of their personnel than civilian doctors) do not recommend prevention with antibiotics, even on short missions. The best precautions are to travel with '*peel it, boil it, cook it, shell it or forget it*' in your mind, knowledge of rehydration procedures, and perhaps a course of *ciprofloxacin*.

Natural preventatives

A preventative option that is natural and unlikely to cause side effects are the so-called **probiotic products**. The idea that it is beneficial to eat certain kinds of fermented foods goes back centuries, and today there is a vogue for eating live yoghurt or other products containing 'friendly' bacteria. They probably help prevent travellers' gastroenteritis and are also of benefit if you are struck with the squits. In a bout of travellers' diarrhoea, the bacteria normally inhabiting the bowel take a hammering, and it is logical to replace battle-worn friendly bacteria with fresh reinforcements in the form of *Lactobacillus acidophilus* or *Bifidobacterium* spp. or *Saccharomyces cerevisiae*. Jeremy Hamilton-Miller, professor of medical microbiology at London's Royal Free and University College Medical School, says these bacteria show promising properties when tested in the laboratory; some even kill harmful, disease-causing bacteria. Pro-biotics seem beneficial in farm animals, and there is plenty of anecdotal evidence to suggest they help keep travellers healthy, but good, solid, well-formed research in people has so far shown rather variable results. Capsules (e.g. **Culturelle**) and powders contain more predictable quantities of desirable bacteria than live yoghurts, and these are also more portable. Pharmacies, drug stores and health food shops sell these lactobacilli-loaded preparations in the UK and the USA. Now becoming more widely available, they can also be found in drinkable form.

Charcoal also has some modest effect on diarrhoea, and some travellers find it helpful, especially if the upset is associated with a lot of bloating, as charcoal absorbs noxious gases. North American travellers often take *bismuth subsalicylate* for their gastro-intestinal symptoms and this probably helps a little.

In infants, the best protection against diarrhoea is **breast-feeding**, so if you plan to travel with small children try to ensure they are exclusively breast-fed rather than offering them formula milk in bottles. Ideally, children should not be weaned off the breast until the age of a year. In many developing countries, it is common for local children to be breast-fed for two or three years; this is an excellent and healthy practice.

TREATING DIARRHOEA

Diarrhoea is a good thing. It is the natural process of expelling the poisons that cause disease. By stopping it recovery may be slowed, which is why I dislike unnatural 'blocking' medicines. A healthy adult is unlikely to come to any great harm from travellers' diarrhoea: a light, bland diet and lots of clear fluids will settle the symptoms of simple travellers' diarrhoea quickly. In the very few travellers who become especially ill, it is adequate fluid replacement that saves life, not antibiotics or anti-diarrhoeal medicines. Passing blood and/or mucus and/or having a fever with diarrhoea probably means you have dysentery, which requires treatment in addition to fluid replacement; *see* p.114. If you have to get on a bus while ill with diarrhoea, beware of the gastro-colic reflex (*see* p.112). Mild diarrhoeal symptoms should respond to a couple of doses of the natural remedy **ispaghula husk**; *see* **Ailments**, pp.279–80.

Treatment of children

When children have diarrhoea, dehydration is a risk. Like adults, they should be encouraged to drink each time they open their bowels; half a glass of fluid is enough for small children. Children can get into trouble with the balance of salts in their blood, especially with profuse diarrhoea. Oral rehydration sachets mixed with boiled and cooled water are the safest remedy. ORS taste awful, though, so it is often more realistic to offer cola with a pinch of salt in it. Otherwise, offer home-made solutions flavoured with fruit cordial or some other tempting cocktail. Getting children to drink is crucial. Babies with diarrhoea need checking over by a doctor.

Important note for parents: Infants and very small children have died from too much salt, so, if in doubt, give too little or none at all. Sugar or glucose and water alone make an acceptable rehydration solution. Babies should continue to be breast-fed. Solid foods should be given as usual.

Replacing lost fluids

Normal diets provide about three litres of fluid a day, so when you stop eating, you need this PLUS anything that is being lost down the toilet. The usual processes of food and fluid absorption become less efficient when you have diarrhoea, yet simple mixtures of sugar, salt and water continue to be well absorbed by the stomach and upper intestine. In fact, they are taken in more efficiently than plain water. Complex carbohydrates (salty crackers, dry bread, plain rice or boiled potatoes) also aid absorption of the fluids you need to replace those you are losing into

Case History: Nepal

Two Nepalis supported a middle-aged American man on a horse. They all stopped at the same teashop as me, so I offered help. The American reported a sleepless night disturbed by diarrhoea; this, along with trekking the Annapurna circuit, had finished him.

'You are quite dehydrated; that makes you feel awful. You need to drink three litres a day to keep your body's fluids topped up – as well as replace all that you have lost to diarrhoea and breathing hard at altitude,' I said.

'I drank a quart this morning and one of those rehydration salt packets, so I'm not dehydrated.' He ordered a cola and I suggested adding a pinch of salt. 'No, I got all the salts I need from that packet.'

I explained that the salt would help him absorb the water in the drink, but he did not want my advice and struggled on. This man suffered unnecessarily. He was dehydrated and needed to drink a lot more. He also misunderstood the role of rehydration packets. They are not a once-only medicine, but a vehicle for fluid transport into the body. They also give a glucose-fired energy burst, which makes you feel really good and enthusiastic enough for serious (non-alcoholic) drinking.

the toilet. The fastest road back to health, then, is to take lots of clear fluids. If you are hungry, take a light, bland diet for 24–36 hours; if you do not feel like eating, do not eat. And avoid milk and alcohol.

Good drinks to take are clear soups, young coconut, drinks made from Marmite, Bovril or stock cubes, herbal infusions, Malagasy *ranovola*, hot lemon, lemon tea and fizzy drinks (cola or Fanta); weak black tea and coffee may also be taken. Combinations of sugar and salt are absorbed best, so add a pinch of salt to sweet drinks or a spoonful of sugar to savoury drinks. Alternatively, drink oral rehydration salts (ORS). These are available in most countries: Electrolade, Dioralyte, Rehidrat in the UK, Oralit in Indonesia and Jeevan Jal (literally 'water of life') in Nepal. ORS are best for children, the frail, those with long-standing medical problems and anyone with very profuse (12 times a day) diarrhoea. Most adult travellers, though, will be fine taking clear fluid and/or their own home-made sugar and salt solution.

Home-made Oral Rehydration Solution (ORS)

Two heaped teaspoons (or a four-finger scoop) of glucose (or sugar) and a three-finger pinch (less than a quarter of a teaspoon) of salt should be mixed in a glass of boiled, cooled water, or eight level teaspoons of sugar and a level teaspoonful of salt in a litre. Otherwise, use a sugar and salt measuring spoon (which may be bought from travel clinics or TALC, *see* **Useful Addresses**, pp.326–30). The solution should taste no more salty than tears.

Most forms of sugar can be used, and raw, unrefined sugars or molasses (*ghur* in Hindi/Urdu) are better than nice white stuff as they are rich in potassium, which the body loses during diarrhoea and vomiting. You can also use palm syrup or honey. A little fresh lemon, lime or orange juice improves flavour and adds potassium.

How much do you need to drink?

Dehydration is a common complication of diarrhoea, and makes sufferers feel really awful. Most people make the mistake of not drinking enough. To maintain fluid balance, a healthy person of normal build who is not eating needs to drink about three litres a day. Fluid requirements are greater in heat, at altitude, in high winds, travelling in cars with the windows open or on a bike, or when breast-feeding. If you have diarrhoea or fever you need still more. Drink two glassfuls each time the bowels are opened, and more if you are thirsty. Those who are vomiting can absorb fluids if they drink slowly, in sips.

Dehydration can make you feel dizzy (or even faint) getting out of bed or a chair. Drink more, move slowly and sit with your legs over the side of the bed before rising. If you are passing only a scant amount of dark-coloured urine, you should also be drinking more.

Case History: Peru

A phone call announced, 'Julian looks awful, feels faint, can hardly get out of bed, terrible diarrhoea, dizzy, splitting headache. Could it be cholera? There's a cholera epidemic in the country, isn't there? Should he fly home?'

I asked a few questions. Most of the chap's symptoms seemed to be due to fluid loss and fear that he was desperately ill: he did, after all, feel deathly. Why else could he hardly stand up? They had rehydration salts (ORS) in the house, and I told him he needed to drink a lot to replace the diarrhoeal losses. 'See if you can drink at least a litre of clear fluids in the next hour; slow the drinking rate if you feel nauseated.'

I called round 90 minutes later to find a stocky man in his twenties looking very sorry for himself. I estimated he had lost 5% of his body fluids: he was badly dehydrated.

'How are you getting on with the drinking?'

'Fresh orange juice gives me stomach ache, but I've had half a glassful.'

He needed to replace 4.5 litres, plus two glassfuls every time he opened his bowels. He was surprised at the volume and by the need to take only clear fluids, but was now convinced enough to settle down to more enthusiastic drinking.He could not stomach ORS. Diluting the juice made it easier on his aching belly, and he made some glucose and salt solution too. Two hours later when I phoned him he said that the headache and dizziness had gone, and he felt much better.

The Gastro-Colic Reflex

Very hot or very cold drinks and foods tend to provoke a reflex bowel action and abdominal pain. This gastro-colic reflex can be useful if you are constipated; a hot drink first thing in the morning often encourages a bowel action. However, if you have diarrhoea with a lot of abdominal crampy pains, take only tepid food and drink to avoid making your bowel even more active. Cramps are more likely if you eat indigestible food when your stomach is upset. Stick to a light, fat-free diet.

Irritable bowel symptoms and abdominal pains are common during or just after an attack of diarrhoea. *Hyoscine* (e.g. Buscopan) 20mg when needed (up to four times a day), *mebeverine* (e.g. Colofac) one 135mg tablet three times daily, or *peppermint oil* (e.g. Colpermin) 1–2 capsules three times daily, can help. If it continues, get a stool test.

What to eat when diarrhoea strikes

Drink plenty, but if you have no appetite, eat nothing. Otherwise, try a little light food; solid, greasy foods often cause abdominal pains as the bowel tries to expel them. Bananas help stop diarrhoea and also contain plenty of essential potassium. Yoghurt can help settle the stomach by replacing diarrhoea-causing bacteria with friendly ones. Dry biscuits or bread can also be comforting to an aching, empty stomach. Children who have diarrhoea should be encouraged to eat what they can.

When to use medicine to treat diarrhoea

Blockers – the 'blocking' medicines such as Imodium, Lomotil and codeine phosphate – are not the cure for diarrhoea that they may appear. Blockers work by paralyzing the muscles of the bowel; they therefore trap noxious bugs and poisons within the body, when what is needed is to expel them fast. Vital fluids may not pour out of your bottom, but they can become pooled in inaccessible pockets. Blockers can be useful if you cannot postpone a bus journey for 24 hours, but they tend to make you feel ill for longer, and should only be taken in combination with an antibiotic. It is dangerous to give blockers to children and anyone with dysentery (diarrhoea with fever and the passing of blood and/or slime). **Enterovioform** was banned as dangerous years ago, yet it is still available in some places (e.g. Thailand). Avoid this, too.

Bismuth appears to reduce the amount of fluids lost during diarrhoea and probably also kills some of the bacteria, yet it does not have the risks of taking antibiotics. It can be taken to prevent or treat diarrhoea and can be taken as *bismuth subsalicylate* tablets twice daily, up to 2.1g in 24 hours. The disadvantages are that it causes an unpleasant taste, nausea and blackening of the tongue and stools. In the UK it is only available over the counter as a liquid and the volumes required probably make it impractical for British travellers to take abroad.

Antibiotics and treatment of severe/bloody diarrhoea

Diarrhoea is generally short-lived (up to 50 hours), so treatment with drugs is often unnecessary. If, though, diarrhoea is accompanied by fever and/or blood in the faeces, or is very profuse, 'blocking' drugs like *loperamide* must be avoided. Instead, it would be sensible to take an antibiotic as well as plenty of rehydration fluids. This should bring relief quickly and safely. *Ciprofloxacin* 500mg twice daily for three days is an excellent remedy for severe and/or bloody diarrhoea, as is *norfloxacin* (which carries the same cautions as *ciprofloxacin*) 400mg twice daily for three days; *levofloxacin* is another good alternative taken as 500mg daily. Different antibiotics work well or less well in different regions; *nalidixic acid* (for adults, 1g four times daily for seven days) is particularly effective for diarrhoea acquired in Nepal, and it is reasonably safe for children; this can be bought as GramoNeg 'oral suspension' in India. With all these drugs you must still take plenty (i.e. litres) of clear fluids: at least two glasses every time you open your bowels. *Ciprofloxacin* is not recommended for young children or growing adolescents, in pregnancy, and probably not for athletes, epileptics or people with other neurological problems. *Ciprofloxacin*, *norfloxacin* and related antibiotics can cause tendon inflammation; tendon ruptures have been reported in competitive athletes after Cipro treatment, so mountaineers and trekkers may also experience problems. For more on the advantages or otherwise of taking antibiotics, *see* pp.83–4.

Even if you have treated yourself with antibiotics, if the symptoms are not beginning to settle after 48 hours it is wise to consult a doctor, or at least arrange a stool test. Persistent abdominal pain, bloody diarrhoea, a fever, confusion setting in, or diarrhoea that goes on for more than three days, suggest that you need medical help.

New treatments

At the time of writing *ciprofloxacin* and related *fluroquinolone* antibiotics are still the drugs of choice for treating gastro-intestinal infections in travellers. However, resistance is developing and it is likely that new antibiotics will become more useful in the coming years.

A new antibiotic to treat travellers' diarrhoea is about to become available in the USA, Spain, Germany, Italy and other countries. This is *rifaximin* (Normix, Flonorm, Redactiv and Zaxine) and appears to cure with few side effects. It is effective in treating gastro-intestinal infections that cause fever despite the fact that the medicine is not absorbed into the body: it stays in the gut in high concentrations killing gram-positive and gram-negative bacteria. It may also have some curative effect on cryptosporidia. The antibiotics *bicozamycin* and *aztreonam* have also been shown to be very effective and safe in the treatment of travellers' diarrhoea, but they have never been marketed and are not currently available; they may reappear in future, however.

Stool tests

Medical laboratories in developing countries are often expert at checking stool samples. Make sure that the sample you give is fresh (preferably still warm). The simplest investigation, which almost any laboratory can do, is look at it under a microscope. If they see mucus or red blood cells (RBC) this indicates dysentery requiring antibiotic treatment (your result may say 'RBC+', which means that some bloodcells have been seen; '++', quite a few; or '+++', lots). The type of antibiotic depends on the symptoms, not the number of + signs. Explosive, profuse diarrhoea and fever means bacillary dysentery, cured by *ciprofloxacin*, *norfloxacin*, *nalidixic acid*; milder symptoms suggest amoebae needing *tinidazole* or *metronidazole* (Flagyl). Worms' eggs can be another finding, but these do not do any harm (and don't usually cause diarrhoea) and can wait for treatment until a much more convenient time. More sophisticated laboratories can identify bacteria and work out which antibiotic will kill them most effectively, but this takes a few days and you may be better or far away by the time you get the result. A look under the microscope is all you need unless a serious problem, such as typhoid, is suspected. With most intestinal parasites, you need three negative checks several days apart to be sure you are not infected.

Diarrhoea that goes on and on

Diarrhoea that goes on for more than 3–4 days should be treated; if no doctor is available try one of the antibiotics suggested above. Diarrhoea can occasionally persist for months (often labelled **tropical sprue**). Sufferers lose a lot of weight. It is not a well-understood disease, but often responds to *tetracycline* (250mg four times daily) and *folic acid* (15mg daily) for a month. Experiment to see whether avoiding milk and dairy products, fatty, oily and spicy foods and alcohol helps reduce the symptoms. Persistent diarrhoea often gets better when you get home, even without treatment.

Nearly all diarrhoea in travellers is due to bacteria and viruses, but in a tiny minority it is due to some other cause. Protracted diarrhoea could be the start of another, non-tropical problem which will need proper medical assessment.

INTRODUCING SOME FILTH-TO-MOUTH DISEASES

Amoebic Dysentery

Dysentery sounds scary but this form can be mild, and will not usually make you feel particularly unwell. However, the blood in your stools means that you need some treatment with *tinidazole* (Fasigyn) 2g (4x500mg tablets) daily for three days or *metronidazole* (Flagyl) 800mg (2x400mg) every eight hours for five days. Do not drink alcohol with Flagyl or you will feel ill. If you have no symptoms, but amoebic cysts are found in your stools (*see* 'Stool tests', facing page), you can take *diloxanide furoate* 500mg every eight hours for 10 days. 'Blocking' drugs like *loperamide* make dysentery worse.

Bacillary (Bacterial) Dysentery

This form of dysentery causes profuse, explosive and bloody diarrhoea with fever, and makes you feel very unwell. *Shigella* is such a powerful microbe that you need only swallow 10 to be struck with severe bacillary dysentery (*see* 'Stool tests', facing page). It needs antibiotic treatment and lots and lots of clear drinks. 'Blocking' drugs like *loperamide* make dysentery worse.

Cholera

The disease rarely causes symptoms in well-nourished, healthy people. There is presently no need to be immunized, but when a better (oral) vaccine is available this advice may change. Profuse watery diarrhoea is often due to ETEC bacteria, not cholera.

Cryptosporidium

This parasite causes a particularly tedious type of diarrhoea lasting between 10 days and two weeks, with a lot of cramps; there is no specific treatment, although the new *rifaximin* (Normix, Flonorm, Redactiv and Zaxine) may be effective. *Cryptosporidium* can be acquired from swimming pools.

Cyclospora

These parasites resemble blue-green algae and were discovered in travellers in Nepal in 1990. *Cyclospora* outbreaks occur there between mid-April and November, with a peak in July. During this season water should be boiled, as chemical sterilization does not kill the microbe. *Cyclospora* diarrhoea lasts 2–12 weeks if untreated. It has now turned up all over the less developed world and the USA. Treatment is with *co-trimoxazole* (e.g. Bactrim or Septrin); *trimethoprim* alone will not help.

Case History: Torquay?

Our luxurious beachside hotel in Turkey offered a wonderful buffet each day. I wanted to avoid putting on too much weight, though, and ate lots of salad. At the end of the second week of the holiday, I developed diarrhoea, which got worse and worse until I was passing almost pure blood. I felt ill, nauseated and developed intermittent feverish shakes. I tried to keep up with fluid loss by drinking, but misjudged it. I became worse and was admitted to a local, small and clean, but isolated hospital for a drip and antibiotics, where they said I'd contracted dysentery from the salad. The subsequent four-hour flight home to the UK was disastrous, with lots of nauseated and bloated trips to the over-popular loo, followed immediately by emergency admission and a week of further in-patient treatment on an infectious diseases ward. The bemused doctor in admissions said, 'So, Simon, I hear you've been to Torquay...?'

Dr Simon B.

Giardia

Giardia lamblia are elegant heart-shaped parasites that swim around the intestine propelled by two splendid whiskers. Infection, called giardiasis, upsets the stomach and causes sulphurous, foul-smelling belches and farts, abdominal distension and often protracted diarrhoea. *Giardia* is probably the most over-diagnosed, inappropriately treated travellers' ailment; if you think you have it, get a stool check before rushing to take antibiotics. First, try 24 hours on clear fluids and a bland, very low-fat diet (*see* 'What to eat when diarrhoea strikes', p.112). Other microbes cause similar symptoms, and untreated giardiasis does little harm other than make you an unwelcome guest. One fairly specific symptom is passing stools that stink, float and are difficult to flush away (there are other causes of this, so if treatment for *giardia* doesn't work, find a doctor).

The usual **treatment** is *tinidazole* (Fasigyn), a single 2g dose daily for two days, or *metronidazole* (Flagyl) 2g (e.g. 5x400mg) daily for three days. Do not drink alcohol with Flagyl or you will feel ill. Treatment failures with *metronidazole* are becoming more common, but a second course often eradicates the parasite. Alternative treatments for recalcitrant giardiasis is *albendazole* 400mg four times a day for seven days or *quinacrine* 100mg three times daily, although the latter is not yet widely available. *Furazolidone* is another treatment that is usually effective against *giardia* and also to some extent against bacterial causes of travellers' diarrhoea. If symptoms return it is best to get another stool sample checked before trying more antibiotics. *Giardia* can be acquired from swimming pools.

On The Ground

Worms, Guts and Nutrition

09

Worms are more alarming than dangerous. Most common is the roundworm *Ascaris lumbricoides*; it looks like a large earthworm and is about 30cm long. They rarely cause problems unless they're present in very large numbers (100 or more) and, since travellers seldom acquire more than a couple, infestations cause – at most – some vague abdominal symptoms. Most people are unaware of their worm until, having died of old age, it emerges a year or so after it stowed away.

Summary

→ Diarrhoea and a great variety of parasites can be acquired from contaminated food that has been inadequately cooked.

→ Eat piping hot, thoroughly cooked food; avoid salads.

→ In regions where sanitation is poor, eating rare or raw steak or pork put you at risk of tapeworm.

→ Pay attention to local cooking methods and eating habits. They have generally been developed to minimize risks to health; the exception is foods that are served raw.

→ Seafood, freshwater crustacea and fish must be thoroughly cooked before eating; most routine cooking will not render them safe.

→ Avoid eating seafood if you are far away from the sea.

→ Reject fish with a peppery or bitter taste or which causes a tingling or smarting sensation in the mouth (but note that some tinned fish prepared in Southeast Asia has pepper or chilli added).

→ Never eat fruits and berries unless you know they are harmless; things that look like tomatoes are often highly poisonous.

→ Vegetables or fruits with a bitter, stinging or disagreeable taste may well be toxic; if in doubt, try them with the tip of your tongue.

WORMS

Where are worms a problem?

Worms infest people wherever disposal of faeces is inadequate. Although they are common in the tropics, they are also found in plenty of non-tropical countries.

Hookworm occurs in all moist, hot parts of the world. Roundworms are especially hardy parasites, prevalent in nearly all unhygienic environments, and can survive the harsh freeze-drying of high, cold deserts like those in Tibet and Ladakh. *Trichinella* and tapeworms exist wherever cattle or pigs eat fodder contaminated with human excreta. Threadworms are universal wherever there are children. Other worms, including a range of unpleasant flukes, are acquired by eating raw or lightly-cooked fish and shellfish, or water plants such as watercress that have been polluted by excrement.

Catching a worm

Few worms are transmitted directly from person to person. Roundworms (and sometimes hookworms) are acquired from contaminated food, via some of the same transmission mechanisms as diarrhoeal diseases (*see* p.99). Worm life-cycles, though, are more complex, as most cannot be passed directly between humans. Most worm eggs need a period of maturation in soil before they can infect people. Tapeworms and *Trichinella* usually need to pass through an intermediate animal host before they can infect man. Threadworms can be transmitted directly from hand to mouth – most commonly among people in close contact with children. These and some tapeworms are the only worms spread directly from one person to another.

There are differences in the ways each type of worm is acquired, but with the exception of hookworm they can be avoided with good food hygiene. Thorough cooking destroys any that lurk in food. Hookworm is mostly avoided by wearing shoes.

Know your worm

There are many to choose from, but those described here illustrate the most common problems.

Roundworm

Roundworms are common; in the developing tropics and sub-tropics they inhabit 80–90% of children. Passing a roundworm is a horrible experience, but in many cases this is a lonely hermit, so no treatment is necessary. It is dangerous to take some worm tablets if you are pregnant, and some treatments are unsafe in children under two, so be careful if you decide to treat yourself. Waiting to take treatment is unlikely to do any harm and is a safe option if you are pregnant. Roundworms cannot be passed directly from person to person.

Hookworm

Hookworm can be acquired from contaminated food, but is more often picked up by walking barefoot in damp, shady places where people have defecated; the pollution need not be obvious. The worms penetrate the skin. Sunshine and dryness kill hookworm; shoes protect you. Hookworms cause few problems, and any stowaways will die out on returning to a temperate climate. Treatment for hookworm is never urgent (I wouldn't bother to get them treated), but for anyone over the age of two, the remedy is *mebendazole* 100mg twice daily for three days.

Expatriate children can suffer significantly from hookworm. Avoid infestation by discouraging them from playing barefoot; any sand used for play should be dried in the sun for a week or two before use. Hookworm cannot be passed directly from person to person.

Strongyloides worms

Strongyloides worms may also penetrate bare feet in unhygienic places. They cause rashes and diarrhoea but, once diagnosed, treatment is easy (*see also* Case History, **Skin**, p.218).

Threadworm

These *Enterobius* are tiny and cause intense anal itching, especially at night. They are a hazard of family life (at home and abroad), usually acquired from children, and transmitted between family members. Expatriates need to treat each member of the household. Intolerable itching will drive you to seek treatment: take *piperazine* (Antepar, Pripsen in the UK; Antepar, Vermizine in the USA) for seven days. Cure rates are improved if a second course is given after a week; *piperazine* should not be taken by people with epilepsy. *Mebendazole* (Vermox, Ovex in the UK; Vermox, Wormin in the USA) given as a single 100mg dose, repeated two to three weeks later, is better, but must not be given in pregnancy (expatriates must take care when treating female employees), nor to children aged under two. Personal hygiene must be scrupulous while the infestation is present. Fingernails must be kept short, and hands washed and nails scrubbed with a brush before meals and after each visit to the toilet. Otherwise, those infected will reinfect themselves and others.

Case History: Bolivia

Sara was 20 and teaching English for a year in La Paz. Suddenly, inexplicably, she began to suffer from fainting fits, and developed little lumps under her skin. Weirder still, she saw shadows passing before one eye. Then a friend noticed that during one of Sara's 'faints' she twitched slightly: this was something more serious than a faint, and she went to hospital for tests. She had **cystocercosis**, cysts of the pork tapeworm *Taenium solium*, in her brain, eyes and under the skin. Hospital treatment cured her and she is now fine.

Sara was careful to avoid drinking tap water, but she enjoyed eating out and had a particular liking for lettuce in salads. Much of the lettuce sold in La Paz is irrigated with the city's effluent. This is also a risk in other cities and towns in the developing world.

Rarer parasites

Tapeworms look like strips of ribbon or pasta in the stools and, alarmingly, may crawl about. They are avoided by eating any meat well done. The **pork tapeworm**, *Taenium solium*, can also be acquired by eating foods contaminated with human excreta: lettuce irrigated with human sewage (as happens in Bolivia, Peru, Nepal and other places) can be a source. Cysts then settle in the brain, eyes or muscles. This **cystocercosis** is worth avoiding; seek medical advice if you think you are infected.

Undercooked pork, wild boar, walrus or polar bear can give you ***Trichinella***, which are also called 'muscle worms'. By eating inadequately cooked pork or lamb you can pick up the parasite ***toxoplasma***, which is dangerous in pregnancy. It can also be contracted by contact with cat faeces. Finally, eating off plates licked by dogs carries a risk of acquiring another difficult-to-treat worm infestation, **Hydatid Disease**.

Guinea worm (*Dracunculiasis* or Medina worm) is caught by swallowing 1–2mm-long freshwater 'fleas'. Water that has been boiled or crudely strained is safe. It is rapidly nearing extinction throughout much of its range: equatorial Africa, eastern India, Pakistan, southwest Saudi Arabia and southern Iraq. Don't worry about it.

PROBLEMS FROM BAD FOOD

The term 'food poisoning' usually suggests the contamination of food with the bacteria or viruses that cause diarrhoea and vomiting; such problems are covered in **Bowels**, pp.97–116. Other 'germs' can also reach you through bad food: an outbreak of streptococcal tonsillitis, for example, was traced to poorly prepared food.

In addition to bacterial food poisoning, it is also possible to become ill by consuming foods containing **chemical poisons**. There is such a range of possible chemicals that can contaminate food that it is impossible to mention them all. However, most naturally occurring food toxins are well recognized wherever they are consumed, and local culinary habits have evolved to deal with them.

One natural source of poison is the **cassava** tuber (manioc), from which tapioca is made. When raw it contains enough cyanide to kill, but local cooking methods (boiling, soaking, washing in running water and pounding) reduce this to a non-toxic level. Do not prepare cassava yourself; get a local person to cook it for you. It is only a risky food during disasters or famine, when there is insufficient time or fuel for traditional methods of preparation.

Expatriates who live abroad for years increasingly worry about the profligate use of **pesticides** on crops. In some regions farmers spray fruit and vegetables just before they send them to market, to make them look shiny and attractive. Large numbers of people suffer from pesticide poisoning (about 40,000 people die and a million are made ill or permanently disabled annually, worldwide), but these casualties are the result of unsafe spraying techniques or suicide attempts. I have not heard of any significant poisoning of expatriates or travellers through foods contaminated with pesticides. Even so, this is another reason to peel or thoroughly wash any fruit or vegetables, to reduce the amount of harmful chemicals ingested.

Local alcohol

A more predictable poison is alcohol. Even in its purest 'Highland Malt' form it is toxic, but when its origin is a still in a shack somewhere, it is likely to contain additional poisons. Be ready to face the consequences if you drink too much. Beware of spirits; distilled drinks may contain extremely toxic methanol, which can cause permanent blindness. Undistilled drinks of lower alcoholic content (less than 40%) are unsafe if (as is usual) they are prepared with dirty water (e.g. Tibetan *chang*). An exception is Nepali *toongba*, where boiling water is poured over fermented millet, but make sure the water is boiling and the pot pre-heated. *See* p.315 for notes on sensible levels of alcohol consumption.

Food for free

It can be tempting, especially in a remote place, to go foraging for free foods such as fungi, berries and salad stuffs. Take great care, though, since some highly poisonous plants may resemble familiar edible plants at home. There is, for example, a plant which provides succulent berries in Madagascar, but looks almost identical to European deadly nightshade (*Atropa belladonna*). Consequently, there have been hospital admissions and deaths among Malagasy people who have innocently eaten deadly nightshade berries in France. Seek local advice.

Avoid red or brightly coloured fruits and berries unless you know them to be harmless. Never eat anything that looks like a tomato (unless you know it is one) even if it smells pleasant, nor any roots, fruit or vegetables with a bitter, stinging or other disagreeable taste. If in doubt, try them with the tip of your tongue. In many regions, wild watercress carries a risk of liver fluke infestation. Seaweeds are all edible, except in highly polluted areas: the tastiest are pink, purple, reddish or green.

Dangerous seafood

Shellfish

Shellfish often harbour parasites and are efficient concentrators of faecal bacteria (including cholera); they should only be eaten if properly cooked and preferably only if they were caught far from sewage outfall. Most normal cooking does not make heavily contaminated seafood safe. For sea-crab to be safe when cooked whole, it should be boiled for 10 minutes (eight is not enough) or steamed for 30 minutes (not 25). In the Philippines you get 'jumping salad', with shrimps so fresh they are still moving; this can give you **capillariasis**, a worm infestation that becomes debilitating if not treated. Capillariasis also occurs in Thailand and Japan and can be caught from raw crabs, snails and fish. Crabs and king (i.e. horseshoe) crabs in Southeast Asia and the Pacific can also be a source of **ciguatera** and **scombrotoxic poisoning** (*see* below). If you decide to eat sea cucumber (it resembles elastic bands in texture but doesn't taste as good), ensure they are peeled; the skin can be toxic.

From time to time in tropical seas there are dramatic blooms of tiny dinoflagellate animals, *Gambierodiscus toxicus*, that make the water look red, known as **red tides**. These dinoflagellates seem to be colonizing species, so they can be a case of nature getting her own back after reef-damage by dynamite, a response to pollution or to storm damage. Red tides are signalled by the deaths of many fish and sea birds. Local fishermen usually know not to catch fish during red tides since they are poisonous, though, as this situation impinges on their livelihood, they may be tempted to sell unsafe fish. Shellfish, being filter-feeders, are especially adept at concentrating red tide poisons, so they must also be avoided at these times. Symptoms develop within half an hour of eating contaminated fish or shellfish, and may lead to fatal paralysis in 12 hours. There is no specific treatment. For other effects of red tides, *see* p.184.

Paralytic shellfish poisoning (PSP) can also occur without a red tide. Symptoms begin (typically within three hours of eating the shellfish) with tingling around the mouth and throat, dizziness and a floating sensation. There can also be headache, nausea and vomiting. The numbness progresses and muscles become affected, so that breathing may stop altogether. It even occasionally occurs in Britain, where the PSP season is May to August, and mussels are usually the culprits.

Seafish

Fish can be risky, although they are not as common a source of disease as filter-feeding shellfish. Skin reef-fish or tropical fish before eating it, and avoid eating the gonads (sexual organs). Choose fish with clear eyes and a firm, intact body that doesn't smell bad. One speciality of the coastal regions of Peru is *ceviche*, raw fish marinated with lemon and chillies; this can harbour cholera. Japanese *sushi*, when it is not properly cleaned, can give you herring worms (*anisakiasis*: fish nematodes), which you can also get from undercooked, salted or pickled fish in California. Fortunately, the worms find man rather an unsuitable host and die fairly promptly after causing a little stomach ache and nausea. Herring worm disease is no longer a problem in the Netherlands as all mackerel and herrings are now deep frozen; worms are killed in 24 hours at -20°C.

Ciguatera fish poisoning is harder to recognize than red tides because there is no obvious change in the sea. It occurs between the latitudes of 35°N and 35°S and is commonly reported in Hawaii, Florida, Puerto Rico and the Virgin Islands. Like red tide poisoning it is due to fish accumulating dinoflagellate toxins as they eat. Fish liver, viscera, sexual organs or roe of large and also scaleless warm-water shore or reef species are most likely to contain the toxin. Moray eels should not be eaten as they carry a high risk of ciguatera poisoning. An early sign a fish is affected is that it causes tingling or numbness of the mouth; reject it at this stage. Symptoms start 30 minutes–30 hours after eating, usually with vomiting, watery diarrhoea and cramps, which all get better in 24–48 hours. Some sufferers experience a bizarre hot-cold reversal where cold objects feel burning to touch and hot objects feel cold. Such sensory confusions can persist for months. There is no specific treatment. Unusually shaped reef fish like surgeon fish, parrot fish and trigger fish (*see* below) – as

Surgeon fish

Trigger fish

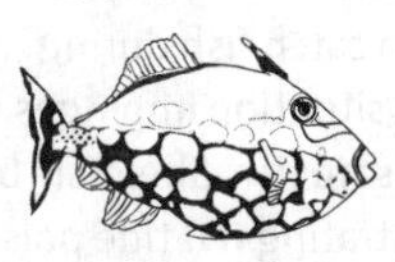

Parrot fish

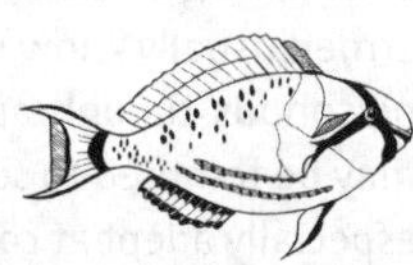

well as moray eels (*see* p.180) – may cause ciguatera poisoning during unpredictable outbreaks. Avoid eating bizarre-looking fish or very colourful reef fish to reduce the chances of ciguatera poisoning.

Scombrotoxic poisoning occurs when the red flesh of tuna, mackerel and relatives (such as albacore, skipjack and bonito), and tinned fish, e.g. sardines, anchovies and others (mahi-mahi, bluefish, amberjack, herring) is decomposed by bacteria to produce histamine poisons. This causes a tingling or smarting sensation in the mouth, or a peppery or bitter taste in the fish. If you continue eating you will experience hot flushing of the skin, sweating, itching, abdominal pain, vomiting and dizziness, all of which usually go away within 24 hours. This is avoided by eating only fresh fish, or by gutting and freezing fish as soon as possible after it's caught. Problems are most common in hot climates, as decomposition begins so quickly. Treatment is not necessary.

The **puffer fish** (*fugu*) is said to be outstandingly delicious, but is lethal if improperly prepared. There are 250 cases of poisoning per year in Japan, with 60% mortality. Other fish in Southeast Asia and the Indo-Pacific can also be toxic, so get a local cook to prepare fish for you.

Finally a word about **large, predatory fish** including shark, marlin and swordfish. These, being at the top of the food chain, accumulate pollutants, and recently it has been realized that they can carry quite high levels of toxic mercury. Adults who eat less than one portion of these fish a week will be in no danger, but pregnant women and children under 16 years old should avoid consuming these fish.

Other hazards of eating exotic dishes

Thailand is renowned for its food, and also for the great variety of exotic parasites you can catch from eating it. Freshwater crabs, raw tadpoles, frogs and snakes are sources of gnathostome worms; raw freshwater fish in Southeast and East Asia harbour *Clonorchis* liver flukes. Eating raw freshwater crabs in central Africa can give you worm cysts and abcesses in the neck, and giant African land snails and freshwater shrimps in Asia, the Pacific and Central and South America, if eaten undercooked, carry a risk of angiostrongyliasis, a nasty little worm that can set up home in the brain or eyes. Always eat your **shrimps**, **beetles** and **snails** well cooked.

One source of travellers' health advice has warned that **armadillo meat** in Mexico and the USA has been implicated in cases of leprosy. Eat your armadillos well done. The only **birds** known to be poisonous are three species of *pitohuis*, thrush-like birds from Papua New Guinea. They produce a very powerful toxin similar to that of South American poison arrow frogs, so that licking the feathers makes your mouth go numb. Locals know where in Papua New Guinea you shouldn't eat small wild birds. **Fruit bats** are tasty, however.

NUTRITION

Some people take **vitamin pills** while travelling. It is better (and cheaper) to take a **varied diet**, including fresh fruit and/or vegetables every day. Even if this is not possible, real vitamin deficiency states are enormously rare in those taking anything like a normal diet. It takes many months of a very poor, unvaried diet before vitamin deficiencies develop, unless you have a long-standing disease of the intestine. In the absence of a nutritional deficiency state, **zinc** is probably the only nutritional supplement with proven clinical benefits as a tonic. It is required by the body in trace quantities and has proven benefits in promoting healing.

One cause of protracted diarrhoea is tropical sprue (*see* p.114). It is treated by taking antibiotics and *folic acid*. This is one time when nutritional supplements have a place and are of proven benefit. Another is when planning a pregnancy. There is some evidence that congenital abnormalities are less likely in children born to women who take vitamins and *folic acid* supplements before and around the time of conception. In addition, women who are pregnant (or planning a pregnancy) and are taking *proguanil* (Paludrine) antimalarial tablets, also need to take *folic acid* 5mg daily (*see* **Special Travellers**, pp.73–4).

Salt tablets are unnecessary and are not a good way of increasing salt intake. If your body requires more salt your taste for it will increase, so shake more on your food. If you are very salt-depleted, salt will not taste salty, so take slightly salty drinks until they do taste salty again.

In parts of the Indian subcontinent and East Africa, water is naturally high in **fluoride**. Long-term residents should avoid fluoride toothpaste and fluoride supplements. Engineers working on water projects will know what is in the local drinking water, but if in doubt, avoid supplements. Fluoride supplements are controversial, but drops may be given to children when water fluoride is less than 0.2 parts per million.

On The Ground

Malaria

10

Malaria is a serious disease: a killer. Fortunately, though, with good information, the right precautions and bite-avoidance measures, the risk is small. Anyone straying into a malarious region should read a little about the disease and try to establish whether the destination carries a significant risk of catching the more serious form: *Plasmodium falciparum*.

Summary

→ Be aware of malaria risks wherever you are travelling.

→ Malaria mosquitoes hunt from sundown at ankle level and they like sweaty feet; have a shower and change into long clothes just before dusk.

→ Take your antimalarial tablets meticulously, including as directed after you have returned home.

→ If you become ill within three months of returning from a malarious region, see a doctor urgently, say where you have been and remind him that you could have malaria.

Sources of advice on malaria

CDC (Attention Health Information), Center for Prevention Services, Division of Quarantine, Atlanta, GA 30333, **US t** (404) 332 4559, *www.cdc.gov/travel*. Offers invaluable travel health information and has an excellent website.

Nomad Medical Centre: **UK t** 0906 822 4100. Gives phone advice and can send information by post, fax or email.

Look at *www.fitfortravel.scot.nhs.uk*, *www.cdc.gov/travel* or call one of the premium phone lines below (costing 50/60p per min) for travel advice, many of which can send you personalized travel health briefs:

Hospital for Tropical Diseases: **UK t** 0906 133 7733.

Liverpool School of Tropical Medicine: **UK t** 0906 708 8807.

Malaria Reference Laboratory: **UK t** 0900 160 0350.

MASTA: **UK t** 0906 822 4100, *www.masta.org*.

WHAT IS MALARIA?

Malaria is the real risk to travellers to the tropics and sub-tropics: you must know about it if you are venturing into the malaria belt. People acquire malaria when they are bitten (and only one bite is necessary) by an *Anopheles* mosquito that has previously bitten someone with malaria. Symptoms follow at least seven days later. It often starts as a 'flu-like illness (fevers, chills, aches and pains), but can appear in various guises: diarrhoea, abdominal pain or a cough.

Malaria is caused by *Plasmodium* protozoa, fastidious parasites that live within the red bloodcells of animals and also inside the body of the mosquito. Bats, rats, deer, monkeys, birds and even reptiles have their own species of malaria – there are over 100 kinds – but only four prefer to inhabit man. The nastiest, *Plasmodium falciparum*, can cause cerebral malaria, and in the extreme form of the disease so many bloodcells become full of parasites that when they rupture in unison, the body (particularly the kidneys) is overwhelmed with bloodcell debris. Death often results however high-tech the medical care is. The death rate from *falciparum* malaria is fairly consistently 1% whether treatment is given in developed or developing countries, although in Japan the mortality rate can be as high as 10%.

The other three kinds of malaria are less dramatic and do not kill, but they can be difficult to completely eradicate from the body. Unfortunately, it is the dangerous form that is on the increase, and it is this form with which resistance to prophylactic and curative medicines is the biggest problem.

Malaria used to be an issue in temperate regions, including Long Island and, until only 50 years ago, Italy. There are five species of *Anopheles* mosquito that are native to southern England and that are able to spread malaria. Oliver Cromwell suffered from the 'ague'; this was, in fact, malaria. The last cases of malaria caught in England were in Romney Marsh just after the First World War – probably spread by local mosquitoes from convalescing soldiers who had returned with malaria. These days the only cases contracted in England are at airports, from mosquitoes that have arrived by plane.

Case History: Africa

A British businessman had been visiting sub-Saharan countries for 26 years, and no longer took antimalarial tablets since he thought that after so much time he must have been immune. He returned from one trip with fever and chills, but delayed seeing his doctor for three days. He developed cerebral malaria and kidney failure, and needed three weeks' treatment in an intensive care unit. He recovered completely.

Balancing risks against inconvenience and side effects

Old Africa hands often say that they've had malaria several times. 'It isn't a serious disease, it is a bit like a mild 'flu. You just take the treatment and soon get better. Besides, taking those antimalarial pills and putting nasty chemical repellents on your skin does your long-term health no good, and isn't it even dangerous to your eyesight? It's better – surely – to just treat the disease as and when you get it? Isn't it?'

There are lots of issues influencing what you decide to do to protect yourself when travelling to a malarious region, and a little simple cost benefit analysis is often required. In order to decide the costs, risks and inconveniences needed to avoid getting malaria, you need to assess the risk of dying from the disease. Perhaps 2.7 million people succumb to the disease each year, and this stark fact should put some of the rather theoretical worries about long-term use of tablets and repellents into proportion. Drug-resistant malaria, in particular, is on the increase, and the proportion due to the nasty *falciparum* form that can cause cerebral malaria is on the increase, which is why well-meant advice from old Africa hands can be misleading, and even dangerous. It is more important than ever to take precautions against being bitten and – where appropriate – to take antimalarial tablets meticulously.

Clearly, of those who contract malaria, most people do not rapidly succumb. It can be mild: the forms that were most common a few decades ago were indeed usually mild, even if they did sometimes niggle on causing health problems that were difficult to cure. This was true for the ague of the English Middle Ages.

Each kind of antimalarial tablet has a range of side effects and the challenge to travellers is to assess the malaria risk, determine whether

The stark reality

→ Malaria can kill within 24 hours of the first symptom appearing.

→ There are about 10,000 reported cases of malaria imported into Europe annually, and amongst the approximately 2,000 people who return to Britain with malaria parasites, around a dozen will die of it.

→ There were 13 UK deaths from malaria both in 1997 and 1999; in 1998 at least 20 Germans died from imported malaria amongst fewer (996) diagnosed cases. In addition, an unknown number of travellers die from malaria abroad.

→ Between 1976 and 1986 the number of malaria cases treated in Britain rose by 50%, a significant number of whom ended up in intensive care.

Risk areas: Malaria

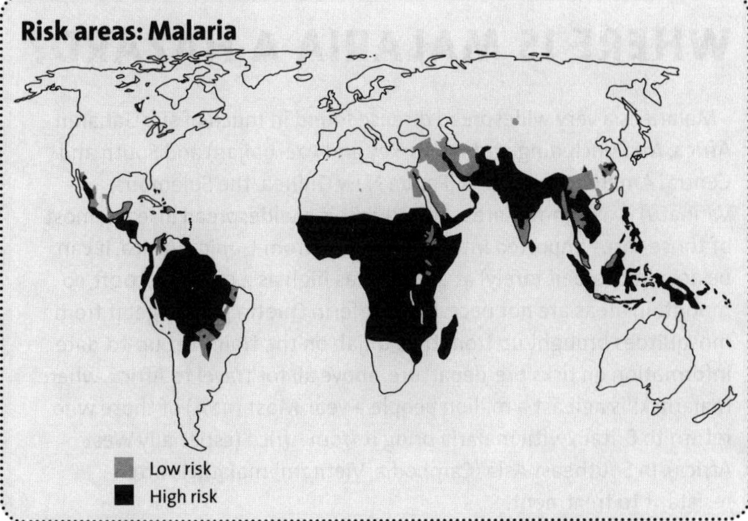

an antimalarial tablet is necessary and then find a suitable one that gives adequate protection for the relevant destination. An understanding of the actual risk should also determine what kind of repellent to use, and what other precautions to adopt. In some regions it would be entirely appropriate to take no tablets, although some travellers would then opt to carry a curative course of medicines. When illness strikes, a local doctor can be sought, who can advise on whether the treatment is necessary, or whether they have some other cause of fever.

Surviving malaria

- → Malaria is a killer but not all malarious regions are high risk.
- → The risk determines what tablets to take and whether prophylactics and/or standby treatment are necessary.
- → The risk should also determine the kinds of repellents required and what other precautions may be necessary.
- → Your style of travel and remoteness of destination will also have some influence on the level of precautions.
- → Babies, young children and pregnant women are at high risk of dying from malaria if they get it.
- → Malaria-carrying mosquitoes mostly bite from dusk until dawn: bite avoidance needs to start at sundown.
- → All antimalarial tablets have the potential for side effects; each traveller must find which of the effective options suits them.
- → Protection against mosquito bites also has the side effect of helping to avoid rarer insect-borne diseases.

WHERE IS MALARIA A HAZARD?

Malaria is a very widespread disease found in much of sub-Saharan Africa, Asia (including parts of Turkey and Azerbaijan) and South and Central America. Melanesia (Papua New Guinea, the Solomons, Vanuatu) is a high-risk area. Although it is a widespread disease, most of those cases imported into Europe come from tropical Africa. It can be acquired (albeit rarely) at altitudes as high as 2,000m/6,500ft, so mountain areas are not necessarily safe: in Quetta people get it from mosquitoes brought up from the Punjab on the train. Get up-to-date information on risks pre-departure, above all for travel to Africa, where malaria kills at least a million people a year. Most (92%) of those who return to Britain with malaria bring it from Africa (especially West Africa). In Southeast Asia (Cambodia, Vietnam) malaria is often resistant to treatment.

Most capital cities in Southeast and East Asia and South America are malaria-free at present, as are the popular Caribbean resorts, Polynesia and Micronesia. Most of South Africa is safe, but in the northeast, including the Kruger National Park, there is still a significant risk.

Pregnant women, **babies** and **young children**, **people who have no spleen**, and anyone who is **immunosuppressed** (e.g. suffering cancer or AIDS, or on high doses of steroid tablets) are all highly susceptible to malaria. Pregnant women who get *falciparum* malaria are likely to miscarry and die. Vulnerable travellers should consider whether they need to enter high risk malarial areas at all. If they really have to, they must be extra-vigilant about bite protection and meticulous in taking prophylaxis.

Case History: Indonesia

A British engineer was working for three years in Surabaya and, knowing that Java is almost completely free from malaria, did not take antimalarial tablets. However, he then spent a weekend on neighbouring Lombok and took no precautions against malaria there either. Three weeks later he died of cerebral malaria.

This man had spent most of his working life in the tropics and had once contracted malaria in Africa, where treatment had soon got the mild symptoms under control. He was not keen to take antimalarials because of side effects, and because he was sure that malaria was not especially serious. It was fine for him not to take malaria tablets while he was in Surabaya, but he needed protection in Lombok.

The big hotels at Senggigi Beach, Lombok, are not keen to advertise the risk of contracting *falciparum* malaria; if word got out it would be bad for business.

HOW TO AVOID MALARIA

Malarial mosquitoes bite from about 5.30pm until dawn. At dusk, put on long clothes and repellents. Sadly, gin and tonic does not contain enough quinine to protect you, but you can take steps to avoid malaria: find out if the disease exists in the region you are going to; investigate the antimalarial tablets available; avoid being bitten; and, on your return, remind your doctor that you have been exposed to the disease.

Antimalarial tablets

Who should take antimalarials?

Taking antimalarial tablets and avoiding bites are your only protection from malaria at present. There is no immediate prospect of a vaccine. Anyone visiting a malarious region must take advice on precautions. They are particularly important for children and pregnant women. *Falciparum* malaria is especially dangerous in the last three months of pregnancy. Antimalarials do not pass into breast milk in sufficient quantity to protect infants, so breast-fed babies also need to be given *chloroquine* syrup or – if they are old enough – *mefloquine* tablets.

People born and/or brought up in malarious regions and who suffer from malaria repeatedly build up a partial immunity, so that if they contract the disease they are less likely to become seriously ill. However, this immunity wanes within a year, so that natives of malarious countries become highly susceptible to malaria, just like other travellers (PhD students beware); hence they also need to protect themselves.

Which antimalarial and what side effects

Most malaria tablets are started one week before your departure and continued for a month after your return. The reason for this is that there is no drug yet known that can prevent the malaria parasite from infecting people. Antimalarials merely slow down the process of multiplication and inhibit the penetration of the parasites into the red blood cells. By taking the tablets for long enough, the parasites fade out.

People taking antimalarial tablets often notice side effects. Up to 40% of those taking either *mefloquine* or the *chloroquine + proguanil* combination will report a problem, although many complaints will be trivial

The four As of avoiding malaria

Awareness (is there malaria in your intended destination?).
Avoidance (of mosquito bites).
Antimalarials (tablets).
Awareness again (remind your doctor you've been exposed to malaria).

and tolerable. Any such symptoms are a price that must be weighed against the major risk of malaria: rapid death. Some side effects can be troublesome enough to make you wish to stop taking the tablets, but in such a case it is important to find an alternative. There is now a good range of prophylactics, so it should be possible to find one that does suit you.

Drug resistance patterns change constantly: get up-to-date advice on what to take. Ask a computer-linked travel clinic or information service (*see* **Sources of advice on malaria**, p.128).

Mefloquine (Larium)

A weekly preparation available on private presription. Anyone with a history of fits, depression or psychiatric problems, severe liver disease or who has a close blood relative who is epileptic should avoid it; it is safe for women during the last six months of pregnancy, but those planning

Case History: Southern Africa

Bad experiences on high curative doses of Larium made me decide against taking any antimalarial prophylaxis on our fabulous 3,000km, five-week journey through the heart of Southern Africa, ending up in the Gonerazhou National Park in Zimbabwe. Knowing the dangers of malaria I took precautions:

→ I applied DEET mosquito repellent on all exposed skin after 4pm.
→ I reapplied mosquito repellent before going to bed (except on my torso, see below).
→ I put on socks, long trousers and long sleeves after 5pm.
→ I burned pyrethrum coils in the hut.
→ I slept under my own mosquito bednet (which was not treated with insecticide).

It was frightfully hot and I slept naked or near-naked. I was probably bitten when I went out in the night to pee in the bush. I began to feel ill 10 days after we left Gonerazhou; then, the morning after a particularly rich butterfish meal, I vomited. The next evening, I felt as if I had bad 'flu. My body felt stuffed with cotton wool; my limbs ached; I had a fever of 38.4˚C; I felt nauseated, had a headache and had the most ghastly, stinky, oily diarrhoea. This was *falciparum* malaria and I started the week-long treatment with *artemesin (artemether)*. The next 48 hours were bad, with symptoms continuing, but worse, with a temperature of 39.6˚C. I felt bad for 3–4 weeks, suffering energy crashes, intermittent headaches and other pains. The scary thing is how terribly fast the disease progresses. My doctor said that even relatively ineffective prophylaxis with *chloroquine* and Paludrine would have slowed and reduced the severity of my malaria.

Barbara Ikin, Maputo, Mozambique

a pregnancy should avoid conceiving for three months after stopping *mefloquine*. In Britain, this is currently only licensed for up to a year, although many people take it for two and, as long as there has been no reaction during the early weeks, it appears safe for such long-term use.

The British press have hammered *mefloquine* (Larium), saying it is a dangerous drug, but it suits many people extremely well, and should not be written off. If *mefloquine* is suggested, begin taking it two and a half weeks (three doses) before departure and stop taking it immediately if it seems to cause vivid and unpleasant dreams, mood changes or otherwise alters the way you feel. Restlessness, dizziness, disturbed sleep and gastro-intestinal symptoms are other reported side effects.

Doxycycline

The antibiotic *doxycycline* is now being taken by some travellers, especially to the border regions of Thailand and Cambodia where resistance to standard drugs is becoming common. It is also suggested for many other destinations, including Africa. One capsule is taken daily, or there is a soluble formulation for those who are not good at swallowing pills. *Doxycycline* is unsuitable for children under the age of 12 and should not be taken by pregnant or lactating women because it binds to growing teeth and bones, and therefore discolours childrens' growing teeth. It should not be taken by people with **systemic lupus erythematosis** nor anyone known to be allergic to *tetracycline*. Travellers who take *carbamazepine*, *phenytoin* or *phenobarbital* need to take double the dose: one capsule twice daily. It is licensed as a prophylactic for up to four months' continuous use, although people taking it to control acne have taken it for up to two years and it has proved safe.

Doxycycline can increase sensitivity to sunburn, so it is not ideal for beach holidays; use ample sunscreen whenever you are outside. Take the capsules with or after a meal and wash them down with plenty of water. If the capsule gets stuck half way down the gullet, it can cause inflamation. Ideally, you should avoid lying down for 30 minutes after taking it.

Chloroquine and *proguanil*

Chloroquine goes under the trade names of Aralen and Resochin in the USA; of the *chloroquine* products available in the UK, Nivaquine tablets are more palatable than Avloclor. *Chloroquine* syrup (Nivaquine) is the only paediatric antimalarial formulation, however, it is terribly bitter and few children tolerate it, even when it is disguised in food.

Two *chloroquine* tablets are taken each week and usually these are taken along with ***proguanil*** (Paludrine in the UK; not available in the USA) two a day; in mainland Europe, combination tablets containing both drugs are marketed as Savarine. *Chloroquine* and *proguanil* are still a good combination for many travellers unless they are visiting areas

Commonly used antimalarial prophylactic tablets

***Generic* drug name**	*Mefloquine*	*Proguanil with atovaquone*
Trade names	Larium	Malarone
Frequency	1 weekly	1 daily with food
Dose	250 mg tablet	100mg *proguanil* and 250 mg *atovaquone*
Start when?	Start 1–3 weeks before travel	Start 1–2 days before travel
Continue until when?	Continue for four weeks after return	Continue for one week after return
Notable side effects	Mood changes; weird dreams; nausea	Nausea; loss of appetite; mouth ulcers
Notes	Avoid in epilepsy, previous depression, breast-feeding, early pregnancy; avoid pregnancy for 3 months after taking	Not recommended in pregnancy or if trying to conceive or when breast-feeding; not for children under 11kg (in the UK for prophylaxis children must weigh at least 40kg)
Approx. cost for two weeks in a malarious region	£25	£90

with multiple drug resistance. The *chloroquine + proguanil* combination is the only antimalarial regime that is available in the UK without prescription, and it is cheap (around £14 for 100 Paludrine and £2.50 for 28 Nivaquine). If *proguanil* is taken by pregnant women, or those wishing to become pregnant, it is necessary to take *folic acid* as well.

Chloroquine can affect the eyes, but only after taking it for at least six years; more frequently, it may cause a slightly queasy stomach shortly after each dose. *Proguanil* (Paludrine) can cause two troublesome side effects. Taken on an empty stomach it often causes nausea, so take it after a meal or with a glass of milk. Secondly, it often causes mouth

Doxycycline	*Chloroquine and proguanil*	*Pyrimethamine and dapsone*
Vibramycin	Nivaquine, Aralen or Resochin and Paludrine	Maloprim (= Deltaprim)
1 daily with plenty of water	2 *chloroquine* weekly and 2 *proguanil* daily	1 weekly
100 mg	2x150mg of *chloroquine* base and 2x100mg *proguanil*	*pyrimethamine* 12.5mg and *dapsone* 100mg
Start 1–2 days before travel	Start one week before travel	Start one week before travel
Continue for four weeks after return	Continue for four weeks after return	Continue for four weeks after return
Rash on exposure to sun; loss of appetite	Nausea; mouth ulcers; heartburn	Has caused bone marrow suppression if two tablets taken weekly
Avoid in children, pregnancy and lactation; take after food with plenty of water	Avoid in epilepsy; may make psoriasis worse. Take after food if possible. *Proguanil* not available in the USA and difficult to find in malarious zones	Sometimes taken with *chloroquine*
£25	Around £15 depending upon preparation chosen	£5

ulcers, so pack something that will ease them (e.g. Teejel or Bonjela). *Chloroquine* and *proguanil* can reduce the appetite and cause heartburn or indigestion.

Malarone

Malarone (*proguanil* with *atovaquone*) is presently licensed in the UK as a prophylactic in people over 40kg and for use in a malarial region up to 28 days, although it is probably safe for up to three months. It is best taken with food or milk. It has the potential to cause some side effects, especially mouth ulcers (as *proguanil* alone does), but also weird

Homeopathic malaria prophylaxis

It's unusual to see practitioners of conventional and alternative medicine united, but both groups would condemn the use of 'homeopathic malaria prophylaxis' as potentially lethal. Such unanimity comes from the fact that 'homeopathic prophylaxis' is actually a contradiction in terms. The founding principle of homeopathy is to 'treat like with like': so only when a patient has symptoms can the practitioner apply homeopathic principles to choose a remedy. Someone who is completely fit and well provides the homeopath with no information on which to base a treatment plan.

I was so worried about this issue that I phoned the Homeopathic Hospital in Glasgow and spoke to Dr Bob Leckridge, who is president of the Faculty of Homeopathy. He told me, "There is no place for notions of 'prophylactic treatment' or 'vaccination' in homeopathy. Such ideas do not fit into homeopathic theory at all. In fact, there are now a number of reports of people who have developed malaria after relying on supposed 'homeopathy' for protection."

Conventional antimalarials are admittedly unpleasant to take, but the homeopathic alternative is not an alternative at all.

Dr Grant Hutchison, consultant anaesthetist, Dundee

dreams, nausea and gastrointestinal disturbance. It is likely to cause malformations in the unborn child, so it should not be taken in pregnancy or if trying for a pregnancy.

Maloprim

Maloprim, aka Deltaprim (*pyrimethamine* + *dapsone* combination tablet), rather went out of favour when several travellers taking two tablets weekly developed bone marrow failure. It is now thought to be safe to take if you have taken it before without problems, although other alternatives are usually considered first by prescribers. It is probably also safe in those who haven't taken it before, as long as no more than one tablet weekly is taken. It might be considered for use in regions were there is a lot of *chloroquine* resistance, such as Oceania. It is also suitable for people with epilepsy, although if they take *phenytoin* or *phenobarbital*, *folic acid* (5mg daily) should also be taken.

No antimalarial is infallible, but the few unfortunates who pick up malaria while taking tablets (perhaps doses are forgotten, or poorly absorbed due to diarrhoea) are less likely to get into serious trouble. Even so, seek medical help.

Hair loss is sometimes blamed on antimalarials, but prolonged flights can also provoke a transient and temporary moult up to three months later (*see* **Flight**, p.91). Menstrual irregularities are also blamed on antimalarials: this may be the case, but it is more likely to be an effect of all the changes that happen during travel.

DIAGNOSING MALARIA

Even experienced tropical physicians cannot reliably diagnose malaria without a blood test: blood is examined either under a microscope or using an immunological test kit. If possible, you should get a laboratory test done before taking any treatment; this only takes 10 minutes, and in Africa costs about US$1. Dangerous malaria is a possibility if you feel unwell, have a fever over 38°C or have 'flu-like symptoms (prostration, aches and pains) seven days or more after arriving in a malarious region, or within three months of returning. Milder forms can take up to a year to cause symptoms. If you are far from medical help, self-treatment is fairly safe, except for anyone pregnant or under 12 years old. Remember that other causes of fever require different treatments; notes to help diagnose them are on pp.271–2.

Self-diagnosis

Several self-diagnostic test kits have been developed recently. These are highly effective immunological tools, which in skilled hands are effective in diagnosing malaria. It was thought that these might be of value to ordinary travellers. When they became ill with a fever travellers could take a spot of their own blood, test it and then decide whether to take drug treatment. Unfortunately, in ill travellers with no laboratory experience, the diagnostic accuracy is very disappointing: in one study 71% were unable to extract blood and a quarter were unable to appropriately put the blood on the slide. In those who managed to complete the test, 10 of the 11 were falsely reassured that they were all right when they were actually incubating serious malaria. So far, then, diagnostic kits are only of proven value when used by doctors, nurses, laboratory technicians and expedition medics, who will have had a little training in the use of the kit and can perform the test for others.

Symptoms of malaria

Unfortunately there is no symptom or pattern of symptoms peculiar to malaria. The most common include:

→ **Fever** (the most common symptom).
→ **Flu-like symptoms**: e.g. prostration and aches (not a cold).
→ **Backache**.
→ **Diarrhoea**.
→ **Joint pains** and **aches**.
→ **Sore throat**.
→ **Headache**.

After: Health Information for Overseas Travel 2001 (UK Dept of Health).

TREATMENT AND CURE

Some travellers to remote places opt to carry a course of malaria treatment. Experts agree that this often leads to over-treatment and to people taking drugs they do not need, yet treatment may also save life. Discuss your trip with a specialist to determine your particular needs and risks; be sure you understand when and how to take the cure. Travel clinics sell treatment kits. In a malarious region, you probably have to assume that any high fever of more than a few hours is due to malaria, so take or seek treatment; if you do self-prescribe, go to a doctor as soon as possible.

Quinine is the basis of most cures, but it is unpleasant to take, so is often combined with other drugs. One fast and effective regime for Africa is *quinine* (2x300mg tablets three times daily for three days) plus *doxycycline* (100mg twice daily) for seven days. Regimes vary according to the prescriber.

Artemether, a drug first used in China 3,000 years ago, is being used increasingly to cure malaria in Africa and elsewhere. In May 2001 a new formulation of *artemether* and *lumefantrine*, aka *co-artemether* (Riamet), was launched in Europe, and this seems as if it will be useful for travellers to carry with them as a stand-by treatment, although it is not as fast-acting as the albeit less-pleasant *quinine* treatment regime. The course is six doses of *co-artemether* taken by mouth over 60 hours. It is licensed for anyone of 12 years or more, providing they weigh over 35kg.

Both **Malarone** and ***mefloquine*** (Larium) can be used as a cure, although not in those already taking these as prophylactics. ***Fansidar*** was a popular alternative, but is becoming less effective. ***Halofantrine*** (Halfan) should no longer be used; it can harm the heart.

Travellers who acquire the dangerous form of malaria will become ill within three months of leaving a malarial zone. Symptoms of fever, sweats, aches and pains should send you scuttling for medical help at once, as people have died of *falciparum* malaria within 24 hours of the first symptoms. If you cannot contact your doctor, go promptly to a hospital accident and emergency department and say that you could have malaria. Milder, non-life-threatening forms of malaria may take up to a year to announce themselves; they also need treatment, although not necessarily the day symptoms begin. Antimalarial tablets are not an absolute protection, and you may contract the disease even if you have been careful in taking them.

Experienced travellers may tell you they have had malaria and that it was trivial; many have contracted it, but many more will have been misdiagnosed. The disease is changing, and more travellers are now acquiring the dangerous and deadly form. Malaria is not a trivial illness.

On The Ground

Biters and Insect-borne Diseases

11

An array of creatures bite for a living and, as a side effect, pass on infection: these are disease vectors. There is an enormous number of wonderfully exotic vector-borne diseases: tick-borne Omsk Haemorrhagic Fever, mosquito-borne *O'nyongnyong* from Kenya and Finland's *Inkoo* virus. Not all are tropical. Most are enormously rare and only of interest to parasitologists. Mosquitoes are the most important vectors of disease, but ticks, sand-flies, black-flies and others are also guilty. The table on pp.150–51 summarizes the main dangerous illnesses. You don't have to travel far to meet vectors: there are tick-borne diseases in the UK and the Mediterranean, and malaria in Turkey. For further information about malaria, *see* pp.127–40.

Summary

→ Avoid being bitten by mosquitoes, especially between dusk and dawn.

→ See a doctor if you have a skin ulcer that will not heal; be especially suspicious if you have visited any American rainforests.

→ Avoid tick and chigger bites wherever you are by wearing long clothes tucked in, and use a repellent.

→ Light-coloured clothes make it easier to spot a tick and also discourage mosquitoes.

→ If you find a tick on you, get it off (without squeezing or damaging it) as soon as you can, then douse the wound with alcohol or a strong antiseptic.

Geographical distribution of vector-borne diseases

Bilharzia (urinary and intestinal Schistosomiasis)	Savannah and semi-arid regions of Africa, the Middle East and South America
Chagas' Disease (American Trypanosomiasis)	Lowland Mexico, Central and South America
Dengue Fever	Spreading throughout the tropics and sub-tropics
Dengue Haemorrhagic Fever	Presently known mainly from Southeast Asia, the Philippines, the Pacific Islands, India and Indian Ocean, Caribbean
Elephantiasis	Humid tropics or coastal regions
Japanese B encephalitis	A problem only in Asia, mainly where pigs are kept and rice is grown
Leishmania	Dangerous forms in lowland forests of tropical Central and South America
Malaria	Widespread throughout the tropics and sub-tropics except at altitude
Plague	A disease of unpredictable outbreaks in very poor living conditions (so unlikely to affect travellers); cases have been reported recently from the USA, Madagascar, China, Myanmar, Vietnam and India
Oriental Schistosomiasis	Patchy distribution in Southeast Asia, China and the Philippines
Onchocerciasis (River Blindness)	West Africa, South and Central America and a few small areas in East and Central Africa
Scrub Typhus	East and Southeast Asia including the Philippines, the Pacific Islands including Papua New Guinea, Australia and South Asia (*see* p.159)
Sleeping sickness (African Trypanosomiasis)	Only in Africa in suitable scrubby habitats between the Sahara and the Zambezi
Tick-borne fevers	All continents, temperate and tropical
Yellow Fever	Tropical Africa, Central and South America; not in Asia

MOSQUITOES

Do all mosquitoes carry disease?

The mosquito is the most deadly animal known to man. It transmits malaria, Elephantiasis, Dengue, Yellow Fever and Japanese B encephalitis (of which the last two are incurable and often fatal), as well as a host of rare and never-talked-about diseases. However, not all mosquitoes transmit disease.

Non-malarial mosquitoes tend to be hump-backed, and their bodies rest roughly parallel to the wall, or their bottoms are slightly closer to the wall than their heads. Males, which don't bite, sport splendid bushy antennae. ***Culex***, the common house mosquito, which causes insomnia and occasionally transmits Elephantiasis but never malaria, rests parallel to the wall. Malaria-carrying ***Anopheles*** mosquitoes rest with their heads close and bottoms far from the wall. Both are evening and night-time biters, so you will be protected by donning long clothes and repellent at dusk, and sleeping under an impregnated bednet.

Aedes mosquitoes, which spread Dengue and Yellow fevers, rest parallel to the wall; they are sometimes called tiger mosquitoes because of their zebra-striped bodies and they also have striking black and white striped legs. They bite from dawn to dusk (inclusive).

Avoiding mosquito bites

You don't have to be bitten, so if bites make you miserable or you are entering a region where insect-borne disease is a real risk, defend yourself. Malarious mosquitoes feed on blood and like to bite from dusk until dawn, so in the tropics and sub-tropics it is especially important to put up some defences against the dusk assault. The mosquitoes that spread Dengue and Yellow fevers bite during daylight hours, but they are also active at dusk, so beware the twilight double shift.

Distinguishing mosquitoes

Culex ***Anopheles*** ***Aedes***

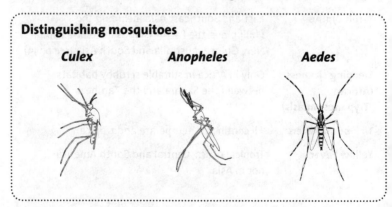

Insects that feed on blood home in on a bouquet of smells arising from a human body, and synthetic repellents confuse mosquito senses. In very buggy regions, take a shower to reduce insect-attracting body odours, then put on long, loose clothes with a good repellent on exposed skin. Alternatively, you could adjourn to the bar where air conditioning and mosquito screens may well protect you. When you do retire to bed, the best protection is to sleep under a bednet that is also impregnated with permethrin.

If you **live abroad**, try to reduce mosquito breeding sites near your house by draining standing water and emptying or covering water tanks and containers. **Travellers** will get bitten less if they select hotels away from accumulations of standing water. Foul black water is where *Culex* nuisance-mosquitoes breed.

Repellents

Choose your repellent according to your risk. Weigh the inconveniences and potential side effects of any repellent against the possibility of dangerous insect-borne disease. A cosmetically less-acceptable product might be necessary in malarious Africa, whereas if itching bites and sensitive skin rather than disease are your main issues, then there are a range of pleasant products on offer. Citronella products (e.g. Mosiguard) are pleasant, safe and non-irritant, while DEET will protect you in a high bite-intensity jungle.

DEET

I am often asked about the toxicity of chemical repellents and in particular, of those based on diethyl toluamide or DEET. This is the gold-standard insect repellent, developed by the US Army in 1946 and registered for general use in 1957. It is now used annually by an estimated 200 million people. Its big disadvantage is that it dissolves plastic and ruins many synthetic materials, including watchglasses, pens, sleeping bags, spectacles and some varnishes. Not surprisingly, this makes travellers wonder what such a compound might do to their skin and insides. Yet this is a safe compound. Serious side effects are uncommon (13 cases amongst the millions of children who have used it), and those likely to have problems are people with very sensitive or broken skin, particularly when lots of repellent is used. Even this ill-advised use will result in little more than a rash or itching. Application under clothes or socks is not recommended, as this will enhance absorption into the body. Test any product on a small patch of skin before travel, so that if there is a reaction, another product can be tried. DEET must be used with extreme caution in small children (a 6.2% time-release DEET preparation for children is marketed in the USA as Skedaddle) and physicians suggest applying no stronger than a 10% solution of DEET to children unless the area of exposed skin is small, e.g. the ankles. DEET is probably best avoided in pregnancy. It should be applied with care if being put on the face since it tastes nasty, makes eyes sore and irritates the linings of nose and mouth. If used sensibly, though, it is unlikely to harm. Most DEET products protect for up to eight hours, but for only 3–4 hours in sweaty conditions. When used in addition to long clothes, though, only a small area of skin needs to have repellent applied to it. This also reduces the problem of needing to frequently reapply repellent when the climate is very humid. There are many DEET formulations on the market, but my favourite is **Ben's 30**, which is water-based and is therefore less likely to irritate, with less absorption than alcohol-based preparations; it also has a neat controlled-flow applicator which dispenses DEET without spillage.

Those who cannot use DEET might try **Mijex Extra** or **Jungle Formula** (containing Merck 3535), which is about as effective as 30–60% DEET. A chemically similar product to DEET, **Odomos** (*diethylbenzamide*), is sold in India; it is effective, although I haven't been able to confirm manufacturers' claims that it is 'baby safe'. The new, non-DEET **Autan** is gentler but does not repel African malaria vectors well enough. It does, though, successfully repel many mosquitoes, as well as stable-flies and ticks.

Vitamin B as a repellent

There is no evidence that taking vitamin B_1 tablets protects against mosquito bites, nor does mixing vitamin B complex in cream nor eating Marmite. There is some evidence that taking vitamin B_1 reduces the itch after being bitten. This might explain why vitamin B is commonly thought to have repellent properties. Reducing the itch might encourage travellers to think they are not being bitten, which in malarious regions

Tips for safe use of chemical repellents

→ Test any new repellent on a small area of skin before travel.
→ Apply only to exposed skin and/or clothing.
→ Do not use DEET under clothing.
→ Malaria mosquitoes bite from dusk until dawn, but other biters can be active during the day.
→ If used with sunscreen, apply repellent 30mins to one hour after the sunscreen.
→ Never use repellents on wounds, on irritated or broken skin, or where there is eczema.
→ Do not spray directly onto the face or apply to the hands of young children.
→ Wash any residual repellent off the skin when it is no longer needed.
→ Consider the risk of serious tropical disease when deciding what precautions you need to follow.
→ Natural oils are toxic if drunk – and so are chemical repellents.

could be dangerous. Don't assume that absence of itch means that you have avoided bites.

Natural oils

There is now a good range of repellents made from strong-smelling natural oils, including the lemony-smelling citronella and eucalyptus. These are pleasant to use. The most effective is **Mosiguard**, which comes in stick and roll-on preparations, but there are others, including the conveniently packed **Natrapel**. Other types of repellent that are less widely available include **Gurkha**, which is milder, but comes in spray bottles that often leak, Scandinavian **tundra oil** and the Chinese **quwenling**; these and many natural oils work quite well and are kind on the skin, but ultimately are not such good repellents as chemical preparations. They are fine for most travel purposes, but are probably not effective enough for use in malarious Africa or other regions of extreme bite-intensity, or where riverine black-flies are a problem.

When selecting a repellent it is important to balance the risk of dying of cerebral malaria, or aquiring some other awful infection on your trip, against the efficacy of the repellent used. I tend to use natural oil products in midgey Scotland or the mosquitoey Mediterranean and also during the day in malarious regions, and then don long clothes and apply DEET (**Ben's**, **Jungle Formula Extra Strength**, **Cutters**, **Repel** or **Off!**) at dusk, or retire to an air-conditioned bar.

Repellents on clothes

DEET and permethrin can be used to treat clothing, in addition or as an alternative to putting repellents straight onto the skin. The disadvantage of skin applications is that the chemicals sweat off quickly and may irritate some skins. Nomad now market a ***Bug Proof*** kit comprising DEET spray for the skin and permethrin contact-insecticide spray for clothes, to make them repellent to biters (especially ticks). This is a particularly effective and useful option in regions where there is a high risk of contracting serious malaria or for those who are really tortured by itching bites. Alternatively, the 'NOsquito' clothing range (*see* below) might be worth trying. In regions where insects are less voracious, DEET-soaked repellent anklets offer some protection from mosquitoes that hunt at ankle level (most *Anopheles* and *Culex*), as long as you are upright. However, they don't stop bites completely. Nor do they repel *Aedes* mosquitoes, which roam around more; this is a pity, since *Aedes* bites are a great nuisance in many warm regions.

Contact information: clothing stockists

Craghoppers Ltd, Risol House, Mercury Way, Urmston, Manchester M41 7RR, **UK t** (for brochure) (0161) 749 1364, **t** (**helpline**) (0161) 749 1310, *www.craghoppers.com*. Stocks 'NOsquito' clothes.

Tips for avoiding night-biting mosquitoes

→ Shower just before dusk.
→ At dusk, either retreat to a screened room or put on long, baggy clothes and a good insect repellent.
→ Take special care to protect your ankles with socks or repellents.
→ Sleep under a mosquito net (preferably permethrin treated), use electric mosquito mats or (the least effective) burn mosquito coils.
→ Try to stay only in screened buildings, and spray the room with insecticide regularly: how frequently you spray depends on how frequently the biters return.
→ Fans help baffle the weaker-flying mosquitoes, but some can fly in turbulent air.
→ Wear light-coloured clothes, since dark colours attract mosquitoes.
→ When there are a great number of small flying insects, wear a cotton neckerchief tucked in like a cravat to seal the neck of your shirt.
→ Avoid using scented soaps or perfumes, or wearing shiny jewellery, as mosquitoes like these too.

Bedtime

Research in Africa has shown that sleeping under a bednet, especially one impregnated with an insecticide such as permethrin, does protect you from attack by night-biting mosquitoes. In fact, a screen of impregnated cloth dangling around the bed is also effective: mosquitoes choose not to fly over the screen to bite their victims. Bednets (costing from about £20/US$32) are a good investment; they can often be bought for much less overseas, although it might be risky to go shopping in-country unless you know about local availability. Nets treated with permethrin will kill any mosquito that lands on the net, so that even if you roll against the net in your sleep (a particular problem with conical nets), mosquitoes won't bite you through it. Impregnation of nets even make those that have got holes in them protective. It also discourages creepies crawling into bed if you leave the net dangling onto the floor. Nets need to be treated every six months or after washing. Specialist travel shops and centres have permethrin net treatment kits, sprays for treating your own net or hotel nets, and so on.

Electrical devices

Small, electric hotplates are available which heat up insecticide-impregnated vaporizing mats. The vapour repels or knocks down mosquitoes. They work well except in very large rooms with high ceilings (common in hot climates). Nor do they work well in a through-draught. Most types work in a room of 30m³ (about 1,000ft³); they are less efficient if the device is a long distance from you. If the hotel has provided only one mosquito killer for a big room, ask for another, or use repellent in addition. The best vaporizers contain synthetic insecticides such as *esbiothrin*. **Electric buzzer devices** are useless against mosquitoes, cockroaches, and (as far as I know) all other insects.

Coils

Where there is no electricity you can burn incense coils. Often made in China, they are readily available in most places where mosquitoes are a problem. In West Africa they have been shown to reduce the bite rate by about half: from over 200 per person per night to a mere 100!

Fans

Ceiling fans may help to baffle mosquitoes a little, although strains are evolving which are expert at flying in turbulent air (they have no difficulty in flying backwards in a rainstorm).

Dealing with mosquito bites

Nothing completely takes the itch out of bites, but **tiger balm**, **alcohol**, **calamine**, ***crotamiton*** (Eurax) and even white, minty **toothpaste** help a little. The convenient marker-pen-sized **After Bite**, containing ammonia, alcohol and even a little mink oil, is also quite effective. Anything that cools the bite area is helpful. Antihistamine creams and potions that contain local anaesthetic are not particularly effective, and often cause allergic rashes. Antihistamine tablets can be relieving, however. Try to avoid scratching bites (cut fingernails short), or you risk skin infection. If you scratch a hole in your bite, clean it with antiseptic and cover with a sticking plaster (*see* **Skin**, p.216). Some unfortunate people are hypersensitive to some insect bites: they erupt into large, watery blisters which should not be deliberately punctured. American sand-flies are particularly potent provokers of blisters. Suffering this in one geographical region will not necessarily mean you will have the problem elsewhere. A slow-to-heal bump that looks like an infected mosquito bite could be a sign of Scrub Typhus, especially if the person is ill. Treatment is with a course of *doxycycline* (*see also* p.159).

Mosquito bites itch a lot during the first six months after you arrive in a new area. Thereafter a kind of immunity develops, so that bites hardly raise a bump. This 'immunity' is geographically localized so that, for example, Peruvians posted from one lowland jungle region to another within their own country, complain of the itching and grief the mosquitoes cause at first in a new place. You must not assume you are not being bitten just because you have no itchy bites. In warm climates, if your skin is exposed between dusk and dawn, you may be taking a risk.

Diseases transmitted by small biters

Vector	Vector habits	Disease	Vaccine?
Anopheles mosquitoes	Evening and night biters	Malaria Elephantiasis Arboviruses Skin infections	no no no no
Aedes mosquitoes	Day biters (dawn to dusk inclusive)	Dengue Yellow Fever Skin infections	no yes no
Culex mosquitoes	Evening and night biters	Japanese B encephalitis Elephantiasis Skin infections	yes no no
Black-flies	Day biting swarms	Nuisance River Blindness	no no
Sand-flies	Evening and night biters	Tropical sores Kala-azar Fever Sand-fly fevers	no no no
Tsetse-flies	Painful day-biters, attack in swarms	Sleeping sickness	no
Cone-nosed bugs	Night biters	Chagas' Disease	no
Rat fleas	Hide in beds etc.	Plague	yes
Bed bugs	Night biters	Pain Skin infections	no no
Mites	Day biters	Scrub Typhus Skin infections	no no
Ticks	Attach in daylight	Dozens	one*

none means *supportive therapy will be given in hospital but that specific treatments that will clear the infection do not exist*
all means *all continents except Antarctica*
one* means *only for 'European' tick-borne encephalitis*

Treatment	Continent	Avoiding action
1% die yes none yes	All Tropics Tropics All	Tablets for malaria; also bite avoidance: long clothes, bednets, repellents and insecticides effective against all *Anopheles*-borne diseases
none none yes	Asia, Africa, Americas Africa, Americas All	Bite avoidance: long clothes, repellents; discard standing water near home
none 30% die yes	Asia Tropics Hot, humid areas	Bite avoidance: long clothes, bednets, repellents and insecticides effective against all *Culex*-borne diseases
no can be dangerous	Africa, tropical America, Tundra, etc.	Avoid rivers; also bite avoidance: long clothes; DEET repellent
difficult difficult none	Tropical Americas, Mediterranean, Middle East, Asia	Bite avoidance: repellents; long clothes; impregnated bednets; fans; sleep above ground
difficult	Tropical lowland Africa	Avoid endemic areas (local advice); repellents; long clothes
90-day course; can be dangerous	Lowland tropical Americas	Use hammock and net if sleeping in wattle & daub housing
antibiotics	Poor housing, mainly tropical	Avoid rats & rodent habitats
yes antibiotics	All All	Better hotel; bed away from wall; light on
antibiotics antibiotics	South & East Asia, Australasia	Bite avoidance: repellents; long clothes tucked in
Often difficult	All	Bite avoidance: repellents; long clothes tucked in

AVOIDING OTHER INSECT-BORNE DISEASES

Elephantiasis

Those who harbour this parasite for years develop elephantine swelling of the legs, hence its name: it's also known as filariasis, because it is caused by microscopic filarial worms. This is a disease men fear, for it can cause the scrotum to become so distended that a wheelbarrow is needed to transport their sorry member; the largest recorded weighed 102kg. However, this takes decades, and any sane traveller will seek treatment long before things have got that far. The worms can be spread by day- and night-biting mosquitoes. Elephantiasis occurs in much of the tropics, but is treatable. The incubation period is from a few weeks to 15 months. The blood test for filaria is done more than six weeks after leaving a risk area.

Loa-loa

Loa-loa is also caused by filaria, but is spread by **horse-flies** (*Chrysops*, *see* below) in West and Central African equatorial forests. Visitors (but rarely locals) experience terrific itching, followed by prickling sensations, swelling, aches and pains. Occasionally a 7cm-long worm meanders across the front of the eyeball, an alarming spectacle. Repellents are not very effective against the flies; avoid bites by wearing long clothes and stay in screened buildings where possible. Loa-loa is never life-threatening; it is treatable.

Chrysops

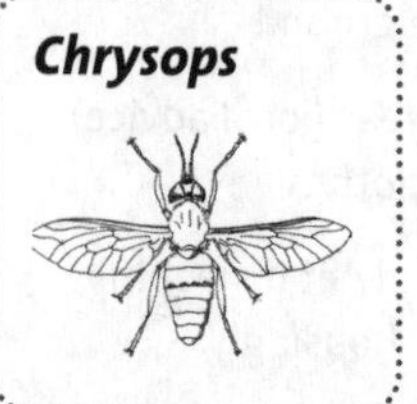

Tularaemia

In the USA and parts of Europe, deer-flies, horse-flies and ticks transmit Tularaemia, a treatable infection causing a range of symptoms from pneumonia to local swellings; often infected people experience no illness at all. In Asia horse-fly bites are merely painful.

Arboviruses

Viruses spread by insects or ticks, arboviruses, are a hazard in many places: 80 cause disease in humans. There is no specific treatment and few vaccines, so prevention is all-important. Avoid bites, and know how to get ticks off quickly and safely (*see* pp.157–8). Arbovirus diseases may not be regarded as much of a problem locally. Natives who survive an attack in childhood develop good immunity to local arboviruses – or die young from them. Travellers, however, may become very ill if infected.

Japanese B encephalitis

This is a dangerous, untreatable viral illness spread by mosquitoes that bite from dusk to mid-evening and early morning to daybreak; they can travel many kilometres from their breeding ponds. Fortunately it is very rare in travellers and tourists. There is a vaccine (for further details and a map showing areas of risk, *see* pp.43–4).

Dengue fevers

Dengue is the most common arbovirus in man. There are about 40 million cases worldwide annually; about two million are caused by **Dengue Haemorrhagic Fever** (**DHF**), which is responsible for 35,000 deaths, almost entirely among local, urban children. Travellers are unlikely to contract this dangerous form. They do, however, risk classical **Dengue Fever** (**DF**) or 'Breakbone Fever'. There have been outbreaks of DF in the USA, Greece, Australia and Japan, but these are sporadic and rare. Dengue has become a big problem in India recently, as well as in Southeast Asia. New outbreaks are likely in burgeoning tropical cities.

The virus is spread by day-biting *Aedes* mosquitoes (*see* p.144), which breed in clean water and are common in tropical gardens, including the gardens of international hotels. Classical Dengue (DF) usually occurs between latitudes 30° north and 40° south: it is endemic in parts of South and Southeast Asia, the Pacific, Africa and the Americas. The incubation period is 2–7 days. DF causes severe muscle and bone pains (hence 'Breakbone' Fever), high fever (40°C/104°F) of abrupt onset and a measles-like rash, but the illness lasts no more than a week and complete recovery is the norm. There is no specific treatment, except *paracetamol* (Tylenol) for the fever and pain; *aspirin* is not given because this promotes bleeding and will make DHF worse. Dengue is

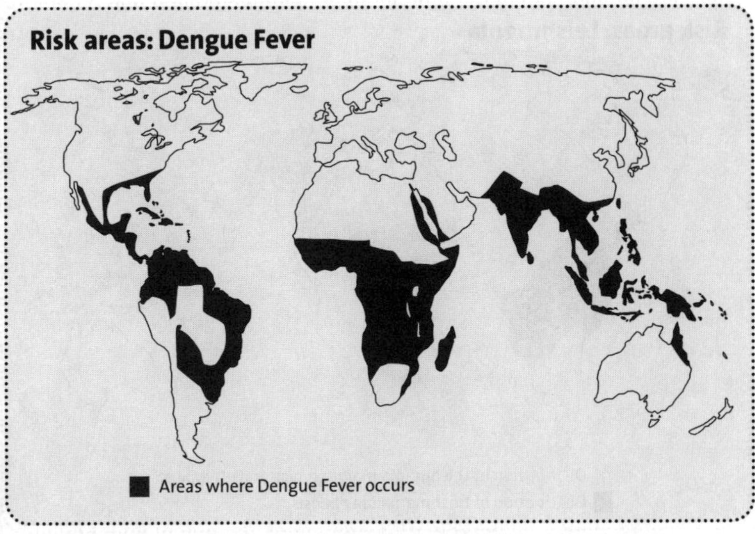

caused by one of four viral subtypes: illness confers complete immunity to further attacks of the same one, but not to the other three.

The dangerous variant, DHF, causes internal bleeding and shock. Left untreated, 50% of all victims die, but with hospital treatment 95% can survive. DHF is a big problem in Southeast Asia, and since 1996 there have been many cases in Latin America and the Caribbean; it is also present in the Pacific, but so far not in Africa. DHF is not completely understood, but Western travellers are at very low risk, although people born in endemic regions who return home are susceptible.

Aedes mosquitoes breed in clean water; discourage biters by emptying out vessels like flowerpots and buckets, and disposing of old car tyres. Expatriates should cover or put fish in water tanks to eat the mosquito larvae. There should soon be a vaccine.

Sand-fly-borne diseases

Sand-flies or 'buffalo-gnats' are tiny, brownish, hairy flies. They are most active at twilight, but bite throughout the night. In tropical America, the Mediterranean and Middle East they transmit **Leishmania**, a protozoan. This either causes painless tropical sores (*see* **Skin**, p.223) or, in hot, dry regions of the Old World, Kala-azar Fever. Sand-flies are so small they can penetrate mosquito nets, though they cannot leave once fed. Permethrin-treated nets keep them out, and repellents work well. They are weak fliers, so ceiling fans also help protect you.

In the New World sand-flies are predominantly moist-forest species, and are most likely to bite during the rainy seasons in the forests of Central America, the Amazon basin and Mexico. Lowland, New World Leishmania is reasonably common and hard to treat, so precautions

Risk areas: Leishmania

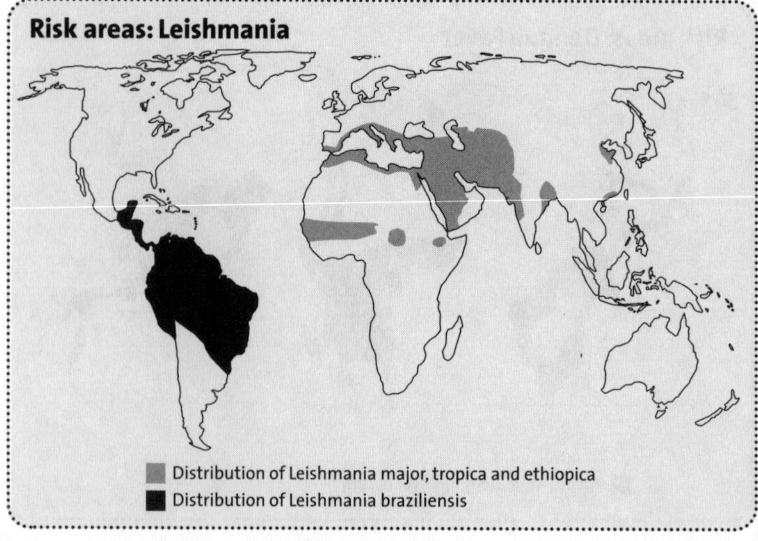

against bites must be taken (*see* pp.144–9). The severe form of the lowland disease is *espundia*. In the Andes of Peru and Argentina, sand-flies stay close to villages, where they bite dogs, people and whoever else seems tasty. Ulcers caused by Andean Leishmania (*uta*) heal by themselves. Seek medical help if you have an ulcer that will not heal, or any kind of wound that seems to be growing.

Sand-fly

African and American Trypanosomiasis

Trypanosome parasites cause disease in man and animals. Disease is rare in ordinary travellers, although there have been some cases of sleeping sickness from Tanzania recently. People are infected by insect vectors that have previously bitten infected domestic or wild animals. Cattle and antelope harbour sleeping sickness parasites in Africa, while in America domestic dogs or forest wildlife are the usual reservoir of Chagas' Disease.

Chagas' Disease and assassin bugs

Chagas' Disease (American Trypanosomiasis) may have killed Charles Darwin, but it is a very rare disease in travellers. It is a problem of the rural poor, occurring from the southern USA through into Central and South America. The parasite is most prevalent in Argentina, Venezuela, Chile, Peru and Bolivia; it has been virtually eliminated from Brazil, which formerly accounted for 40% of cases. It is rare in the Amazon basin, as Indian huts, having no walls, are unsuitable homes for the bug vector.

The trypanosome parasite is happy in almost any mammal, and is spread by bites of **cone-nosed** or **assassin bugs** (right; *see also* p.248). These are substantial (2–2.5cm long), shield-shaped, flying nocturnal bugs. They defecate as they take their blood meal, and the parasite migrates from the bug's faeces into the victim's broken skin; often, it is aided by the victim scratching in response to the bug-bite. If the parasite gets in, an inflamed swelling (a **chagoma**) may appear at the site of entry, and in half the cases there is a typical swelling of the eyelids, but the first stage of the disease is mild and may go unnoticed. Symptoms generally begin after several years, by which time treatment is difficult. Avoidance of bites, then, is all-important. Avoid sleeping on the floor of a wattle and daub house. A hammock helps protect you, particularly if it has a built-in mosquito net (these are sold in Latin America). There are several other species of cone-nosed bug that bite, usually in self defence; their bite is painful, but they do not feed on blood or transmit disease.

Cone-nosed bug

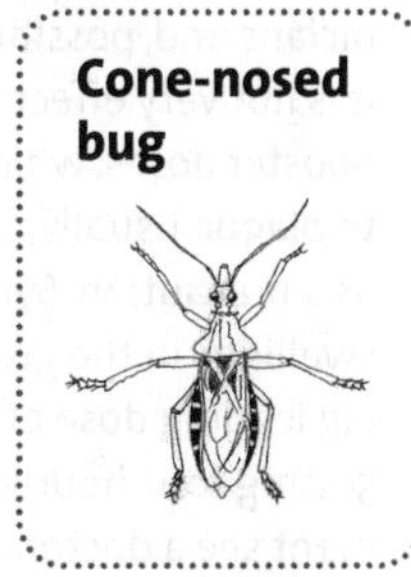

Tsetse-flies and African sleeping sickness

Tsetse-flies (*Glossina spp.*) transmit **sleeping sickness** (African Trypanosomiasis) in a patchy distribution over parts of sub-Saharan Africa,

mostly on forested lake shores and river banks or in forest-savannah mosaic. They like leafy habitats, but one, resplendent in the name *G. longipennis*, survives almost into the Sahara. Local knowledge about the disease is good, so ask before you venture into the bush. Tsetse-flies are active during daylight hours, fly in vast swarms, have a painful bite and are attracted to blue. They are about twice the size of a house-fly.

Visitors to African game parks have been infected recently. A small scab appears at the site of the bite and within a few days there is usually a fever which comes and goes. There is also headache, loss of appetite and swelling of lymph glands, especially in the neck. Eventually parasites invade the brain, causing the apathy, sleepiness and then coma that gives the disease its name. By this time treatment is difficult.

Plague

When plague infects rats living amongst people inhabiting unsanitary, poor accommodation, the rats die of the infection and they are deserted by their fleas. These then go off in search of a new host to bite. People bitten by these fleas acquire bubonic plague, which is treatable with antibiotics. Travellers are most unlikely to catch the plague (*see also* the feature 'Plagues, pestilences and paranoia' on pp.13–15). Those at risk are nurses caring for patients dying of plague, medical laboratory technicians and, possibly, mammal ecologists. Although there is a vaccine it is not very effective and side effects are unpleasant, especially after booster doses, which need to be given every six months. Those exposed to plague usually take antibiotics (*tetracycline* 500mg four times daily) as a precaution. Symptoms of plague (fever and, usually, painful swellings in the groin or other body 'junction points') require treatment (3g loading dose of *tetracycline* then 3g daily by mouth, or 1g then 500mg four-hourly by IM injection). If you think that you need treatment see a doctor.

TICKS AND TICK-BORNE DISEASES

Ticks are small, slow-moving animals with eight short legs. They attach themselves to larger hosts in order to dine on their blood. They are very widespread, and remarkably well adapted to surviving on an intermittent food supply: the American Relapsing Fever tick can live without feeding for 10 years. Unfed adult ticks are 3–6mm long, like a sesame seed with legs, but after feeding become the size and colour of a chilli bean. Catching a tick in the act of feeding off you is unattractive in itself, but its bite can be very itchy, particularly if bits of broken mouthparts are left embedded in the skin. Ticks can also carry serious infection, which gets transmitted more easily because the bite site is itchy and open; some ticks can cause a transient but life-threatening paralysis.

Cattle tick

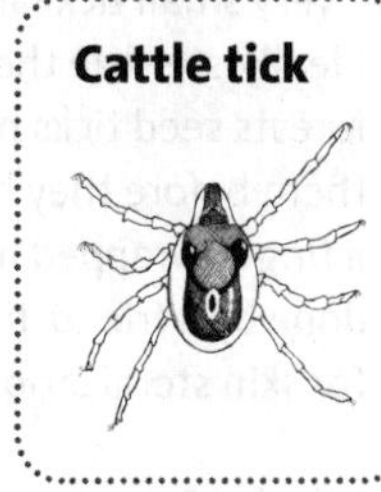

Ticks are master cat-burglars; they crawl undetected over your skin before settling down to feed in some cosy corner near the genitals, or where the clothing is tight. In tick country wear long clothes, tuck trousers into socks and shirts into trousers. Remember, too, that insect repellent is effective against ticks, itch mites, other insects and leeches, as well as mosquitoes (*see* pp.144–9 for bite avoidance measures).

Removing ticks

Prompt removal – as soon as you find a tick – will reduce the chance of disease transmission. If the tick is squeezed, crushed or damaged, infection is more likely to be passed on. Some tick-borne pathogens can get in through intact skin, so protect the removing hand in a plastic bag (or surgical gloves if possible).

Why ticks are undesirable

- ➜ The sight of an engorging tick attached to one's warm and tender parts is unattractive.
- ➜ Most are able to transmit serious infections.
- ➜ The bite site is often itchy and broken skin allows skin infections in more easily.
- ➜ If mouthparts are left in the skin, they can cause long-term itchy discomfort.
- ➜ Some cause a transient but life-threatening paralysis.

Ticks are tenacious: a barbed snout and a kind of cement hold them in place, so unless they are still in the process of settling down to feed they are hard to remove. The best method is to grasp the tick with finger and thumb as close to the skin as possible, and pull steadily. This often hurts, since the mouthparts are cemented in. Do not jerk or twist. Once it has been removed, disinfect the skin with alcohol (gin and whisky are fine) and wash your hands with soap and water. It's not necessary to put anything on the tick to make it let go, nor is it wise to apply a flame: this could singe your pubic hair, or make the tick spit, thus increasing the chances of infection.

Very small tick larvae or 'seed ticks' can be scraped off with a knife; ideally, sterilize the skin with alcohol afterwards. In Central American forests seed ticks may crawl on you in enormous numbers. Remove them before they have had a chance to attach by stroking the skin with a finger wrapped in masking tape, sticky side out. This is most easily done by a friend. If the ticks have not been damaged there is less need for skin sterilization, which may not be a practical proposition.

Tick-borne infections

Ticks are efficient disease transmitters because of their longevity, because they feed on blood at each stage of their life cycle and because some diseases (like Tularaemia) live in the tick from one generation to the next. There are at least nine tick-borne infections in the USA; Britain's only surviving vector-borne illnesses are spread by ticks and they are **Louping Ill**, from sheep ticks in the Scottish borders, and **Lyme Disease**. Others occur in Africa, Asia, South America, even Siberia. Some are easily treated with antibiotics. Most are geographically localized, and local doctors know them. They tend to start with fever, aches and pains and headache.

'European' tick-borne encephalitis (TBE)

'European' tick-borne encephalitis is a viral disease of warm, low-lying forests in central and eastern Europe and Scandinavia (*see* map, inside back cover). The ticks live in the undergrowth of deciduous woods, so campers and orienteers are most at risk and might consider immunization. A post-exposure injection can be given within four days of a bite; this is advised if you develop a fever after a tick has attached itself in TBE regions. For more details and a map showing the areas of risk across Eurasia, *see* p.45.

Lyme Disease

Lyme Disease was only first described in Old Lyme, Connecticut, in 1975, but has almost certainly been around for centuries, wherever *Ixodes* ticks are found. It occurs in Britain and there is a risk where sheep or deer graze amongst trees and bracken; Lyme Disease ticks favour border habitats between woods and meadows and sparsely wooded forest paths. A vaccine against the American strain of the disease was recently developed and licensed in the USA and proved 76% effective (i.e. not very effective), however, it is currently under review and has been withdrawn temporarily due to some safety concerns having been raised.

Even in regions where there is a lot of Lyme Disease transmission, only 1–2% of people bitten will be infected. Then, 7–10 days after a person is bitten by a tick or seed tick, a slowly enlarging red patch, ring or weal usually appears (in 70% of cases); this does not usually itch. It spreads to a diameter of about 15cms (6in) over a couple of weeks, and may persist for months or disappear after a few weeks. Other common symptoms are aching joints (in 80% of cases), fever, aching muscles and headache. Untreated, the disease slowly progresses, developing into a serious illness that can affect the heart and brain, but antibiotics (usually as *tetracycline*) taken within four weeks of the bite are effective. If diagnosis is made later intravenous antibiotics are given in hospital.

Rocky Mountain Spotted Fever and other spotted fevers

Rocky Mountain Spotted Fever is a misleading name, as in the USA this is now mostly a problem east of the Rockies, although it occurs in every US state except Maine, Alaska and Hawaii. The disease also occurs in Mexico, Columbia and Brazil. Pets can bring ticks into homes, so this is occasionally an urban problem; there was even a case acquired in New York city. Victims become unwell with fever, aches and pains, and may become delirious; they usually develop reddish-purple-black spots on the soles of the feet, palms, lower legs and forearms. The rash may spread onto the trunk. It responds to antibiotics.

There are **other tick-borne 'spotted fevers'** which occasionally cause dangerous haemorrhagic (bleeding) disease. These are rare, but occur as close to home as the Mediterranean, as far south as South Africa, and in southern Russia, India and northeast Australia as well as the Americas. They can be treated with antibiotics.

Scrub Typhus

Scrub Typhus is a treatable rickettsial infection usually spread by ticks (but mites or lice can be the vectors), which is widespread in the scrubby countryside of Oceania, northern parts of Australia, southeast Asia and westwards to southeast Siberia. There are similar tick-borne infections in Columbia and Brazil, and also in the Mediterranean. The site of the tick-bite often leaves a slow-to-heal bump (an **eschar**) that looks like an infected mosquito bite, but the victim is also ill. Treatment is straightforward and is with a course of *doxycycline*. **African Tick Typhus** is similar, but usually very mild, with the fever lasting only a few days. It requires no special treatment.

Tick Paralysis

Tick Paralysis is a strange condition, most often described in people bitten by *Dermacentor* ticks in the American Pacific Northwest, but known to exist in every continent. It comes on 4–6 days after a tick attaches. Paralysis begins in the feet and hands; loss of co-ordination follows, then paralysis of the face, slurred speech and uncontrolled eye movements. By about the eighth day breathing becomes irregular, then stops. Children under two are most commonly affected. It seems to be due to a toxin secreted by the salivary glands of the tick in a period of rapid egg development.

Fortunately, though, as soon as the feeding tick has been found and removed, symptoms usually disappear in reverse order to that of their appearance. There are no long-term after-effects. There is an antidote in Australia, where paralysis may continue after the tick has been detached.

On The Ground
Hot Places

12

Strong tropical sun and intense heat cause a range of health problems: heat stroke can kill or permanently disable; sunburn can make life wretched and lead to skin cancer; failing to adapt to heat will make you plain miserable. The main way of avoiding these problems is to change your behaviour. It's what you do rather than physiological adaptations that protect you – or not. This chapter also deals with desert and forest environments.

See **Water**, pp.171–90, for healthcare on the beach and other hazards encountered in and around rivers, lakes and the sea.

Summary

→ Consider the risks before heading into an unfamiliar environment; make suitable preparations and take sensible precautions.

→ Protect yourself from the sun with a hat, suitable clothes and sunscreen. Avoid sunbathing in the middle of the day: the best sunscreen is shade.

→ Use a high-protection factor, waterproof sunscreen and/or protective clothing, especially when snorkelling or swimming.

→ Apply any repellent 30–60mins after sunscreen.

→ When outdoors, wear shoes or some other kind of foot protection.

HAZARDS OF HEAT AND SUN

The hottest place in the Indian subcontinent is northern Sindh, where summer shade temperatures reach 53°C. For Sindhis, the pace of life slows dramatically as temperatures rise: they realize that reducing the amount they expect to achieve is the only way to cope with extreme heat. People sit around and sip tea or bottled drinks, and there is more time to chat. Otherwise, if they are too poor to take shelter and rest, they may succumb, as more than 2,500 Indians did in the bad 'Hot Season' of 1998. Foreigners who follow the local example, though, can protect themselves from physical and mental burn-out.

Case History: India

I travelled to India during an unusually hot pre-monsoon when more than 2,500 Indians died of heat stroke. Temperatures were in the forties (110°F), yet I needed to work, walk, think and run a workshop. I found myself struggling up a hill at midday to look at a village water supply. At a point way above the village I cursed bringing neither hat, umbrella nor water with me. Sweat streamed off me; I was parched, scorched, light-headed; my heart was pounding and my head was throbbing.

When I suggested discussing the water problems of the village sitting under a tree, everyone looked relieved. I had forced the pace, trying to show off what a mountain goat I was, and how I was used to Asian heat. They knew the right strategy was to slow right down. People most likely to be struck by heat illnesses are those new to heat who exercise hard within the first week of arrival. It takes at least that long for the body to adapt, by producing more sweat and moving fat from beneath the skin to around the central organs. Babies are not good at regulating their body temperature, so they can get into trouble, while older people, especially those taking heart medicines, also need to be extra wary.

After overdoing it the first day I slowed down, and found my main problem was to drink enough. And although I felt I was drinking plenty, I rarely slaked my thirst. American soldiers on desert manoeuvres are required to drink eight litres of fluid a day, and Israeli troops in the Sinai are told to drink 10. British Army doctors recommend a basic five litres a day plus half a litre for every hour of physical exercise. My strolls around villages were not on a military scale, but these figures do emphasize the huge volumes that can be lost and need to be replaced. If I gulped down a litre all at once, it felt as if it just stayed in my stomach, so I put rehydration salts into drinking water to increase absorption and replace a little of the salt I lost in sweat. Taste for salt increases when you are salt-depleted; in my case, local curries and the occasional fresh lime soda (with salt) were enough for my salt requirements.

The body adapts to heat by increased sweating and reducing how much salt is lost in sweat; this change takes 1–3 weeks. So, when you first arrive, don't try to do too much, and avoid exercise around midday. Wear 100% cotton clothes: even 30% artificial fibre feels uncomfortable in the heat.

You must increase water intake in hot weather, so as to pass a good volume of urine at least three times a day. Passing small amounts of dark, tea-coloured urine usually means you are dehydrated. Make a conscious effort to drink more, as the body's thirst mechanisms are not good at encouraging enough drinking. Drink at least a large glass of water with every meal. Avoid the temptation to rehydrate with beer: top up with water or soft drinks before alcohol, which is dehydrating. If you let yourself become dry, you will feel awful, and risk kidney stones (*see* p.229) and constipation. Even in extreme heat, it can be difficult to drink enough when all you have is warm plastic-and-chlorine flavoured water. I therefore favour a metal (e.g. Sigg) water bottle, iodine if I am using a chemical water treatment, and I often add a squirt of fresh lime juice or a little drink powder. When the heat is so intense that you cannot keep up with water loss from sweating, **oral rehydration sachets** enhance absorption of water into the body.

Skin care in the sun

Tropical sunshine is powerful, so be very careful about exposing your skin, especially at first. Sunlight radiation not only ages the skin prematurely, it can also stimulate unpleasant-looking warty growths called solar keratoses, and increase the risk of skin cancer. Consequently, some say that sunbathing at all in the tropics is daft. If you must do it, build up your exposure from 15 or 20 minutes a day, and avoid being out in the midday sun (11am–3pm); short shadows indicate that the sun is at its fiercest. Seek shade when your shadow is shorter than you. Untanned skin can burn in 15 minutes in tropical midday sun. A deep tan only gives as much protection as a factor 3 sunscreen, and sunscreens are by no means an absolute protection: factor 12 delays burning for about three hours. You will burn faster if the sun is reflected off water or other light surfaces, such as a beach, the sea or snow (*see also* **Water**, pp.173–4, for skin care on the beach). The processes leading to skin cancer are not entirely understood, but it seems certain that while sunscreens protect skin from burning, they do not eliminate the risk of cancer.

The number of skin cancer cases has risen steadily since people from temperate climates began travelling more to sunny places. At special risk from skin cancer are fair-skinned people living in the tropics; it is particularly important for white-skinned children to be protected. The Australian campaign to protect people from skin cancer has a useful ditty – *Slip Slap Slop* – to help remember the precautions to take:

Slip on a shirt – Slap on a hat – Slop on some sun cream.

Sunscreens

The **ultraviolet** (**UV**) radiation that reaches us on earth consists of **UVA** (wavelength 320–400 nanometres) and **UVB** (290–320nm). Shorter wavelengths (UVC at 100–290nm) are still intercepted by the ozone layer. UVB causes sunburn, but both UVB and UVA cause skin cancer and skin ageing. Even one episode of severe sunburn appears likely to greatly increase the risk of skin cancer.

Sunscreens either absorb UV energy or reflect it. Absorbent ones only protect against UVB, although some offer minimal UVA reduction. Reflectant sunscreens (also called sunblock) contain inert pigments (often zinc oxide or titanium dioxide) that protect against both. Their disadvantage is that they often form a white film on the skin, but many now contain 'microfined' particles of titanium dioxide that are less visible.

The **Sun Protection Factor** (**SPF**) of a sunscreen is a measure of the difference between the dose of UV radiation that produces measurable redness in protected skin and in unprotected skin. Manufacturers' SPFs mainly refer only to UVB protection. Unfortunately, there is no standardization of SPF tests, so direct comparisons between brands are hard to make. In addition, SPFs take no account of a sunscreen's actual performance in real conditions. Nevertheless, SPF does give a rough guide to the degree of protection from UVB. People with sensitive skins should choose an SPF of 15–20, others about 10. It is unnecessary (even undesirable) to use preparations with very high SPFs (25 or more), since even at the Equator the dose of UVB radiation received in a day is not 25 times the amount that will cause sunburn, and very high SPF screens allow extended periods of sunbathing and thus invite longer-term damage from large doses of UVA.

There are now excellent clothes and swimsuits that give good protection from UV radiation and, just as sunscreens boast their SPF, **clothes** have an ultraviolet protection factor (**UPF**). Most summer clothing has a UPF of under 15, whereas these special fabrics have UPFs of about 50, higher than the protection offered by the average sun cream. In Britain, several stores (Boots, Mothercare, Marks & Spencer, BHS, Rohan) sell this protective clothing, and it is becoming more widely available.

Sensible clothing and other skin protection

Shirts with collars (rather than T-shirts) protect the back of the neck from burning. Wear trousers, safari shorts or long, full skirts, not short shorts, and keep the sun off your head: umbrellas are cooler than hats when walking or trekking, and more comfortable in tropical rains than a cagoule (black umbrellas get hot, white ones don't screen out enough sun; mine's a grey collapsible). A cotton bush hat can be dunked in water when you're overheating, and a wet neckerchief draped around the neck is very cooling. Cover up when riding on trucks, bus roofs or motorbikes; the cool breeze disguises the fact that you are burning.

Case History: cycling through the Americas

Weight for weight the cyclist uses less energy to cover a given distance than even superbly designed salmon or dolphins, birds, great cats, the motor car, or any form of jet or rocket engine (*Scientific American*, 1973). Perhaps this explains why the use of bicycles for expeditions has increased so dramatically over the past few years. Certainly, there is no more versatile vehicle known to man. One of its greatest advantages is that once a cyclist has become fit, he or she is far less likely to get ill. On a long expedition, a cyclist's immune system soon gets beefed up, and so long as food-poisoning or serious accidents are avoided, it is possible to cycle for months without having any health disorders. And with good bicycle gearing, climbing hills is no longer a problem, for fitness keeps the cardiac and respiratory changes to a bare minimum and the onset of muscle fatigue is greatly reduced. It is the wind that is the enemy of the cyclist, not mountains! On long expeditions, through such areas as Patagonia or Tibet, it is helpful to cycle during the least windy times of day – and these are often predictable.

I pedalled over 17,000 miles – from California to Tierra del Fuego – for a combined period of three years. Much of this time was spent in the high Andes visiting potters and weavers, sometimes in the remotest villages with no public transport or electricity, and I was never seriously ill. I kept fit by boiling or pilling all my water (and by NEVER getting dehydrated), by cooking most of my own meals (on an Optimus, low-grade petrol cooker) and, when in markets or cafés, only ate meals that I could see boiling before my eyes. I carried a small but comprehensive first-aid kit on the basis that 'a stitch in time...', and for me it worked!

Hallam Murray, Battersea

Skin cancer and sunburn are not the only reasons for keeping the skin covered in the tropics. Being reasonably well-dressed helps protect from stinging and biting wildlife (*see* pp.144–9 and box, p.248). It is also culturally sensitive and appreciated by locals.

Eyes, as well as skin, suffer from too much sun. Wear sunglasses if there is a lot of glare, or you will suffer from a soreness of the eyes like mild snow-blindness. Use only sunglasses that claim UV protection and carry a national quality mark. A hat with a brim sometimes helps, too, unless glare is being reflected up at you from sea or snow.

Treating sunburn

Calamine lotion, or preparations containing calamine, soothe sunburn. They are often unavailable abroad, so take some with you. *Aspirin* helps calm sunburn, and *silver sulphadiazine* (Flamazine) is also said to help if applied to burned skin. Oily skin treatments, though, trap heat in and make sunburn more uncomfortable. Do not deliberately puncture sunburn blisters. Fluids and heat can be lost through badly burned skin, so drink plenty; you may also develop a degree of hypothermia (reduced body temperature) if you are in a climate with hot days and cold nights.

A new, emollient cream called ***tretinoin*** is claimed to repair years of photo-damage to the skin. Sadly the effect is only temporary, and reversible, so this is no elixir.

Medicines and sun sensitivity

If travelling in hot climates, be careful about what you do with any essential medication. If it is put in a bus hold next to the engine it may get cooked or stolen.

A range of medicines can sensitize the skin to the sun. If you develop a rash that seems sun-sensitive and are taking any non-essential medicine, try stopping the medicine to see if the symptoms settle. Common offenders are high-dose (150 or 200mg daily) *doxycycline* antimalarial tablets (e.g. Vibramycin), and *ciprofloxacin* and Bactrim, used to treat diarrhoea. Non-steroidal anti-inflammatories such as *ibuprofen* (e.g. Brufen) and *diclofenac* (e.g. Voltarol) and many other medicines can also cause this reaction. Unfortunately some tablets prescribed to control diabetes (e.g. *glipizide*, Glibenese, Minodiab, *chlorpropamide*) can also cause this super-sensitivity to the sun, yet clearly these cannot be stopped on suspicion in the middle of you trip. It should, however, be possible to change to a different prescription drug. In this case, seek competent medical advice well before travel.

Cold Sores

If you suffer from cold sores (due to the herpes simplex virus), exposure to strong sunlight may reactivate them. *Aciclovir* cream (formerly *acyclovir*; Zovirax in the UK and the USA, Cyclovir in India) is very effective in preventing them, if applied early. Apply it when you notice the sensation of an incipient cold sore, even before it appears.

Heat illnesses

Heat exhaustion

Heat exhaustion is a particular risk in hot, high-humidity environments, especially following strenuous exercise in the sun. Overweight people are more prone to it than the very fit, and new arrivals are far more likely to suffer than those who have been in the environment for two weeks or more. There is profuse sweating (which keeps the body relatively cool), but this loss of fluids causes weakness, dizziness, exhaustion, muscle cramps, restlessness, rapid pulse and vomiting. The skin is very flushed with blood as the body attempts to increase heat loss, but this is at the expense of blood flow to the brain. The body temperature rises but stays below 40°C (104°F).

Take the sufferer to a cool, shady place, where they should drink plenty of water. They will probably be very fluid-depleted and may need to drink as much as 2–4 litres in the first hour. If their temperature is 39°C (102°F) or above, they should be actively cooled by removing clothes, fanning and sponging with a cool (not ice-cold) cloth. Cooling should be continued until the victim's temperature is below 39°C.

The sufferer should do no more physical exercise that day; some would say they should be evacuated to hospital. The point at which you decide to evacuate must depend on the competence of the first-aider; if you have no experience of the problem, evacuate. If not taken seriously, heat exhaustion can rapidly lead to heat stroke, which is a medical emergency.

Heat stroke (also called sunstroke)

Heat stroke can come on suddenly, or can follow heat exhaustion. It is responsible for some deaths, and sometimes permanent disability. The body temperature is usually above 40°C (104°F), but the most important sign of heat stroke is that the victim becomes confused or behaves irrationally. There may be a lack of coordination or delirium, and eventually even convulsions or unconsciousness. Sweating usually decreases, but the skin is not often dry. Pulse and respiratory rates are higher than normal (worrying rates in adults are a pulse-rate of over 100 beats/min, or a respiratory rate over 30 beats/min). The respiratory rate is the number of times the chest rises; note that people who know you are taking their breathing rate are unlikely to breathe normally.

Unconsciousness implies a very grave condition. If the victim has been unconscious for more than two minutes, evacuate him to a hospital while continuing cooling. Unconsciousness for longer than two hours is usually followed by permanent disability. Heat stroke is a very serious and dangerous condition.

For **prickly heat** and **heat rash**, *see* p.217.

Treating heat stroke

Treatment is as for heat exhaustion:

→ Place victim in the shade.
→ Remove clothing (the victim's, not yours, silly) and fan the victim.
→ Sponge with a cool, wet cloth (but do not apply ice).
→ Gently massage limb muscles to encourage heat dissipation.
→ Encourage drinking, if possible.
→ Monitor the temperature; stop cooling when it is below 39°C (102°F).
→ Beware of the temperature rising again.
→ If the victim is unconscious, raise the legs above the level of the heart.

JUNGLE, FORESTS AND SCRUB

Tropical and sub-tropical forests are hot, humid places where you can lose a surprising amount of body fluids very quickly. Take it easy at first, and build up the pace of activities over at least a week (even if you're fit).

Wear long, loose cotton clothes and insect repellent. They keep off mosquitoes, other insects and ticks (*see* pp.165–6) and also protect you from noxious plants (*see* below and pp.217–19). Although most malarial mosquitoes bite at night, some forest-dwelling insects are day-biters, including vectors of Dengue and Yellow fevers and tropical American sand-fly-borne diseases (*see* table on pp.150–51). Asian rainforests and deciduous forests in the monsoon are often alive with leeches, which are also kept away by repellents and long clothes (*see* pp.251–2). Wear proper boots if you expect to stray from paths: you need to be especially cautious about snakes, centipedes and, after dark in dry forests, scorpions. Try not to grab at plants to steady yourself; many have thorns, or harbour hordes of aggressive ants. Never put your hands or feet where you cannot see them. Tropical wasps and bees readily get cross with lumbering humans and the more you flail, the more they will sting and call in further reinforcements (*see also* pp.256–8). And shake out your boots before putting them on.

Noxious plants and wee furry animals

Tropical plants have evolved an impressive array of unpleasant ways to protect themselves. Some plants are covered in barbed thorns that you may not notice until you come into contact with them; they can be difficult to pull out. Furry-looking seed pods are covered in little hairs that penetrate skin and cause discomfort, only relieved by painstakingly removing each hair with a fine pair of tweezers. Prickly pears, young bamboo and a host of other plants have similar defence mechanisms.

There are also plants that secrete irritant oils, such as the New World poison ivy and poison oak. The **giant hogweed**, *Heracleum mantegazzianum*, causes a sunlight-sensitive rash (*see* pp.218–19). Avoid any plant that secretes a milky sap; some species cause blistering if the sap gets in your eyes. Others are extremely painful stingers. Nepalese **nettles** (called *sisnu* or *allo*, which look like malignant mutants of the English stinger) are exceedingly unpleasant. Antidotes which, like the European dock, grow with it, include *Artemisia dubia*, a straggly, chrysanthemum-like shrub called *titepati*.

Some small animals, such as the cute little **tenrecs** (Madagascar's equivalent of a hedgehog), can deposit masses of very fine spines in the skin, as can furry caterpillars (*see* pp.253–4). Mosquitoes and larger predators love dense undergrowth; do not go into the jungle scantily clad or ignorant of local wildlife hazards (*see* **Animals**, pp.264–5).

DESERTS

The risks of heat and sun are more obvious in deserts than many other environments. If you are driving through desert, consider the possible consequences of vehicle breakdown and carry plenty of water. Body-fluid losses are huge, especially when you are receiving a cooling breeze through an open window; make an effort to drink more. If you are stranded without water, do not drink urine but look for other water sources, such as the car radiator (so long as no antifreeze has been added), or condensation, which will collect under plastic at night. A major hazard of desert travel in vehicles is coming across unprepared travellers who scrounge water and leave you short. Carry plenty.

Avoid undue heat exposure by wearing a hat and long, loose clothing. Avoid vigorous exercise when it's very hot: the siesta is a very sensible adaptation to the intense heat of midday. Your appetite for salt will probably increase; shake more on your food to replace the lost salt your body is requesting. Salt tablets are not recommended.

The major animal hazards of deserts are snakes (*see* pp.259–63) and scorpions (*see* pp.255–6), although some deserts have larger dangerous species, like the lions in the Kalahari.

Responsible desert relief

Many dry environments are deceptively fragile, and for this and aesthetic reasons, defecating and urinating should leave no disturbance. Dig a small, deep hole. The toilet paper should also be dropped into the hole and burned as much as possible; it should then be covered over thoroughly with earth and sand. In the desert the wind will sooner or later uncover buried paper, which will then merrily fly around, littering the environment and leaving unhygienic calling cards. Faeces present less of a problem because, especially when covered up, they decompose naturally. After urination, women may either 'drip-dry', burn the used paper or, best of all, collect the used paper, place it in a plastic bag and dispose of it when they reach the next garbage disposal facility. Toilet paper does not decompose, so simply dropping it behind a bush or under a stone will leave it to be whirled around by the wind for weeks, if not months.

Barbara Ikin, Maputo, Mozambique

On The Ground

Water

13

Many of the attractions of sea and shore are in themselves among its dangers: the vibrant coral, beautiful fish and blazing sun can turn a beach holiday into a misery if you are stung, bitten or burned. On top of these hazards, many accidents occur because swimmers and revellers don't take enough care: many underestimate the power of sea and river currents; others attempt watersports without the right equipment or training, or after they have eaten or drunk too much.

However, being aware of the hazards is what allows you to avoid them; wearing the right clothes and footwear reduces the risk of being stung, while applying adequate sunscreen should protect you from too much sun, the effects of which are increased by reflection off water.

See also **Hot Places**, pp.161–70 for skin care in the sun and guidance on coping in hot weather.

Summary

→ Consider the risks before entering an unfamiliar environment; make suitable preparations and take sensible precautions.

→ Protect yourself from the sun with a hat, suitable clothes and sunscreen; the best sunscreen is shade.

→ Use high factor, waterproof sunscreen and/or protective clothing, especially when snorkelling or swimming.

→ Apply any repellent 30–60mins after sunscreen.

→ When outdoors, wear shoes, 'jellies' or some other kind of foot protection, even when bathing, strolling along the beach, swimming or paddling.

→ Heed warnings. Think twice before bathing where locals say it is dangerous to do so.

→ Do not attempt a dangerous sport for the first time anywhere if the outfit does not seem geared up for beginners; check on instructors' qualifications.

HAZARDS OF THE SEA

The salt concentration of sea water is not high enough to act as a disinfectant, and many disease organisms, including cholera, thrive in it. Swallowing sea water may be hazardous (you can catch hepatitis A) if you swim in heavily contaminated, land-locked or poorly flushed seas. The Mediterranean and many British beaches are especially unhealthy despite European laws forbidding the dumping of untreated sewage. Faecal coliform counts (measuring numbers of faecal bacteria) are now published for many UK beach sites and our record is poor. Skin problems are another consequence of bathing in heavily polluted waters (*see also* **red tides**, below, p.184).

A depressing number of tourists drown each year while bathing in idyllic, inviting tropical seas. Many have been drinking alcohol before they drown. People worry about sharks and scorpion fish, but undertows and rip-tides are far more effective killers: in the USA you are 1,000 times more likely to drown than be killed by a shark. Listen to what locals advise about swimming, and if no one else is bathing, pause to think why.

Even in summer, temperate seas are rarely warmer than 15°C, and at these temperatures swimmers easily get into trouble and drown. Beware of swimming too soon (less than two hours) after a heavy meal. Cramp can sink even the strongest swimmer. It comes on much more readily if your stomach is very full and if you have any alcohol in your system; the risk is greatest in cooler waters.

Water droplets act like lenses that magnify the burning power of the sun. Even waterproof sunscreens wash off or are sweated off quite quickly, so swim wearing a shirt (preferably one with a collar), as well as a good, water-resistant sunscreen. Being out all day in tropical sunshine – especially reflected off water or other light surfaces – can give you soreness of the eyes as well as sunburn. Protect yourself with good sunglasses. It is often wise to retire to some shade during the hottest part of the day, but beware that falling coconuts kill a suprising number of holidaymakers each year.

Case History: Central America

In three months working at a rehabilitation centre for disabled children on the Pacific coast of Mexico, I was called three times to the beach to resuscitate people who had drowned. All had been drinking alcohol and swept out by rip currents. Despite proper mouth-to-mouth resuscitation, none survived.

Don't get drunk and swim.

Jean Sinclair RGN, MSc

Wearing **shoes** or 'jellies' on tropical beaches helps protect you from injuries caused by treading on sharp pieces of coral and sea-urchin spines, and also used hypodermic needles, which are increasingly common on beaches. Scuba 'fins' offer a little protection, but they do not protect from venomous fish.

Snorkelling and scuba diving

When planning a trip to explore the submarine world, manta rays, sharks and giant squids might worry you, but the most significant hazard that you must plan for is probably the sun. Tropical and sub-tropical sun burns fair skin in minutes and, if you are snorkelling, you can get the skin of your back, back of the neck, thighs and calves badly burned and blistered while you are keeping cool just below the surface. Water doesn't protect the skin from damaging sunlight radiation, indeed, water droplets can act like magnifying lenses to increase the possibilities of damage. Scuba divers too risk sunburn, especially when in the boat travelling to a dive site, since sun seems to be stronger and more damaging when it is reflected off water. So protect yourself with a waterproof sunscreen and by wearing a T-shirt or, even better, an old polo shirt with a collar. When snorkelling, wear long 'shorts' and ensure that there is high-SPF sunscreen on any exposed parts of your body, including the nape of the neck and the backs of the legs. Thus you reduce your chances of skin cancer and premature wrinkling caused by too much exposure to the sun. Note that it is now possible to buy **swimsuits** made from special fabrics with their own ultraviolet protection factor, which offer better protection from UV radiation than the average sun cream (*see also* **Hot Places**, p.165).

A large number of **diving centres** now exist all over the tropics. Many, however, do not expect any previous training in the sport, even though they may offer only minimal tuition themselves. They have a vested

Sea and shore tips

→ Wear shoes on the beach and when swimming to avoid getting bits of coral and worse in your feet.

→ Protect yourself from sunburn when swimming and snorkelling by wearing a shirt and waterproof sunscreen.

→ Take local advice about where it is safe to snorkel or swim – there may be estuarine crocodiles, risk of shark attacks or rip tides.

→ Try to avoid alcohol or recreational drugs before entering the sea. Drowning is much more likely if you are intoxicated.

→ Be very careful when picking up any tropical sea creatures – lots are armoured and venomous.

Case History: Central America

A strong swimmer and life saver from Ontario, Canada, was standing on rocks on the Pacific coast of Costa Rica, watching the sea for the first time ever. He was well used to large bodies of water – the Great Lakes – but didn't realize that not all waves are the same size. He was washed off his feet by a big "seventh" wave, and had to swim for nearly half an hour before he struggled back on land, suffering in this time a badly gashed knee that required several stitches. However experienced you are on home ground, local conditions elsewhere may be very different and challenging.

Jean Sinclair RGN, MSc

interest in renting equipment out to you. Remember, though, that in tropical waters you can see a tremendous amount with only a mask and snorkel; stick to these unless you know what you are doing. If you have no scuba experience, do not be tempted to 'have a go' unless you are offered training to a recognized standard. The PADI certificate is the most widely recognized international dive-masters' qualification; NAUI or the British Sub-aqua Club Sports Diver certificate are equivalent. Avoid dive centres that do not boast such qualifications. You can burst a lung and die of air embolism while ascending from a depth of as little as three metres, and this kind of injury is common in people learning to use compressed air but who are not properly supervised. And don't forget to check the equipment before use.

It is possible to suffer from decompression sickness if you **fly** soon after scuba diving. If you have a single dive each day, it should be safe to wait just 12 hours before flying. If you have dived several times a day for several days or you have made dives with decompression stops, an extended time on the surface of 24 hours or more is necessary. If there has been treatment of decompression sickness in a chamber, it may be necessary to wait as long as seven days before flying, and expert advice should certainly be sought. The **British Institute of Naval Medicine** run a 24-hour emergency helpline for divers (*see* below).

Gloves give useful protection if you must collect anything from beneath the waves, although keep in mind that there are some seriously be-weaponed little beasts that demand respect (*see* below, p.176). Some of the most attractive cone shells of the tropics possess a venomous harpoon that packs enough poison to kill an adult. And rummaging around in rocky crevices might have you disturbing a moray eel, which can inflict a savage bite.

Contact information: diving emergencies

Divers' 24-hr emergency helpline: **UK t** 07831 151 523.

Coral

After the sun, probably the next most likely hazard when plunging into warm seas is from coral. Coral is attractive because of its gorgeous colours and because it is a haven for all kinds of marine life, but in tropical seas creatures need to be able to protect themselves, or they end up in something else's stomach. Even just brushing against coral causes a nasty abrasion and these scrapes usually become inflamed and easily infected. Be wary of even the softest looking coral; don't get too close and consider wearing some protection: a T-shirt and gloves, perhaps, since a snorkeller wearing gloves can do a little to fend themselves off a coral reef in choppy seas. Coral can cause several problems. There are varieties of **stinging corals**, known as fire corals, which inflict extremely painful and persistent stings, but these are less common. Probably the most common problem is caused by the small fragments that make up many idyllic palm-fringed beaches; these readily penetrate the soles of the feet, and even a small piece is painful and remarkably difficult to extract, so wear shoes when paddling or swimming. Live coral looks soft, inviting and beautiful, but is actually highly abrasive; scratches you get by brushing against it will suppurate and be particularly uncomfortable, sometimes for weeks. Wash any abrasions thoroughly, remove any coral, sand or debris and apply antiseptic (*see* p.216). Remember that sea water isn't salty enough to be antiseptic and so continuing to sea-bathe after sustaining abrasions is asking for trouble.

Nasty sea creatures

All marine animals should be assumed to be venomous and treated with great respect. Swimmers and paddlers are stung by venomous fish even in temperate regions, and noxious creatures abound in tropical seas. Fish toxins are inactivated by immersion in very hot water; prevention and treatment are described in detail below. Touch nothing unless you are sure it is harmless, and wear stout gloves if you are collecting anything or rummaging around in crevices. Collecting living creatures is not only bad news for them, it could be for you too.

Cone mollusc (*Conus* spp.)

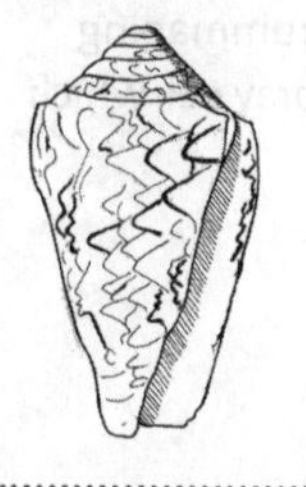

Cone shells

The attractive cone molluscs of the Indo-Pacific seas feature a venomous, tongue-like, harpoon tooth. They range up to about 23cm in length, although the majority are much smaller. They have stung collectors through the trouser pocket. Stings can cause unpleasant tingling and numbness, and sometimes even paralysis and death from respiratory arrest. Resuscitation can be life-saving, but there is no antivenom. Do not collect live specimens.

The Octopus family

Octopus saliva contains a vicious toxin that can be introduced into the skin by a bite from the animal's powerful beak, between the tentacles. Bites are painful and bleed, swell and become inflamed. Blue-ringed octopi, *Hapalochlaena maculosa* and *H. lunulata* of Australia, Indonesia and the Philippines, possess such toxic nerve poisons that they can cause fatal paralysis within 15 minutes of a bite. They are only the size of a human hand (10cm long) and can be found in shallow waters.

The flying squid, *Onychoteuthis banksi*, is also dangerous, but since it only comes up to shallow waters after dark it rarely comes into contact with people. Those bitten are almost always fishermen. They are sold as food throughout their range; exercise care when preparing them for the table, in case they are still alive.

Jellyfish and their kin

Jellyfish, sea wasps, Portuguese men-of-war, fire coral, sea anemones and sea nettles all have venomous stinging capsules called **nematocysts**. Jellyfish stings are most common when there are onshore winds. Fortunately, very few species are dangerous and in the region where they commonly cause trouble – the northern coasts of Australia – coastguards warn people if dangerous jellyfish have come inshore.

Sea wasp

Worldwide, there are about 30 deaths a year due to jellyfish, and although this is 30 deaths too many, the chances of such a fatal sting are very small indeed. Just six species are responsible for these deaths. Three are the **box jellyfish** (*Chironex* spp.), also called 'sea wasps'. These are box-shaped, with tentacles hanging from the four corners of the squarish 'bell'. The largest, most venomous and fast-swimming is ***Chironex fleckeri***, which occurs along the tropical coasts of Australia and Southeast Asia. They have bodies as big as basketballs (20cm diameter) and tentacles that trail out for 3m. The tentacles (which carry the sting-cells) are translucent and difficult to see and thus are easy to brush against. Those who are stung experience incredible pain and may collapse and die, sometimes within four minutes. Flooding the stung skin with vinegar inactivates any undischarged stingers. There is a specific antivenom in Australia, which is given by lifeguards. The **Irukandji** (*Carukia barnesi*) is another box jelly that has been causing grief in tropical Australia, yet it is only the size of your

Irukandji

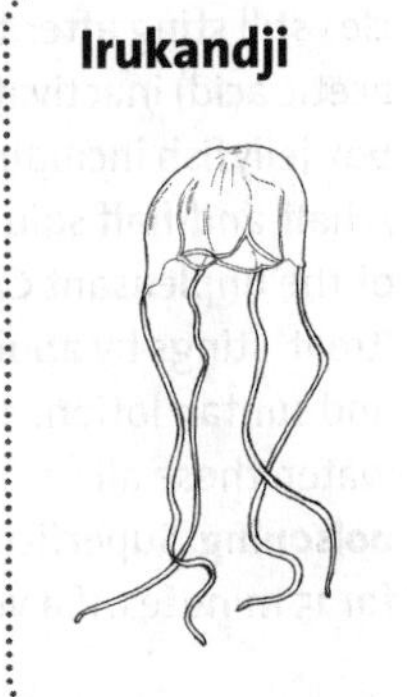

thumb. Often, contact with these goes unnoticed, but if people are stung by lots of them, they do collapse and may not survive (*see* below for prevention and treatment).

Portuguese man-of-war

The **Portuguese man-of-war** (*Physalia physalis*), which is common in warm waters of the Atlantic, Pacific and Indian Oceans, occasionally causes deaths. It possesses a 10–30cm-long, bluish float, with tentacles beneath that trail for 20m. The smaller Indo-Pacific species has just one large tentacle and is called the bluebottle in Australia. Vinegar must not be applied after portuguese man-of-war stings as this will make the situation worse by making more nematocysts fire.

Chiropsalmas quadrigatus inhabits the seas of Indo-China, from the Maldives to the Philippines. It also occurs in the Atlantic, from Brazil to North Carolina. Finally, there has been one reported death in southeast China by stings of *Stomolophus nomurai*, which has a 1.5m diameter bell. Stay away from big jellyfish wherever you are.

Australians recommend wearing two pairs of tights/panty-hose as **protection** from jellyfish stings. You put one pair on conventionally and then by cutting a hole in the crutch and cutting the feet off the other pair, you can put your arms into the legs, head through the crutch hole and your hands emerge where the feet of the tights were. Then, you tape the two waistbands together to make a whole outfit: I am not sure, however, that I'd feel much like swimming in such garb, so I think I'd wear a proper protective suit, which is available in Australia and makes a more chic alternative.

Treatment of jellyfish stings

Try to remove any fragments of clinging tentacles with your fingers or, better still, scrape them off with a credit card, remembering that tentacles still sting after they have broken off the jellyfish. Vinegar (4–6% acetic acid) inactivates the stingers of the Indo-Pacific and Australian box jellyfish including the Irukanji, but do not use this on other species. A half-and-half solution of baking soda in water inactivates the stingers of the unpleasant *Chrysaora* sea-nettle jellyfish of the Atlantic. **Never** 'treat' stings by applying alcoholic solutions, such as methylated spirits and suntan lotion, nor by applying kerosine, urine, hot sand or fresh water: these all causes massive discharge of stingers and **exacerbate poisoning**. Superficial pain usually responds to cold packs or ice applied for 15 minutes. If a victim has stopped breathing, give mouth-to-mouth

Case History: Australia

I like the big landscapes of North Queensland, but swimming was an amazing palaver: either you put on tights and T-shirts, or you invest in a 'stinger suit', or you use the town beach which is dragged with a net every day. Not having thought to pack tights, ever, or a Lycra suit, we went for the town beach. This was fine, except that it still seemed like swimming in jellyfish soup with added stingy bits. The next day we went again, but the beach was closed. We watched the 'surf rescue person' drag a small net along the shoreline with his four-year-old helper and then pick out the 'deadly' box jellyfish with his fingers; there's a knack, obviously. What was interesting was:

a) the difference between what sweeping the beach sounds like and what it actually means; i.e. the 'official' procedure was stunningly underwhelming;

b) you can pick up deadly jellyfish;

c) actually, they're not usually deadly but they hurt a lot;

d) the best medicine is vinegar (up-market tourists should use balsamic);

e) they sting children mainly because it's mostly children who seem to gather alongside them at the shoreline;

f) that you don't need to worry about big box jellies that much; it's the Irukandji that'll kill you...

g) ...except that it may not kill you, but it'll sting like hell for weeks;

h) none of the local info on jellyfish seems to be consistent, nor does it give one confidence in its reliability;

i) after weighing all this up, how much do you want to swim anyway?

When we subsequently went snorkelling we had to rent Stinger Suits (dead or weeping tourists are bad PR) and apart from the fact that you no longer pay the jellies any mind at all, or can swim up and peer at them, you don't get SUNBURNED or have to faff around with any of those ghastly waterproof SPF unctions.

Edward Howarth, Melbourne

resuscitation and, if necessary, cardiac massage. The effects of the venom are remarkably short-lived, so that keeping the victim alive for a few minutes with mouth-to-mouth resuscitation means that they will probably come around and recover completely, albeit with scars. After a Portuguese man-of-war sting, itching can persist for months, and is best treated with a mild steroid cream like hydrocortisone.

Sea anemones, starfish and sea urchins

Anemones sting their prey, so treat them with respect. One species, *Anemonia sulcata*, found as close to home as the Adriatic coast, can inflict painful stings.

Starfish and **sea urchins** have venomous spines and grapples, which can produce dangerous poisoning. Spines embedded in the skin are at best a painful nuisance. Remove them after softening the skin with 2% *salicylic acid* ointment, or *acetone* or *magnesium sulphate* paste (readily available in pharmacies). This technique may also be useful for extracting deeply embedded pieces of coral (*see* p.176).

Saltwater crocodiles and sea snakes

Saltwater crocodiles (*Crocodilus porosus*) are said to be the most vicious killers in the world: they are bloodthirsty and insufficiently imaginative to fear anything. They are the biggest of the crocodiles, with reliable records of beasts seven metres long and many claims of others in excess of 10m. They are found in the sea, mangrove swamps, tidal parts of rivers and estuaries in Southeast Asia, India, Sri Lanka and Australia. Seek local advice before you bathe.

Sea snakes are highly venomous, but fortunately, they rarely bite. Of the few people bitten by sea snakes, some 80% receive no venom and suffer no ill effects. Sea snakes are easy to see because they have striking markings and their vertically flattened, oar-like tail distinguishes them from **eels**. Snakes are sluggish and loll around in warm seas, rocking with the swell. If you happen to be snorkelling above one when it surfaces for a breath, you might get bitten, but the only time that they are commonly provoked into aggression is when they are caught in a fishing net or otherwise harassed. Sea snakes go in for orgies, gathering in numbers to mate; if disturbed at this time they can also be aggressive. If you find a group, stay clear. Afford individuals respect and they will leave you alone.

Sea snake

Moray eel

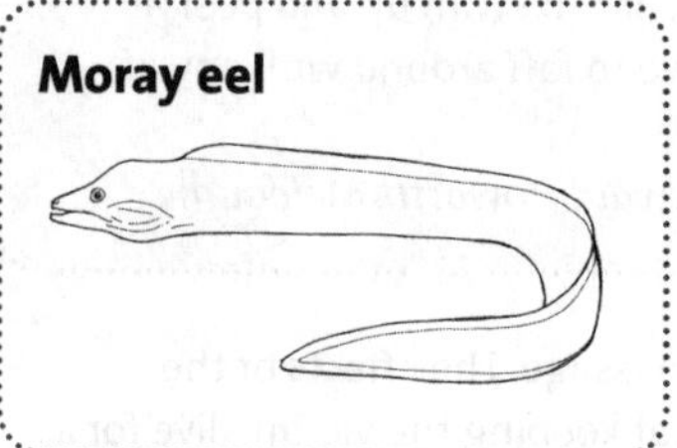

Dangerous sea fish

About 100 species of fish can administer dangerous stings, and a selection (barracuda, moray and conger eels, garfish, groupers and sharks) are able to inflict severe bites. Fish stings are common, and it is estimated that there may be as many as 1,500 stingray stings and about 300 scorpion fish stings a year in the USA alone. However, fatalities from fish stings are rare, and so are deaths from shark attacks.

Stonefish, scorpionfish and their relations

Stonefish often lurk in shallow water, well camouflaged, half-buried and looking like stones. Impaling a bare foot on their venomous fins or spines is an excruciating experience, but there is a stonefish antivenom. The equally venomous **scorpionfish** and **lion fish** make themselves more conspicuous, and may charge if threatened.

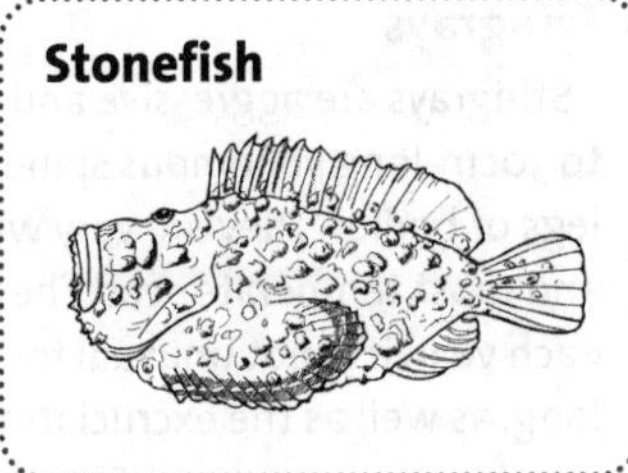
Stonefish

Lion fish

Weever fish

Weever fish

Venomous fish are not peculiar to tropical waters. European weever fish are common around Britain, especially Cornwall, where they cause many excruciating stings. It is an undistinguished but tasty little brown fish used to make *bouillabaisse*. Like scorpionfish they have venomous dorsal fins, and often lie partially buried in sand in shallow water, so that it's easy to tread on them. The sting is so painful that a Welsh trawlerman cut off his toes to get relief. They also occur in the Mediterranean.

Treatment of fish stings

Fish venom is inactivated by heat, so the treatment (whether the sting is from a tropical or temperate species) is to immerse the affected limb in water that is hot but not scalding (45°C). Pain relief is usually immediate, but pain may return. Continued soaking will probably be needed, including a topping up with hot water, for 30–90 minutes; by this time most of the pain will have gone. Repeat the hot soaks if pain returns. Antivenoms exist for some species, and doctors can also inject local anaesthetic, which also gives some relief. *Morphine* and *pethidine* (*meperidine* or Demerol in the USA) do not really help the pain; even where modern medical facilities are available, hot water treatment will bring the quickest relief. Subsequently, any pieces of your assailant must be removed, or infection is bound to set in. Foreign bodies, be they fish spines, pieces of coral or rusty nails, will all lead to infection if left in a wound. Some debris will also tattoo the skin.

Rays and Sharks

Stingrays

Stingrays are aggressive and very common. They are equipped with up to 30cm-long venomous spines on their tails, which lash out against legs or bodies. They are very widespread in all tropical and sub-tropical and most temperate seas. They inflict many injuries in North America each year: it is not unusual for victims to receive lacerations 13–17cm long, as well as the excruciating venom. Stingrays occur as far north as Scandinavia and are found in the Mediterranean. In Australian coastal waters there is a species that reaches a length of about five metres and a weight of 350kg. There are also nasty freshwater rays in South America. Any ray sting causes awful pain and swelling, which is at its worst 30–60 minutes after being stung. Stings can also sometimes cause collapse and even death.

Stingray

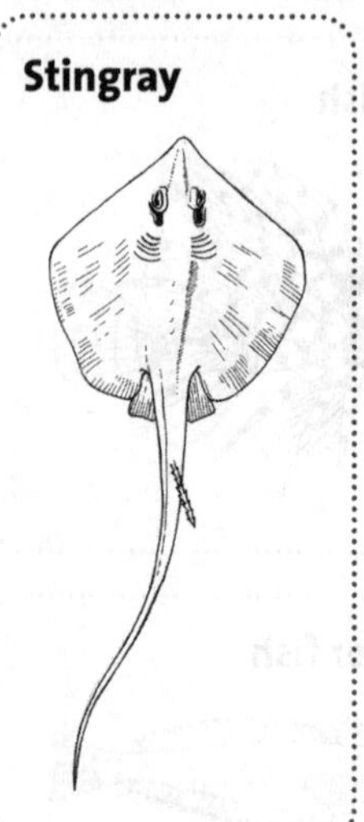

Few animals, though, choose to attack unprovoked, and stings are the rays' defence when surprised by someone. Wearing shoes will give you little protection from stingrays (although you will avoid other venomous fish), but adopting a shuffling walk (the **stingray shuffle**) when paddling in shallow water will efficiently advertise your presence. The fish will then swim away before you tread on it.

Sharks

Being eaten alive by a shark is an image that nightmares are made of, yet the risk of shark attack is extremely small. There are perhaps 50–100 deaths a year worldwide due to sharks, compared to about 400 deaths annually from drowning in Britain's chilly waters alone. You are more likely to be struck by lightning than end up in a shark's belly. And compare the 50 or so human deaths due to sharks to the 100 million sharks that are killed annually by people – mainly for shark's-fin dishes. In Australia there are an estimated 15 deaths a year due to shark attack and 150 from falling coconuts!

I have also been told that the nearer you are to the Equator, the less dangerous sharks are likely to be. Equatorial waters are so overstocked with fish that sharks do not usually trouble to attack something as large and indigestible as a snorkeller or swimmer. The problem with sharks, though, is that they are unpredictable. Most attacks seem to be from 'rogue' individuals, or they occur when someone is unfortunate enough to precipitate or get caught up in a 'feeding frenzy'. Sharks then become so mad that injured individuals turn to eat their own entrails. Hungry sharks smell blood and damaged flesh (especially fish oil) from half a kilometre away. Spear-fishermen who carry their catches on their belts may be more at more risk of attack, and menstruating women may also attract sharks.

A common prelude to an attack is the shark circling its victim. Try to keep calm and swim away steadily, as thrashing will excite the shark. Keep it in view, and if it comes close try banging it on the nose, poking it in the eye and shouting under water: these techniques sometimes work. Be aware that shark skin is highly abrasive, and will tear your skin if the shark brushes past you, which could precipitate a feeding frenzy.

Most shark attacks occur between latitudes 30°N and 30°S. Take local advice before swimming. If there have been shark attacks, or if there are nasty currents or other dangers, locals will know about them.

Other sea hazards

Stinging sea

Swimmers notice stinging sensations in tropical seas including Indonesia, Sri Lanka and East Africa. Unlike 'sea lice' (*see* below) this seems to affect everyone in a similar way, and immediately. Expatriates blame it on stinging seaweed since the problem is most apparent when there is a lot of weed in the water. It is probably due to jellyfish larvae or segments of jellyfish stingers which come in to the beach with the onshore winds and are mixed up in the weed debris. It is an unnerving sensation, but transient.

'Sea lice' or Sea-bathers' Eruption

This has only recently been recognized; it is also known as **Ocean Itch**, ***Caribe*** or **Sea Poisoning**. Swimmers notice raised, red weals a few hours after bathing in tropical seas; these last several days. The rash appears most usually on skin that has been covered by bathing suits or in places where the skin is rubbed, such as the armpits, the backs of the knees and, in surfers, where skin has been in contact with the board. In Florida, where it is best-known, 'sea lice' seems to be caused by stings from larvae of the **thimble jellyfish**, *Linuche unguiculata*. These are tiny, near-invisible creatures half a millimetre long that get caught between swimsuits and the skin.

Not everyone is affected the same way; people who have never met the larvae before will have no rash. The disease seems to be an immune hypersensitivity reaction to jellyfish venom, and those who have encountered larvae several times notice a mild stinging sensation as they swim. They can give an early warning to other swimmers.

The thimble jellyfish is a widespread species, occurring off Central and South America as well as in the Indo-Pacific, including the Philippines. Other jellyfish larvae are probably capable of causing similar problems anywhere in warm seas. On the Florida coast 'sea lice' is only present between April and July (inclusive). It only occurs in some years and, as with other jellyfish stings, usually when there are onshore winds.

Treatment of 'sea lice'

'Sea lice' inject venom under the skin, so nothing you put on the skin will go deep enough to counteract it. The only action that is really likely to help is to remove bathing suits and take a shower (preferably in salt water initially) after swimming. Showering in fresh water with the swimsuit on will make the venomous cysts of the larvae discharge, aggravating the situation. Anyone who has an attack of 'sea lice' will probably experience another when they wear the same swimsuit again. It is therefore advisable either to throw the swimsuit away or machine-wash it with detergent and tumble-dry it.

Red tides

This phenomenon occurs at unpredictable times in warm seas, turning the ocean red, and can happen anywhere in the tropics. In a red tide there are abnormal accumulations of tiny dinoflagellate organisms, which produce toxins that are released into the sea and sometimes into the air, due to the action of the surf. These aerosol toxins can cause slight irritation of the airways, a cough, a runny nose, sneezing and sore eyes, and asthmatics tend to wheeze. There is no treatment except to stay away from the red surf; you should also avoid swimming near a red tide. For problems associated with eating seafood during a tide, *see* **Worms, Guts and Nutrition**, pp.123–4.

DANGERS OF RIVERS AND LAKES

The principal risk of bathing is **drowning**. A surprising number of riverside beauty spots and apparently tranquil pools have claimed the lives of careless revellers. Be wary, especially in limestone areas where rivers could suck you underground.

In the UK more people drown **inside vehicles** than while swimming. Here is what to do if your car ends up in deep water. When a car plunges into water it settles nose down, as the heaviest bit, the engine, is usually at the front, while the boot (trunk) remains full of air. The submerged car will begin to fill with water, but it's not until it is reasonably full that you will be able to open a door and get out. If you are in the front seats you may be submerged inside the car before enough water has entered to allow you to escape. **Wind down windows** to let the car fill up quickly, so that you can open the doors or exit through a window.

If you **fall out of a boat** and are swept into a rapid, or are white-water rafting and are taken downstream out of control, ensure that you are travelling feet first; that way, if you hit any boulders or obstacles, your feet will take the impact, not your head. Even if you feel you can make headway by swimming against the current, resist the temptation to swim across the river. You will just get swept downstream faster. **Swim heading upstream**, pointing just a few degrees towards the bank you wish to reach. You will slowly progress across in a 'ferry glide'. Ducks and other experienced river users adopt this technique.

Finally, **if you get caught up in a standing wave** at the bottom of a small watershoot or waterfall, you will be held in the water, unable to breathe, just below the surface. The only way to escape is to **swim downwards**. The water at the bottom of the standing wave (canoeists call them 'stoppers') will flush you out and allow you to surface. This is one rare situation where a life jacket may reduce your chances of escape; jettison it if you are caught in a stopper and the jacket prevents you from swimming downwards.

Some white-water rivers may be quite polluted, so keep your mouth shut when you fall in and promptly sterilize even the slightest graze with a good drying antiseptic, such as dilute iodine or *potassium permanganate* crystals dissolved in a little water.

Bilharzia (Schistosomiasis)

Napoleon called Egypt the land of menstruating men. Bilharzia was so common that mothers were said to consult doctors if their boys did not 'menstruate'. Passing blood in urine is the major symptom of one of the three kinds of Schistosomiasis.

Avoiding Bilharzia

→ If you are swimming, paddling or wading in fresh water which could carry a Bilharzia risk, try to get out of the water within 10 minutes.

→ Dry off thoroughly and vigorously with a towel.

→ Avoid bathing or paddling within 200m of villages or places where people use water, especially reedy shores or where there is lots of weed.

→ If your bathing water comes from a risky source try to ensure that it is taken from the lake in the early morning and stored snail-free; otherwise it should be filtered, or have Dettol or Cresol added to it.

→ It is safer to bathe early in the morning than during the last half of the day.

→ Cover yourself with DEET insect repellent while swimming.

→ If you have been exposed to Bilharzia arrange a blood test more than six weeks – but ideally less than 12 weeks – after your last contact with suspect water.

It is caused by a minute worm, which spends part of its life-cycle in freshwater snails and the other part in people. The parasite causes 'swimmers' itch' as it burrows through the skin while you paddle or bathe in infected water. The species that occur in Africa and the Middle East (*Schistosoma haematobium* and *S. mansoni*) and in America (*Schistosoma mansoni*) are slow penetrators. Since it takes at least 10 minutes to get through the skin, a quick splash across a suspect stream should do you no harm; vigorous towelling after bathing also kills any parasites caught in the act. Unfortunately, oriental Schistosomiasis (*Schistosoma japonicum*) penetrates within a few minutes and is a much nastier parasite altogether.

From the skin, the worm rides the bloodstream, traverses the lungs – where it often causes coughs 2–3 weeks after the swimmers' itch – and finally sets up home to cause an illness with fever. If left untreated, this will settle, but over years, and fired by further infections, this disease

Case History: Malawi

Bilharzia is a growing concern for travellers to Africa. Many lakes, rivers and irrigation canals carry a risk of infection if people swim, wade or even shower in contaminated water. Blood tests on Malawi expatriates show that two-thirds of them have been exposed to Bilharzia, and in 1995 there was an outbreak in a group of people scuba diving off Cape Clear in Lake Malawi for only a week; three-quarters of them acquired the disease. Diving off a boat into deep off-shore water should be a low-risk activity, but showering in lake water or paddling along a reedy shore near a village is high-risk for catching Bilharzia. This was how the divers became ill.

becomes debilitating, and it can kill after a couple of decades. Travellers are mostly diagnosed and cured in a couple of months; the real sufferers are the poor, who are repeatedly infected and have no access to treatment. A single dose of *praziquantel* cures Bilharzia at present, but drug resistance may be developing. Avoidance is better than cure: avoid bathing in high-risk areas.

'Swimmers' itch' is even an occasional problem in Britain; schistosomes penetrate the skin, but are unable to complete their life-cycle. An example is *Trichobilharzia* of Loch Lomond, which causes mild, short-lived itching and needs no treatment.

Bilharzia country

Bilharzia snails like well-oxygenated, still or slowly moving freshwater with some plant life in it. The snails must first be infected by someone who has the disease urinating or defecating into the water; the risk of infection is therefore greatest in water that is close (less than 100m) to human settlements. Bilharzia is a growing problem in some irrigated areas, mainly in Africa; some criticize irrigation projects for causing epidemics, but projects that are properly built do not cause problems.

The disease afflicts perhaps 200 million people worldwide (*see* map below), and is prevalent in much of Africa including Madagascar and Mauritius. It also occurs in the Middle East and the tropical Americas (NE Brazil, the Guianas, Surinam, Venezuela and some Caribbean Islands). The Indian subcontinent is clear except for a tiny area in Maharashtra. The oriental form has a patchy distribution: it occurs in parts of China, Taiwan, Vietnam and the Philippines, but Indonesia is free of it except for two remote valleys in central Sulawesi. Bilharzia is never acquired from sea bathing.

Risk areas: Bilharzia (Schistosomiasis)

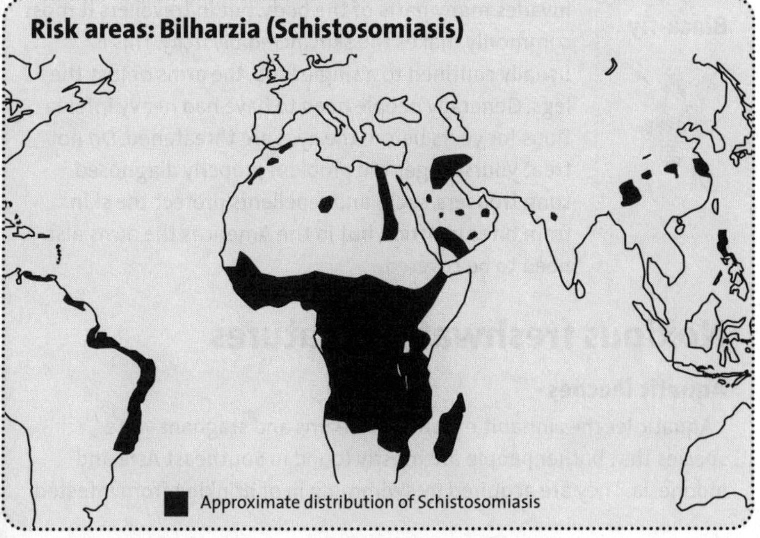

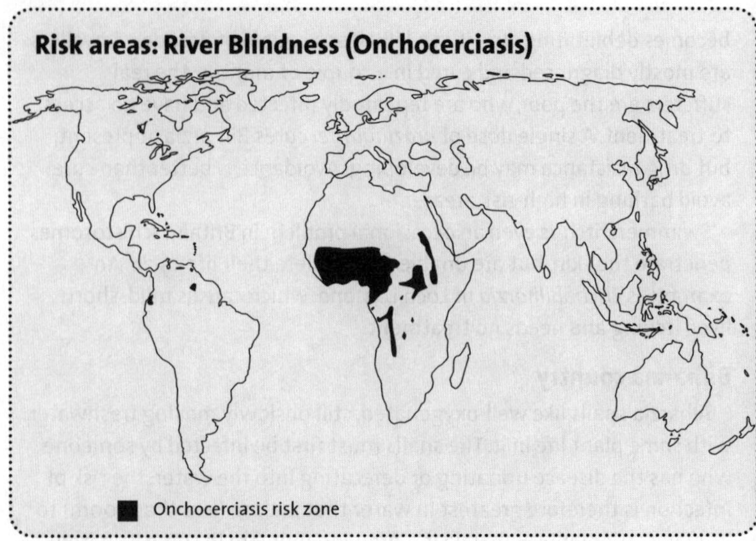

Black-flies and River Blindness (Onchocerciasis)

River Blindness is a problem in much of tropical sub-Saharan Africa, between 19°N and 17°S, and in central and tropical South America (*see* map above). The unpleasant worm is transmitted near to fast-flowing rivers where small black-fly vectors breed. These *Simulium damnosum* are a nuisance even in regions (like Asia) where River Blindness is absent; their bites cause big lumps in the skin with a bloody speck at the centre, and are itchy for days. Black-flies bite during the day.

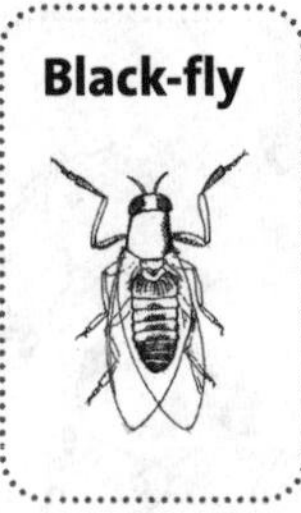

The disease has a variety of manifestations, since it invades many parts of the body, but in travellers it most commonly makes the skin incredibly itchy. This is usually confined to a single limb, the arms or just the legs. Generally people need to have had heavy infestations for years before the eyes are threatened. Do not treat yourself; get the problem properly diagnosed. Long trousers, socks and repellents protect the skin from bites in Africa, but in the Americas the arms also need to be covered.

Noxious freshwater creatures

Aquatic leeches

Aquatic leeches inhabit mountain streams and stagnant water; species that bother people are mostly found in Southeast Asia and Indonesia. They are acquired by swimming in or drinking from infested streams or pools, so drink only boiled or filtered water. Some are slow feeders and stay attached for weeks. If one invades a body orifice (this is enormously rare in travellers) it will probably have to be removed in hospital, but complications are unlikely. If a leech is attached inside the mouth, throat or nose, gargle or sniff a strong salt solution.

Candiru (*Vandellia cirrhosa*)

If you urinate in South American rivers, there is a fish, it is said, that follows the stream to its source, swims inside, sticks out barbed fins and stays put. It can then only be removed surgically, perhaps by penile amputation. The tiny candiru (also called the Carnero fish) is 40–60mm long (1–2 inches) and only 4–6mm broad. It is known to embed itself inside the gills of other fish; the tale of it parasitizing man seems to be a myth.

Crocodiles

Crocodiles are merciless killers, taking about 1,000 lives a year worldwide. New World crocodilians seem to be less dangerous: most deaths are due to the Nile crocodile (*Crocodilus niloticus*) in Africa (including Madagascar) and the saltwater crocodile (*see* above, p.180) in Asia and Australia. The mugger crocodile (*Crocodilus palustris*) of the Indian subcontinent is said not to be aggressive, but in Sri Lanka, in 1988, the remains of a man were found in one very big mugger living in a freshwater reservoir.

Crocodiles usually hunt victims who are drinking (or washing) at the waterside. The reptile speeds towards the riverbank and, just as it is about to run aground, launches itself at its lunch, exploding out of the water unexpectedly. The only hope for escape is to attack the animal's eyes, its only vulnerable spot. Even if you have a Crocodile Dundee knife to hand you will not be able to sink it through its thick skull.

Freshwater stingrays

Freshwater stingrays of South America are very unpleasant and can inflict severe wounds. Avoidance and treatment are as for saltwater rays (*see* above, p.182).

Piranhas

Piranhas have a nasty reputation stemming originally from a fanciful account written by Theodore Roosevelt. Most species are nearly exclusively vegetarian, while others daintily nibble the ends off fins or scales of other fish. Reliable reports of human deaths are lacking, but the occasional aquarist has been injured by a pet piranha, and their sharp teeth are used by Indians as razor blades. Larger members of the *Serrasalmus* genus may possibly threaten someone who has been injured or otherwise weakened; this is only likely if the piranhas' natural food is scarce, if they have been provoked by waste being dumped in their river, or if they are trapped in a receding pool just before the rains. Most are about 20cm (eight inches) long; the largest piranhas reach 60cm (two feet). They are not the peril of South American rivers that Roosevelt and other tale-tellers make them out to be.

Electric eels and fish

Electric eels and fish are a hazard in tropical South America and a few rivers in West Africa. Camaroonian electric fish can cause unconsciousness and South American eels have been reported to be able to stun a horse. Take local advice, and send the horse in ahead of you when making river crossings.

Water scorpions

Some **true bugs** live in fresh water in temperate and tropical regions (backswimmers and water scorpions). They have a surprisingly painful bite for their size, but do not usually bite unprovoked. There is an exception: the giant *Belostomatidae* water bugs from the Guianas can reach lengths of 10cm, and can inflict deep, painful wounds. They sometimes attack swimmers, and so have the common name of 'toe-biters'.

Infections

Itching can be a problem after bathing in polluted waters, and there are at least two nasty bacterial illnesses – ***Leptospirosis*** (Weil's disease; *see* p.212) and ***Shigella*** (bacillary dysentery, *see* p.115) – that can get you if you swallow water while swimming, white-water canoeing, etc. **Hepatitis A** may also be acquired this way. If you suspect water is contaminated, try to stay in moving water, and keep your mouth closed while swimming.

On The Ground

High, Cold and Dark

14

The biggest hazard when venturing into the mountains, caves or other cold, hostile environments, is an accident, and it is the poorly prepared and inexperienced who are most likely to fall or injure themselves. And, once injured, cold and remoteness can be responsible for taking life. Preparations, adequate clothing and footwear, and a little fitness training will contribute to the success of any trip. Anyone planning to ascend above 3,000m or 10,000ft should read enough on altitude sickness to recognize the symptoms and know what to do about it.

Summary

➜ Many accidents in hostile environments arise from poor planning and research, and/or being poorly equipped.

➜ Get the right clothes and footwear for the environments you are exploring.

➜ In cold conditions, wearing wet socks can easily lead to frostbite. Carry spares.

➜ Remember sunscreens may be necessary even in cold conditions.

➜ Check possible threats from unseasonal weather from local sources.

➜ Above 3,000m (10,000ft) be careful about altitude illness, and descend immediately if anyone's health is deteriorating. Do not try to ascend too rapidly.

➜ When venturing high, it is best to be in the company of people you know, so that if someone begins to act strangely you will realize that they are developing high-altitude cerebral oedema.

➜ Many deaths in mountains are due to falls and accidents: take care.

➜ Exposure and frostbite hit poorly equipped travellers: take precautions.

➜ Any limb that has suffered cold injury, or even chilblains, should be rewarmed gently; rubbing is damaging.

➜ Do not venture into the dark zone of caves unless you are an experienced caver with reliable lights that will last for 10 hours.

➜ If entering tropical bat caves ask locals about them first and consider the risk of Histoplasmosis.

➜ Trek with a small first-aid kit. And take enough socks so that you can change them whenever they get wet.

HAZARDS IN THE MOUNTAINS

More and more people are venturing high. About 50,000 trekkers a year visit Nepal alone, and during the trekking season more than 50 people a day cross the Thorong La (a 5,400m/17,700ft pass) near Annapurna. Most of these people have little or no mountaineering experience. This section comprises tips for people who are going to altitudes up to 6,000m (20,000ft), but who are not experienced mountaineers and may not have done much mountain walking at lower altitudes. High altitude trips (above 6,000m) need specialist advice and training. Consider attending a course at an approved centre; this will also give you a chance to try out or break in any new equipment.

Trekking in the Andes or Himalayas combines all the problems of hill walking, plus special altitude risks compounded by the challenge of limited facilities. Sedentary individuals who decide to take up trekking should start slowly. Fitness makes for a more enjoyable trip; even doing just 100 step-ups on a chair each day will strengthen all-important thigh muscles. It is easy to be misled by conditions in the mountains: bright clear skies and warming sunshine make foul weather seem an impossibility, so people get caught out. Of 148,000 trekkers who visited Nepal over three and a half years, 23 died, mostly by falling off cliff paths, and there were 111 helicopter rescues, many for cases of simple exhaustion. Deaths from altitude illnesses are now fewer than some years ago, and it is accidents that take the most lives. Between 1993 and 1997 there were 23 notified deaths of British citizens in Nepal; nine were from accidents, eight from natural causes (mostly heart attacks), four due to altitude illnesses and two to filth-to-mouth diseases. A surprising number of visitors are pushed off cliff paths by pack animals: always stand on the uphill side of the path if you meet a yak or mule, and they will walk around you.

Allow enough time. Rushing makes any trip miserable and exposes you to altitude illnesses, injury and accidents. Nor do you see as much. Only half of the trekkers who set out intending to walk to Everest base camp actually arrive. The others turn back, disappointed, having run out of time and having found themselves unable to cover the distance they expected because of sickness and the strenuous nature of the trek. In Nepal, particularly, you do not need to rush up to great heights to see extraordinary things; lower altitudes are just as interesting, and there are often fewer tourists.

Who should not ascend?

Not many medical conditions impose an absolute ban on climbing to high altitude, but there are two: **sickle cell disease**, and a propensity to recurrent **pneumothorax** (burst lung). It is probably unwise to climb above 3,500m (12,000ft) when pregnant. Those who have had laser surgery for short sight (radial keratotomy) may experience dramatic changes in their vision, sufficient to render them functionally blind, at altitudes over 15,000ft (*see* below, **Snow Blindness**, p.198).

The right way to walk

Walk with a steady rhythm, and pace yourself so that you do not need frequent rests; you should be able to keep going all day. If you have to stop for breath or pause because you are tired more often than five minutes each hour you are trying to walk too fast. Go at your own pace, enjoy the scenery and don't try to keep up with macho show-offs. At altitude (e.g. above 4,000m) trekkers need to make a conscious effort to walk slower than their natural rhythm suggests. This is not easy. When forced to walk slowly by shortness of breath, it is important to slow down even further.

Taking proper care of your feet is also, naturally, of the utmost importance. The lightest possible footwear is most comfortable in mountains. Unless you are going very high or expect to be walking in snow, almost any robust, comfortable shoes will suffice, but a big range of trekking shoes, boots and socks is available. Take specialist advice on the best shoes for your particular trip and, whatever you wear, ensure they are comfortable before you go. Remember that many waterproof climbing boots need to be dried out every evening: they do not 'breathe' like leather boots.

Case History: Nepal

Trekking during the monsoon, I walked some of the way with a Nepali. While scrambling down a landslide, I slipped and scraped my knee. When my new acquaintance saw the dribbling blood, he suggested slapping on a handful of a scruffy little weed with blue flowers. He scrunched them up a little and applied the poultice. Not only did the graze stop bleeding immediately, it didn't get infected; yet wounds always go rotten in the monsoon.

I looked the plant up later and discovered that it is called *Stachys* or woundwort. A very similar plant grows on English lawns and heaths.

Simon Howarth

Change your socks whenever they get wet, especially in snow, as it's very easy to get frost nip without realizing it. Remove footwear when crossing rivers: wet boots are more likely to rub and cause blisters. If a stiff pair of boots is giving you trouble, try the old technique of wearing two pairs of socks (one thick, one thin) to reduce friction and blisters. Any broken skin must be carefully cleaned and incipient patches of infection treated (by soaking feet in hot salty water) before bacteria have a chance to get a hold. Do not puncture blisters: pad them with sticking plaster or moleskin cut into a doughnut shape. Big toenails easily 'ingrow' and become infected. To avoid this, cut the nails straight across: leave sharp corners and do not round them off. Keep other nails short. For advice on **Athlete's Foot** and **cracked heels**, *see* p.225.

'Sahib's Knee' and other walkers' problems

In the days of the Raj British administrators often pranged their knees visiting the hills. They got '**Sahib's Knee**'. Sahibs and tourists sustain knee injuries because of unfitness and poor walking technique. Walking down is more strenuous than climbing, and requires more awareness of technique. Fatigue makes people step down onto a straight leg. This jolts the knee joint. To protect the knee and develop a controlled walking rhythm, you need to step down onto a slightly bent knee. The muscles and tendons of the thigh then absorb the repeated impacts. It is hard to do this for long if you are unfit – and you risk injury. Stop when you are no longer able to take your weight on a slightly flexed knee, and rest overnight before long descents. Many trekkers find poles very helpful when walking down, and they are especially useful if anyone in your group is in difficulties and needs to be supported.

The **treatment** for knee injuries and other strains and wrenches is rest. If you must continue walking, reduce your daily distance considerably and, if possible, employ someone to carry your pack. Tight strapping with a crêpe or ace bandage will help, although crêpe bandages need to be washed frequently to retain their stretchiness. The treatment of wrenches, sprains and sore joints is dealt with on pp.302–3.

Some **swelling of the feet**, **ankles** and **lower legs** (oedema) is common in mountain walkers even at low altitudes, especially if they are overweight. So long as you continue to feel well this is no cause for concern. If the swelling becomes uncomfortable, rest with your feet above heart height. If it is accompanied by pain or illness seek medical help, if possible; certainly do not go any higher, but descend at a gentle pace.

COLD, WIND CHILL AND OTHER ASPECTS OF MOUNTAIN WEATHER

In the low temperatures that prevail at altitude it is easy to get seriously cold. Chilling happens most quickly if conditions are windy and/or you are wet. Carry a change of clothes packed in a plastic bag. Mittens protect the hands better than gloves (and carry spares, since mitts often get lost). The skin can also become uncomfortably dry and scaly even at modest altitude, but particularly in the high, cold deserts of the Andes or Transhimalaya. Pack moisturizing cream, as well as sun cream and lip-screen to protect you from the sun. If you have no moisturizer, use butter or some other locally available cooking grease. Equally, nosebleeds are common in high, dry climates. Prevent them by anointing the inside of the nose with a greasy non-perfumed cream such as petroleum jelly, Vaseline, emulsifying ointment or even yak butter or cooking oil.

Mountaineers and trekkers walking in snow will know to protect themselves from the sun with sunscreen and goggles but it is also possible to get sunburned inside the nose from sun reflected up off the snow if sunscreen isn't applied there too.

For the effects and treatment of **frostbite** and **exposure**, *see* pp.206–9.

There have been a few deaths from mountaineers being poisoned with **carbon monoxide** from butane stoves left burning in badly ventilated tents all night in order to keep out the cold. Others have been burned alive. Beware.

Fluid loss

The body loses more fluid at altitude and in windy conditions, so you must make a conscious effort to drink more. With any fever, diarrhoea or bad sunburn you need more again. Thirst is no guide to whether you are drinking enough.

Effects of the sun at altitude

In Ladakh (where winter daytime temperatures can be -20°C), it is supposedly possible to get sunstroke and frostbite simultaneously, by lying with your feet in the shade and your head in the sun. It is easy to get sunburned despite the cold; even dark-skinned people need to wear sunscreen, suitable clothing and a hat. The sun may provoke cold sores, if you are prone to them (*see* p.167).

Case History: the Himalayas

It was winter in Ladakh, and the temperature during the day was −10°C. I met two Frenchmen who had wandered to the wrong side of a 5,300m/17,500ft pass. When they set out, the sun was bright and warming despite sub-zero temperatures. They had no packs or spare clothes, so that when the weather closed in unexpectedly they narrowly escaped getting into serious trouble.

In East Nepal, four tourists ventured high in good weather dressed only in sandals and summer clothes. There was then an unseasonal snowstorm, and had they not found a hut in which to spend the night they would all have died. In the morning, the least frostbitten of the group struggled down for help and they all made it to safety – minus a few toes.

Snow blindness

Nepalis describe snow blindness as like having your eyeballs rubbed in a mixture of chilli and sand. It is painful and disabling. This most frequently occurs at altitude and in snow. It is dangerous because it temporarily blinds in a situation where you may need to see to stay alive. The right treatment is to cover the eyes (tape them closed if it's bad) and descend to recover. Cold compresses may help the pain.

Snow blindness is prevented by filtering out UV radiation with good quality (expensive) glacier goggles; sunglasses aren't good enough. Poor Nepalis protect their eyes by tying on a strip of cloth with slits cut for them to see through.

Another form of temporary blindness, which has been recognized recently, happens in climbers who have undergone a radial keratotomy laser operation for short sight. Altitude temporarily alters the shape of the eyeballs, resulting in extreme long-sightedness that renders the victim unable to perform many tasks. This has led to at least one climber being left for dead and getting badly frostbitten on Everest.

Disturbed sleep: Periodic (Cheyne-Stokes) Respiration

When people first climb high they often sleep poorly. Some are woken up by a nightmare feeling of being suffocated. During sleep, breathing becomes progressively slower and shallower until it actually stops for a few seconds; then there is a deep sigh and breathing restarts, sometimes waking the sleeper. This is alarming to witness, because as you lie in the darkness you begin to wonder whether your friend is ever going to start breathing again. Then, when you're just about to struggle across to shake them back to consciousness, a deep sighing inspiration starts them breathing again. This is normal in people newly arrived at altitude, and is no cause for concern. *Acetazolamide* (*see* below, pp.204–5) speeds up acclimatization and reduces sleep disturbance.

ALTITUDE ILLNESSES

Mountains kill a lot of people. One-tenth of mountaineers who climb above 6,000m (20,000ft) on serious expeditions die. Yet most of those who are killed in the mountains are not on expeditions: they include many tourists and visitors in the Himalayan region, the Andes, on Mount Kilimanjaro and Mount Kenya. Although falls and other accidents are the major killers, ignorance about mountain sickness makes a significant contribution to the risks and is another important reason why people die in the high ranges.

In South America it is called *soroché*, in Nepal, *aye-lagio*; whatever you call it, mountain sickness is frightening and can kill. Mountain illnesses have been known for a long time. Chinese travellers in 35 BC described the Himalayas as the 'Headache Mountains'. The symptoms, though, are unpredictable and the disease complex, and still not completely understood. Altitude illnesses are caused by an imbalance of acid and alkali in the blood; this affects breathing controls that normally maintain fluid balances in the body. You need to breathe faster at altitude to take in enough oxygen from the thinner air, but initially the drive to breathe lags behind the body's need for oxygen. When oxygen supplies to the brain are not maintained, headaches and confusion begin. The headache is a sign that the brain is swelling. The imbalance can also allow fluid to build up in the lungs, which causes breathlessness and coughing and can lead to death by drowning.

With sensible rates of ascent, though, and adaptation to altitude over a few days, other longer-term mechanisms switch in: enzyme and hormone changes that allow breathing to settle back to a slower rate. This is acclimatization.

Bad headache, disorientation and breathlessness (especially if associated with coughing up frothy or even bloodstained spit) are signs of severe, dangerous problems. These can lead very rapidly to death. The treatment is to descend at once. Going down as little as 500m can be sufficient to save someone's life, but descend as far as you can or until the victim is clearly well again. It is rare to be in a situation where you have to ascend before descending, so most deaths are unnecessary.

Altitude illnesses are dangerous because they can come on rapidly, and do not necessarily progress from milder mountain sickness. The early symptoms are non-specific, and the victims are often too disorientated to recognize how sick they are; they may even argue about descending, or can be too apathetic to help themselves. Overruling them can be difficult, but may save lives. Do not wait until morning to see if the victim feels better. If in doubt, descend.

Diagnosing significant altitude illness

Assume any illness at altitude is altitude sickness – especially if it keeps getting worse. And 'treat' significant illness with descent. If the problem reveals itself as another disease you will happier to be closer to home and medical help. Several doctors have produced guidelines for diagnosing mountain illnesses to help decide when descent is necessary, but the symptoms of severe altitude illness so often overlap with other common problems of mountain walkers that none is foolproof.

Symptoms of mild AMS (Acute Mountain Sickness)

➜ Poor performance.
➜ Slight headache.
➜ Fatigue.
➜ Chest discomfort.
➜ Insomnia.
➜ Loss of appetite.
➜ Nausea.
➜ Vomiting.

Action: watch out for increasingly severe symptoms. If you are planning to go higher consider stopping for a rest day and acclimatization. Descend to sleep lower down if possible, or dramatically slow your ascent. Ascend no further until the headache gets better.

Symptoms of moderate to severe altitude illness

Severe altitude illness may not necessarily lead on from mild AMS, but can cause rapid deterioration over a couple of hours 'out of the blue'. Only some of the listed symptoms will be present.

➜ Mood changes.
➜ Severe headache.*
➜ Disorientation.
➜ Confusion* and memory loss.
➜ Strange behaviour.*
➜ Difficulty with balance, stumbling, acting drunk, etc.*
➜ Hallucinations.*
➜ Drowsiness (person is difficult to wake up).*
➜ Severe nightmares.
➜ Unwarranted breathlessness, perhaps even at rest (compared with companions).*
➜ Nausea and vomiting.
➜ Severe fatigue.
➜ Dry cough, frothy spit and even bloodstained spit.*

Note: symptoms marked * are very worrying and should precipitate immediate descent, whatever the time of day or night.

Action: descend at once.

Lists of symptoms are also less useful than deciding whether someone looks ill or not. Headache is worrying, and weird or uncharacteristic behaviour can also be warning symptoms. There are no signs (except perhaps frothy or bloodstained spit) that are especially characteristic of severe altitude illness. It can be difficult to differentiate, say, dehydration and exhaustion from mountain illness: both can cause headache, dizziness, confusion and nausea, but if there is any doubt, the wise action to take is always to descend. People who are suffering from mountain illnesses should improve dramatically with descent. Diagnosis in children is even more difficult; pay close attention to any complaints.

Treatment of altitude illnesses

Descent is the only treatment for significant mountain illness. If in doubt, descend while the victim can still walk rather than waiting, as the wait may mean having to evacuate someone who is unconscious or uncooperative after dark. Go down as far as you possibly can. Repressurization bags (the **Gamow** weighs 8kg/18lb) are no substitute for descent, and if using them delays going down it may actually do more harm than good. I have been horrified to hear of people suffering bad enough altitude illness to be repressurized in a bag and then, once 'cured', continuing to ascend. This is dangerous.

The headache of mild AMS can be treated in adults (not children, who should descend, *see* pp.202–3) with *acetazolamide*, in a 'loading dose' of 750mg (three tablets) for small adults (less than 60kg/125lb) or 1,000mg (four tablets) for large people, then 500mg daily. AMS headache will respond in a few hours; do not climb higher if you still have a headache. If someone appears to be 'drunk' and disorientated, *dexamethasone* (8mg, then 4mg six-hourly) may help enough for them to walk down; similarly, if someone is having severe trouble breathing, *nifedipine* (20mg slow release six-hourly) should improve their condition enough that they can be evacuated. None of these drugs is an alternative to descent.

If you have to descend, breathe out by puffing against pursed lips. This increases air pressure in the lungs, and acts as a kind of short-term repressurization technique. It also gives someone who is feeling awful something on which to focus their attention.

Who is at risk from altitude illness?

At greatest risk are those who arrive at altitude by plane, helicopter, train or bus, and then climb further without acclimatizing. Lhasa in Tibet (at 3,658m), Cusco in Peru (at 3,415m) and La Paz in Bolivia (at 3,625m) are dangerous: tourists fly in and expect to ascend the next day. Similarly, in Peru you can ascend from Lima to nearly 5,000m (16,400ft) by train in half a day. Sleeping at the lowest possible altitude helps protect from altitude illnesses. Mount Kenya, at just over 5,199m (16,400ft), is not particularly high, but it kills people: the first day's climbing takes you to 3,000m, and on the second day there is a 1,300m climb to the second refuge. People feeling bad at the second refuge should go back to sleep in Refuge One, and continue when they feel better. Kilimanjaro, at 5,895m/19,340ft, is one of the highest mountains climbed by ordinary tourists without technical mountaineering skills, and is also dangerous.

The fitter you are the faster you can ascend, so the more likely you are to suffer from mountain illness. Clearly, though, there are other risks if you are unfit. Mountain illnesses are unpredictable. If you have escaped once you may suffer the next time you ascend, and if you suffered once it does not mean you will suffer every time, although it probably does indicate a propensity. It is impossible to give absolute rules about when a climb or walk must be slowed down or abandoned, but if there is any doubt, descent – or at least taking an extra day to acclimatize – is the wise course. In some regions, immediate rapid descent may not be possible. This might happen (e.g. in the Himalayas) if you have climbed over a ridge and then come down with the intention of camping in a relatively high valley. Thus you would need to ascend before you could lose any significant amount of height. Or, if you are exploring the Andean *altiplano* on local buses or trucks, you may find that a lift is just not available when you need to descend. When over 3,000m (10,000ft), it is vital that you plan an escape route in case one of your group is struck by mountain sickness. If you or a companion seems to have early symptoms, ascent must be slowed and plans changed.

Drinking alcohol at altitude

It is unwise to imbibe large quantities of strong alcohol at altitude. It tends to exacerbate broken sleep and, if the drinker is already suffering mountain sickness to some degree, it reduces the drive to breathe to a dangerous level. It will also contribute to poor performance while trekking, as well as increasing the dehydration caused by altitude. That is not to say it is necessary to be teetotal when in the mountains, but if you are already feeling 'rough' because of altitude, don't drink spirits as a cure. Be wary too of locally distilled spirits: *pisco* is of vary variable quality and *raksi* is fermented and distilled anything. Maize brews have the worst hangover potential, while the connoisseurs say that the best *raksi* is made from millet: even this is fairly toxic.

Altitude sickness in children

There are several issues to consider when trekking with children. Most parents worry about mountain illness, but as you climb high it also becomes difficult to keep small children warm (*see* p.206) and they get bored, too, if mountain lassitude sets in. I have done 12 treks to modest altitude with children from the age of three months, and I would advise against taking young children above 3,000m (10,000ft). Even at this altitude you must be meticulously cautious; you must know what you are doing and be prepared to descend rapidly at short notice. The younger the child, the more careful you must be, as it can be very easy to overlook significant altitude illness in an infant. Experts in mountain medicine caution against going above 2,000m with children under two; in any case, small children enjoy treks better if you stay well below 10,000ft; there is more to entertain them and the climate is kinder. Children must not be given *acetazolamide*; descend even if symptoms of AMS are mild.

Case History: Kanchenjunga base camp

Four of us, walking together over a couple of weeks, had got up to 5,000m. We felt well at this altitude, made two trips to around 5,400m, then decided to climb a 6,200m peak. As we began this ascent there was an argument about the route; Alan was uncharacteristically short-tempered, but finally we went on up with Alan striding strongly ahead. From a vantage point on a ridge we realized that next we had to descend a difficult scree slope to reach our first campsite at the foot of a glacier. I arrived first; the others straggled in over the next hour, Rick carrying Alan's pack and, last of all, Alan supported by Gill. It was 3.30pm and we were at 5,500m. Alan was cold, had a headache and was exhausted. Rest, painkillers and hot soup did not revive him but the prospect of descent was horrendous. Alan's headache got worse; then he vomited and became confused. I forced him to get up and was shocked to see him staggering like a drunk. He clearly had cerebral oedema. It was 5pm but I knew that we must descend. I gave him 8mg of *dexamethasone* and 1,000mg of *acetazolamide* but he vomited the tablets.

We headed down a steep gully, with two people at a time taking turns to support Alan, trying to keep him upright. It was soon pitch dark with a thick mist and no moon. Our progress was excruciatingly slow, managing barely 20 metres between rests, while Alan's breathing was growing weaker. Whenever he sat down, he fell asleep immediately. I gave him more *dexamethasone* which he kept down, but it didn't seem to help. Fortunately, we were able to radio friends at base camp and at 9.30pm we met a rescue party. They brought oxygen and injectable *dexamethasone*. By 11.40pm we had all reached the valley, low enough to save Alan. Had we stayed at 5,500m he would not have survived.

In retrospect it is easy to see that we should have started down again as soon as we'd reached camp, but we were tired and conditions were difficult. Alan's moodiness was uncharacteristic and alarm bells should ring when a fit man suddenly becomes disproportionately exhausted. And, since we ascended at more than the recommended rate of 300m a day, we also might have expected trouble.

Dr Mark Howarth, GP in West Sussex

Avoiding altitude illnesses

Mountain illnesses are generally only a problem in adults above 3,000m (10,000ft), but some have died of it even at this modest altitude. The only way to avoid it is to allow plenty of time for acclimatization and, if you notice any symptoms, stop or at least slow down your ascent. A recommended safe rate of ascent is to take several days to reach 3,500m (11,000ft), then a further week to reach 5,500m (18,000ft). This gives an average of about 300m per day, but take rest days and – as always – pace yourself according to the slowest member of the party. Even at this rate not everyone is able to go high. Many people are too impatient to ascend at this rate, or it may be that the terrain or the need to reach accommodation makes it difficult to slow down. If you exceed the recommended rate watch carefully for danger signs. Be especially cautious on a first ascent, or if you have had problems before. Even at recommended rates, half of trekkers suffer symptoms of mild to moderate AMS (headache, poor appetite, nausea). Some people are inexplicably sensitive to even slow rates of ascent.

Local advice on mountain illness may be misleading. Local guides and porters who live at intermediate altitude may not realize how much more susceptible foreigners are to these problems. Conversely, with increasing numbers of tourists there are greater opportunities for inexperienced lowlanders, who may know less about the hazards than you do, to work as porters. Some die each year from altitude problems. Take responsibility to ensure that porters you employ directly or indirectly are properly equipped (with shoes, jumpers, blankets, shelter) and watched. Headaches should probably be treated with *acetazolamide* (*see* p.201), rather than painkillers. Allow time for rest if porters flag; they will feel they cannot rest however ill they are.

Some trekking agencies proudly announce that they can arrange Gamow bags (*see* p.201) for treating altitude sickness; it is worth asking why they feel this is often necessary: does it indicate poor planning on their part, and/or slowness to descend when symptoms begin? Ask agencies what they know about altitude illness, and what they might do in hypothetical problem situations.

Prevention of altitude illnesses with medicines

The benefits of taking *acetazolamide* tablets to hasten acclimatization are debated. It increases oxygen availability to the brain in the critical first few days at altitude, which helps the traveller until longer-term mechanisms take over. It reduces the headache, nausea and insomnia that bother many people above 3,000m (10,000ft), and is therefore excellent if you are ascending rapidly to altitudes of 3,000–4,500m by vehicle and cannot slow down your ascent. The argument against it is that it may encourage people to go higher faster and less safely. It is not an alternative to descent in cases of severe mountain illness (especially when symptoms seem to be getting worse). Symptoms more serious than headache or disturbed sleep warrant descent.

My late friend and colleague Tony White ran a test during our expedition to 4,000m in the Andes. Some of us took *acetazolamide* and others a lookalike placebo. Those of us taking the drug felt better, slept better and had more stamina on caving trips, and our ability to perform psychological tests was much better; unlike those taking placebo, our judgement was as good as at sea level. Clear thinking can be vital in mountains, so I am a fan of *acetazolamide*. Other drugs (*benzolamide*) against altitude illnesses may also become available. *Acetazolamide* cannot be given to children.

Acetazolamide is only available on prescription in the UK (and, like any drug provided for foreign travel, will not be covered by the NHS); a private prescription costs about £10/$16 for 100 tablets of 250mg. It is available over the counter in some pharmacies in Nepal, for about one UK penny a tablet. Take two 250mg tablets or 'sustets' in the morning, beginning three days before ascent and continuing for two more days at altitude. Assuming you try the medicine before ascent (a two-day trial several weeks beforehand is wise, to make sure you are not prone to intolerable side effects), each traveller needs a minimum of 14 tablets.

Side effects of *acetazolamide*

It is unusual for people to notice any dramatic reactions but, like all drugs, *acetazolamide* has side effects. Those who are allergic to sulpha antibiotics or medicines are likely to be allergic to *acetazolamide* as well, and should not take it. If you take it as a trial several weeks before ascent you will be forewarned of any unpleasant reaction. The most common side effect is tingling of the hands and feet, occasionally sufficiently annoying to make people want to stop taking the medicine; missing one or two doses should solve the problem. *Acetazolamide* is also a diuretic, so be prepared to produce more urine than usual while you are taking the drug. Some people complain of taste disturbance, especially when consuming carbonated drinks.

Further information: mountain medicine

The BMC runs mountaineering courses and advises on other courses and insurance.

Himalayan Rescue Association, *www.gorge.net/hra*.

Union International des Associations d'Alpinisme, Mountain Medicine Centre, British Mountaineering Council, 177–9 Burton Road, West Didsbury, Manchester M20 2BB, **UK t** (0161) 445 4747, **f** (0161) 445 4500. Publishes information sheets on the medical aspects of mountaineering. Most are aimed at climbers; a few are for doctors.

OTHER HAZARDS IN THE MOUNTAINS

Exposure (Hypothermia)

Exposure (Hypothermia) is most likely when you are cold, wet, exhausted and hungry. As the body temperature falls, you feel inappropriately comfortable. Content, you lose the drive to get to somewhere safe. Sometimes the confusion of exposure makes people act in bizarre ways: they take off their clothes or sit in puddles. This is why it is so dangerous: people die of cold without ever realizing they are in trouble.

Heat is lost more rapidly when the body is wet or chilled by wind. Drinking alcohol also increases heat loss. Make sure you are adequately equipped for your journey. Ask about local conditions before ascent, and be prepared for the worst possible weather: in particular, ensure that everyone has adequate footwear. Wear mittens (*see* p.197). Carry a change of clothes in a plastic bag so that you can get warm and dry once you reach a safe place. The next day, change back into the previous day's sweaty, damp clothes and keep one set dry for night-time. Rest for a day and dry out if you cannot face this.

Watch the people you are walking with and be forceful if you think they are getting into trouble. Stumbling is an early warning sign. People with early exposure shiver, but this ceases as the temperature continues to fall. Exposure and altitude sickness both cloud judgement, so it is up to the unaffected to protect sufferers. They are dangerous enough in themselves, but they also make people prone to accidents, especially in combination with exhaustion. Plan carefully, and be cautious.

Children cool quickly, and are at particular risk of hypothermia if you carry them; exercise keeps you warm while they chill out. Make sure they are warmly dressed, and check often that they feel warm to the touch, especially if it is windy. If their feet and hands are cold but the trunk is warm, they are cold but coping; if their body feels as cold as their extremities the child is seriously cold and you must stop and get them warm. Children carried in backpacks by skiing parents quite often freeze to death: a handful of such deaths occur in the Alps each season.

Treating exposure

The treatment for exposure is slow, gentle rewarming. One technique is to put the victim in a sleeping bag with someone else. Making them too warm too soon can make things worse, so hot baths are not sensible (even if available), nor is alcohol. The recommended rate of rewarming the body is only by about 1°C per hour, but this can be doubled if shivering starts. This is a good sign, as it shows survival processes are returning to normal. Even so, it takes hours to rewarm someone thoroughly. Space blankets help the body to rewarm slowly and steadily, but do not work well if the wearer is lying uninsulated on the ground. Hot drinks also help in rewarming.

Action: insulate from the ground; shelter from wind; change into dry clothes.

Frostbite and cold injury

Trekkers most often get frostbitten when they try a high pass on a whim. Frostbite means that living tissue has become frozen; in deep frostbite the toes (or other members) look like a piece of chicken from the deep freeze. It is more likely at altitude (where there are high, chilling winds), at extremely low temperatures (below -10°C), if you are wet, if your boots are constricting, in those with altitude illness and in smokers. Contact with metal makes the skin more susceptible, since it conducts heat away. Beware of metal glasses or earrings in very cold conditions.

Cold injury starts as frost nip, usually of the ears, nose, cheeks, fingers, toes or chin. It makes the part numb and blanched (white/very pale), but this is entirely reversible and no damage has been done yet. As the

Case History: Chile

I was supposed to be the leader of the group but I was right at the back on the descent from seeing the lava bubbling in the crater of Volcán Villarrica. I watched the others glissading speedily down on their backsides in the snow, resisting the temptation to join in until the last one – the longest and fastest of all. In waterproof trousers it was great fun, and I then rolled over to make a perfect ice-axe self-arrest. Just as I stopped, though, a crampon spike caught the snow and something snapped! Never glissade down a volcano in crampons. Sergio, the group's real technical leader, organized the group to tow me downhill, holding hiking poles. Then, when the snow ran out, Sergio made a rope stretcher, and after wrapping me up and giving me food and water, they carried me down to a four-wheel-drive vehicle. I was in the hospital in Pucón within two hours of the accident. They thought it might just be a sprain, but plastered it anyway, and next day the X-ray showed a broken fibula. Three days later the group flew south while Sergio and I took the overnight bus to Santiago, thence to Heathrow where I used my luggage trolley and hiking pole to support me and my plastered leg as far as the bus. It was not a serious break, and two months after flying out of Chile I was back with another hiking group.

Tim Burford

skin rewarms it becomes red and tingly. If the part is not rewarmed the tissues next suffer superficial frostbite, with the surface layer actually frozen: the skin looks yellow-grey and is leathery to the touch, but the tissues underneath are still soft. On rewarming the skin is mottled with red-purple patches and some blanched areas. If freezing continues the tissues go on to suffer the most serious end of the spectrum of cold injury, deep frostbite.

Climbers will know times when their feet and hands have been numb for hours. Unfortunately, deep frostbite feels no worse; it is not painful until rewarming begins. The painlessness of frostbite makes it dangerous, as it is easy to injure a frostbitten limb and feel nothing. This is a primary reason why gangrene and infection often set in, with amputation the final result. In deep frostbite the flesh is hard, white or very pale and obviously frozen. The response should be immediate evacuation and the abandonment of a climb. Do not climb again for several months after suffering frostbite.

Treatment of frostbite

The basic treatment is evacuation to a lower, safer place (walk on the still-frozen foot if necessary); do not thaw if there is any chance of it refreezing. Once in a safe haven, rewarm the affected part by immersion in a saucepan of warm (not hot) water (40°C) for periods of 20 minutes. Deeply frostbitten skin will look mottled blue or grey. Do not knock or even rub the limb. Never immerse in hot water.

After the limb has been defrosted, the skin must be kept clean and the limb used as little as possible. The greatest danger to frostbitten skin is infection, which can enter through any small breaks in the skin. A few hours after thawing the limb swells, and over the next two days huge blisters erupt. These should be left intact; they will be reabsorbed over the next week. The frostbitten limb becomes horribly discoloured, even black and shrivelled if there is gangrene. If frostbite has been superficial, new pink skin will form under the dead shell. If there was deep frostbite the toe or fingertip will eventually, painlessly but revoltingly, fall off.

Case History: Nepal

Climbing over a high pass in Nepal, the snow was deep and wet for five days, and my boots were not as good as they should have been. I didn't really notice that my feet were always damp until we were warming up in front of a fire after we'd come down. Then the skin of my big toe and the nail slid off like a glove from a finger. It wasn't painful at the time, but it festered in the heat and became very sore on the 10-day walk to the nearest road. I wasn't carrying any dressings and the toe was smelly and infected by the time I'd hobbled to the nearest clinic.

Simon Howarth

If surgery is required, there are advantages in waiting at least a few weeks, and it is best done by a surgeon experienced in frostbite damage. Return to a hospital in the developed world if possible. A frostbitten limb suffers permanent damage that makes it more likely to be frostbitten again so, once frostbitten, twice frost-shy.

Trench (or Immersion) **Foot** was a problem in the First World War, when soldiers were cold, immobile and wet for days. The feet do not freeze, but the condition and its treatment are similar to frostbite. Recovering feet are also prone to infection.

Altitude effects on pregnancy and the contraceptive pill

Do not climb above 3,500m (12,000ft) when pregnant, and be extra careful to allow plenty of time for acclimatization. If you are trekking during the first three months of pregnancy, consider the possibility of a miscarriage (unpleasant in any circumstances) happening in a remote mountain village. The middle third of pregnancy is the best stage to be intrepid if you want to be, although there may be risks to the unborn child from long stays at high altitude. For more on travelling while pregnant, *see* **Special Travellers**, pp.72–4.

Women taking the combined contraceptive pill are theoretically at increased risk of pulmonary embolus, deep vein thrombosis and other blood clotting problems at altitude. Women climbing to extreme altitude (above 7,000m) may therefore consider stopping the pill for six weeks beforehand. In this case, don't forget to pack some condoms or try Depo-Provera or another injectable progestogen contraceptive, but start it several months before your trip (*see* 'Delaying menstruation', in **Sex**, p.240).

Avalanches and cross-country skiing

Avalanche accidents have become a major cause of injury and death even in Scotland (where wet snow and slab avalanches commonly occur). If you are going out in the hills in snow it is important to know that it is dangerous to climb in gullies or on steep, open slopes, especially convex ones, during or immediately after heavy snowfall. Most avalanche accidents happen within 24 hours of a heavy fall of snow; thereafter, snow usually settles sufficiently to reduce the danger. If out in a heavy fall of snow, keep to safe buttresses or ridges.

Most people who are killed or injured by avalanches are skiers, and true cross country skiers (not those using prepared pistes) are at the highest risk. Avalanches can occur in many kinds of terrain, even including tree-covered slopes at angles as little as 15°, and skiers have been killed by avalanches less than 20m wide and which flowed only 100m. Knowing about avalanches will protect you.

Loose snow avalanches happen when new loose snow slips off the old snow base; provided the slip is slow, these are not usually dangerous, although if the slope is long and the speed of the avalanche builds up it can develop into the next, highly dangerous kind of avalanche.

Air-borne powder avalanches occur when the flowing snow gains momentum and becomes terrifically powerful. They can travel up to 200mph, when they uproot trees, shatter buildings and sweep buses off the road.

Wet snow avalanches are most common in the spring when snow is melting. They are heavy, so that skiers trapped in them die from being crushed. However, they are rather slow, predictable beasts and can therefore be avoided by those who know the mountains.

Slab avalanches occur when a complete slab of snow breaks away; frequently they are a feature of open, grassy slopes, from snow packed by wind. Slab snow is dangerous because it slips off the underlying snow so easily, yet the smoothed nature of the snow attracts skiers – at their peril.

Avoiding avalanches

Avalanches mostly kill the reckless. Take local advice before setting out. If you choose to venture into avalanche country, travel in a party. Test any slopes by shouting and throwing stones or snowballs ahead of you and then cross one at a time. It is wise to loosen ski bindings and remove the hands from the pole loops since, in an avalanche, it is the moving snow pressing on your equipment which causes fractures. Ideally the leader should be roped to her mates or should have a length of red cord trailing behind so that if she does disappear into the snow, the cord should still be visible and will lead rescuers to her.

If caught in an avalanche, try swimming to stay near the surface. Keep your mouth closed and, as the slide slows, try to clear a space around your mouth and chest to give you room to breathe. Once the avalanche stops moving you will be unable to move and, if rescue doesn't come, suffocation will occur in less than an hour. When I asked mountain rescue experts for tips on increasing the chances of survival once buried, they all said: 'avoid the avalanche'.

Equipment should be familiar to you before you head off into the mountain wilderness on your skis and realize that tight, ill-fitting boots predispose to frostbite. Take a map and compass and make sure you know how to use them. Consider taking emergency food and a small survival pack, too.

CAVES

Caver's Lung and other hazards

Straying more than a few metres into caves takes you into absolute darkness, and it is foolish to enter unless you have reliable specialist lights. If you don't have such equipment or any caving experience, you should only visit 'show caves' with a local guide. It might surprise readers to know that exposure (also known as **Hypothermia**, *see* above) is a significant risk even in caves that are situated in reasonably warm climatic zones; this is because cavers get wet, which speeds up the loss of body heat. Flash floods are also a peril, especially in regions of high rainfall; I have seen tree trunks stranded a kilometre inside a tropical cave and dread to imagine the forces that transported them so far.

As with many hostile environments, accidents are a big risk but in addition, there are three special cave diseases: **Histoplasmosis**, **Leptospirosis** and **rabies**.

Histoplasmosis

This yeast-like fungus is as happy growing on bat or bird dung as in human lungs, so it is contracted by those venturing into enclosed spaces where a great deal of guano has been deposited. Disease is only suffered on first exposure to the fungus, and thereafter there is immunity. The illness may be quite mild or, at worst, there is fever, headache, cough and chest pains, which last between 10 days and three weeks. Usually the illness needs no treatment except *aspirin* or *paracetamol* (Tylenol). Occasionally there can be serious pneumonia and certain caves in particular regions (including Mexico and South Africa) are known by locals to be dangerous. Cavers in South Africa have worked out which caves to enter first; thus they become 'immunized' against the serious disease that they would otherwise suffer if they entered a 'malignant' cave first. **Smog masks** give some protection, by reducing the number of fungal spores inhaled, although these are uncomfortable to wear in high-humidity, tropical caves, especially if exercising hard.

Where to find *Histoplasma*

The *Histoplasma* fungus grows in soil contaminated with bird or bat dung or in accumulations of such offerings in barns, chicken houses and beneath bird roosts, as well as in caves. In the Americas it is principally a tropical microbe, although it has been found in the extreme southeast corner of Canada, in Alaska and in sub-tropical Argentina. It has been isolated in Italy but is not known to have caused disease there. It occurs in Africa, in many parts of Asia and in Australia and should probably be expected in any unsavoury-looking habitat. Fortunately, however, the risk of serious disease is very small unless you enter a small, confined space where a lot of excreta is disturbed and thus inhaled. Almost everyone who has lived in Tennessee, Kentucky and Ohio will have become naturally immune to the fungus through inhaling small quantities of spores lurking in the soil.

Leptospirosis

This infection, which is also known as Weil's disease, most often comes from rat (or bat) pee. Infection can arise from drinking infected water, via a skin scratch, or it can get in across the membranes of the nose or eyes in swimmers or sump-divers. Cavers should therefore wear sufficent clothes to protect them from abrasions. The illness begins abruptly with high fever, headache, chills, vomiting, diarrhoea, muscle aches and reddening of the eyes. It responds to penicillin and *doxycycline* antibiotics. Those taking *doxycycline* as malaria prophylactic should also be protected from Leptospirosis. The illness can be quite serious, so if it is suspected, get it properly diagnosed and treated.

Rabies, bats and caves

Rabies is the scariest and nastiest of the cave-related infections, and like the other two cave-related infections is transmitted via unpleasant media: bat urine and saliva. Large numbers of bats roost in tropical caves and they often carry rabies. In a high-humidity cave atmosphere, it is possible to catch rabies just by inhaling contaminated cave air. There have been two deaths in the Americas in people who had entered bat caves but who had no direct contact with rabid animals. Anyone entering caves in the Americas should be immunized against rabies (*see* **Immunizations**, pp.47–8; for more on rabies, including the common route of infection, *see* **Animals**, pp.265–8).

Other animal hazards in caves

Caves may be cool refuges for troublesome or dangerous animals, so be particularly careful of what you find inside, especially if you are merely sheltering from the sun or taking a discreet leak. Hornets commonly build nests in cave entrances and you are likely to get stung if they decide you are a threat. Big animals, including large carnivores, also shelter in caves: I've found fresh puma prints in a cave in Peru. In northern Madagascar, large, hungry Nile crocodiles take refuge in the caves of Ankarana during the dry season. Caves can be home to snakes, too. Even something as small as a European badger would be quite formidable if you encountered it face to face in a low passage. If cave entrances are used by cattle or other mammals to shelter from the heat, they could also be places to pick up a tick.

On The Ground

Skin

15

Skin infections are common in travellers to hot, moist climates and regions where it is difficult to keep clean. Sunburn is one very common but avoidable affliction; ***Slip, Slap, Slop*** precautions for avoiding sunburn and its treatment are given on pp.164–7. Body-piercing, acupuncture and tattooing can give you hepatitis B or HIV if needles are improperly sterilized. Beware.

Summary

→ In warm climates, bathe even the smallest wounds in a good, drying antiseptic.

→ Use repellent and long clothes; bites go septic fast in hot, moist climates.

→ In hot climates it is best to wear loose, 100% cotton underwear.

→ Wear shoes, sandals or flip-flops as much as possible: bare feet are prone to injury and they invite parasites and fungal infections.

→ A washcloth/face flannel is an indispensable aid to washing essentials (crutch, armpits, beneath the breasts) when it's cold or there is little privacy.

→ A sarong, too, aids modest bathing.

SKIN INFECTION

The skin is very prone to infection in hot, moist climates and filthy environments. Even the slightest cut or abrasion allows bacteria in, causing infections which can be difficult to cure – especially in the rainy season. Mosquito bites – particularly if you scratch them and break the skin surface – are a very common route of infection; apply cream to reduce the itching. Tiger balm or calamine preparations help, and so does toothpaste if you have nothing else. Clean and dress any wounds carefully, and keep them covered; flies love snacking on oozing wounds.

In hot, damp environments tropical ulcers can develop within hours, so look hard at your legs before retiring for the night. Start treatment as soon as you notice any ulcer. Clean the wound with a good antiseptic, rest with the limb raised above heart height (e.g. raise the leg on a pillow in bed) and consider whether antibiotic treatment is needed (*see* below). Skin infections can spread rapidly, so seek medical help early.

Dermatology made simple

Antiseptic creams are not the best thing to use in hot, moist climates, because they keep wounds wet, therefore feeding infection. What you need is a powerful antiseptic that also dries the area. I favour old-fashioned *potassium permanganate* crystals dissolved in water (*see* recipe on p.216). Diluted tincture of iodine or *povidone-iodine* preparations are excellent too: Videne powder (Riker Labs) is most convenient, but Betadine products are also good. Aerosol *povidone-iodine* is useful but bulky. You can also use antiseptic wipes (alcohol wipes are good, but they sting open wounds), or *chlorhexadine* (e.g. PHiso-hex or Hibiclens) solutions. **A warning**: both *potassium permanganate* and *iodine* stain disastrously if they spill in your luggage.

Skin infection and what to do about it

An early sign of infection is the skin feeling hot, looking red and perhaps throbbing. Lymph glands often enlarge and become painful at 'junction points' in the body (neck, groin or armpits) and sometimes red tracks appear on the skin. If the redness and heat begin to spread, and especially if you feel feverish (hot and cold), you probably have an infection that needs treatment with antibiotics. If medical advice is not to hand, take a week-long course of *flucloxacillin*, 250mg every six hours (or *cloxacillin* 500mg every six hours). If you are allergic to penicillin you should take *erythromycin* 500mg (or 250mg if you are of very small

If a rash is dry and scaly it should be moistened with greasy creams or ointments. If oozing and wet, it needs to be dried out with an antiseptic, such as *potassium permanganate* or an iodine-based preparation.

Signs of bacterial skin infection

Some or all of:

→ **Spreading redness.**
→ **Increasing pain.**
→ **Throbbing.**
→ **Itching.**
→ **Pus** or **fluid discharge.**
→ **Painful lymph glands.**
→ **Fever.**

build) four times a day for seven days. Regular *paracetamol* (Tylenol) or *aspirin* (every four to six hours) will help control the aches and pains that accompany fever. They will make you feel better even before the antibiotics start working (within 48 hours). It is also therapeutic to rest with the affected part raised to heart height to drain away any swelling.

For more on the treatment of cuts, wounds and abrasions, *see* p.290.

Boils

Boils and abscesses do not need antibiotic treatment unless you have lots of them. They are also hot and red, but the infection is confined to one small area with no 'streaking' or spreading of the redness. Never squeeze a boil: let it break by itself. Applying *magnesium sulphate* paste under a waterproof dressing will make the boil or abscess come to a head and expel the poisons. Hot compresses (for 15–20 minutes every four hours) are also soothing and helpful. If there are crops of boils in different parts of the body, antibiotics will probably be needed (*see* above); see a doctor if possible, as things that look like boils can be something very different (such as tumbu maggots, *see* p.244).

Preventing and treating skin infections

If you have minor skin breaks or blisters from walking, soaking the feet in hot, salty water will often prevent infection; it is also very refreshing for tired feet. Bathing in sulphur springs also cures mild skin infections; I can vouch for the efficacy of the springs near Tingo María, Peru, even though they turn silver jewellery black.

Treating minor cuts, abrasions and insect bites

Bathe any wound at least twice a day (more if you can) by dabbing it with cotton wool dipped in a solution of half a teacup of boiled water containing a few *potassium permanganate* crystals; it should be about a 0.01% solution. *Potassium permanganate* is very cheap and readily available in most developing countries. It also prevents infection far better than Dettol or any cream. Diluted *iodine* or gentian violet are also good drying antiseptics and have similar advantages.

RASHES AND ITCHES

A rash can be a sign of many diseases, from harmless heat rash through measles and syphilis to serious typhoid. If you have a widespread rash, it is probably worth consulting a doctor to determine the nature of the problem. In general, if the disease causing the rash is serious, you will feel terribly ill.

Itching without a rash can be due to many causes, and you will probably need a doctor to get the correct treatment. Calamine lotion or antihistamine tablets such as *chlorpheniramine* (e.g. Piriton in the UK) or *diphenhydramine* (e.g. Benadryl in the USA) will help but remember that these cause drowsiness. Itchy rashes become itchier when the skin is hot, so cooling the skin with tepid sponging or fans will help. If you itch, cut your fingernails very short, so that you do not do so much damage when you scratch. Some rashes indicate particular illnesses.

Prickly Heat

Many people are troubled by an itchy, prickly heat rash in hot climates. Typically it is a fine, almost pimply rash, often spread over the chest. It is difficult to control. It is usually worst where clothing is tight or adherent, where clothing or bedsheets rub the skin, or where skin rubs skin.

Treatment of Prickly Heat

Wear loose, 100% cotton clothes; sleep naked under a gentle ceiling fan; take frequent cold showers (without soap) followed by careful drying (avoiding rubbing skin with a towel). This usually gives some relief. Calamine lotion can be very soothing, and spending time in air-conditioned rooms may also reduce discomfort. If you can't afford an air-conditioned hotel, try hanging out in some public building or the lobby of an international hotel.

Allergic rashes

If the skin erupts in a series of raised, red, itchy weals, it may be a sign of an allergic reaction to something you have consumed recently. This can be caused by newly-started medicines, or unusual foods. Antihistamine tablets help settle the symptoms, but cause drowsiness; the best are *chlorpheniramine* (e.g. Piriton in the UK) or *diphenhydramine* (Benadryl in the USA). Consider what could have caused the reaction, and avoid it in future; the next reaction will probably be worse. If a rash appears a few hours after being in the sea, it may be due to 'sea lice' (*see* **Water**, pp.183–4).

Brushing against **poison ivy**, **poison oak** and **sumac** plants commonly causes rashes in North America. They appear several days to a week after contact with the plant and usually begin as red streaks or patches.

Case History: Madagascar rain forest

I woke up feeling as though my body had been through a mangle: muscles I didn't realize I possessed ached. I also had technicolour sores covering my feet, an irritating rash around my middle and dramatic rumblings in my gut. Over the following days, my health deteriorated further: stomach rumbles became severe abdominal pain, intestinal volcanoes erupted with gasesous emissions to match.

Back home, my blood count showed a high eosinophil count and I was soon the centre of much interest at the Infectious Disease Unit of the hospital; samples were taken and, finally, they took me up to the lab to look down the microscope: at hundreds of *Strongyloides stercoralis*.

These are ingenious and unique amongst human worms in having a free-living cycle that can persist in soil for several generations. The larvae burrow through the skin of the feet (especially between the toes). I had been wading around in rainforest streams and flooded rice fields in Masoala and Marojejy. From the skin they enter the blood-stream and lymphatics, causing itchy rashes anywhere. Once in the lungs (where they cause a transient cough and wheeze), the larvae moult to become 2mm-long adult worms. They are coughed up, swallowed and end up in the small bowel, their final retirement home. In this warm, nutritious environment they flourish and live for up to four months. Their eggs are then passed in faeces and hatch into new larvae. The adults can also climb out of the rectum (causing itching) and penetrate the skin to boost the internal infestation again. In this way, the parasite can maintain itself inside someone for 30 years.

After taking some 'horse pills' my visits to the loo became less frequent and eating became a pleasure once more. However, there were still thousands of little corpses floating around my body and my immune system continued to send out the heavy artillery to combat the apparent invasion. I suffered rashes and skin sores for a further couple of months. I recovered fully – but perhaps now I'll think twice before paddling in the tropics.

Nick Garbutt, zoologist and wildlife photographer

These develop into blisters which break down, ooze and crust over; there is often swelling of the underlying skin. The problem usually settles down in four to seven days. There is no special treatment, but cool compresses or calamine lotion can ease it. The **cashew tree** is a relative of poison ivy, and contact with it quite often causes allergic cashew nut dermatitis.

Contact with the stem or the seeds of the **giant hogweed** plant (*Heracleum mantegazzianum*) can, in some people, also cause blistering. This seems to be due to the plant toxin sensitizing the skin so that it becomes highly susceptible to sunburn, and it can leave pigmented patches that persist for seven years. Wearing long clothing whenever you go into jungly areas should protect you from this and other noxious plants and animals. **Primroses** in Europe also cause blistering in some allergic people, causing a reaction not unlike the poison ivy rash. **Nettles** are discussed on p.169.

'Nairobi Eye' and blister beetles

Rove beetle (*Paederus* spp.)

Some species of small, slim, earwig-shaped **staphylinid beetles** (*Paederus* spp., right) cause skin problems in many regions. If crushed or damaged they cause irritation and blistering on contact with the skin, but this begins after a one-day delay. If they fly into an eye and are damaged, inflammation, irritation and swelling starts after 12 hours or so and continues for several days. The delay makes the problem particularly difficult to recognize and avoid, until it is too late.

These beetles are found in East Africa and Thailand, but also exist in southern Spain. Any outdoor lighting after dark can attract them in plagues. Even in temperate climates, small staphylinid beetles can fly in great numbers and may enter the eyes of cyclists and motorcyclists, causing a burning sensation. Antihistamine tablets may help. Unless affected skin is close to the eye apply *silver sulphadiazine* (Flamazine) or calamine to help control the burning feeling.

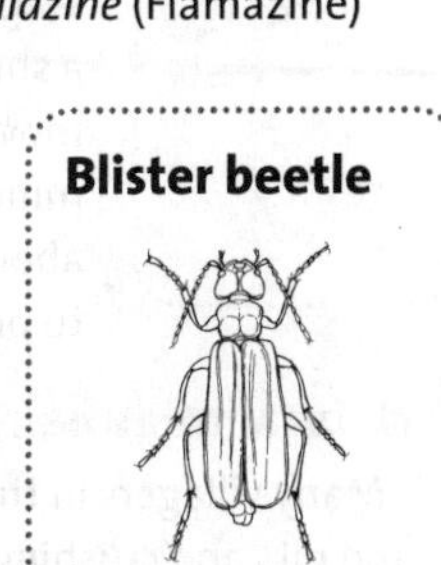

Blister beetle

Blister beetles (of the *Meloidae* family, right) are another widespread family of insects that cause blistering, although without the one-day delay in symptoms. These medium-sized beetles are mostly black or brown, but can be bright metallic blue or green. Again, they only cause blistering if beetle body fluids come in contact with human skin. The **coconut beetles** (family *Oedemeridae*) of the Gilbert Islands also cause severe blistering.

Scabies

This is an intensely itchy rash caused by tiny mites, *Sarcoptes scabiei*, burrowing beneath the skin. It tends to be worse at night, and does not affect the head unless the sufferer is under two years old or is very debilitated. Scabies is acquired from prolonged close contact with an infected person (often a child). It is therefore a risk if you sleep in communal accommodation or share a family bed. Symptoms take up to eight weeks to emerge, and in four-fifths of victims are confined to the wrists and hands. The best treatments are preparations containing *malathion* or *permethrin*, applied twice. The solution must be painted all over the body except the face and scalp, including under the nails; it is then left overnight and washed off the next day. Treatment is repeated after seven days. *Benzyl benzoate* is available in many countries, but it is more unpleasant to use and less effective; it usually needs three applications. Expatriates should treat all members of the household, wash all clothes and bedding in very hot water and dry them in the sun. *Malathion* is safe for all. *Benzyl benzoate* and *permethrin* should not be used in pregnancy. *Crotamiton* (Eurax) cream is an anti-itch preparation that also has some anti-scabies effect.

Itching can actually increase for 24 hours after treatment, and persist for as long as two weeks after the treatment has been successful. Hot baths or other things that heat the skin make the itching even worse.

Lice

Itching of the head and/or body may be caused by lice (*Pediculus humanus*), however clean you keep yourself. Lice of all kinds are generally caught by direct contact with someone who has lice, although you can get headlice from a shared brush or comb. Adult lice are translucent and difficult to spot, but the egg cases (nits), firmly cemented to hair, are white and easier to see. They resemble dandruff, but unlike dandruff cannot be picked out of the hair. Fine-toothed combs remove and reveal lice at all stages, so they are a great diagnostic aid. Comb over a sheet of white paper and you will see small things moving amongst the fallout; they vary in size from minuscule up to a length of about 3mm and breath of about 1mm. Combing nightly (with a fine comb) is said to prevent lice colonization.

Louse

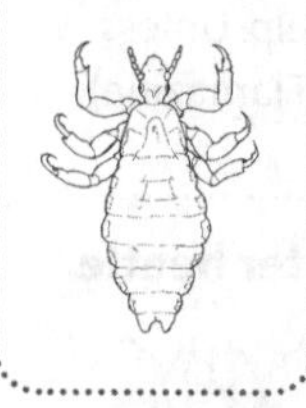

Natural treatments for headlice

Many villagers in the developing world are skilled at combing out lice and nits and crushing them between the fingernails. A more high-tech treatment is to wash the hair with a lot of conditioner, then comb it meticulously before rinsing; wet combing is more effective than dry, because the lice find it difficult to cling on to wet, conditioner-covered hair, and using a fine-toothed comb designed specifically for louse removal is best. Wash brushes and combs as well, and dry them in direct sunlight or on a radiator. You'll need several long sessions of combing to be effective. Shorter hair makes this process easier, and in Asia, children are often treated by shaving the head. **Natural oils**, including neem and tea-tree oils, have insecticidal properties and would be excellent alternatives to combing with conditioner.

Body lice are most common in very poor living conditions. There are many louse treatments available, but be particularly careful of what you apply in pregnancy or to small children. Treat bad infestations of head and body lice with *malathion*, *carbaryl* lotion (Quell in the USA; Carylderm in the UK), *permethrin* or *phenothrin*. *Malathion* is the safest and least irritating of the preparations but it is still very strong-smelling and stings if you get it in the eyes; in any case, it can be hard to find. *Benzyl benzoate* is used to treat lice but is less effective than other treatments. Body lice can spread the nasty **Louse-borne Relapsing Fever**. This is very rare in travellers but could be a hazard of spending winters in the Ethiopian highlands or if you sleep in crowded, very poor accommodation in any less developed country. There have been outbreaks in Sudan, West Africa, Vietnam, the Balkans, the Andes and China. For pubic lice (crabs), *see* **Sex**, p.229.

The Geography Worm or *Larva Migrans*

This causes another very itchy, localized rash, which affects people whose skin has been in contact with soil or sand polluted with dog (or cat) faeces when walking barefoot or sitting on beaches, notably in the Caribbean and Sri Lanka. The dog (or cat) hookworm larva penetrates the skin, then wanders in vain looking for some dog-flesh in which to set up home. It does so for weeks, leaving a dry, flaky, red, itchy track, until it finally dies unfulfilled. The head advances millimetres each day; the map-like pattern it leaves behind explains why it is also called the geography worm.

The worm will do no harm, but it can be dispatched by freezing the head of the parasite with an ethyl chloride spray or carbon dioxide 'snow' (used against warts, and most likely to be found in clinics used by the affluent). An alternative (recommended in medical texts, but messy) is to crush a few *thiabendazole* tablets, mix them with a bland skin cream and apply it to the area, keeping it in place for 12 hours under a waterproof dressing. Anthelmintics (*thiabendazole* or *albenazole*), taken orally for a few days, are also effective, especially if there are several tracks. If a track is on the trunk (between the neck and knees) and progresses faster than a few millimetres a day, this is probably strongyloidiasis and it is best to arrange treatment with tablets within a few weeks.

Fungal infections

Fungal colonization of the skin often causes itching and flaking. The infected area usually has a well-defined, slightly raised edge, redder than the paler centre. Infections in moist areas (under the breasts, within the vagina) may not look the same. Fungal infections are common in sweaty corners, such as the armpits, groin and between the toes. With all these symptoms, wash the affected area, then apply *clotrimazole* (e.g. Canesten in the UK and Asia; Mycelex or Lotrimin in the USA) cream, *miconazole* (e.g. Daktarin in the UK; Monistat Derm

Case History: Pakistan

It was the hot season in southern Pakistan; Jim was very unwell with fever, aches and pains, which he labelled 'flu. Prompted by questions on other aspects of his health, he volunteered that he had uncomfortable lumps in his groin. These are often active lymph glands fighting an infection, and that was the cause in Jim's case. He had not noticed that red streaks were tracking up his leg above a tiny cut in the shin.

Jim's 'flu was actually a skin infection that had sneaked in through a trivial break in the skin. Prompt disinfection would probably have prevented it, but by now he needed a course of *cloxacillin* (500mg four times daily for a week), with which he felt better in 36 hours. Resting with his leg above the level of his heart (lying in bed with his leg propped up on pillows) also aided healing.

in the USA) or *nystatin* 2–3 times a day. Fungal infections encourage bacteria, so if antifungals do not seem to be working an antibiotic may be needed; *see* pp.215–16 for warning signs.

If you have an itchy, red area with a well-defined border in the groin or other sweaty corner, smear on an antifungal cream 2–3 times a day. If this does not work, see a doctor, or consider a course of antibiotics (*see* pp.215–16). Soreness and/or itching around the vaginal opening can be treated the same way, but will often need treatment with antifungal pessaries. Both **crutch rash** and **thrush** are less likely if you wear all-cotton clothing. Underwear is best worn loose: boxer shorts for men and French knickers for women. If you are an expatriate working at a desk, use a cane chair that lets air circulate (but note: bed bugs like cane chairs too).

Impetigo

This is a very common superficial infection of the skin, which often begins in a scratched mosquito bite or a crack at the corner of the mouth. It is an oozing, blistering, golden, crusting, slightly itchy sore that is highly contagious but easily cured. Remove crusts with a mild antiseptic, such as *povidone-iodine* if you have it or salt water if you don't, and treat with an antibiotic cream or powder: *chlortetracycline*, *fucidin*, *framycetin*, *polymyxin* or *neomycin* (e.g. Cicatrin in the UK; Neosporin in the USA). A dilute solution of *potassium permanganate* crystals is also quite effective, and often easy to buy locally, if less convenient to apply while travelling.

OTHER SKIN PROBLEMS

Painless tropical ulcers

A superficial painless ulcer that will not heal over months, particularly one acquired in Central or South America, needs medical assessment. It may be *espundia* (Leishmania), transmitted by sand-fly bites (*see* **Biters**, pp.154–5), which requires expert treatment in a tropical disease hospital. Do not let anyone cut it out, as drug treatments are difficult and the ulcer is a useful monitor of how well treatment is succeeding. In other regions, especially the Pacific Islands, rapid-growing tropical ulcers are often due to bacteria; again, seek medical help. The usual treatment is antibiotic tablets and rest, keeping the affected limb raised above heart height. Both types of ulcers seem to arise from nothing. A skin sore that will not heal over several months could also be a skin cancer (*see* below). It is important that any non-healing wounds are properly diagnosed.

For **Lyme Disease**, initially a non-itchy weal around a tick bite, *see* p.158.

Case History: Peru

I spent four months working in the Peruvian rainforest, at Tambopata. We also explored tributaries by canoe when we slept out in a hammock with no mosquito net. We'd been warned to wear long clothes and apply repellent in the forest but sometimes, especially when labouring, I removed my shirt. Some three months after returning home, I became concerned about a crusty ulcer an inch across on my wrist that just would not heal. Fortunately for me, a friend from the same trip had already been diagnosed with Leishmania and I realized that I too might have the disease. I soon had two more lumps further up my arm.

Eventually I ended up at a military hospital, where they took a sample of the ulcer (leaving most of it – to help monitor whether treatment was working). The wound was dressed and packed and I received antimony intravenously three times a day for a week. This treatment was frightening: antimony affects the heart and once, when an impatient junior doctor gave the injection too quickly, I felt as if I'd been kicked in the chest! That treatment did not clear the parasites, so I returned to hospital for a further three weeks of intravenous treatment. This was intensely boring since I felt very well and had nothing to do.

Four of the 30 people on this particular trip contracted Leishmania *braziliensis*, and the friend who sought medical help last needed six months' treatment to eradicate the *espundia* parasites. Soldiers are given a card about ulcers that don't heal; other adventurers beware – keep those little biters away.

Rupert Howes, Brighton

Skin cancers

There are around 40,000 new cases of skin cancer in Britain annually. Fortunately, most of these are either rodent ulcers (also called **basal cell carcinoma**) or **squamous cell carcinoma**. BCCs don't kill and SCCs are eminently curable. Both are painless and often start with a red or pearly bump which goes on to crust and scab over but, even over months, it never quite heals. These are easily treated, usually by surgical removal under local anaesthetic. Such tumours are common in older, white expatriates or people who have spent a lot of time in sunny places.

Amongst all those who get skin cancer in the UK, about 5,000 suffer from **malignant melanoma** each year, of whom about 1,500 die. This can be an aggressive tumour, which is difficult to treat if caught late. It is becoming more common with increasing tropical travel and its incidence is doubling every 10 years. It is now Britain's second most common cancer in women under 45. Short bursts of intense exposure to strong sun – as in a two-week beach holiday – are a particular risk factor for melanoma in white people.

Moles

Moles are slightly raised, pigmented areas of skin. Some skin cancers arise from a mole that changes, or appear in the guise of a new mole. The worst form of skin cancer, malignant melanoma, can kill, but if diagnosed early is curable.

Those most at risk from skin cancer

→ Fair-skinned people.
→ Those with freckles.
→ Those with red or fair hair.
→ Those who burn easily and tan with difficulty.
→ Those who have been badly/often sunburned, especially as children.
→ People with large numbers of moles (more than 50).
→ Those with existing sun damage (called solar keratoses or 'sun spots').
→ People with a close blood relative who has had malignant melanoma (but not just those who have had moles surgically removed).
→ Anyone who has already had a skin cancer diagnosed previously.

Signs that should make you seek treatment

→ A mole that grows larger or becomes thickened.
→ A mole that becomes irregularly shaped or asymmetrical.
→ Development of different colour shades in the same mole.
→ A mole that itches, bleeds, oozes or develops a crust.
→ Dark pigment appears to start streaming out of the mole.
→ Moles over 1cm in diameter are more likely to be of concern.

Leprosy

Leprosy is still a common problem in people living in poor, overcrowded conditions in many parts of the world; the disease causes slow destruction of the extremities so that people lose fingers, toes and noses. It first appears as patches of depigmented skin that lack sensation. Lepromatous beggars sometimes touch foreigners deliberately, presumably in the hope that you will be terrified into buying them off, but you cannot contract the disease by touching a leper, or by brushing past people in the bazaar. It is only caught after prolonged and quite intimate contact with an infected person, so the risk of a traveller or expatriate catching it is minuscule. In South America, a similar-looking problem is caused by Leishmania (*espundia*; *see* above and pp.154–5).

Foot problems

Athlete's Foot is a dry, scaly rash, often with soreness and itching between the toes; if the skin cracks there may be some oozing too. If you think you have it, get it treated before departure. It is cured by thorough washing and drying, and then applying *clotrimazole* cream (e.g. Canesten), *miconazole* (e.g. Daktarin) or *nystatin* 2–3 times a day. To prevent reinfection from sweaty shoes and socks, sprinkle an antifungal powder (e.g. Mycota) into your shoes every night and into your socks each morning. Even the worst Athlete's Foot may clear up with antifungal powder alone.

Using lots of antifungal powder protects against reinfection, and is a sensible precaution. Wearing sandals (and going barefoot indoors), when possible, also helps. If you have to wear shoes, ensure that your socks are 100% cotton or wool. Severe athlete's foot can become secondarily infected, so if it becomes hot and throbbing, or you feel feverish and unwell, you may need antibiotics (*see* pp.215–6).

One expedition doctor recommends soaking feet in a 4% formalin footbath for 10–15 minutes three times before travelling to hot, moist regions. This hardens the feet for 2–3 months and may be worthwhile if you are going on a tough trip. However, too much formalin treatment will cause the skin to crack, so exercise care.

Sandal-wearers are greatly troubled by **cracked heels**. If this is your problem, keep the offending area of skin fairly thin by abrading it with a Scholl skin-grater or pumice after soaking in a bath (do not try this if the skin has already begun to crack). Wearing shoes and socks (the sweat softens the skin) helps too. Otherwise, apply a greasy lubricant: the Body Shop's peppermint foot lotion does the job and smells delicious.

The small parasitic fleas known as **jiggers** can also cause painful swellings between the toes; for these, *see* p.245. For tips on care of the feet when walking, *see* pp.195–6.

TO BATHE OR NOT TO BATHE...

In Westerners medical problems are often caused by too much bathing rather than too little. In hot climates you may take several showers a day, and if you use soap each time the skin loses protective oils. Cool water alone is good enough much of the time. If conditions make bathing difficult, just to wash armpits, between the legs, between toes and under the breasts with soap and a washcloth.

Squat toilets are a challenge: wet the pan before dumping – then they flush easily. In much of the world people do not use toilet paper, but rinse themselves with water after defecation: a primitive bidet. This takes practice (and is near-impossible on Western-style WCs). You need to use lots of water. While you are 'a learner' remove all clothes below the waist otherwise water will go all over everything. Squat down low and pour – preferably using a vessel with a spout – directly onto your bottom to flush all the lumpy stuff off. That way you hardly need to use your fingers, except for a quick final rub. In a warm climate washing like this is hygienic, will help reduce fungal infections, and the damp area dries quickly even without a towel. It also frees you from carrying toilet paper.

Wash your hands with soap after visiting public toilets. You can acquired others' faecal flora from a door handle. Your own faecal flora will not harm you, but others' will. Air-dry hands by waving them around rather than using a dirty towel.

Showers and Legionnaires' Disease

The first recognized outbreak of Legionnaires' Disease attacked 182 American Legion members in a Philadelphia hotel; 29 died. The symptoms were 'flu-like with a pneumonia that did not respond to antibiotics that are usually prescribed for chest infections. Since that first outbreak effective treatment has been identified, so that it generally only causes grave problems in the infirm, immune deficient, frail elderly or heavy smokers. Over 95% of people exposed to the bacteria do not suffer any illness. It is contracted mainly in First World or Western-style hotels, and big institutions like hospitals. Running a shower for a few minutes before bathing will flush out the Legionnella bacteria and further reduce any chances of infection. Rainforests are an occasional source of human infection. Direct sunshine kills the bacteria; they survive best in above-65% humidity.

On The Ground

Sex

16

Not all genital disease is sexually transmitted. Fungal infections around the genitals are common in the tropics – even in nuns (*see* pp.221–2 for treatment). If you have an intimate problem, clinics specializing in sexually transmitted diseases will be quickest to sort it out. In many developing countries dermatologists (skin specialists) are also venereologists. This chapter deals with genital symptoms, contraception and how to avoid HIV/AIDS.

Summary

→ Wearing tight, mixed-fabric clothes around the nether regions predispose to fungal infections. Wear 100% cotton underwear and dress to allow air to circulate as much as possible.

→ Consider the possibly dire consequences of casual sex anywhere. Both men and women would be wise to carry a supply of condoms.

→ Condoms are invisibly damaged by contact with sun creams, insect repellents and moisturising creams, so wash your hands before unwrapping and touching a condom, otherwise an unwanted pregnancy or infection may result.

→ Remember that alcohol and other drugs affect your judgement.

→ Get a check-up in a special clinic promptly if you have any symptoms of sexually transmitted infection: discharge, pain on urinating or genital ulcers.

→ Drink plenty of water to avoid cystitis and kidney stones.

EMBARRASSING BITS

Waterworks

Passing blood in the urine usually denotes a bladder infection, requiring antibiotic treatment. Be aware, though, that Bilharzia can cause bloody urine (*see* pp.185–7). Some foods and medicines alter urine colour: eating beetroot colours urine red, which can make it look as if you are bleeding. Very dark urine suggests dehydration (*see* p.111) or hepatitis infection (*see* p.278). In dehydration, drinking a great deal more should lighten the urine colour; try this before seeking medical advice. Travellers should pass good volumes of urine at least three times a day; fewer means you are not drinking enough. Men with pain on passing urine may have a sexually transmitted infection, and must have a medical check-up at the appropriate clinic. Women who have pain on passing urine probably have cystitis (*see* below, pp.233–4).

Kidney stones

Kidney stones are hard deposits that build up in the urinary system. They are more likely to occur if you become dehydrated. They cause excruciating pain somewhere along a line drawn between one side of the small of the back, around the loins, through the groin to the point where urine emerges from the body. The problem needs treatment in hospital with intravenous fluids and powerful painkillers. If you have had kidney stones once you are more likely to get them again. Drink plenty of fluids.

Crabs or pubic lice

These look like minuscule crabs; they feed on blood, and therefore cause a great deal of itching. They are usually acquired from direct (sexual) contact with someone who is infested. Crabs or pubic lice rarely leave the body unless damaged or dying, so transmission via dirty bedding is unlikely. If you are hairy, crabs will not necessarily be confined to the pubic region: they can get as far as the eyelashes by way of chest hair and beard. **Treatment** is to apply an aqueous lotion of *malathion*, *lindane* or *carbaryl* to all hairy parts of the body and leave it on for 12 hours or overnight; it is best to apply a second treatment a week later. If you have crabs, you may have other sexually transmitted infections, so you should have a check-up at a special clinic.

SEX

There are often opportunities for pleasant romantic encounters while travelling, but the risks of acquiring HIV (*see* facing page) are considerable. Unprotected sex also exposes you to hepatitis B and a selection of more than 25 other sexually transmitted infections. It is sobering to realize that in the UK, half of all heterosexually acquired HIV is caught abroad. It is foolhardy to have unprotected sex anywhere. A doctor practising in a port in Madagascar told me that 10% of his consultations were for gonorrhoea, a figure not untypical of communities where many people are passing through. So, if you too are passing through, think about the consequences of unsafe sex. Using a condom or femidom (female condom) reduces the risks, and employing spermicidal pessaries or creams in addition to a 'barrier' diminishes them further, as these sperm-killers are also toxic to viruses. However, beware of contact with other creams, as many oil-based lubricants, and even sun creams and insect repellents, can invisibly damage condoms, making them porous and allowing sperm to escape.

Sexual appetite may be enhanced or reduced by travel. Many factors that are common in travellers, including fatigue, illness, depression, anger, alcohol consumption and being at altitudes above 3,500m (12,000ft), can temporarily, but reversibly, reduce **libido**.

Symptoms of Sexually Transmitted Infection (STI)

In women

→ Discharge from the vagina that is thicker or smellier than normal.
→ Itching around the vagina or pubic region.
→ Pain on passing urine (but usually this is due to cystitis, *see* pp.233–4).
→ A painless ulcer or warts in the genital area.
→ Pain during sex.
→ Pain low in the abdomen.
→ Bleeding between periods or increased pain during periods (though travel often does weird things to women's cycles).

In men

→ Discharge from the penis.
→ Itching around the genital region.
→ Pain on passing urine.
→ A painless ulcer, spots or warts in the genital area.
→ Pain in the testicles.

HIV/AIDS

The human immunodeficiency virus (HIV) that causes AIDS cannot be acquired from mosquito bites. It is commonly spread through sexual contact and less often via contaminated needles or unsterile medical equipment or transfusion. AIDS is a disease of heterosexuals as well as of homosexual men. It is very common in Africa and is increasing in Asia and most other parts of the world, especially in major cities. Some countries deny its existence, but it is unlikely any are free from the disease. About 100 British travellers each year pick up HIV overseas, and the rate is rising.

Condoms offer some protection, although oils – and oil-containing sun creams and insect repellents – damage rubber and make microscopic holes that might allow viruses acess. Spermicides can be used safely with latex or rubber condoms. Although spermicides destroy the AIDS virus and so should help reduce transmission, frequent use increases the chances of ulcers forming, and any such broken skin allows easy access for the virus. Ulcers due to STIs or any areas of broken skin therefore make HIV infection much more likely. Get any genital infection treated promptly, by consulting a doctor in a special, genito-urinary or skin clinic.

See also **Special Travellers**, p.68, for further details on travelling with immunosuppression and **Medicines**, pp.82–3, for information about dealing with emergency exposure to HIV.

MEN'S HEALTH

A painful testicle

A testicle that becomes hot, red and painful needs medical attention. There are two likely diagnoses. If the problem has come on suddenly, it is most likely **torsion** or **twist of a testicle**, when the blood supply is cut off and the testicle dies within a matter of hours. Seek help from a surgeon urgently. More common is ***epididymitis***, an infection in which the discomfort tends to come on more gradually; this can be cured with a course of antibiotics. The pain of both conditions will be helped by wearing underwear (or a jock strap) that gives some support.

Discharge or sores

Discharge from the penis or an ulcer on the genitals may be due to a sexually transmitted infection (STI) and, even if you do not think you have been exposed to infection, a special clinic is the best place to go for a check-up. Self-treatment is not wise until the problem has been properly diagnosed. Seek help promptly; if the symptoms seem to get better without treatment, it does not necessarily mean the problem has gone away, but it will be more difficult to diagnose if and when it re-emerges later.

Useful condoms and the International Organ Standard

It is sensible to pack a supply of condoms for several reasons. Firstly, penile sizes vary: Southeast Asian condoms, for example, may be rather small, while African ones are large. Condoms bought in developing countries may not be made to the same stringent quality controls as they are in Europe or North America. The shape of penises is also very diverse, so not all condoms fit all comers; specialist shops such as Condomania can help if you are non-standard, or you can try a mail order company like **Quick and Direct** (*see* below). Travel with a brand of condoms you know. Note that carrying them in wallets or jeans' pockets shortens the effective lifespan of condoms, especially in hot climates.

Other considerations aside, condoms are also useful items of travellers' equipment. Infantrymen and seasoned jungle travellers say they can be used to carry surprisingly large volumes of water. They are also good waterproof covers or containers. They can be used as temporary fan-belts in cars, washing machines and vacuum cleaners, and can be filled with ice and placed on swollen, painful joints or haemorrhoids (piles) to reduce inflammation and discomfort.

Contact information: stockists of condoms

Quick and Direct, 137a Hersham Road, Walton-on-Thames, Surrey KT12 1RW, **UK t** (01932) 232 443, *info@QuickandDirect.com*.

WOMEN'S HEALTH

Sexually Transmitted Infection (STI) in women

Women should carry condoms or femidoms when they travel so that they can protect themselves from infection (and unwanted pregnancy) in case of unplanned romance. They are also a useful contraceptive back-up if diarrhoea stops absorption of the contraceptive pill. STI in women usually causes an unpleasant vaginal discharge. It may compromise future fertility and makes you more vulnerable to acquiring HIV. If you suspect you have an STI, get it treated promptly; most big towns have special clinics.

Discharge from the vagina is not always due to an STI; thick, white discharge is common in thrush and fishy-smelling discharge is probably bacterial vaginosis (treated with *metronidozole* 2g as a single dose, or with *clindamycin cream* a 5g applicatorful for three to five nights). Tampon-users may notice foul-smelling, dark-coloured or black discharge if they forget to remove the last tampon.

Thrush

Thrush causes itching and sometimes white plaques around the entrance of the vagina. Sometimes there is also cheesy white discharge. It is common in moist, warm climates. Washing the genital area too much, too often with soap or shower gels aggravates the problem: thrush can therefore be a problem for women who keep themselves too clean. Treatments are as for other fungal infections (*see* pp.221–2), although antifungal pessaries such as *clotrimazole* (e.g. Canesten) are often necessary. *Fluconazole* (Diflucan) capsules, taken by mouth, are available over the counter in the UK. Air circulation helps to clear the infection, so when social circumstances allow it, women should wear skirts or loose-fitting clothes, and not wear underpants. Grapefruit-seed extract has been promoted as a cure for thrush, but not for any natural reason; the antifungal effect of grapefruit comes from chemicals used as preservatives – organic grapefruit has no effect.

Cystitis

Women often suffer from a 'water infection' of the urinary tract and bladder. Such attacks of cystitis can become much more frequent in the tropics, possibly because most people do not drink enough when in hot climates, or perhaps because holidays just allow more time for more sex. Cystitis makes women feel they want to pass urine very frequently, but only small volumes are produced and there is usually great pain at the end of urination. If the only symptom is pain and frequency of urination, try drinking a glass of water containing a teaspoonful of bicarbonate of soda (baking powder), then a glass of plain water every 20 minutes. This has the effect of flushing out bacteria. The first couple of times you pass urine you will notice stinging, but the more urine you pass the less it will hurt. The pain should subside after three hours of this routine. If it does not get better with this treatment, if there is blood in the urine or if you have a fever, antibiotics will probably be needed. In this case, take a three-day course of *trimethoprim* 200mg twice a day (not safe in pregnancy) or *co-amoxiclav* (Augmentin) 500mg every eight hours (but not for those allergic to penicillin). Women who are allergic to penicillin and are pregnant should take *cephalexin* 500mg (unless allergic to *cephalosporins*) or *nitrofurantoin* 100mg every six hours (unless close to the baby's due date). And drink plenty.

Cystitis is not a sexually transmitted infection but, like thrush, is common in women who are sexually active. A design fault in the female has positioned the opening of bowel and bladder too close together, so that infection passes from the back passage. Wiping from front to back after using the toilet can help reduce the frequency of attacks, and so does passing urine after intercourse. Also, avoid using antiseptics or perfumed cosmetics in the genital region or cosmetics in bath water. Tight-fitting garments, especially jeans and leotards, can aggravate the problem too.

Cystitis in men or children needs a proper medical assessment.

CONTRACEPTION

Although the pill is available in most countries, your regular brand may not be. The progestogen-only '**mini-pill**' is certainly hard to find in many Asian countries. In Japan 'normal' steroid hormones, although available, were only licensed as oral contraceptives three years ago; they are very expensive there (¥2–3,000 per cycle, equivalent to about £1,000 per year), and can be hard to find (the International Clinic in Tokyo might be able to help). In general, you should ensure you have enough supplies for your entire time away. If you are planning an extended trip it may be worth considering using a **progesterone implant** (Implanon), which gives three years cover, or an **intrauterine contraceptive device** (IUD; also known as the **coil**), which gives 3–5 five years' cover depending upon the device used. Alternatively, an **intrauterine contraceptive system** (*Mirena*) gives five years of contraception and usually causes monthly bleeding to cease. Injectable '**depo**' **contraceptives** have the advantage that they give contraceptive cover for twelve (Depo-Provera) or eight weeks (Noristerat); after some months of use, these usually have the pleasant side effect of reducing or stopping menstrual loss. As with all medicines they have their disadvantages, which need to be discussed well in advance – preferably months ahead – of your trip. A family planning clinic or your usual doctor will advise on depo injections, implants and IUDs. Whatever method you decide to use, plan well ahead to ensure that any new contraceptive method suits you several months before departure. Some methods intially cause erratic bleeding.

The pill

Sort out any contraception well before travel. Even in those women who are happy with regular oral contraceptive use, it is still wise to carry condoms, femidoms or possibly a cap to protect themselves from sexually transmitted infections. These are also a useful back-up in case of forgotten pills, a major stomach upset or profuse travellers' diarrhoea.

Problems of pill-taking while travelling

Contraceptive pills may not be absorbed properly if you vomit within three hours of taking the pill or if you have very profuse diarrhoea. A slightly upset stomach with a couple of loose bowel motions is not a cause for concern. Taking antibiotics and certain other medicines can also reduce the efficiency of pill absorption. In these cases you should take alternative contraceptive precautions (condoms, femidoms or a cap) for the rest of the cycle, or as described below. It is also worth carrying condoms as a back-up in case you need to stop taking the pill because you have developed jaundice (when the whites of the eyes and then the skin go yellow), *see* p.278. You may also like to consider stopping the pill if you experience a great deal of swelling of the ankles. This happens to some people in hot climates and contraceptive pills tend to increase the swelling. Finally, there are some theoretical additional risks to taking the pill when ascending to altitudes over 4,500m. With ascents to very high altitudes (over 7,000m/23,000ft) it may be wise to avoid this method of contraception; *see* **High, Cold and Dark**, p.209.

Rules for taking missed pills

If you forget a pill, are late taking one, or vomit within three hours of taking one, following the guidelines in the box below will ensure your contraceptive safety.

Women on the pill are most likely to conceive around the pill-free break, so a break of longer than seven days is risky. If you discover that you are more than a day late starting the next pack of pills and have had sex in the previous few days, it is advisable to take emergency pills.

Clots and the combined pill

Taking the combined oral contraceptive pill increases the risk of a blood clot, and the newer pills carry a higher risk than the older ones (*see* box, facing page). Women who fly frequently may decide to choose a second generation pill (containing *levonorgestrel* or *norethisterone*, e.g. Microgynon) rather than a third generation pill (which contains

Rules for taking missed pills

For the mini-pill (progestogen-only pill)

If less than three hours late there is no problem; if more than three hours late:

→ Take the forgotten pill.
→ Take the next pill on time.
→ Use condoms or do not have sex for 48 hours.
→ Keep taking the mini-pill.
→ If you have already had sex before realizing you were late taking your pill, consider taking emergency contraception.

For the combined oral contraceptive pill

If less than 12 hours late, there is no problem; if more than 12 hours late:

→ Take the forgotten pill.
→ Take the next pill on time.
→ Use condoms or do not have sex for seven more pill-days.
→ Keep taking the combined contraceptive pill.
→ If fewer than seven pills remain in the current packet, start taking the next packet without a pill-free week.

The combined pill and the risk of a clot

Statistics comparing the background average risk of a thrombosis in the general population – travelling or not – compared to those taking hormones or in pregnancy:

Risk in healthy, non-pill-taker	5 in 100,000 women/year.
Risk in second-generation pill-taker	15 in 100,000 women/year.
Risk in third-generation pill-taker	25 in 100,000 women/year.
Risk associated with pregnancy	60 in 100,000 pregnancies.

desogestrel or *gestodene*, e.g. Femodene, Cilest or Marvelon), or consider other methods of contraception. This might be wise if long-haul travel is planned and the traveller is a smoker, overweight, or there is a family tendency to clots. There is no increased risk of clots in women taking the progestogen only 'mini pill'.

The background risk of deep vein thrombosis in the general population is 50 in one million, with an estimated 1–2% death rate. The increased risk of pill-taking is equivalant to the increased risk of death when taking a two-hour drive one Sunday afternoon a year compared to sitting at home. People who have several risk factors for clots and then take a long flight should be aware that risks multiply. They must pay special attention to the precautions and prevention strategies described in the feature on pp.6–9.

Emergency contraception

So-called 'morning after' emergency contraception is an option for up to 72 hours after unplanned, unprotected intercourse. In the UK it is available from GPs, family planning clinics and hospital casualty departments, under the brand name Levonelle-2. Take the first dose as soon as possible (but within 72 hours of intercourse), and the second dose 12 hours later. Levonelle-2 contains only progesterone and carries no risk of clots. It would be wise to travel with this as a back-up if condoms are used as a contraceptive method. An intra-uterine contraceptive device may also be used for emergency contraception up to five days after unprotected sex.

Unwanted pregnancy

Mifepristone or RU486 is now licensed in many regions to terminate an unwanted pregnancy up to the first nine weeks. This is an abortifacient (terminates a pregnancy) so it is not available everywhere and is under stricter legal restrictions than emergency contraceptives. In the UK it is only administered in hospital and leads to a miscarriage with some associated discomfort. In some overseas locations, including

China for example, doctors will prescribe it to be taken unsupervised at home; however, it would be advisable in this situation to ensure that adequate pain-relief is provided. In the UK, referrals for this kind of medical termination, or for surgical removal of a foetus under general anaesthetic, are made by GPs or family planning clinics. Procuring such a termination of an unwanted pregnancy is possible in most European Union countries, excluding Ireland and Malta. It becomes medically and legally more difficult after the 12th week of pregnancy. Although strictly illegal in many other countries, it is often possible to arrange a termination of pregnancy, although this depends upon the reasons for the request and the attitudes of individual doctors as well as national laws. Arranging and going through with this unpleasant procedure is difficult in the absence of psychological support and medical back-up. Have a check-up afterwards.

For information about travelling during pregnancy, *see* **Special Travellers**, pp.72–4.

Information resources: contraception

For country information on emergency and other contraception, abortion and helpline numbers, look at the websites below:
www.mariestopes.org.uk/abortion.html
http://ec.princeton.edu/worldwide/default.asp

MENSTRUATION AND TAMPONS

Tampons can be difficult to find abroad, so take a supply unless you are prepared to make do with local sanitary towels. It is easy to introduce infection when inserting tampons, yet it is sometimes difficult to find washing facilities when travelling; if possible, be especially careful about washing your hands before insertion, or carry wet wipes.

Travel can mess up periods; they may stop or become erratic, but also be aware that the most common reason for periods to stop is pregnancy. **Period pains** may become more of a problem during travel; pack a remedy, assuming you will have the worst period pains you have ever had. Reducing the quantity you drink for a day or two before the period and for the first day of bleeding often helps reduce pain, particularly if there is some bloating during this time, although beware of getting dehydrated if you are still acclimatizing in a hot destination. *Ibuprofen* (Brufen in the UK; Motrin in the USA), other non-steroidal anti-inflammatory medicines (*see* **Medicines**, p.82) or *paracetamol* (Tylenol) also help. Otherwise, the contraceptive pill should reduce such symptoms. If periods appear to restart more than a year **after the menopause**, a gynaecological check is needed.

Note that menstruating women are considered unclean in many religions, and it would be blasphemy to enter a temple or mosque while you are bleeding.

Disposing of sanitary towels

Proper disposal of sanitary towels is difficult. If they are put into the ordinary rubbish disposal system, they may end up being scattered by wind and dogs. The only sensible option is to burn them. Otherwise, washable sanitary towels can be purchased from the sources below.

Contact information: washable sanitary protection

Green Baby, 345 Upper St, London N1 3QP, **UK t** (020) 7226 4345, *www.greenbabyco.com*.

Plush Pants, 55 Newlands Ave, Cheadle Hulme, Cheshire SK8 6NE, **UK t** (0161) 485 4430, *www.plushpants.freeserve.co.uk/FOR_MUM.html*.

Twinkle Twinkle, Briley Cottage, Beggars Hill Rd, Lands End, Twyford RG10 0UB, **UK t** (0118) 934 2120, *www.twinkleontheweb.co.uk*. Produces pretty patterned ones!

Yummies, 52 Holland St, Brighton BN2 9WB, **UK t** (01273) 672 632, *www.yummiesnappies.co.uk/PROD_cloth_pads.html*. Produces washable sanitary cloth made in soft unbleached flannelette. A set comprises two winged outer pieces that 'popper' around your knickers, and 10 inners (of various sizes) that you fold into a pad and insert into the outer.

Delaying menstruation

Women who are already taking a combined contraceptive pill can miss a period by continuing one 21-pill packet straight after finishing the previous one, without the normal seven pill-free days' break. This is convenient on a short trip or special holiday. Even in established pill-takers, extra or 'break through' bleeds are common if the pill is poorly absorbed due to diarrhoea, so it is wise to pack extra sanitary supplies. Starting the pill simply to control or delay menstruation or miss a period is probably not worth the effort and inconvenience: a study of young women on six-week-long expeditions suggested that many of those who started taking the pill just before the expedition suffered unpredictable bleeding. Packing more tampons, in good, waterproof containers, is a better strategy. Do pack plenty of sanitary protection; it can be hard finding such products overseas, although Tampax seems to be very widely available.

It is also possible to ask your doctor to prescribe *norethisterone* 5mg thrice daily to delay menstruation; it is started three days before the period is expected to start and then the period comes two or three days after stopping these hormone tablets. Injectable contraception (e.g. Depo-Provera) could be especially useful for women planning trips of up to three months. After two or three cycles of this method periods usually cease and, since this is a progestogen-only method, it side-steps the slightly increased risk of thrombosis (a clot) associated with the combined pill. As such, provided this was initiated four to six months before a trip, Depo-Provera would be an ideal contraceptive for mountaineers (*see* **High, Cold and Dark**, p.209) and other travellers who are at increased risk of clots (*see* **Features**, p.6).

On The Ground
Animals

17

Many of the animals described in this chapter are venomous, but the actual danger they present to the traveller is usually disproportionate to the fear they engender. The beasts that people most fear exist in insignificant numbers and the risk they pose to the health of the average traveller is slight. Most hazards from tropical animals are vastly overstated, and it makes more sense to worry about road accidents than snake bites. The most common injuries from animals, when travelling or at home, are domestic dog bites. In the USA, home of many dangerous animals, most of the deaths due to venomous creatures are from honey-bee stings. Worldwide, most of the deaths due to animal bites are caused by diseases spread by mosquitoes. This chapter, then, mainly covers animals that are revolting or scary rather than truly harmful.

Many noxious animals advertise themselves with bright colours and markings, so do not handle anything strikingly marked unless you know it is harmless. Avoid patting unknown dogs, however cute.

Summary

→ Insect repellents deter six-legged assailants, and also leeches, ticks and chiggers. The best repellents are based on DEET (diethyltoluamide) *see* pp.145–6.

→ Stop leeches climbing up your ankles by applying repellent to shoes.

→ In leech country carry salt in a film canister; a dab will get a leech off.

→ Protect yourself against all biters by wearing long, baggy, cotton clothing – with trousers/pants tucked into the socks, and shirt tucked into the waistband.

→ Wearing shoes will protect you from jiggers, as well as hookworm, an assortment of venomous animals and injuries to the feet.

→ When walking outside at night, wear shoes and carry a torch (flashlight) so that you do not stumble upon a snake or scorpion and provoke it to defend itself.

→ If bitten by a snake, splint the limb, keep it low and get to hospital; never incise the wound and do not apply a tourniquet.

→ When removing jiggers, fly-maggots, ticks or leeches, make sure they leave in one piece.

→ If a dog bites you in an unprovoked attack, assume it is rabid, clean the wound thoroughly and then seek medical advice promptly.

→ Consider rabies immunization before travelling to remote places.

→ Never handle wild animals that are inexplicably tame, and do not stroke or pet unknown tame animals.

SKIN INVADERS

Some insects lay eggs on human skin so that, as they hatch, the young eat the living tissue. Accounts of such horrors are just what some travellers like to dine out on – or write books about. The good news, though, is that only two animals commonly invade human skin, and only in small, discreet areas: you will never be eaten alive. These are tumbu flies and jiggers (not to be confused with chigger-mites). In numbers, they can be very unpleasant. Bot-flies in South and Central America also invade skin. Old and New World screw-worms feed on living tissue in wounds, and the Congo floor maggot sucks blood from skin. Other fly maggots can cause benign (if revolting) infestation of dead tissue, and have been used medically for centuries to clean up wounds.

Tumbu flies

Tumbu flies or *putsi* (*Cordylobia anthropophaga*) are African relatives of blue-bottles or blow-flies. The maggots develop in human skin, causing an inflammation like a boil. These 'boils' usually come in crops, often on the back, arms, waist and scrotum. The adult fly lays her eggs on clothes that have been left drying in the shade, and maggots usually get to victims by way of clothes or directly from the soil. Eggs or young maggots also contaminate laundry left to dry on the ground. When the clothes are put on, the maggots invade the skin and grow to a maximum size of 15mm in about eight days. The mature grub, which is club-shaped, then falls out through a small hole in the centre of the boil and the inflammation settles down.

The maggot can be encouraged to leave before its eight days are over, but this is not a pleasant spectacle. It first has to be suffocated by placing a drop of mineral oil over its two breathing tubes; these appear as a pair of black dots on the surface of the boil. If gentle pressure is then applied, the maggot should pop out. Otherwise, as it suffocates it will wriggle violently, and when it emerges it can be grabbed with tweezers and removed. Too much force at this stage will damage the maggot, and if any part of it is left in the skin there will be an unpleasant reaction. Be firm but gentle. You will come to no harm by leaving the maggot alone, although you probably will not want to.

Avoiding infestation

The way to avoid infestation is to be careful about where you dry your clothes. Hang them on a line in the sun, or inside where flies cannot reach them. Only take washing in when it is so dry that it is crisp, for the maggot is unlikely to survive a thorough baking in the sun. Iron clothes inside and out. The waistbands of underclothes, bedsheets and babies' nappies (diapers) must also be ironed. Tumbu flies are a problem in hot and high-humidity regions of East, West and southern Africa.

Removing unwanted lodgers

When dispatching unwanted guests, be they jiggers, fly-maggots, ticks or leeches, they must always leave intact. If any part of the beast is left behind, it will cause inflammation, which will be difficult to clear and worse than anything the parasite would have done to you if you had left it in peace.

Jiggers

Jiggers, also known as chigoes or sand-fleas, are degenerate fleas. They are picked up by walking barefoot in endemic areas, usually where soils are fairly dry and sandy; it is even possible to acquire them indoors. The most troublesome species, *Tunga penetrans*, occurs in tropical Africa, Central and South America. Eight to 10 days after a pregnant jigger has set up home in you, she will have swollen to the size of a small pea, which causes a painful swelling at the side of a toenail, between the toes or on the soles of the feet. Left unmolested she will shed several thousand eggs and then die, and her remains will eventually be expelled with a load of pus.

Treatment of jiggers

Pick away with a safety pin or needle until you can remove the whole, very pregnant, egg-filled body of the lady jigger. Afterwards, the hole must be doused with antiseptic and a dressing applied to stop infection. If the animal bursts during removal, the eggs will go everywhere and probably re-infest you. Douse with spirit, alcohol or kerosene to kill the remaining eggs (do not smoke while doing this!).

Bot-flies

Bot-flies (*Dermatobia hominis*) lay their eggs on mosquitoes. When the mosquito takes her blood meal, the hitchhiking fly eggs hatch and the maggots penetrate the victim's skin via the bite hole or a hair follicle. Covering up with long clothes and repellents protects against bot-flies. Once under the skin, they grow until, after two or three months, they measure 2cm. They are unpleasant and unnerving parasites because as they move about you can feel (and sometimes hear) their fidgeting.

Removal techniques

One technique is to poison the maggot with nicotine from the base of a used, non-filter cigarette. This throws it into quease-making convulsions before it gives in, but subsequently the beast can be squeezed out; get a local who is practised in maggot-evictions to do this if you can. In Belize, Barb McLeod has developed a technique that avoids the dying paroxysms. Cover the fly's breathing hole with a generous amount of non-water-based glue: without waiting for this to dry, place a circular patch of adhesive tape on top. The tape should be 1–2cm in diameter, depending on the size of the 'boil' and its location. Apply a second seal of glue along the edge of the tape, and allow to dry well. The bot-fly may try to force a new breathing passage by secreting lymph under the edge of the tape. Leave the tape on overnight; by morning the larva should have asphyxiated and can easily be squeezed out or removed with tweezers.

Medical texts say that the only way to extract bot-flies is surgically. However, a paper in the prestigious *Journal of the American Medical Association* (1993; **270**: 2087–8) suggests applying strips of bacon over the 'boils'; the maggots love bacon, come out to feast, and can then be caught and removed with tweezers. I go for the McLeod method, because any attempt to grab the live animal risks pulling it apart, which will provoke a nasty inflammatory reaction and infection.

Animal hazards and where they occur

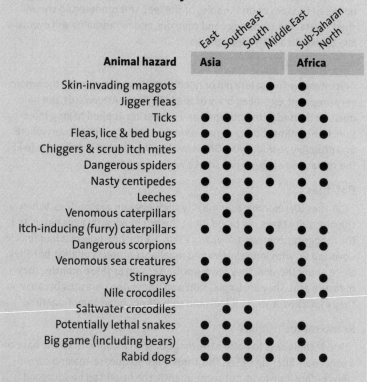

Animal hazard	Asia				Africa	
	East	Southeast	South	Middle East	Sub-Saharan	North
Skin-invading maggots				●	●	
Jigger fleas					●	
Ticks	●	●	●	●	●	●
Fleas, lice & bed bugs	●	●	●	●	●	●
Chiggers & scrub itch mites	●	●	●			
Dangerous spiders	●	●	●	●	●	●
Nasty centipedes	●	●	●	●	●	●
Leeches	●	●	●		●	
Venomous caterpillars		●	●			
Itch-inducing (furry) caterpillars	●	●	●	●	●	●
Dangerous scorpions			●	●	●	●
Venomous sea creatures	●	●	●		●	
Stingrays	●	●	●		●	●
Nile crocodiles					●	●
Saltwater crocodiles		●	●			
Potentially lethal snakes	●	●	●		●	
Big game (including bears)	●	●	●	●	●	
Rabid dogs	●	●	●	●	●	●

Asia, East: Japan, China etc.
Asia, Southeast: Indonesia, Thailand, Malaysia
Asia, South: Pakistan, India, Nepal, Bangladesh, Sri Lanka
Pacific, Australasia: Australia, New Zealand
Pacific, Islands: Fiji, Solomons, Papua New Guinea, etc.

SMALL BITERS

Mosquitoes, ticks, sand-flies and other little beasts that transmit vector-borne disease are covered in **Biters**, pp.141–60. For human head and body **lice**, *see* **Skin**, pp.220–21; for **crabs** (pubic lice), *see* **Sex**, p.229. 'Bugs' refer to those insects that entomologists call **true bugs**, the *Hemiptera*.

Six-legged biters

Insects have six jointed legs; many have wings. There are more insect species than all other animals put together. Most make a contribution to the earth's ecological balance; a few make a nuisance of themselves.

America		Pacific		
Caribbean	South & Central	Australasia	Islands	Habitat
	●		●	rural lowlands
	●			dry, sandy
●	●	●	●	rural
●	●	●	●	poor housing
●	●	●	●	scrub & forest, especially secondary forest
●	●	●	●	warm regions
●	●	●	●	most tropical & sub-tropical rural areas
				moist forest
●	●	●		forest, scrub, plantations
●	●	●	●	rural areas
●	●	●		dry forests, scrub, desert
●	●	●	●	tropical seas
●	●	●	●	shallow sea; tropical South American rivers
				rivers & lakes
		●	●	estuaries, mangrove swamps, coastal regions
●	●	●	●	scrub & forest
	●			scrub & forest
●	●		●	villages and towns

Note: This table should only be used as a rough guide, since accurate information on animal hazards is difficult to obtain. Small biting animals which transmit disease are listed in the table on pp.50–51.

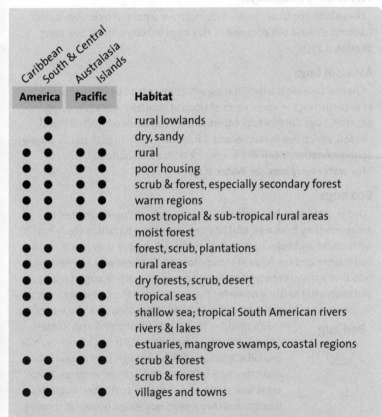

Fleas

Fleas are dynamic jumpers. They may be acquired in cheap hotels; they tend to leave a line of bites across the abdomen, then settle down in your sleeping bag. Turning bedding inside-out and leaving it out in direct sunlight usually makes them go elsewhere. If this doesn't get rid of them, insecticides may be necessary. Fleas are difficult to see and even more difficult to catch, for they are small and fast-moving; they are flat side-to-side, dark nut-brown and look as if they are made from polished leather. In a very few regions, rat (rarely human) fleas transmit **plague**, a very rare disease in travellers (*see* p.156).

Flea

Stable-flies (*Stomoxys*)

These look like small house-flies, but have a painful bite. They do not transmit disease but occasionally lay eggs in body orifices (*see* **dung beetles**, p.255).

Assassin bugs

Chagas' Disease is a debilitating affliction spread by bites of barber or assassin bugs in some parts of tropical South America (*see* p.155). Assassin bugs are flat-backed, brown, nocturnal insects, often shield-shaped, which live in wattle-and-daub houses; if you plan to use simple accommodation, sleep in a hammock with a mosquito net.

For **water scorpions**, *see* **Water**, p.190.

Bed bugs

Bed bugs (*Cimex lectularius*) are true bugs (*Hemiptera*), related to assassins; they have a painful bite, too. They are a hazard in seedy hotels with cracks and holes in plaster or brickwork; by day they lurk in walls, bed frames and the folds of mosquito nets. The best way to avoid them is to find a smarter hotel, but if you are unfortunate enough to discover bed bugs after settling down for the night, move the bed away from the wall and keep a light on, if possible. One bed bug takes 10–20 minutes to drink its fill of blood and, if interrupted, will bite repeatedly until it has had enough or you kill it. Bites are painful enough to keep you awake, and often very inflamed and itchy afterwards. There are seldom long-term problems after bed bug bites, though, and they spread no disease (except insomnia).

Bed bug

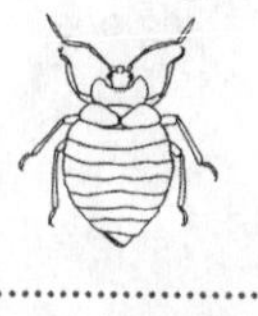

Preventing mite bites and tick attachments

To avoid mites, leeches, chiggers, ticks and the diseases they carry, put on insect repellent; the best are DEET-based (*see* pp.145–6). Wear long sleeves and trousers, and tuck trousers into socks in high grass or scrub.

Eight-legged biters

Chiggers and mites

Chiggers or red bugs are little red mites known in Britain as harvest mites. They do not enter the skin or suck blood, and should not be confused with the Jigger-flea. Only 20 of the 700 species are important, as they cause scrub itch. In Asia and the Pacific Islands they transmit Scrub Typhus (*see* below). Chiggers are well known to people who walk in long grass, especially in the tropical Americas, for although they are only 1mm long they make their presence felt. To **keep them off**, apply repellent and tuck trousers into socks, or they will latch on to ankles, the groin, armpits and wherever clothing is tight. They stay on for four days, but welts and severe itching last for 10 days. This is because they leave behind a stylosome (drinking straw), created partly as the body's reaction to their saliva, which continues to irritate and inflame the skin. If you scratch as much as you'd like to, you will get a nasty skin infection.

Scrub Typhus mites

The bites of the small Asian mites that transmit Scrub Typhus (a rickettsial disease that responds to antibiotics) do not itch and so often go unnoticed. True to their name, these mites are common in scrub and secondary forest. Scrub Typhus mites occur within a large area of East Asia and the Pacific Islands, down to Queensland, Australia in the south and Sri Lanka and Pakistan in the west.

Other more localized mites

Australian whirligig mites (*Anystis* spp.) are also red and impressively large for mites: up to 1.35mm long. They are fast-moving predators, producing painful bites with a small area of inflammation, which may persist for several days.

Also worth mentioning is the **Mauritian red poison mite**. Its toxic secretions, if conveyed to the mouth via the hands, are sufficiently potent to cause unpleasant and sometimes dangerous swelling of the mouth and throat. Wash your hands well if you come into contact with red crawlies in Mauritius.

Spiders

Almost all spiders are venomous, but most are unable to bite into human skin. As a general rule, those that spin elaborate webs need less venom to immobilize their prey, so are less likely to be dangerous. Cold compresses or applying ice is sufficient treatment for most spider bites but, in Australia, apply a broad, firm compression bandage and immobilize the entire bitten limb in a splint to slow the spread of venom. Dangerous spiders either dispense toxins that kill a discreet area of skin (*Loxosceles*, *Lycosa*), or nerve poisons (*Lactrodectus*, *Phoneutria*, *Atrax*). These five genera are described below. Most spiders harm by biting.

However, some of the very large, hairy spiders flick off body hairs towards the source of their annoyance, and these cause itching; they are particularly unpleasant if they get into the eyes.

Brown recluses or fiddle spiders (*Loxosceles*)

These are long-legged brownish spiders that are widely distributed throughout the Americas, and have also bitten in the Mediterranean, North Africa and Israel. The fiddle describes the violin-like mark on the back of many species. Bites cause localized death of skin tissue and underlying structures. Occasional fatalities occur; there have been about six this century in the USA. Men have been bitten on the genitals while on outdoor toilets, so check before you sit. Antivenom is made in Peru, Brazil and Argentina.

Brown spider

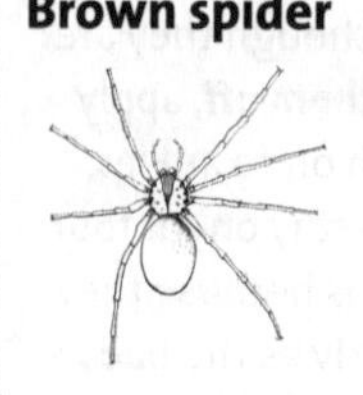

South American wolf spiders (*Lycosa rartoria* and *L. pampeana*)

Wolf-spider bites can cause tissue death resulting in a scar up to 20cm long. There is an antivenom in Brazil. The European wolf spider, *Lycosa tarentula*, was once blamed for epidemics of bites that, supposedly, could only be cured by dancing the tarantella. However, feared though it is, it rarely kills anyone except the infirm.

Black and brown widows (*Lactrodectus*)

Widows have a very bad reputation but, again, deaths are unusual. They are small black or blackish-brown spiders with a red, hourglass-shaped design on their backs. They are very widespread and occur in much of the Americas, Africa, southern Europe, warm parts of Asia and Australia. Bites are usually on an extremity and, if venom is dispensed, pain spreads from the site up the limb to the lymph nodes in the groin or armpit, and then to the muscles, which suffer cramps and spasms. The victim can become exhausted and dehydrated. Pain is difficult to control even with painkillers, but hot baths may help. Recovery usually takes one or two days, or half an hour if antivenom is given. Deaths are rare but occur occasionally in small children, the elderly or those with long-standing heart or respiratory disease. Antivenom is made in the USA, Australia, Russia, the Balkans, Italy, South Africa and South America.

Huntsman spiders (*Phoneutria*)

Also called **wandering** or **banana spiders**, huntsman spiders are from South America. They are big – with 4cm bodies and 13cm leg-spans – and aggressive, with rather threatening red colouration around the jaws. Bites cause intense pain, sweating and cramps, but recovery is usually complete in 12 hours. Deaths are unusual, and occur in children and weak adults. Antivenom is made in Brazil.

Funnel-web spiders (*Atrax*)

The nastiest funnel-web spiders fortunately have a very restricted range: they only occur in an area immediately around Sydney, Australia. Because antivenom treatment is available, deaths from funnel-web bites are now rare and, despite its fearsome reputation, the Sydney funnel-web has killed just 13 people in 80 years. They are medium-sized, heavily built 'tarantula'-like spiders that either give a series of superficial bites, or grasp firmly with their legs and drive their chelicerae in with sufficient force to pierce the skull of a chicken.

Many-legged biters

Centipedes

Centipedes are fast-moving predators. Most of their segments have a single pair of legs that protrude to the sides. Bites by big, tropical centipedes are very painful but, worldwide, only one person is recorded as actually having died from a centipede bite. The usual treatment is to inject local anaesthetic, but injections of *morphine* or *pethidine* (*meperidine* or Demerol in the USA) may be required.

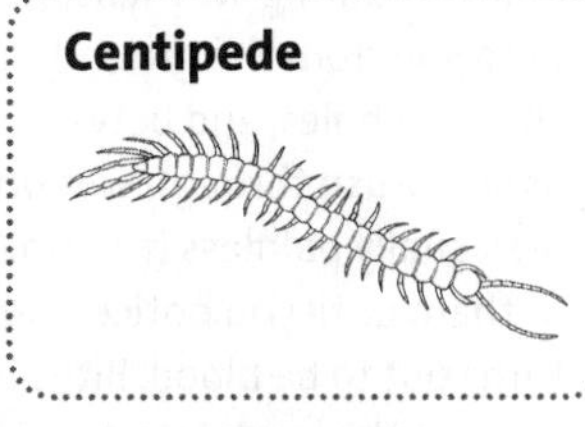

Millipedes

Millipedes do not bite and are sedate, dignified animals. They are rounded, with legs (two pairs per segment) tucked beneath their bodies to give them an almost snake-like look. When annoyed, sat on, or rolled on in your sleep, some tropical species secrete an irritant fluid that will inflame the eyes and perhaps even the skin.

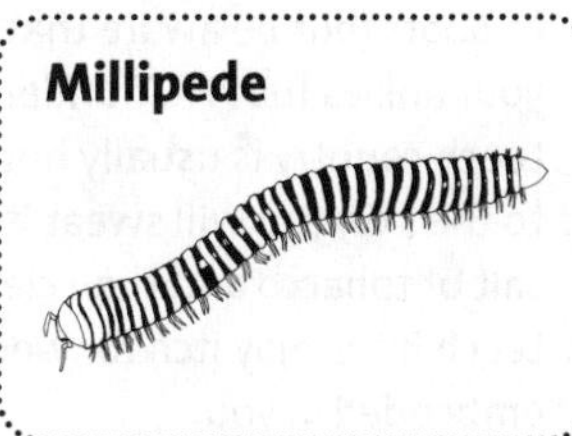

Legless biters

Leeches

Leeches do not transmit disease; they harm only if the bite becomes infected. But they are nightmarish creatures – British troops serving in Malaya wore condoms at night because they were so worried about leeches crawling into their urethra. Freshwater aquatic leeches very occasionally enter body orifices to cause bleeding from unusual places (*see* **Water**, pp.188–9), but this is rare and happens only in swimmers.

Case History: Madagascar

The warm rain was pouring down in the forest of eastern Madagascar, we were soaked to the skin, and repellent didn't seem to stay on for long. I was wearing stout walking boots and thick socks, but my socks were a squelchy, sticky mess of pink rainwater. I did an experiment and plastered my right boot thickly with DEET, while the left boot received none. At the end of the day my left ankle was ringed with leech bites and my right was unscathed. Applying repellent to boots protects for longer, reduces direct skin contact with the insecticide and means that your protection isn't sweated off.

Leeches are common in rainforests, including in Australia, and in scrub or forest during wet seasons, particularly in Asia. They usually climb onto you from the ground. They can squeeze through small holes like shoelace holes, and between the fibres of socks. They may hitch a ride as you brush through wet undergrowth, or drop down from trees. Bites are usually painless (they inject local anaesthetic). You may be unaware of them until you notice a squelching or stickiness in the socks that turns out to be blood. Bites bleed for some hours because of the anticoagulant the leech injects, and often, leeches have left by the time you find blood.

Avoidance and first aid after leech bites

You can avoid leeches by applying DEET insect repellent to the outside of boots (but be aware that DEET dissolves plastics), putting DEET on your ankles (but NOT under your socks) and tucking trousers into socks. Leech country is usually hot and steamy, so if you only apply repellent to the skin you will sweat it off in an hour. Get leeches off with a dab of salt or tobacco and then clean and cover (if possible) any broken skin. Leech bites may itch for weeks, especially if the mouthparts remain embedded in you.

OTHER SMALL ANIMALS WITH BAD HABITS

What is dangerous?

Local information about dangerous animals is not always accurate. I was told in Sulawesi, for example, that I would be dead in 24 hours after handling a very large, rather attractive millipede. While centipedes have extremely nasty stings, the only noxious property this millipede has is that the juice it might have secreted if upset (which it wasn't) can inflame the eyes if rubbed in. So will snail and slug slime. The secretions of a few tropical millipedes and contact with some damaged beetles in many regions (including southern Spain) may blister skin (*see* p.219).

Squirters

Tail-less whip scorpion

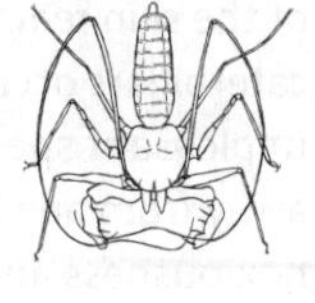

Tail-less **whip-scorpions**, **cicadas** and a range of other creatures squirt or spit irritant juice when annoyed. If any goes close to your eyes, wash it out with plenty of water. In North America there are a couple of hundred insects known as **walking sticks**; some are known as musk phasmids, as they exude a white liquid with a pleasant musky smell. These are insects to be wary of, however. One species, *Anisomorpha buprestoides*, a 7–12cm-long, yellow-and-brown-striped insect also known as the **Florida Stick**, can spray its 'musk' a distance of 40cm. When inhaled, this substance causes pain, and if it gets into the eyes the severe burning sensation it provokes takes 36 hours to go away.

Florida Stick insect

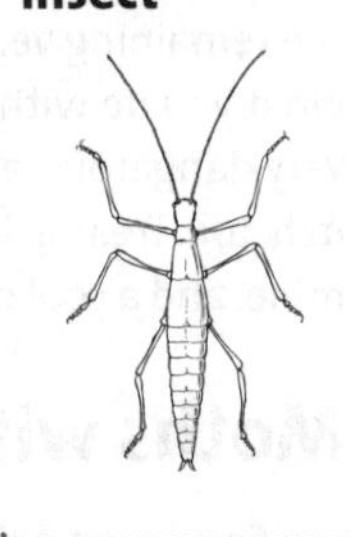

Caterpillars

Furry caterpillars cause great discomfort if you lean on them or they get caught up in your clothes and their hairs are forced into your skin. In rural areas there can be plagues of these attractive-looking insects, and in houses it is easy to lean on one, or pick something up on which one is perched. The fine 'hairs' inject irritant chemicals akin to histamines, which cause irritation for between a few hours and several months.

Hairy caterpillar

In Nepal, locals say the 'hairs' can be removed by rubbing the affected part in the hair at the back of someone's neck (if you try it, make sure there's no risk of hairs entering the eyes), but this does not work with fine, Western hair. Some caterpillars have large, eye-like markings and spiny-looking appendages to warn you they are unpleasant; these induce blood blisters if you brush against them.

Caterpillar species to watch out for

Hairy moth caterpillars are common all over the world, but only the South American species are really noxious. In Brazil there are very nasty spiny caterpillars. The worst is *Lonomia achelous* (family *Saturniidae*), whose spines deliver a toxin that interferes with blood clotting and can make people very ill. Similarly armed caterpillars are known in Venezuela. Stings by the long-haired caterpillar *Premolis semirufa* (*Arctiidae*) can cause such deep inflammation around the joints that the victim may be permanently disabled (a hazard for South American rubber tappers). In Peru there are rufous funnel moth caterpillars (*Megalopyle superba*) that are so large and 'furry' they are known as the ***cuy rojizo*** or 'reddish guinea pig'. They are notorious for the severity of the skin reactions caused by coming into contact with them. Related caterpillars occur in the southern USA and the Caribbean. Similarly unpleasant species exist in the Old World tropics and subtropics. Keep away from any furry or spiky caterpillars; striking markings advertise noxiousness and venom.

First aid for removing caterpillar hairs

Sit down in good light and pick each hair out – one by one – with pointed tweezers. Do not use eyebrow tweezers as they will squeeze the remaining venom into the skin. Sticky tape is no help. Be careful what you do with the hairs you pull out; if they enter the eyes they are very dangerous, and if they fall onto your lap they may make that part itch, too. Treat irritation with *paracetamol* (Tylenol) and/or an antihistamine, and a cool or tepid bath.

Moths with unusual habits

In Southeast Asia and the Southwest Pacific, some moths drink tears from the eyes and also enjoy saliva and other body secretions. This could presumably introduce infection, particularly conjunctivitis. The *Calyptera* genus of moths, from the mountains of Southeast Asia and Papua New Guinea, has a taste for blood and occasionally attack people at night, usually at or above an altitude of 1,000m (3,000ft) and in the rainy season. Initially the wound is painless, but it hurts when the moth empties saliva into it, and later there is transitory inflammation. The only likely problem arising from this is infection, as these moths also dine on cattle dung.

Small spiny creatures, dung beetles and flesh-flies

The smallest **tenrecs** (Madagascar's equivalent of the hedgehog) will deposit their very fine spines in your skin if you handle them (*see* p.169). Each spine has to be painstakingly removed with fine tweezers. It takes hours to do this.

Dung beetles have unpleasant egg-laying habits, and mothers attending my clinics in Sri Lanka commonly complained that insects flew out of their toddlers' faeces as they were deposited on the ground! This bewildering but harmless affliction needs no treatment, and is most unlikely to befall even the sleepiest of travellers.

House-flies, **bot-flies**, **blow-flies**, **flesh-flies** and **hover-flies** occasionally deposit eggs in open wounds and in body orifices so that their maggots can infest the ears, nostrils, eyes and genitals, but this occurs almost invariably in children or very debilitated people.

Stingers

Scorpions

Scorpion

Brontoscorpio is my nightmare creature; it was a metre-long scorpion that fortunately became extinct 300 million years ago. The largest survivors, *Heterometrus* spp. of Southeast Asia and *Pandinus imperator* of West Africa, look terrifying, but their sting is only painful; few scorpions are dangerous to adults. Today there are species capable of lethal stings, mainly to children, in North Africa and the Middle East, South Africa, India and North, Central and South America. Scorpions are most common in dry, arid regions, but do not tolerate extreme heat. They are most in evidence after rain. They are attracted by humidity and so wander into shower rooms. Outside, they hide under stones or rotting logs, so if you ever need to move any, lift or roll them so that anything lurking underneath flees away from you. Scorpions are nocturnal, so most stings happen at night or when a slumbering specimen is disturbed after it has settled down in your shoe or rucksack. They are occasionally a problem in cities, notably in big towns in lowland Mexico and also in India.

Generally, scorpions with big claws and slim 'tails' rely on claws as their principal weapon, so they are less venomous. Those with small claws and a more substantial 'tail' and stinger are more likely to be seriously dangerous. Exceptions exist: the Middle Eastern *Hemiscorpius lepturus* has a very long, slender stinger, but is very dangerous.

Seek medical help promptly if a child is stung. Mexicans suffer more deaths from scorpions than any other nation, over 1,000 per year, mostly in children under five. Even in Mexico, though, most stings are painful for up to four hours, and only eight of the 25 local species are a serious threat. Antivenom is available for the dangerous ones, like the 5–8cm narrow-bodied, elongated *Centruroides* 'bark scorpions'. These species also occur in Arizona, but rarely kill there as antivenom is readily available. Antivenom is also available for species in Saudi Arabia, although it should not be administered by amateurs.

Scorpion toxins attack the heart and circulation; some are nerve toxins. The red scorpion of South India causes deaths (unusually, **in adults** rather than children) by poisoning the circulatory system. My own finger is still numb after a sting 13 years ago in Madagascar. A dangerous sting provokes a feeling of being very unwell, profuse sweating, the shakes and a rapid heartbeat. Seek medical help if you can; otherwise rest, let the storm pass and avoid immersing the stung part in cold water, as this increases pain.

Scorpion antivenom and other treatments

Scorpion antivenoms are manufactured by institutions in the USA, Germany, Mexico, Brazil, Turkey, Algeria, South Africa, Egypt and Iran. In the UK, the **Lister Institute of Preventative Medicine** stocks some. Scorpion haemolymph (the scorpion equivalent of blood) neutralizes scorpion venom. A child in Israel was saved by a haemolymph injection when antivenom was unavailable.

Applying ice packs, immersion in water or cooling by hanging the affected limb out of a car window **increases** the pain. Avoid rubbing or other friction and keep the stung part warm and cushioned. Injecting local anaesthetic in or around a stung finger may give temporary pain relief, but an injection of a powerful, morphine-like drug may be required. However, this treatment will be risky if there are respiratory complications, as there may be after a red scorpion sting, which causes flooding of fluids into the lungs (pulmonary oedema). Seek medical help if you can.

Contact information: stockists of antivenom

Lister Institute of Preventative Medicine, Elstree, Herts WD6 3AX, UK.

Hymenoptera (thin-waisted insects: bees, wasps, hornets, ants)

Normal insect repellent is ineffective against stinging insects such as bees, ants, wasps and hornets, although there are now some products to deter wasps. On encountering air-borne stinging insects, back off calmly; never thrash or flail about. Even a swarm of the feared killer bees should not attack if you stay cool. As they sting, wasps release alarm pheramones which summon other wasps to help in the attack.

Wasps and their kin are attracted by sweet things, perfumes and brightly-coloured floral patterns.

Honey-bees

When a bee stings, its stinger (complete with venom-sack) remains in the skin and continues to pump venom in after the bee has gone. Bees empty 90% of their venom within the first 20 seconds and the remainder within a minute, and the longer you take to get the stinger out the more painful the sting will be. Speed of sting removal is more important than technique. Try to scrape or flick it off with your fingernail. Fussing about to find a knife or pin with which to scrape or pick it out will lose time, while grasping stings with tweezers will inject the remaining venom left in the stinger.

Once the sting is out, **treatment** is to apply ice or a cold compress (wet cloth), elevate the part that has been stung, and take antihistamine tablets and/or *aspirin* or *paracetamol* (Tylenol). As a **natural remedy**, applying papaya – or extract of papaya in the form of meat tenderizer (at the ratio of 1:4 tenderizer to water) – probably relieves some of the pain through destroying the venom. It is worth trying.

A severe allergic reaction to stings causes a great deal of swelling and can provoke breathing difficulties; this can be fatal in minutes. Such a severe reaction is unlikely unless there have been previous stings. A hypersensitive individual will usually notice that with each sting they suffer, local swelling becomes increasingly extensive and persistent. Be warned. Most people in Britain who are allergic to bee stings are bee-keepers or their relatives (i.e. people who have been stung lots of times). Allergy is less likely in children than in adults. Those who are allergic should carry an *adrenaline* (*epinephrine*) Epipen or injection (*see* p.66), or a 'medihaler'.

Wasps and hornets

Wasps and hornets are not always yellow and black and stripy. The common Asian field wasp is plain orange, and there are other species that are navy blue. Wasps do not leave their stingers behind, but otherwise their stings require similar treatment to bee stings.

Fire ants (*Solenopsis* spp.)

Fire ants originated in South America but have spread to the USA, where large numbers of people are stung all year round. They have recently colonized Queensland in Australia, too, where they are also becoming a great nuisance. The ants are reddish-brown to black and they are small (less than a quarter of an inch/5mm long), but when

Fire ant

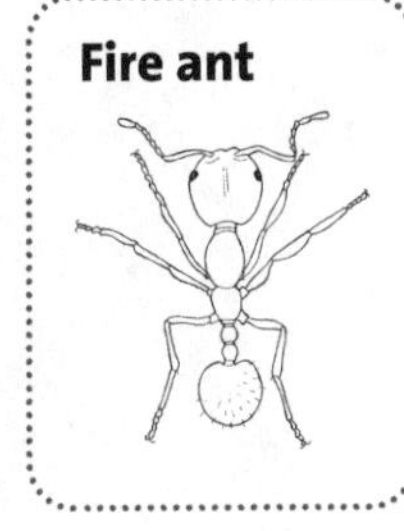

their colonies are disturbed the ants will attack in thousands. Victims suffer pain, itching, swelling and redness around a central weal or welt, which lasts for up to a few hours, and then a small blister containing clear fluid will form. Over the next half day or so, the fluid in the blister turns cloudy and the area begins to itch. As with stings from wasps and bees, fire-ant stings can cause dramatic and dangerous allergic reactions.

Sweat bees

These are small (3–4mm long) black bees which are attracted, often in large numbers, to sweaty skin, mouths and nostrils. They are annoying, slow moving and easy to kill, and their stings are trivial. However, if one gets crushed it will release pheromones that stimulate its friends to attack. They can then become intolerable. They live in many parts of the tropics and sub-tropics, and have pestered me in dry, deciduous forests in both Madagascar and lowland Nepal.

VENOMOUS SNAKES AND NASTY REPTILES

Venomous land snakes

Few snakes are dangerous. Of a possible 2,400 species worldwide, 500 are venomous, but fewer than 200 ever cause severe envenoming in humans leading to death or permanent disability. A good proportion of the snakes that are venomous do not have the capability or temperament to be harmful; even those that are venomous and aggressive more often than not give a 'dry' (harmless) bite. However, as the division between harmful and harmless species is far from clear, anyone bitten by a snake should be assessed by an expert. Snake venom is a kind of meat tenderizer produced by modified salivary glands; it partially digests the prey prior to being eaten, so it has some very unpleasant effects. There are about 40,000 deaths worldwide per year (mainly in India, from cobra), but it is exceptional for travellers to be envenomed. Those at high risk are agricultural labourers, who disturb happily basking snakes, or people who are foolish enough to tease snakes – teasing can cause the snake to increase the dose of venom. Peninsular Malaysia boasts a particularly rich array of venomous species but, even here, only about one in a thousand people bitten by a snake actually dies. It is 'energy-expensive' for a snake to make venom: it takes 2–3 weeks for a snake to recharge its venom gland, so it is reluctant to waste it on anything but food-hunting. In India snakes are most mischievous during the rains, and in most geographical regions they become active at dusk.

Case History: Nepal

I arrived at the district hospital in lowland Nepal after the outpatients clinic had finished, but one patient remained. An emaciated little boy squatted in the corridor, quivering in terror, with a string tied tightly around his arm, which was soaking in a bucket. He was scared to death, his fear aggravated by the fact that the local medical staff were scared to touch him. The child had been romping in leaf litter, and the snake he had disturbed had bitten the fleshy part of his hand, near the thumb. Someone had cut into the wound and applied the anus of a beheaded chicken, because the decapitated corpse is supposed to draw out the venom. I asked, 'Is there any antivenom in the hospital?' The Nepali staff laughed. 'No, but you can find it in the bazaar.'

'Can you get some, and we'll take off the tourniquet and observe the child with antivenom ready...'

I took off the tourniquet and the child was fine.

Cutting into a snake bite does not flush out venom, but it can sever arteries; **tourniquets** are also dangerous (*see* facing page). However, the chicken's arse treatment – where the anus of a decapitated chicken is applied to the wound in the belief that it will draw out the venom (*see* Case History above, p.259) – is based in perverse good sense, in that it may help the victim by preventing him from panicking. People bitten by snakes are so scared that they often thrash around in a blind panic, enabling venom to be distributed more quickly and effectively. A complicated ritual helps the victim stay calm, and this is an important but difficult part of snake bite treatment. Those managing the situation must appear confident and cool, even if they are panicking inside.

Snake bites and treatment

Snakes use their venom to hunt and so are often reluctant to waste it in unnecessary aggression. They can control whether they dispense venom or not and often bites are 'dry' and harmless – even if the snake

If a snake bites

1. If you are the victim, try to get someone to help you get help. The less you do the better.
2. Keep the victim still. Promote a calm atmosphere. It is likely to have been a 'dry' bite.
3. Clothes should be rolled up or cut, and not removed, because undressing encourages movement, which disperses venom.
4. The bitten part should be washed with clean water and soap, and wiped gently with a clean cloth to remove any venom from the skin surface. In Australia, the venom in the cloth may then be used to identify the snake and then the correct antivenom can be administered.
5. If venom has entered the body there may be swelling, so any rings, watches and jewellery must be removed.
6. If you have a crêpe bandage, apply this firmly over the bite-site as soon as possible and extend the bandaging to wrap up as much of the bitten limb as you can.
7. Then, splint the bitten limb to slow absorption of the venom and reduce pain.
8. Keeping the bitten limb below the level of the heart also helps slow the spread of the venom and is a useful maneouvre if if bandages and splints are not available.
9. Prompt evacuation to a doctor or hospital is the next priority. If the victim begins to show signs of envenomation, antivenom will then be administered in a safe clinical environment. Administering antivenom carries its own risks (*adrenaline/epinephrine* should be available); it can be dangerous, particularly if venom has not actually entered the body.

is venomous. Travellers are rarely unlucky enough to suffer a dangerous bite, but everyone wants to know what to do if they are on the wrong end of a pair of fangs. Try to get to a clinic or hospital where they know about snake bites. Many 'first aid' measures can make things much worse but, while evacuation is being organized, the rules in the box below will help protect the victim.

Tourniquets

A tourniquet is a tight band designed to cut off the blood supply to a limb. Using a tourniquet may be appropriate occasionally, but only under certain circumstances (*see* 'When to use tourniquets', below). A great many limbs are lost through incompetently applied tourniquets. Too often they are applied after a bite by a harmless snake or by a venomous one that has dispensed no venom. Home-made tourniquets do little to stop venom spreading through the body, yet can still cut off circulation enough to risk losing the limb. Applying a broad, firm crêpe bandage around the bitten limb and splinting it is a safer option than a

10. Finally, if the offending snake can be captured without risk of someone else being bitten, take it to show the doctor, so that it can be identified to help define proper treatment. Beware, though, that even a severed head is able to envenom in a reflex bite.
11. Never cut into the bite or suck the wound, and avoid using 'Venom-ex' or similar first-aid devices that cut the skin; they are dangerous and do no good.
12. If prompt evacuation is not going to be possible, release the crêpe bandage every half-hour for 15 seconds and remove it completely after two hours.
13. Do not take *aspirin*, but *paracetamol* (Tylenol) is safe.
14. Do not apply ice packs.
15. Do not apply *potassium permanganate*.
16. Don't panic: it is likely no venom has been dispensed.

When to use tourniquets

Tourniquets are only appropriate under the following circumstances:

→ The delay in getting to competent medical help is going to be more than 30 minutes but less than three hours.
→ The biter was an elapid snake (cobra, krait, mamba or coral snake), a sea snake (*see* p.180) or an Australian snake.
→ You know what you are doing and feel competent and calm enough to take charge of the situation.
→ The tourniquet is released for 15 seconds every 30 minutes.
→ The tourniquet is removed after two hours.
→ You have a watch, and can write down what you are doing.

tourniquet. Even the splinted bandage must be released every half-hour, to let blood reach the body tissues.

Electric shock or stun guns do not inactivate venom, nor do the 'snake stones' of India and Sudan, although they may be useful – like the headless chickens – by helping everyone to stay calm.

Snake habits

It is worth repeating that not all venomous snakes are dangerous. Many of the brightly coloured coral snakes have such small mouths that they are only capable of getting their teeth into an earlobe or finger web. In a review of snake bites in peninsular Malaysia, the only record of coral snake envenoming was one case, back in 1937 (the victim survived). Some South American species are big enough to bite a finger, if offered.

Other species, like the black-fanged snakes of Madagascar, can only inject venom as their victim is being swallowed, so they can only envenom those who stick a finger down their throats! Others do not have the temperament to attack. **Sea snakes**, for example, have a very powerful venom, but attacks by them are virtually unknown (*see* p.180). The highly venomous **krait** and much-feared **bushmaster** are similarly unlikely to bite, even if provoked (don't try it: kraits still claim a few lives).

Most deaths from snake bites are in the Indian subcontinent, because snakes there are often forced into contact with man. Most feared is the huge **king cobra** or hamadryad (*Ophiophagus hannah*), which can be 4.8m long and, in threatening mode, may stand 2m off the ground – looking you in the eye. When they attack they do so with enthusiasm, and are efficient dispensers of venom. However, they are a scarce day-active species that live in dense forest, and you are unlikely to meet one. They are fast movers, but cannot outrun a man. The Indian cobra (*Naja naja*) claims more victims than any other snake in the world, but is not usually aggressive, and often timid. It may attack when disturbed. The young can be real delinquents; they appear during the monsoon and are much more dangerous than adults, because they haven't learned to fear people, are more easily excited and are always

To avoid snakes

➜ Do not sleep on the ground, unless you are inside a tent with a sewn-in groundsheet.

➜ Sleep under a mosquito net that is tucked in.

➜ When walking around after dark, carry a torch and wear boots or strong shoes and long trousers.

➜ When collecting firewood, tip it away from yourself as you lift it to give the snake an easy route of escape.

ready to strike repeatedly and with determination, especially when cornered in a house. Indian cobras are active in the late afternoon, evening and at night.

One of the difficulties of treating snake bites in most regions is that the first aid required is different depending upon the kind of snake that bites you. **Viper** venom, for example, mainly harms by destroying tissue around the bite-site, so tourniquets make viper bites worse. Slowing down the circulation of venom, however, is life-saving in snakes whose venom attacks nerves or muscle, including heart tissue; this is the case with bites from **cobra**, **krait**, **mamba** or **coral snake**, **sea snake**, and all **Australian snakes**. In these situations, tightly wrap up as much of the bitten limb as possible with a stretchy bandage (you may need three crêpe bandges for a leg) and get yourself to a hospital or clinic that stocks antivenom.

Other health hazards from snakes

The most common problem caused by snake bites is **infection**. Even non-venomous British grass snakes will inflict a deep dirty wound that is hard to clean, so there is a risk of sepsis, tetanus and gangrene. Seek medical help after any snake bite.

Pythons and other large, non-venomous constrictors should be treated with respect. They can reach a length of 10m, and the largest occasionally kill people. A colleague has a gruesome portrait of a python (*Python reticularis*) killed in Sulawesi, which was sliced open to reveal the body of a man consumed on his wedding night. Pythons (*P. sebae*) have swallowed people in Africa and in South America (*Eunectes eunectes*). South American anacondas can weigh up to 230kg and have also been known to attack people.

Poisonous and dangerous lizards

In Madagascar I have been assured by local people that chameleons are deadly; in Thailand, geckos are also believed to be poisonous, as are cute little skinks in Nepal. All are harmless. There are only two venomous lizards: the **Gila monsters** and the **beaded lizard**. Both are big (45–80cm) and live in the Southwest USA and Mexico. There is no antivenom, but humans are rarely bitten and there are no reliable reports of deaths. The **Komodo dragon** of Indonesia, a flesh-eating monitor lizard that grows to 3m long, is not venomous; however, it has killed at least one careless tourist.

DANGEROUS LARGE MAMMALS

Man-eaters

Wildlife documentaries allow us to watch from our armchairs while animals dispatch their prey, and it's easy to forget that predators can hurt us, too. Few animals will pick a fight, but most will defend themselves if surprised or cornered, and females will be aggressive if they are with their young. Large primates, especially chimpanzees and baboons, are very dangerous. Do not go walking through dense scrub or long grass that could hide a rhino or buffalo. Big carnivores are probably best faced: running away will do you no good, since they can outrun you, and this is exactly what prey species do. Do something a prey species would not, such as throwing rocks, or running at the animal shouting and waving a big stick. The predator will (you hope) be so confused it will retreat. Don't sleep in a tent containing anything a big animal might relish; bears often rip open tents if they smell food inside, and carnivores or scavengers help themselves to meat.

Dangerous African animals

If venturing into wildlife country on foot, be sure to take a guide who understands animals. Many 'Africa hands' consider buffalo, hippopotamus and large primates (chimps and baboons) the most dangerous species.

Buffalo

Buffaloes are very aggressive, and hippos are likely to trample you by mistake if you frighten them and are between them and a river, their refuge. Hippos come out of the water to graze at dusk, during the night and on overcast days. Crocodiles are the other significant predator to respect if you are relaxing beside an African river (*see* p.189).

Large Asian species

In Africa there is generally space for both wildlife and man. In Asia, with more pressure on land, wild animals are in much closer conflict with farmers. Elephants can be very disgruntled and ill tempered, and they often attack: they kill about 250 people a year in India. Large cats (leopards and tigers) in the subcontinent seem to become man-eaters more frequently than in Africa, perhaps because they are so often close to villages and their protected areas are too small; talk to people before camping in big cat country.

The great Indian rhinoceros is dangerous if you meet it at close quarters on foot. Beware of walking through elephant-high grass in reserves

Case History: North America

I was on a solo camping trip to the Adirondack National Park in the USA, where bears have lost their fear of man and like to scrounge from campers. I was dropping off to sleep when I heard a large animal sniffing around outside the tent. Fortunately I had taken good advice. I had used a rope to hang my food (including tinned food, foody rubbish, even toothpaste) up in a tree away from where I was sleeping, so the bear soon lost interest in the tent. He was also perhaps put off a little by my banging of pots and pans. Bears have quite frequently clawed into tents after smelling food inside. In bear country, wash up plates and pots promptly, away from your camp, and burn any rubbish.

Dr Matthew Ellis, paediatrician, Bristol

where they are common and, if you meet one, climb a tree (adrenaline will rapidly improve your climbing skills), get behind a tree or lie down. And beware of picnicking near Asian temples; the rhesus monkeys may bite to persuade you to part with your lunch.

Bears

Bears are a hazard in places as far distant as the Himalayas and the Rockies. There were eight bear-related deaths in Alberta in the 15 years up to 1995, but compare this with 38 horse-riding deaths in the province over the same period; you are also 25 times more likely to be struck by lightning than killed by a bear in North America. Rural Nepalis are wary of their bears, which are short-sighted and may attack without provocation if they smell someone.

Dangerous domestic animals

Because humans have so much contact with domestic animals, they are much more likely to injure us than wild animals. Dogs kill hundreds of people, while healthy wolves have never killed anyone. There have been reports of deaths or severe injuries after attacks by camels, cattle, water buffalo, elephants, pigs, cats and even sheep and ferrets. Be wary of domestic animals you do not know. If you need to pass a pack animal on a cliff path, stand uphill, so that it does not push you over. Domestic animals and pets also act as disease reservoirs; parrots with runny noses harbour pneumonia-causing bugs, while pet terrapins, tortoises, snakes and even African pygmy hedgehogs are a common source of exotic Salmonella infections.

Dog bites and Rabies

The most common injuries inflicted by any largeish animal, at home or abroad, are dog bites. In England and Wales over 200,000 people

Case History: Peru

Matthew was visiting the Ashaninka Indians of the Peruvian Amazon as part of an anthropological research project. They were generous in their hospitality and the party went on late, until he and most of the tribe lost consciousness in the village plaza. Next morning he was disturbed to see two deep tooth-marks in his big toe, from which a puddle of blood was oozing. He could not decide which was more impressive, the power of the local hallucinogen (*ayahuasca*) or the vampire's local anaesthetic, which it administers before it dines. Vampire bats, like any mammal, can transmit rabies and, because of the anticoagulant they secrete, bites bleed a lot and easily become infected. These are two unexpected consequences of losing your inhibitions through recreational drugs. Luckily the vampire was not rabid.

Despite misleading Transylvanian legends, vampires only occur in the New World, and here they are small mammals. The rabies risk is another reason, when camping in tropical America, to sleep in a zippable tent or hammock with a mosquito net. In a rare plague of vampire bites in a Brazilian village in 1991, 314 people were bitten, three of whom died.

attend hospital for dog bites annually, and there are about 10 deaths. Worldwide, hundreds of people are killed by domestic dogs. If threatened by dogs, stoop as if to pick up a stone to throw at them; most dogs will retreat if they think you are armed with missiles.

Dog bites abroad are bad news because of the nasty injuries they inflict, because wounds frequently become badly infected, and because of the risk of tetanus and, in many countries, rabies. Even if you have both tetanus and rabies cover (*see* p.40, pp.47–8), bites can still become infected: they must be carefully cleaned and dressed, and medical help sought (or antibiotics started) if infection sets in (*see* pp.215–16).

Rabies is a huge problem in much of the developing world. More than 25,000 people die from it each year in India alone, and most are infected by stray dogs. Never handle wild animals that are unusually tame; they may be dying of rabies (*see* 'First aid for animal bites', below).

Cats

Cats can be quite vicious, and even trivial scratches or bites carry a risk of Cat Scratch Fever, caused by *Rochalimaea henselae* bacteria. This is usually a mild illness causing enlargement of the lymph nodes 2–3 weeks after a cat bite, scratch or a cat-flea bite. Perhaps one third of American cats are infected with the disease, but it will only cause significant problems in the elderly or debilitated. It can be treated with a course of *co-amoxiclav* or *clarithromycin* antibiotics. Recently, some Americans have also caught bubonic plague from their cats.

Rats and other rodents

Rodents can damage your health. They are a reservoir of bubonic **plague**, **Leptospirosis** (Weil's disease), **Tularaemia** and the dangerous **Hantavirus** in the Far East, North America and Europe (*see* pp.156, 212, 152, 272). Zoologists planning to handle wild rodents should consider these risks and that of rabies, and wear leather gloves.

First aid for animal bites

Clean any animal bite by scrubbing with soap under running water for five minutes, then liberally apply *povidone iodine* or alcohol (at least 40% – gin and whisky will do) or 0.01% *aqueous iodine*. Then seek medical help for further wound care (but do not allow anyone to suture the bite). If you are far from a clinic you may need to self-treat with a course of *co-amoxiclav* or *clarithromycin* antibiotics.

If you are in a region where **rabies** is a risk, **even if you have had pre-trip rabies immunization**, you should have two booster injections, or a course if you are not immune (*see* pp.47–8).

Tetanus cover is also necessary if you have not been immunized in the previous 10 years (if in doubt, get boosted, *see* p.40). If the usual tetanus injection that protects you long-term is given at the time of the bite, it may not become effective fast enough to protect you. A special, post-bite immunoglobulin needs to be given if you are not immune, and a course of immunization started for future protection.

The WHO recommends that dogs that have bitten people should be tied up; if the dog survives for 10 days it is said to be free from rabies, so there is therefore no risk to the bitten person. These guidelines were developed when the only treatment for suspect bites was the dangerous and painful series of 'Semple' vaccines (5% suspension of mouse or monkey brain) given into the abdomen on 21 consecutive days, followed by booster doses. Serious reactions to it happen as frequently as one in 76 courses (with 41% of those affected dying) and its efficacy is poor. Today the logical treatment is to vaccinate all people with suspect bites using the new, safe, effective vaccines.

If bitten, you need cover with the **Merieux inactivated rabies vaccine** or other tissue-culture product. Some embassies can arrange supplies; otherwise you should travel to an international clinic or fly home for treatment. The Semple vaccine may be all that is immediately available in some regions, but it is not worth the risk.

Getting treatment in time

I have met a surprising number of people who have been bitten by dogs or other animals that they feared might be rabid, but, since they were far from medical help, have just hoped for the best and had no

Case History: United States

On 13 April 1990 a man in Texas picked up a bat that he'd noticed lying on the ground; it bit him on the finger. The bat was small, and had only just broken his skin, so he did not wash the bite or see a doctor. He became ill on 30 May, and died of rabies on 5 June despite excellent medical care. Since 1980, 12 of the 25 confirmed rabies deaths in the USA have been blamed on bats. This man's mistakes were to handle an animal that was abnormally tame (it was dying of rabies); having been bitten, he then failed to clean or sterilize the wound and, finally, he failed to arrange protective, post-bite injections.

treatment whatsoever. Yet, once symptoms of rabies appear, it is an incurable, invariably fatal disease, and the mode of death is horrible. The incubation period between the bite and the onset of symptoms depends on the distance of the bite from the brain and the severity of the bite. Generally it is between two and eight weeks, but it can be a little as four days, and as long as seven years. The virus travels along the nerves and only causes encephalitis and hydrophobia when it arrives at the brain. At this point there is no treatment that will save the victim. Most adults are bitten on the leg, so the incubation period for the disease (and thus the interval they have to be vaccinated) may be weeks. It is pure madness, then, not to seek help, even if it is long after the bite. The days of painful injections into the abdomen are long gone, and the post-bite treatment is a series of ordinary injections with fewer side effects than pre-trip immunizations.

Act as soon as possible. Clean the wound thoroughly and do not delay seeking medical treatment. Those with an ostrich-like, head-in-the-sand approach to protecting their health should realize that it is never too late to have post-bite injections. Bites closer to the brain need urgent action. Small children are often bitten on the face by dogs, in which case treatment must be immediate.

On The Ground

Ailments

18

Few of the illnesses people catch abroad are serious. This chapter covers treatment of ailments that often trouble travellers whether close to or far from home. Sore throats and colds are common everywhere; coughs and chest infections are probably even more frequent than at home.

Rare and exotic diseases are such a topic of conversation among travellers, though, that I have also included a few notes on the most talked-about pestilences. Illnesses detailed elsewhere can be found by referring to the index. I have deliberately avoided mentioning every possible disease by name, but the prevention strategies recommended will protect you from almost all problems. Taking precautions against malaria, for example, will protect you from Japanese encephalitis; eating well-cooked foods rather than salads or raw fish will help you avoid filth-to-mouth diseases as well as all those wonderful unpronounceable parasites.

Summary

→ Avoid all unnecessary medical treatment which involves injections, and also do all you can to avoid situations that make medical treatment necessary.

→ Take care to reduce the chances of road accidents; motorcycles are the most hazardous form of transport.

→ Injecting drugs carries the risk of acquiring AIDS and hepatitis B.

→ Carrying illicit drugs in many countries is a very serious crime, even a capital offence.

→ Intoxication and addiction in itself kills a fair number of travellers each year.

FEVERS

Fever is a common symptom of many diseases; it makes most people intermittently feel uncomfortably hot, then chilled to the marrow. Fever causes lethargy, aches, pains and headache. Taking *aspirin* or *paracetamol* (*acetaminophen*/Tylenol) regularly (every 4–6 hours) and drinking plenty will help these symptoms. Children and those with ulcers or stomach problems should not take *aspirin*. It's easy to become dehydrated with a fever, especially in a hot climate, which will make you feel even worse.

If drinking plenty and taking *aspirin* or *paracetamol* does not make you feel much better, think about the cause of the fever and consider further treatment. Do you, for example, have a cough or an inflamed area of skin? Infections that often cause fevers are **colds**, **'flu**, **chest infections** and **skin infections**. In women, **cystitis** is common (*see* pp.233–4), and in children, **middle ear infections** or **tonsillitis**: the sore throat of tonsillitis usually puts children off their food. Usually you will know what is causing the fever, so you can refer to the relevant section of this book. Whatever you have is probably trivial or treatable but, if in doubt, and if simple rehydration and *aspirin* do not have much effect, seek a medical opinion. Seek help as soon as possible if a child is ill.

There are two serious but treatable infections that cause high fever and significant illness without many other symptoms to help locate the source of the trouble. **Malaria** and also **Leptospirosis** can cause fever and severe illness without any obvious focus and with diagnostic tests often staying 'normal' initially. The treatment of Leptospirosis is with *doxycycline* or another a tetracycline antibiotic. Malaria treatment is detailed in **Malaria**, p.140.

Case History: Out of Africa

I was called to see a five-year-old girl who had returned to England from Kenya a month previously, and had just stopped taking her malaria tablets. She was very unwell with a high fever. Her parents were sure she had malaria, because they had friends who had developed malaria on stopping antimalarial tablets a month after leaving Africa. When I examined her I found she had huge, inflamed tonsils and swollen, tender lymph glands in her neck. Her bacterial tonsillitis responded to a 10-day course of penicillin.

The parents were right to consult a doctor. East Africa is a high-risk area for malaria, but their care with taking tablets and using mosquito nets and repellents had paid off. The child merely had a common, treatable childhood illness.

Some rarities

Anthrax

Anthrax is a disease that can occasionally be caught from animals and the people who are occasionally infected are agricultural, tannery and other workers involved in processing bone, hair and hides. It can enter the human body by inhalation, when it can cause a **high fever** and severe illness, but more common is the skin form, where, over a period of 2–6 days, a painless swelling (on the hands, forearms or head) breaks down, weeps and develops a black centre. The illness is treated with one of several readily available antibiotics and is not spread from person to person. Occasionally, travellers are infected from poorly tanned or cured animal skin items from the developing world. There is a gastrointestinal form, but proper cooking kills anthrax and renders infected foods safe.

Ebola virus

Ebola occurs in outbreaks in Congo (formerly Zaïre), Sudan, the Côte d'Ivoire and Gabon. It makes people very ill suddenly with a **high fever**, after an incubation of about seven days; half of its victims die. Since most cases are infected through direct contact with body fluids, this is rarely a disease of ordinary travellers, but it can involve development workers in hospitals.

Hantavirus

Hantavirus has caused concern in the Americas, but also occurs in the Far East and elsewhere. Infection comes from mice, if an infected mouse excretes on or nibbles uncooked food that you eat. Symptoms are **fever**, aches and pains, which can progress to breathing difficulties that may kill up to half those affected. It does not respond to antibiotics. Prevent it by ensuring that all food is peeled, boiled or cooked.

OTHER INFECTIONS

Lots of infections – both tropical and mundane – cause rashes and spots. Those who notice spots but have no fever and who feel well otherwise are unlikely to have anything nasty.

Chickenpox

Most adults (90%) are immune to chickenpox or varicella virus and in the USA children are immunized. People in the infectious stages of the disease (which is two days before the onset of the rash and until all spots become dry scabs) should not fly. Pregnant women who are exposed to chickenpox and who have not had the disease or been immunized need to seek medical advice; chickenpox is likely to be more severe in adulthood, especially in pregnancy, and there are implications for the baby. Chickenpox is dangerous to those with compromised immune systems, e.g. those who have had cancer or cancer treatment within the previous six months.

'Slapped Cheek' Disease

This is a common parvovirus infection, which causes fever and characteristic red cheeks, but the infected child remains well and there is not much of a rash elsewhere. Most adults (60%) are already immune, having had the disease mildly in early life. However, if a non-immune mother gets it during the first 20 weeks of pregnancy, there can be severe foetal anaemia which needs careful monitoring and possibly treatment with foetal blood transfusions. A blood test done at the time of exposure to the virus will determine the mother's immune status.

Case History: Peru

When my sister and I were medical students we organized a scientific expedition to Peru and, being keen and ignorant, carefully read up about the nasty tropical diseases we might catch. About 10 days after arriving in the Andes, my sister began feeling ill, and one morning awoke with spots. She diagnosed fleas, and furiously hurled her sleeping bag into the river. I disagreed with her diagnosis (the pustules were not in the typical breakfast–elevenses–lunch–tea–supper pattern of fleas), but my mind started sifting through the tropical diseases she might have. We were most worried about Verruga or Oroya Fever: a rapidly fatal, incurable disease (we vaguely remembered) infamous in the area.

Then, one of the non-medical members of the team said, 'That rash looks just like one my little sister had with chickenpox!' And chickenpox it was. Later we discovered that Oroya Fever is not only very rare, but that it responds to antibiotics and is not that dangerous after all.

Foot and Mouth Disease

Foot and Mouth is an infection of cattle and is not a risk to humans. The stringent controls that are put in place during a foot and mouth outbreak are to prevent the spread of infection between livestock. There have been one or two cases of agricultural workers becoming infected but these people are in direct and often very close contact with infected animals. Although perhaps aesthetically unattractive, eating cooked meat from an animal infected with Foot and Mouth is not hazardous to human health. This is a completely different microbe to the virus causing Hand, Foot and Mouth Disease, a benign illness that is common in children.

COUGHS AND CHEST AND BREATHING PROBLEMS

Coughs or colds may be the last thing you expect to catch while in hot places, but they are as common there as anywhere and, if you are mixing with more people (including on planes), you may be more at risk of catching a mild respiratory infection. Moist, warm, tropical atmospheres also allow germs to survive for longer between victims. The fever these infections cause can largely be controlled by taking *paracetamol* or *aspirin* every 4–6 hours or *ibuprofen* eight-hourly. Gargling (and then swallowing) soluble tablets helps relieve a sore throat. Sore throats and colds are usually caused by viruses, so antibiotics are no help. If you are feverish increase the amount you drink, as even mild dehydration will make you feel worse. The common cold lasts about a week. If it goes on longer, suspect an allergy and try antihistamine tablets (e.g. Piriton or Benadryl), or see a doctor. If you have a cold and a drippy nose, buy cloth rather than paper handkerchiefs or your nose will get sore.

The rate at which someone breathes can be a helpful guide to significant disease in the chest. Unfortunately it is near-impossible to record your own breathing rate accurately, or the rate of someone who knows you are timing them. The normal respiratory rate of an adult is about 12–20 breaths a minute; a rate of 40 a minute implies something may need treatment, or that the person is hyperventilating through anxiety. If the person is asthmatic, remind them to use their inhaler. Normal respiratory rates in children are below 30, and in babies below 40.

If there are breathing difficulties and/or a cough, humidified air helps; in hotels with hot water, fill the bathroom with steam. This is useful in children with croup (which causes a characteristic, rough-sounding cough). Small babies with colds may get cross at being unable to breathe and feed simultaneously. Put a drop of boiled-and-cooled water into each nostril and the baby will sneeze out or sniff in the offending snot.

Coughs without fever

Honey (by spoonful or in drinks) is a pleasant, soothing, natural remedy for coughs. Cough medicines offer some comfort, but beware of what you buy abroad as some contain bizarre and even addictive concoctions. If available, stick to *simple linctus* (a soothing syrup), or make your own with equal amounts of fresh lemon/lime juice, honey and rum or whisky in a little hot water. Inhaling infusions of eucalyptus oil, Vicks or tiger balm in hot water also helps. Drinking plenty of water, tea or similar drinks helps to loosen a cough and expectorate phlegm, while gargling with warm water helps settle a tickly cough and can be very soothing.

Case History: Nepal

John had been travelling rough in Nepal for four months and was feeling very unwell. He told me that he'd had bad luck with his health during this trip. He had a splitting headache, a severe stabbing pain in the right side of his chest and aching limbs and back. He had a fever and felt a little disorientated. He had a slight tickly cough, made worse by cigarettes. He looked very unwell, was trembling and was very distressed by pain in his chest whenever he moved, breathed in deeply or coughed. His temperature was 40°C (104°F). He had pneumonia. He was a lot better after 18 hours of penicillin, lots to drink and regular *aspirin* (two every four hours).

Coughing up blood

Blood-stained spit, or larger quantities of blood brought up by coughing, is a reason to seek medical help and probably have a chest X-ray. See a doctor, also, if you have a cough for more than four weeks.

Chest infections and chest pain

A chest infection may be indicated by a cough and fever (especially if you produce a lot of discoloured, thick spit), or a fever with chest pain (especially if it is worse on breathing in), or by a feeling of tightness in the chest. Treatment with antibiotics is likely to help. Take *penicillin* 500mg four times a day or *amoxycillin* 500mg three times a day for seven days, unless you are allergic to penicillins; in this case, you can take *cephradine* 1g twice daily, or *erythromycin* 250mg four times daily, or *clarithromycin* 250mg twice daily. Otherwise, try *trimethoprim* 200mg twice a day (safe for those allergic to penicillin, but not for pregnant women). In addition, take *aspirin* (or *paracetamol*) every 4–6 hours to control fever and pain. If symptoms do not improve in 48 hours change antibiotics: penicillin takers should add *erythromycin* or *clarithromycin*. Penicillin is the first choice antibiotic in pneumonia; however, resistance has become common in the Far East, Papua New Guinea, South African and Spain and so *clarithromycin* would probably be the best choice in these regions.

Severe central chest pain, especially if crushing in nature and without fever, needs urgent, careful medical assessment. Heart problems are most common in men over 50, especially if heavy smokers and over-weight. Smokers suffer more chest infections in general, and are more at risk from illnesses like Legionnaires' Disease (*see* p.226). A burning pain at the bottom of the ribcage ('heartburn') is likely to be indigestion. If the pain is severe or is not relieved by taking antacids, seek medical help urgently.

Tuberculosis (TB)

TB is a potentially serious infection that usually begins in the lungs and is very common in those who live in overcrowded housing. Travellers on a short trip to a developing country are unlikely to risk infection, but there is some risk for expatriates. TB is spread by infected people coughing over others, but since it is not very infectious TB is only caught after a great deal of exposure over a long period. Walking through a market puts you at no risk, but those living in the Indian subcontinent, Africa, Southeast Asia and some countries in Eastern Europe may catch TB from sharing a small, poorly-ventilated office with ailing colleagues, or from ill staff at home. Medical personnel looking after the sick in a hospital or refugee camp are at risk. TB can also be contracted from infected cows' milk, but not from insect bites, drinking water, food or crockery, nor from touching an infected person. BCG immunization gives about 80% protection; it is not commonly used in the USA (*see* pp.40–41). People with TB often look quite well, and symptoms tend to come on gradually and insidiously; they include fever, night sweats, lethargy, a cough and, eventually, blood in the spit. Expatriates might ask staff or potential staff if they ever cough up blood, so that treatment can be arranged. Not all persistent coughers have TB, but it is more likely in people who have been coughing for more than three weeks. Even if you have been sharing a house with local coughers, do not worry about TB in yourself unless you notice symptoms. Then, seek a check-up and chest X-ray when convenient. Treatment is easy and effective, but tablets need to be taken carefully for a full six months.

HEPATITIS AND JAUNDICE

Hepatitis means inflammation of the liver. The common causes in travellers are three viruses: **hepatitis A** (also called infective hepatitis), **hepatitis B** (serum hepatitis) and newly recognized **hepatitis E**. Jaundice (yellowing) due to the hepatitis A or E virus is frequently acquired by travellers, especially in the Indian subcontinent and tropical Central and South America: it is one of the many filth-to-mouth diseases (*see* p.101). Hepatitis B is acquired in the same ways as HIV: dirty needles, blood transfusions and sex. It will need hospital treatment. For information on hepatitis A and B immunization *see* **Immunizations**, pp.41 and 46.

Hepatitis A usually begins with feelings of profound lethargy, lack of appetite, nausea and generally being unwell. As this begins to go away the whites of the eyes and the skin turn yellow. At this point, you look worse but feel much better. It is a variable illness, which leaves some people feeling very debilitated for many months, but is not dangerous. **Pregnant women**, though, can become profoundly ill with hepatitis E, so they must be very cautious about avoiding filth-to-mouth infections.

Western medicine can do little for sufferers of hepatitis A and E, but people experience dramatic improvements by taking ayurvedic medicines (on the recommendation of a Western-trained doctor) and Tibetan *amchi* medicines. There are ayurvedic hospitals in Kathmandu and many Indian cities. During recovery from hepatitis, experiment to see what you can eat and drink. Fatty foods (e.g. fried food, peanut butter, avocado, mayonnaise, coleslaw) and alcohol commonly upset jaundiced people, and it may be necessary to be teetotal for six months or so. Your level of activity should be built up slowly; overdoing it causes profound fatigue. Rest as much as you need, avoid alcohol and, if fatty foods upset you, do not eat them.

SYMPTOMS RELATED TO THE GUT

Episodes of **nausea**, poor appetite and feeling vaguely unwell are common in travellers. This may be a mild assault by diarrhoea-causing pathogens, in which case 24 hours on a bland, light diet will help settle the problem. *Proguanil* (Paludrine) and several other antimalarial tablets also cause nausea if taken on an empty stomach, so take them after a meal. Whole yoghurt or *lactobacillus* capsules (*see* **Bowels**, p.108) should help. Constipation can also be a cause of queasy feelings. It is worth noting that the way English-speakers describe nausea differs on either side of the Atlantic. The British talk of feeling sick, which to an American simply means feeling unwell. Brits talking to American doctors need to explain that they feel like vomiting.

Constipation

Constipation is a common problem in the tropics, since it can be difficult to eat enough fibre. Wholemeal flour is rarely available in the developing world, but the coarse wheat flour (*atta*) used to make Indian chapattis is wholemeal, and I have made very good bread with it. Cornmeal tortillas in Latin America are also a good source of fibre. Dehydration and immobility make constipation worse (going for a run may help get things going), and painkillers and many other medicines can aggravate it. Uncomfortable constipation can be caused by anti-diarrhoea medicines, especially Paregoric. Even without 'blockers', travellers often oscillate between diarrhoea and constipation. Bananas and eggs exacerbate constipation, but other fruits help relieve it.

Natural remedies for constipation

Ispaghula husk, which originated in South America but is available in Britain (as Fybogel, Regulan) and sold in India as flea-seed husk or *saat ispagol*, is a useful regulator. Mix it with a glass of water and swallow it down quickly; if you hesitate, the solution turns the consistency of wall-paper paste and is difficult to get down. You'll need to drink more water or juices while taking this remedy. If you're very constipated it takes a few days and several doses to take effect, but it works very well and counteracts the see-sawing between diarrhoea and constipation; it is often suggested to help the symptoms of irritable bowel syndrome. Increasing your **bran** intake will also help, but this is very difficult to find or identify in many destinations. In Indonesia it was sometimes available but the label of brown/chocolate-coloured powder/flour seemed to cover bran, wholemeal flour and also chocolate powder.

If eating more fruit and increasing the amount you drink does not get the bowels moving, and you cannot get bran or ispaghula husk, then take **lactulose syrup** 15ml with breakfast. This is a gentle, natural laxative which takes a day or two to work. With severe constipation you can take twice this dose twice a day (i.e. 60ml a day), but build up the dose gradually. Lactulose syrup is bulky and heavy, so it is not an ideal medicine for backpackers, but if constipation is really getting you down you may wish to stop and rest for a few days. Constipation remedies draw water into the bowel to loosen the stool, so you must also increase yet more the amount you drink.

Senna is a powerful stimulant laxative. Once you have started to re-establish a normal pattern try to ensure that you go to the toilet whenever the urge strikes (usually after food or hot drinks). This may be easier said than done, but the constipating effects of dehydration are exacerbated by 'hanging on' too long.

Piles

Haemorrhoids or piles may begin during exotic travel. They are caused by anything that increases pressure within the abdomen. A common factor in travellers is constipation, so drink plenty, eat lots of fruit, avoid constipating food (like eggs and bananas) and take regular exercise. Obesity can also bring piles on or make them worse, so keeping slim and fit is advisable (spending a long time reading on the toilet is also said to encourage them). Mountaineers sometimes get piles because of the strain of heavy packs combined with exercising and breathing hard at altitude.

Piles are small bulges in the lining of the rectum. Some hang out through the anus like the fleshy end of a little finger. Most itch, and some will bleed. They are harmless, but can be very painful, or at the least, uncomfortable. Treatment while travelling can be difficult. Keep them clean (their shape and position means they are easily soiled, and makes them even more itchy and uncomfortable), keep them lubricated with some bland cream (e.g. Anusol, Sudocrem) and try to ease them back inside the rectum. If they are very painful you will need to rest (lying on your side or face down, propping the bottom up on a pillow). Warm baths or cold compresses (crushed ice in a condom) may help.

Occasionally a small blood vessel can leak into a pile so that it becomes intensely painful and looks purple. Purple piles more than 2cm in diameter need to be lanced with a scalpel (perhaps surprisingly, it brings great relief), and smaller ones that are very painful may also be lanced. If there is no one available to do this, it will take over a week for the pain to subside, but there will be no long-term damage.

Abdominal pain

Pains in the abdomen (tummy) frequently accompany diarrhoea, but are often relieved by passing wind or a motion. If diarrhoea is the cause, pain usually comes in waves. If pain is severe, constant, of sudden onset, worsens rapidly, is associated with a high fever, long-lasting (more than four hours) or not accompanied by diarrhoea, it may be a sign of serious disease and a doctor should be consulted. **Appendicitis** often starts as a central, umbilical pain, which moves to the right lower corner of the abdomen and settles there. **Diarrhoea** and **constipation** can both cause pain spasms in the lower left abdomen. A competent medical opinion should sort out the trivial from the serious. New or persistent symptoms are always worth a consultation. For burning pains or discomfort below the rib cage (**heartburn**) and other stomach symptoms, *see* below.

Stomach or **duodenal ulcers** tend to cause a gnawing pain between the navel and the bottom of the rib cage, in the pit of the stomach. If simple antacids do not give relief, *ranitidine* or *cimetidine* should help. When you return home, consult your doctor.

Heartburn and indigestion

A burning pain at the bottom of the ribcage should respond to simple antacids (such as *magnesium trisilicate* or *aluminium hydroxide*, e.g. Amphojel, Aludrox, Maalox, Tums and Magalan) or with alginates (such as Gaviscon or Algicon), which put a raft of seaweed extract onto the stomach contents to decrease reflux. Yoghurt can be settling too, and cutting alcohol and cigarette consumption usually helps. Try *ranitidine* or *cimetidine* if antacids don't work.

Stomach acid is the body's first line of defence against any pathogens you have swallowed; taking antacids reduces stomach acid and so makes you more prone to diarrhoeal disease. It is likely, too, that acid-reducing medicines, including *ranitidine* (Zantac), *cimetidine* (Tagamet), *lansoprazole* (Zoton), *omeprazole* (Losec) and related drugs, increase susceptibility to intestinal or other infections. Antacids too will increase the risk of acquiring Brucellosis, so veterinary surgeons should think twice about taking them. Boiling milk products before consumption will eliminate Brucellosis organisms.

Vomiting blood

Vomited blood can look like coffee grounds; it is a serious symptom that needs prompt medical assessment. If, however, the blood has been swallowed after a nose bleed, this need cause no concern and no treatment is required. Often, smears of blood are apparent with tonsillitis; a doctor can confirm this for you.

PROBLEMS OF THE HEAD, NOSE AND THROAT

A severe headache of an unusual type, or one associated with fever, profuse vomiting or inability to look at light, needs urgent medical help: it could be caused by meningitis or another infection (*see* below). **Headache** is more often a symptom of dehydration, and people new to hot climates are often surprised by how much they need to drink. Do not worry about replacing salt lost in sweat, but drink plenty and, if vomiting, take sips of oral rehydration solution.

Carbon monoxide poisoning over weeks, from faulty gas appliances or kerosene fires, can also cause troublesome headaches. If headaches start after a head injury, or you experience recurrent headaches of an unfamiliar type, seek medical help promptly. Headaches caused by altitude are covered in **High, Cold and Dark**, pp.199–205. Expatriates with recurrent headaches should consider whether they need an eye test for spectacles or whether they are overworking, stressed or drinking too much alcohol.

Meningitis (*see* pp.44–5) causes fever and such an intense **headache** that you won't want to roll over in bed or look at light. It is a medical emergency.

Typhoid and **paratyphoid fevers** are filth-to-mouth illnesses common in South Asia and tropical Latin America. Vaccine is only partially effective (*see* pp.41–2). The incubation period is about two weeks; then there is **headache**, aching limbs, tiredness, constipation, cough and fever. Fever increases over the first week to 39–40°C; there may then be a rash of tiny, rose-pink spots on the abdomen or chest. Without treatment, the disease is likely to become very serious by the end of the second week, when diarrhoea starts. By the third week there is a real risk of intestinal perforation and bleeding. The illness responds well to antibiotics, so seek medical help if this description fits.

Brucellosis is transmitted by drinking infected unpasteurized cows' or goats' milk. Illness begins after an incubation interval of 1–3 weeks, with **headache**, loss of appetite, a feeling of being unwell, constipation, often a cough, fever and profuse sweating. It settles down after about 10 days, but the fever returns repeatedly for months. There may also be pain in the joints. It is treatable with antibiotic injections.

Feeling faint

Feeling you are about to faint is a common symptom if you are unwell. Feeling dizzy on standing up or getting out of bed is known as postural hypotension, which implies you have insufficient body fluids circulating to get enough blood to your brain. The most common cause of postural hypotension in travellers is dehydration – from diarrhoea and/or drinking insufficently in hot weather. Try drinking two litres of water (or ORS solution, *see* pp.109–111); carry on until you need to pass water. Until you are topped up with fluids again, sit with your legs over the side of the bed for a minute or so before standing up. A serious but rare cause of hypotension is blood loss. If you think you may have lost blood due to an injury or internal bleeding – if you have vomited 'coffee grounds' (*see* p.281) or passed blood (*see* pp.113–4) – get medical attention urgently.

Occasionally, women with very heavy periods become anaemic and notice dizziness on getting up; a doctor may be able to sort this out, but it is not an urgent matter.

Sinusitis

When the normally air-filled sinuses in the skull fill with mucus, there is pain at the front of the face, and sometimes even toothache affecting several top teeth on one side. Sometimes it can cause intense pain in an eyeball. The best treatment is to liquify the secretions, by leaning over a large bowl of steaming hot water with a towel draped over you and the bowl. Aromatic additions help e.g. natural oils, tiger balm, friars' balsam, menthol, eucalyptus. Antihistamines (*see* motion sickness table in **Flight**, pp.92–3) may help, especially if you tend to suffer from hay fever. Decongestants like *pseudoephedrine* (Sudafed or Actifed in the UK and the USA) are sometimes recommended by doctors and pharmacists, but these thicken mucus and – especially if several doses are taken – tend to make things worse. Flying increases sinus pain, so if your sinuses are clogged you might need to delay the trip; alternatively, you could try lots of steam inhalations and then, two hours before take-off, one dose of *pseudoephedrine*. If sinusitis makes you feverish and very unwell, take a seven-day course of *doxycycline* (e.g. Vibramycin), 200mg on the first day, then 100mg daily, with plenty of water during a meal. Do not use *doxycycline* if you are pregnant. *Trimethoprim* 200mg twice daily or *co-amoxiclav* 250mg three times a day are good alternatives.

Nose bleeds

Nose bleeds should be treated by rest and cold compresses on the bridge of the nose. Lean forward and pinch the nose, releasing the pressure every few minutes. Leaning back will make you swallow blood and provoke a vomit. Recurrent nose bleeds can be a problem in very dry conditions, especially in high, cold deserts (*see* p.197). Bleeding from the nose, gums or elsewhere when you are feverish requires urgent medical assessment.

Earaches and itches

Earache in both ears is more likely due to mucus congestion than infection. Steam inhalations plus *aspirin* can help; one dose of a decongestant like *pseudoephedrine* (Sudafed) might help, and is often useful before a flight, but taking this medicine regularly tends to thicken mucus and aggravate the problem. If earache is on one side only, with fever, take penicillin 500mg every six hours at least half an hour before food, or *trimethoprim* 200mg twice daily for five days.

If an ear becomes inflamed, swollen, distorted or very itchy, there is probably an infection of the ear canal. This is common, especially in hot, moist climates. Treat (2–3 times daily) with drops of a combination of an antibiotic (*neomycin*, *gentamicin*, *chloramphenicol* or *framycetin*) with a mild steroid, 0.5% *hydrocortisone* (Otosporin, Audicort, Framycort in the UK; Cortisporin otic drops in the USA). Useful alternatives are drops that acidify the ear canal (*aluminium acetate* 8% or *boric acid* in very dilute form). They work well, are cheap and are less likely to cause allergy than antibiotic combinations. Introducing anything into the ear can stimulate infection, so never, ever use cotton buds or put anything smaller than your little finger in your ear. On objects in the ear, *see* p.307. People who are prone to recurrent infections of the ear canal would be well advised to pack a remedy in their medical kit.

Sore throats and throat infections

Sore throats can be a problem in very dry environments, especially at altitude when you may find yourself breathing through your mouth rather than the nose. The best treatment is to suck boiled sweets or pastilles, and drink plenty. In adults, throat infections and tonsillitis are usually caused by viruses, so antibiotic treatment is unhelpful. Viral infections are the most likely diagnosis if the sore throat is accommpanied by symptoms of a cold. Keep drinking; gargle every 2–3 hours with one soluble *aspirin* or *paracetamol* (Tylenol), then swallow the gargle (take no more than eight *paracetamol* in 24 hours). Even gargling with warm water can be soothing. Treatable, bacterial throat infections cause fever, you often feel very unwell, there are swollen painful neck glands, obviously inflamed tonsils covered in white pus, and no cough. If you take an antibiotic it should be for a full 10 days (even though the symptoms will settle in about two). Take *penicillin* 250mg four times daily for 10 days, or *erythromycin* if allergic to *penicillin*.

Diphtheria has virtually disappeared in the West but is still a problem in many tropical and temperate regions, including the ex-Soviet countries. It starts with a sore throat and can progress rapidly to cause difficulties with breathing; it can also damage the heart and nervous system and, if untreated, can kill. Immunization gives excellent protection (*see* p.40) but, even so, prophylactic *erythromycin* is advised if there has been close contact with someone with diphtheria.

Sore throat and mild feelings of being unwell can also herald one serious infection: **Lassa Fever**. This is acquired in rural West Africa. In many cases the disease is mild, and indeed, children who are exposed to the infection often experience few or no symptoms at all. Infection can come from swallowing urine of the multimammate rat (usually via contaminated, uncooked food), so it is theoretically a risk for travellers staying in villages and eating uncooked food, but most cases are in health personnel working in unsanitary hospitals. In adults, the first symptoms are an undramatic sore throat, aches and pains; then, after 3–6 days, there is a sudden deterioration. Those who die succumb 7–14 days after the first symptoms. Seek medical help promptly if you are, or have been, in West Africa and develop a sore throat within three days of arriving or within 30 days of leaving the region. Lassa Fever is one of a clutch of very rare, highly infectious and serious viral haemorrhagic fevers that cause bruising and bleeding. Avoid it by eating properly cooked food.

At home, anyone suffering from a **hoarse voice** for over three weeks would see an Ear, Nose and Throat specialist. If there is no obvious cause of prolonged hoarseness (such as a harsh, dry climate), it's wise to do so while travelling too.

EYE PROBLEMS

Black and yellow eyes

A black eye consists of simple bruising around the eye, so the best treatment is cold compresses, as for bruising anywhere else (*see* p.302). If there seems to be any injury to the eye, or headaches begin after sustaining the black eye, seek medical help immediately. Double vision on looking up after an eye injury is a symptom that needs medical assessment reasonably promptly.

If the whites of your eyes turn **yellow** you have jaundice, probably due to infectious hepatitis (hepatitis A); there is no specific treatment (but *see* above, p.278).

Red eye, conjunctivitis and other irritations

Superficial eye infections or pink-eye are very common, especially in the tropics. Infection usually starts in one eye but rapidly spreads to both, making them feel sticky, gritty, red and painful.

Conjunctivitis

The first thing you may notice is the eyelids stuck together with green gunk in the morning. This is usually caused by bacterial infection, and treated with antibiotic drops into both eyes, initially every two or three hours. *Chloramphenicol* or *neomycin* are fine; newer, fancier antibiotics cost more but are probably no better. If symptoms do not start to improve after 36 hours, try *tetracycline* drops or ointment; if this does

Case History: UK

Alexander, aged 11, awoke on a Monday morning with a painful red eye. He'd just returned from a weekend with his cousins and they'd been romping in grass and throwing sticky burdock seeds at each other. He had a slight cold. His family doctor diagnosed viral conjuctivitis and prescribed some antibiotic drops. The doctor explained that mild viral conjuctivitis often accompanies colds. Alexander's other symptoms improved but the eye steadily got redder and felt worse. It was uncomfortable to look at light, and the eye watered a great deal. Alexander saw the doctor again on Wednesday, who sent him to the eye specialists at the hospital. The ophthalmologist removed a slender spicule, presumably part of a burr, and the eye immediately started feeling better. The 'foreign body', which was tiny but stuck into the underside of the upper lid, had slightly scratched the intensely sensitive front of the eye. The eye recovered completely within a few more days.

It is very unusual indeed for conjuctivitis to affect only one eye and where one eye is red and painful, expert assessment by a specialist is usually necessary.

not work seek medical help. Avoid eye preparations that contain extras, especially *hydrocortisone*, *betamethasone* or other steroids. If you notice a change in your ability to see, or if there is great pain in the eyeball or behind the eye, you should consult a physician or specialist in eyes or internal medicine. If the problem remains confined to one eye only, it is unlikely to be simple conjunctivitis: it could be iritis or a foreign body in the eye. See an eye specialist.

Conjunctivitis can be caused by viruses. In that case, inflammation will be less, there will be less green discharge and you will probably have a cold and/or sore throat. This will get better without treatment (antibiotic drops do no harm, if in doubt). In bacterial and viral conjunctivitis, bathing the eye in warm, slightly salty water will aid removal of any discharge. Getting noxious chemicals in the eye such as slug slime, cicada spit, whip-scorpion squirt or centipede ooze can also cause conjunctivitis. Again, bathe the eye in warm, slightly salty water. If the inflammation is bad, tape or pad the eye closed and see a doctor.

Sore, gritty or burning eyes

Eye discomfort of this sort can be caused by insufficient tears. This is a common problem in all climates, but is even more frequent in hot and dry regions. Hypomellose or artificial tear drops are useful and safe, and can be applied as often as necessary – half-hourly if you wish.

Subconjunctival haemorrhage

This is bleeding that turns the white of the eye red; it does not affect the coloured iris of the eye. It looks horrendous, but is harmless (unless after a bad head injury, *see* p.299) and needs no treatment. Very rarely, it can be a sign of widespread disease (e.g. Louse-borne Relapsing Fever or a viral haemorrhagic fever), but if so, other symptoms will be present and it will be obvious that you are very ill.

Redness and swelling around the eye (Periorbital Cellulitis)

A very painful, red, puffy eye accompanied by fever requires medical attention. If you are somewhere remote, take *flucloxacillin* 500mg four times a day (or *erythromycin* if you are allergic to *penicillin*) and find a doctor immediately. If there is no fever the problem may be due to a mosquito bite (*see* **Biters**, p.149) or insects flying into the eye (*see* **Skin**, p.219). Inflammation will be greatest if the insect's body is damaged when you try to remove it from the eye.

Styes

Styes are small boils on the eyelid, which are treated by applying a hot compress (use a face cloth). Pluck out the eyelash at the centre of the stye with tweezers, if possible, since this will aid draining of the pus. Antibiotic creams or drops are unlikely to be helpful with a simple stye.

If the infection starts to spread elsewhere on the face, take antibiotic tablets, in the same way as for skin infections (*see* **Skin**, pp.215–6).

If you get a stye that does not discharge and go away, or if one keeps recurring in the same place, this is probably a cyst in the eyelid that is getting repeatedly infected. It can be dealt with as a non-urgent matter with a minor operation under local anaesthetic.

Glasses and contact lenses

If you wear glasses or contact lenses, carry your lens prescription with you. Replacements are usually available and cheap in the tropics, but eye tests can be unreliable. Lens wearers should also carry with them as much as possible of their preferred solutions, as they may not be able to find them at their destination.

Remove contact lenses on long flights to reduce soreness. Contact lenses can introduce infection into the eye and this is more likely to happen in a hot, dusty, dry climate, especially if you are travelling rough and hygiene standards are difficult to maintain. There are a selection of bugs that may cause eye problems, of which the most worrying is *Acanthamoeba*. Consider wearing glasses instead of lenses, or at least carry a pair of glasses with you so that as soon as any hint of irritation or infection begins you can change over. At extreme altitude (above 8,000m/26,000ft) contact lenses can deprive the eye of oxygen.

TOOTHACHE AND OTHER DENTAL PROBLEMS

If several top teeth hurt, this is probably sinusitis (*see* above, p.283). Toothache is more likely to be due to a cavity if you can see a hole (although those brought up on fluorinated water will have less obvious holes), and cavities tend to hurt only after eating and drinking and not if you tap it. If the tooth hurts all the time – even when you are trying to sleep – and it is worse on tapping, this is likely to be an abscess. There is often soreness of the gums near the abscess and there can be swelling of the face on the same side as the bad tooth. A course of an antibiotic (usually *penicillin* or *erythromycin*) will be needed. Treatment by a dentist is then usually necessary, but this should take place after the infection has been cleared.

If a **tooth** is **knocked out** and the tooth is a baby tooth, stop the bleeding by getting the child to bite on some cotton wool. There is no need to put a baby tooth back. The permanent tooth that grows in its place may be a little late coming through. If a permanent tooth is knocked out, wash the tooth gently in clean water and ensure that the tooth is clear of bits of dirt. Gently push the tooth back into the socket until the biting edge of the loose tooth is at the same level as the tooth beside it. Hold it in place with the fingers. Next either find a dentist to fashion a guard to hold the tooth in place or see if you can improvise support with two thin rolls of beeswax or some similarly malleable material moulded in front and behind the row of teeth. If a tooth can be put back within an hour of being knocked out there is a good chance that it will survive. After 12 hours there is little hope.

CUTS, WOUNDS, BITES AND ABRASIONS

Does it need stitches?

In the sterile, high-tech West, we are used to cuts being stitched promptly in hospital casualty departments. In hot, steamy, unhygienic environments this can cause a great deal of trouble, especially if the wound is deep or very dirty, or the result of an animal bite. Sometimes stitches are required to stop massive bleeding, but otherwise, in tropical environments it is often safer to allow even quite big wounds to heal naturally or delay stitching for a week. Animal bites should not be sutured and need expert attention, since infection is almost inevitable and rabies is a big risk. Keeping wounds clean is more important than closing them (*see* below).

Deep or very dirty wounds should be washed under a running tap or by pouring on water from a bowl or jug. There is no need at this point to worry about water sterility – just use lots of it. Make sure there is no mud, gravel or glass in the wound, since these will guarantee infection and delay healing. Pick out any bits with clean fingers.

If there is a lot of bleeding, do not apply a tourniquet. Stop bleeding by elevation and firm, direct pressure (*see* **Accidents**, pp.298–9). You will be unable to assess the extent of the injury (or discover the whereabouts of a persistent bleeder) while everything is covered in blood, but do not

Case History: Sri Lanka

It had been a long, hot morning, and when I found an ice cream parlour in a fancy shopping mall in Colombo, we were all ready for a break. The place was stylish and newly painted in soft green, with large potted trees on the floor, and the glass-topped wicker tables sparkled with cleanliness. I was cautious about eating dairy products, even those with recognized brand names, while in unknown tropical places, but when I saw a western family (with the children wearing local school uniforms) inside enjoying treats, I decided that we could eat here safely. Four-year-old Bernard, who had been arguing about what size ice cream he could manage, angrily put his bowl down on the table. The entire top shattered, and splinters flew everywhere. Fortunately, only his middle finger was actually implanted with shards of glass. Bernard had not used any great amount of force, but I will never again trust a glass table without some kind of band or border edging the glass – nor do I travel anywhere now without a plaster.

Iris Gowen, Beijing

Case History: Indonesia

Ray slipped in remote rainforest on the island of Sumbawa. As he fell he impaled his arm on a cut bamboo shoot that had been left sticking out of the ground; it went clean through the muscles of his forearm. He took himself to a local clinic and the paramedic on duty sutured the entry and exit wounds. A few days later he consulted me, because his arm was becoming increasingly painful and swollen and he was feverish.

By now, the stitches were under tension, so I removed them. This immediately made the arm more comfortable because it allowed the pus that had built up inside to drain away. I dressed the two little wounds but left them unsutured; Ray started a taking course of antibiotic capsules and he cleaned and bathed the wounds three times a day. His tetanus immunization was up to date. The whole thing settled down over the following week. Ray's injury was impossible to clean because it was so deep. Suturing the wound was asking for trouble, because it was stitching in the dirt. Leaving a wound like this open allows it to expel any foreign or noxious material naturally, so the healing process is faster and infection is less likely to set in.

be too enthusiastic about clearing away blood clots, because bleeding will restart. Wash wounds thoroughly but, during this initial clean-up, don't worry about sterility or about applying antiseptic. Then, once you feel that most of the dirt is gone, bathe the wound in dilute *potassium permanganate* solution or another antiseptic (*see* pp.215–16) and change dressings once a day for the first few days.

All wounds (especially deep, dirty wounds and bites) carry a risk of **tetanus**. You should have been immunized before travel (*see* p.40); if you are not covered, you will need both active and passive immunization as soon as possible after injury (*see* p.267). Animal bites also carry a risk of rabies (*see* pp.265–8). Bites should not be sutured; this will seal in infection.

Muscle cramp

Cramp can be due to poor fitness, overdoing unaccustomed exercise in the heat, or lack of salt. Stretch the cramped muscle gently but firmly and stimulate circulation by massage. Drink a couple of glasses of water with a teaspoonful of salt (if it does not taste salty, drink more). In the longer term, shake more salt on your food. Increasing salt intake is generally necessary in hot climates. Health educators discourage salt consumption in temperate climates, but it is a necessary part of the tropical diet. Salt tablets are not a useful way of taking in salt. One treatment that is prescribed for nocturnal cramp, usually in older people, is *quinine* 200–300mg at bedtime. This is worth a try if salt depletion has been excluded and cramps are a persistent problem.

EVACUATION AND MEDICAL TREATMENT

A serious mishap may curtail your trip. However, you still need to be reasonably well to be medically evacuated: the last thing a seriously ill person needs is to be confined in an aircraft with relatively little oxygen and no emergency care. Flight constraints can make it difficult or slow to evacuate, so sometimes – and assuming that you are not too unwell – it may be quicker to get to a safe hospital on a scheduled flight rather than by air ambulence. Otherwise you may have to make do with local facilities, at least in the short term. It is perhaps worth noting that often, the more you have paid for an airline ticket, the easier it will be to reschedule your flight home. In most developing countries you will probably find the best medical care in the capital, but ask embassies, expatriates, an international clinic (if there is one) or hotel staff where to go for the best facilities. Embassies are generally wonderful in such emergencies, and they are also the people to approach should you need to organize a funeral, cremation or repatriation of a body.

For anyone taken ill in the Indian subcontinent, the best medical care is in private hospitals in Bangkok; treatment is good (as is the food!),

Healthcare in Rome

Most minor complaints, say a tooth abcess or cystitis, can be dealt with at the pharmacy (*farmacia*), and some will give appropriate antibiotics (although they are not supposed to). The Accident and Emergency (*pronto soccorso*) departments of all major hospitals are usually good for more serious problems such as possible appendicitis or a child with a fever, however standards of care depend on the particular doctor on duty at the time. Those admitted to hospital may have less predictable treatment. You'll need to take everything with you, including toilet roll, knife and fork, etc. Apparently the nursing care on the wards is not as good as in the UK because of very low staff levels; the patient or the patient's relative might, for example, need to remind nurses to give prescribed medication – even nebulizers for an acute asthma attack. Treatment in Accident and Emergency departments is free in Italian hospitals, although, if you are sent home with a prescription, you have to find a pharmacy open in the street to dispense your medicines and there is then a prescription charge, which is often higher out of hours. Many expatriates in Rome favour using **Rome American hospital** (Via Emilio Longoni, 69, **Italy t** (06) 22551) where the staff speak English, but the care is at American prices. They do not have an A & E department.

Dr Mary Styles, Rome

Reminder: accidents and emergencies

Accidents are the health hazards that most often kill or seriously harm travellers. About half of the deaths that occur while travelling are due to accidents; many are avoidable. Consider the risks of accidents at all times when travelling.

acceptably high-tech and relatively cheap. Thai government hospitals are also good, but not quite as good as private facilities. Hong Kong and Singapore are also quite good but more expensive. In Africa, head for South Africa or Nairobi; in South America, go to any capital city.

Pharmacies are a great source of immediate medical help and advice; in many countries, including in much of Southern Europe, appropriate antibiotics or other remedies will be sold for specific problems.

Risks of medical treatment

Medical treatment, including blood transfusions after serious accidents, or transfusions of blood products for serious illnesses, are routes of HIV infection that are difficult to avoid. If you need any such treatment, try to select expensive hospitals and clinics where staff say that blood is screened (you can only take their word), and try to ensure that intravenous equipment and syringes are new. In Asia, people replace or re-seal packets so that the contents look new: many travellers carry their own and ask local doctors to use them. Many Third World doctors give unnecessary injections, too, so be wary. The pros and cons of carrying an 'AIDS' kit (containing needles, syringes and intravenous fluid) are described under Blood and blood transfusions, below.

Blood and blood transfusions

After a major accident the victim may require a rapid blood transfusion. The dangers of transfusing unscreened blood and blood products are now well known, but many developing countries do not have the resources to carry out this screening. The situation in Bolivia is not untypical: only 30% of its hospitals screen blood, and a survey found that 54% of blood was contaminated with Chagas parasites (*see* p.155), hepatitis B, syphilis or HIV. The Red Cross has introduced a system of accreditation to monitor hospitals claiming to screen blood, which means that it should be possible to identify clinics or hospitals where screening is reliable. These kinds of projects are currently functioning or starting up in many developing countries. Also, screened blood is now available in almost every capital city throughout the world, although there may not always be enough of every group. The **Blood Care Foundation** (*see* below) sends safe, screened blood with a paramedical

Case History: Indonesia

A serious motorcycle accident befell a member of a small expatriate community (in an area where hepatitis B was prevalent). Not only was the AIDS kit spurned but expats offering to donate blood were turned away. In the event the patient survived without being infected, but nearly died because he was given blood of the wrong group. The best way to escape such risks is to be safety conscious, avoid accidents and realize that riding a motorcycle abroad could be the death of you.

courier to members who have suffered an accident; they have blood banked in Europe, Hong Kong, Florida and Lagos, and so far have always delivered within 12 hours. This is covered by some insurance policies.

Because of the dangers of infection with HIV or other diseases from blood or contaminated needles some people travel with 'AIDS kits'. These kits (sold by MASTA, *see* below), comprise needles, syringes and a small amount of intravenous fluid which could be used in case of an emergency admission to hospital. The largest AIDS kit is bulky, because it contains 500ml of intravenous fluid along with the 'giving set' and other useful items.

Although it would seem reassuring to carry intravenous fluids, the volume required in a real emergency is large, and it is impractical to carry enough saline or plasma expander to be really useful. I also know of situations where an AIDS kit has been produced but was not used by the local medical staff.

Many doctors regard a comprehensive AIDS kit as a useful precaution and, clearly, if you are travelling with someone with at least paramedical skills, it could be life-saving. I never carry intravenous fluids, but it is probably sensible to carry a few needles, syringes and sutures, and to ask the local doctors to use them if you go to hospital.

The risks associated with emergency treatment make it doubly important to avoid accidents in the first place. Many sane people become reckless when away. They do not wear motorcycle helmets or car seat belts, and they drive drunk and travel in unsafe vehicles. It's much better not to take the risk.

Contact information: medical treatment

Blood Care Foundation, *www.bloodcare.org.uk*.

MASTA, *www.masta.org*.

See also **Useful Addresses**, pp.326–30.

Emergency telephone numbers

In the European Union (EU): t 112.

In the UK: both **t** 999 and **t** 112 will reach emergency services.

In the USA and Canada: t 911.

On The Ground
Accidents

19

This chapter is not a complete first-aid course, but should remind those with some knowledge of first aid and offer tips to complement well-known procedures. Anyone planning a trip to somewhere lacking an ambulance service should go on a Red Cross, St. John's or other course, and gain some knowledge and confidence about what to do in a medical emergency.

For information on suggested medicines to bring with you, *see* **Medicines**, pp.77–9.

Summary

→ Drunk driving or accepting being driven by a drunk is foolhardy. Check that your bush-taxi driver is sober and has functioning eyes and limbs before trusting your life to him.

→ Travel with a small first-aid kit and know how to use it.

→ Accidents away from home are scary since you may not know where to find help or treatment.

→ The challenge to a traveller is that you may be able to adminster good first-aid, but there is not necessarily any ambulance to call to administer second-aid or to take you to tertiary care in a big hospital.

→ It is wise to have read a little about basic first-aid, and preferably to have attended a course.

→ Be assured that immediate treatment after an accident is often straightforward and rarely complicated.

→ Travellers to regions with less effective healthcare services would be wise to become safety conscious and avoid accidents.

SERIOUS ACCIDENTS AND RESUSCITATION

If there is a serious accident, drowning or a major medical crisis (such as a heart attack), people die through one of two causes:

→ **Air** fails to get into the lungs;
→ **Blood** fails to get to the brain.

This makes resuscitation a simple process. Read on to see what to do.

Immediate responses and safety

Take time to assess the situation: consider your own safety. Check whether you might put yourself in danger by trying to help. Is the casualty still connected to an electricity supply? Is the foul air in the well that overcame him also going to poison you? Ensure that you do not make the situation worse in any way. See if the victim is in any danger of further injury. Remember that if there is a chance of a spine or neck injury, movement might be harmful. If anyone else is on hand, get them to help; it is hard to resuscitate someone single-handed – even for an expert. Use your first-aid course techniques and the **ABC mnemonic** (*see* below) to remind you what to do. If you have any broken skin you can acquire hepatitis B or HIV infection by contact with blood; use surgical gloves if possible.

ABC for emergencies

Send for help, then:

A is for **Airway**: check that the mouth and throat are clear; people often vomit in a crisis, or inhale teeth or debris, or the accident can crush part of the face. Clear the airway with your fingers as far as possible. If there is damage to the face that seems to be interfering with breathing, pull the jaw forward (away from the face), hook the tongue forward with your fingers if necessary and tip the head up and back.

B is for **Breathing**: check that the victim is breathing by placing your cheek close to their nose and mouth. If they are not breathing give mouth-to-mouth artificial respiration, or another method of assisted ventilation if this is more familiar to you.

C is for **Circulation**: check that the heart is beating by feeling the chest, or (if you are used to finding them) pulses in the neck or groin; wrist pulses are difficult or impossible to feel if someone has lost a lot of blood or is in shock. If there is no pulse, give cardiac massage. If there is a great deal of bleeding this must also be staunched, or your cardiac massage will soon be to no avail.

Emergency telephone numbers

Emergency numbers vary throughout the world:

In the (European Union) EU: **t** 112.

In the UK: both **t** 999 and **t** 112 will reach emergency services.

In the USA and Canada: **t** 911.

Miraculous recoveries have happened after apparent drowning through people continuing resuscitation for a long time; do not give up after a few minutes.

It is dangerous to move an unconscious patient who may have a spine or neck injury, and moving a fractured limb is undesirable as well as agonizing. Someone who is conscious but has a back injury will generally be in such pain he will realize he must not be moved. If a casualty experiences a great deal of pain when you try to move him, stop and think; you may be making things worse.

Severe bleeding

Establish where the blood is coming from (gently clear away blood with a clean cloth) and press on the bleeding point. Blood loss always looks more dramatic than it is, and gentle mopping often reveals a modest wound. Cuts on the scalp or face bleed copiously and always look horrendous (you may think the victim is close to death), but after cleaning you will find only a tiny nick in the skin. If bright red blood spurts out with each heartbeat, an artery has been severed and you should press hard on the bleeding point until it has stopped (more than 10 minutes). Fortunately, in most accidental injuries crushing and tearing of arteries puts them into spasm, so they often stop bleeding spontaneously. 'Clean' wounds, such as those from glass or stab-wounds, often bleed more because the incision is neat.

Stop the bleeding by applying a clean cloth, if available, and pressing on the bleeding point; pressure with two thumbs (one on top of the other) often works well. Bleeding from a long cut can be reduced by pressing the sides of the wound together with your thumbs, then holding it together with Steri-Strips (*see* below). If lots of blood is coming out of a large, fleshy area (buttock or thigh) you may need to put your hand into the wound to try to get hold of the source of the bleeding.

Press hard for a long time (at least 10 minutes), then put on some kind of dressing and tie or strap it firmly in place; crêpe bandages are useful, or you can use an ambulance or military field-dressing pack. If it gets soaked with blood, put on more cloth and apply firm, direct pressure

Press where the blood is coming from and raise the bleeding part above the height of the victim's heart. Never use a tourniquet.

again. Do not remove the blood-soaked cloth and do not peek to see if bleeding has stopped.

Steri-Strips or **butterfly closures** can be a very useful way of closing a wound, but it is hard to get them to stick if the skin is wet or there is a lot of blood. Use direct pressure during the initial flow, then pull the wound together with Steri-Strips when the blood is dry. Once bleeding has stopped there is not such an urgent need for qualified medical help, but when you do reach a clinic try to discourage the attendant from stitching the wound (for more on this and on blood transfusions, *see* **Ailments**, pp.292–4). If there is a deep **scalp wound** that is bleeding profusely, pull the wound edges together by tying strands of hair together across the wound. Also try to ensure that there isn't any hair in the wound, since this will delay healing. Wait at least five days after the accident before cutting away the blood-caked tangle of hair; doing this too soon will encourage bleeding to restart.

If something is sticking out of the wound, do not remove it unless it is small and superficial like a splinter. Pad the area and apply pressure around the object to staunch the blood flow. Get to competent medical help as soon as you can.

Unconsciousness and fits

Head injury and concussion

Any period of unconsciousness after a fall or accident suggests trauma to the brain (concussion) and, the longer the period of unconsciousness, the more likely the possibility of serious damage: unconsciousness for over a minute or so is worrying. Nausea and vomiting are common after a head injury. Confusion, a change in the victim's normal behaviour, sleepiness or persistent headache after a bash on the head may indicate bleeding within the skull and needs urgent medical assessment. Unconciousness or extreme drowsiness with fever is very worrying: it could be **cerebral malaria** (*see* p.129) or **meningitis** (*see* p.282, pp.44–5). Get to a doctor urgently.

Convulsions or fits

People who are fitting may bite their tongue, but this will probably happen in the first moments of the attack, so trying to force something between the teeth will do more harm than good; it is not recommended. The victim will usually be incontinent, and will be sleepy and disorientated after the fit. Gently reassure them, but realize that they may not really be aware of what is going on and will just want somewhere to rest and sleep for a while. It is very rare for people to have a fit for the first time in adulthood; if this occurs, it could be a sign of serious disease like **cerebral malaria** or **meningitis**, so the victim must be taken to see a doctor urgently.

Dealing with fits and convulsions

In adults

If an adult is having a fit or convulsion, take the following action:

1. Clear the area of hard objects (chairs, tables, etc.) so that the person does not injure himself by thrashing against them. Drag the victim away from any danger. Do not force anything into his mouth.
2. Loosen any tight clothing (if this is easy to do) and wait for the fit to subside.
3. Place the victim in the recovery position (*see* below).

In children

Fits, seizures or convulsions are common under the age of five. If a child has a fit:

1. Turn him on his side so he is less likely to choke.
2. Do not force anything into his mouth.
3. Wait for the fit to subside; then, if the child is hot, give a dose of *paracetamol* (Tylenol) syrup, strip off clothes and cool by sponging with tepid water.

The most likely cause of the fit is a rapidly rising temperature due to some kind of infection. Seek medical help promptly to determine the cause of the fever, as it could be meningitis or cerebral malaria, or simple tonsillitis. Do not worry; children grow out of fits induced by fevers, and they do not lead on to epilepsy later.

See the box above for how to treat adults and childrens having fits.

Fainting

If someone **faints**, lie the victim down and elevate legs above heart height; if you have nothing to prop legs up on, simply bend them at the knee. Check for the heartbeat by feeling the chest, or find a pulse in the neck or groin if you know how to do this; pulses at the wrist are very difficult to feel in someone who has fainted. If there is no pulse, start resuscitation. If a victim has simply fainted, get them to lie flat for a few minutes after recovery. People are embarrassed by fainting, and often reluctant to lie down to prevent a faint, or to stay down when they are recovering. If they do not, they will then faint again.

The Recovery or Unconscious Position

Someone breathing but unconscious is at risk of vomiting. Vomit may enter the lungs and choke or drown the victim (drunks are especially vulnerable). It is important not to leave an unconscious person on his back, unless injuries make moving difficult.

Kneeling beside the casualty, tilt the head and lift the chin to make breathing easier. Straighten both legs, and place the arm nearest you out at right angles to his body, elbow bent and with the palm of the hand uppermost. Bring the other arm across his chest and hold the hand against the side of his face nearest to you, palm outwards. With your other hand, grasp the thigh furthest away from you, and pull the knee up to bend the leg so that the foot stays on the ground. Keeping his hand against his cheek with one hand and your other hand on the leg, roll him towards you until he is propped on his side supported by his bent arms and leg. Check the head is tilted so that the chin is up and the neck extended, to help him breathe freely (remember **ABC**, *see* p.297). This is easier than it sounds; try it.

Recovery Position

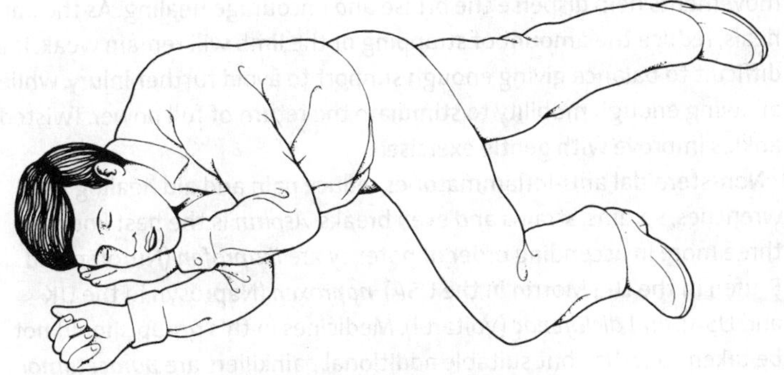

This information is reproduced by kind permission of St. John Ambulance.

STRAINS AND SKIN AILMENTS

Sprains, bruises and wrenches

Badly **strained muscles** and **wrenched joints** are best treated with **RICE**: **R**est, **I**ce compresses, **C**ompression and **E**levation. The best cold compress is ice cubes in a plastic bag or condom, wrapped in cloth. If there is no ice, bathing in cool water while gently moving the limb will help. Compression means strapping; elevation means supporting the damaged part above heart height. Use pillows to chock it up if you are in bed. Strapping an injured limb firmly with a crêpe bandage provides comfort and allows mobilization (wash bandages frequently to maintain their stretchiness). Rest and *aspirin* (or another non-steroidal anti-inflammatory medicine) relieve pain in the short term, and gentle movements help disperse the bruise and encourage healing. As the part heals, reduce the amount of strapping or the limb will remain weak. It is difficult to balance giving enough support to avoid further injury, while allowing enough mobility to stimulate the return of full power. Twisted ankles improve with gentle exercise.

Non-steroidal anti-inflammatories reduce pain and aid healing in all wrenches, sprains, strains and even breaks. *Aspirin* is the best known; three more in ascending order of potency are *ibuprofen* (Nurofen and Brufen in the UK; Motrin in the USA), *naproxen* (Naprosyn in the UK and USA), and *diclofenac* (Voltarol). Medicines in this group should not be taken together, but suitable additional painkillers are *paracetamol* (Tylenol) or *codeine*.

With **bruising**, apply cold compresses immediately, and after 12 hours or so use hot compresses or hot baths and elevation, followed by gentle mobilization with a crêpe bandage as support. As a bruise begins to disperse it changes colour, through lurid red, purple, black, brown and green to yellow. If there has been internal bruising or bleeding after an operation, these colours may appear a week or so after the initial injury, and gravity takes them below the wound. They can be quite alarming. Significant bruising or bleeding – for instance, into the knee – can also result in bruising appearing below the site of injury and this new, migrating bruise is tender to touch. This surprises many people but it is

Treating sprains and wrenches

Badly strained muscles and wrenched joints are best treated with **RICE**:

Rest
Ice (or cold water) compresses
Compression
Elevation

all part of the healing process. Bruising, when there has been little to provoke it and if it is not usual for you, can be a sign of serious illness. Easy bruising that is associated with a fever is sometimes a sign of some very serious, but rare, tropical infections. See a doctor.

Pain is a useful sensation: it says something is wrong and that something needs to be done. The action usually required is rest. If you do wrench something, try to stop travelling for a while; car travel is very bad for backache. Strapping the affected area and taking a non-steroidal anti-inflammatory will help joint pains. However, try to avoid taking pills just to carry on, especially if there is no need to carry on.

Deep wounds

Deep or very dirty wounds should be washed under a running tap or by pouring on water from a bowl or jug. Don't worry about water sterility – just use lots of it. Make sure there is no mud, gravel or glass in the wound, since these will guarantee infection and delay healing. Pick out any bits with clean fingers.

If there is a lot of bleeding, raise up the bleeding part above heart height if possible and apply firm, direct pressure (*see* above, pp.298–9). Once the bleeding has stopped, resist the temptation to clear away blood clots, because bleeding will restart. Wash any wound thoroughly, wrap it all up and seek help if you can (*see* **Ailments**, pp.290–91, for more on wound care). If you are somewhere remote, refer to p.299.

Burns and scalds

Remove the victim from the source of the injury. If it is an electrical burn, beware of being electrocuted yourself: turn off the supply, kick the victim free, or use a broom handle or similar non-conductor to disconnect him from the supply. Electrical burns are often very deep and readily become infected, so seek medical help if you can.

To treat **minor burns**, pour on or immerse in cold water until the burn or scald no longer feels hot to the victim. Do not apply creams, lotions or other potions. If clothes are fused into the burn, as often happens with man-made fabrics, trim away loose pieces; do not pull away adhered cloth. Cover the burn with a clean, dry, non-fluffy dressing. *Aspirin* helps reduce pain and burning, and so does raising the burnt area above heart height.

In **superficial burns**, skin sensation remains and the skin appears red and mottled. Deep, severe burns are generally less painful, because nerve endings have been destroyed. The skin looks white or charred. In cases of extensive burns, the immediate threat to the victim's survival is loss of fluids through the burn site. If the victim is able to drink, offer sips of water (or oral rehydration solution). Encourage drinking a cup an hour (in sips will be easiest); a remarkable amount of heat and water can be lost from burnt skin. Keep the victim warm: there is also a risk of hypothermia.

The next serious problem in severe burns is **infection**; in this case, evacuation home is advisable. Signs of infection include: increasing pain, spreading redness, pus dripping from the wound, itching or a bad smell. It sets in rapidly in warm climates.

Allergic reactions

Severe allergic reactions are scary and can be life threatening. Allergy tends to be announced by dramatic and often wide-spread swelling, itching and redness of the skin. The tissues around the eyes and mouth become swollen and the airways can become constricted. The best treatment is injection of *adrenaline* (*epinephrine*) and many allergic people carry an Epipen in case of this eventuality. Less dramatic allergic reactions can be treated with an antihistamine tablet (*see* motion sickness table in **Flight**, pp.92–3) and hydrocortisone is also of value, although – even when given by injection – this takes a couple of hours to have much of an effect. Tests are possible to identify allergens.

Bleeding under a nail

Injuries to fingers or toes can cause bleeding under the nail. Even a tiny amount of blood trapped in such a confined space is intensely painful. Heat the end of an uncurled paperclip in a flame until it is red, and place it firmly on the black nail, at right angles to it, so that it burns through the nail but not to the nail bed. You do not need to apply much pressure; the paperclip should just burn through. Do not use a pin or needle; they are too sharp and you will push through to the sensitive nail bed (ouch!) before making a hole big enough to let the blood out.

The paperclip technique is a very satisfying piece of first aid because as soon as the blood is released, there is immediate relief of pain and you have a very grateful patient. The nail comes off eventually and a new one will grow in its place.

FRACTURES AND DISLOCATIONS

Often the victim will have heard or felt a bone break; they will feel faint and unwell despite the fact that initially there is not always much pain. There will be swelling, an unnatural shape or position, and a reluctance or inability to move the fractured limb. Movement of one end of the fractured bone on the other causes intense pain, so immobilize the limb with whatever you can improvize. You can bandage a broken leg against the good one (with plenty of padding in between), or one finger against another. Cushion the broken limb as much as possible; any movement is excruciatingly painful. Broken limbs swell, so check that any bandaging is not compromising blood supply. Third World paramedics are often very competent bone-setters, but evacuate to hospital if you can. Fingers or toes going numb and/or blue after the bone has been set and plastered is a sign that the limb is in serious trouble and the cast is too tight. Get someone to cut the cast off urgently and replace it.

If you **break your nose** it will probably be obviously crooked. It will not be all that painful at first, but take some painkillers and then apply a thumb to either side of the nose and straighten it as best you can. All you need to do is to get it reasonably straight. You will get no better treatment in hospital. Cold compresses will help to reduce bleeding from the nose and will soothe the pain somewhat.

Dislocations are usually hard to treat unless they happen frequently to an individual: some people habitually dislocate knee caps or shoulders. It may be possible to relocate fingers or toes without anaesthetic. The principle is to pull the digit slowly, steadily and firmly back out straight until it jumps into place. Any rough grinding sensations imply there is also a fracture, best splinted and treated by a professional.

SOMETHING STUCK...

Something in the eye

If something is protruding from the eye, you need to find a doctor; if evacuation is going to take some time, you need to protect the eye. Large objects that have penetrated the eye tend to fall out. Small objects can generally be wiped out gently, using wet cotton wool twisted into a point or the corner of a clean handkerchief.

Usually the victim's own instincts will protect the eye sufficiently, but if a difficult evacuation is foreseen it may be sensible to protect the eye from further damage. One way to do so is to make a cone-shaped shield from cardboard, stiff paper or plastic. Cut a circle which is larger than the eye socket, and cut a radius (like the first cut when slicing a cake). Then overlap and stick the edges of the cut to form a flattish cone. Many first aid books suggest gently packing around the eye with bandages so that the injured eye is covered, **without** any pressure on it. This can be very difficult in practice and may do more harm than good. Even if the other eye is undamaged, the victim will not want to open the good eye and so will need a great deal of help and support during evacuation.

If there is something small in the eye, such as a grain of sand or an eyelash, first ensure that the outside of the eye is clean by wiping with a damp cloth, then, while looking up, grasp the eyelashes of the top lid and pull the upper lid over the lower one. Blink. If this does not work, get a friend to pour water into the eye while blinking as much as possible. Use tepid water and pour from close to the eye, or trickle water in from a syringe without a needle. The coloured part of the eye is very sensitive, so pour gently onto the white part. Looking away from the water makes the procedure more comfortable. If this doesn't work grasp the top eyelashes, roll the upper lid back over a cotton bud and inspect under the top lid where grit often lodges. The surface of the eyeball should be checked too, and any particles gently brushed away with another cotton bud. Even the tiniest of foreign bodies can be very painful; a magnifying glass will help you search.

CS Gas and the eye

If you are exposed to tear gas the best treatment for the discomfort in the eyes is to blow dry air on them; use an electric fan if possible, otherwise get someone to blow on them. Washing or irrigating with water will make the symptoms worse. Meanwhile spit out (do not swallow) saliva containing the gas (it will make you nauseous, and you may even vomit). Get into a ventilated area and strip off excess clothes (and wash them in due course). The discomfort will disappear in minutes.

Something in the ear

Inexpert attempts to remove objects or insects from the ear canal usually push the offending item further in, which may damage the ear drum. Lie on your side with the problem ear uppermost, and fill the ear with water; the object should float out. Straightening the ear canal by pulling the ear flap towards the crown of the head may help the object float out, and soaking in a bath with ears under water can also help. If this does not work you will need medical help. A medical worker with an ear syringe may be able to flush out the object, but many foreign bodies need to be removed in a hospital Ear, Nose and Throat department.

Something in the throat

If you swallow a fish or meat bone, it may feel as if the bone has stuck, but this is rare: more often the throat has only been scratched. This requires no treatment. If a foreign body really has stuck in the throat it will be almost impossible even to swallow saliva, and large quantities of additional saliva that are secreted will be spat out. The neck will often also feel very tender on prodding from the outside.

The definitive test of whether it is a scratch or whether there is something stuck is to wait for 12–24 hours while taking a cool, soft diet (but not ice cream unless you are somewhere hygienic). People with a scratch will improve, while those with something stuck will feel worse. The treatment for something stuck in the throat is removal of the object in hospital under general anaesthetic.

If someone is choking on an inhaled object or piece of food, stand behind him, put your arms around him, linking hands to form a fist in the middle of the upper abdomen beneath the rib cage, and pull towards you and upwards sharply. The idea is to force air out of the lungs and with it the object.

Getting small objects from up a child's nose

If a small child has pushed a small object or piece of food up their nose, here is a painless way for the parent/carer to get it out. It doesn't always work but it doesn't hurt to try. The parent tells the child that they are going to get a big cuddle and kiss. Close the unaffected nostril with one finger, seal the child's lips with your own and give a short sharp blow into the child's mouth. With a bit of luck the offending object will pop out of the nostril. I found this particularly useful when my youngest daughter developed a temporary fondness for pushing little beads up her nose.

Dr Deborah Mills, The Travel Doctor – TMVC, Brisbane Australia

If the victim has collapsed, roll them onto their back, get astride them facing their head, put your hands (one on top of the other) just under the rib cage and repeatedly force down and towards their head: this should propel the item out. A small child can be held upside-down and smartly slapped on the back. If you are the victim you can achieve a similar effect by slumping forward onto a chair back; this forces air and the object out.

On The Ground
Expatriates

20

Most of the information in this book applies equally to independent travellers and expatriates. Expatriates also need to be careful about food hygiene and water quality, but it's relatively easy for them to protect themselves from infections. They may be at risk of catching TB (*see* p.277), so should consider BCG (*see* pp.40–41). The risks facing expatriates vary according to where they are based – cities, rural areas, jungle, desert or refugee camps – and on their kind of work. Diplomats, development consultants, businessmen, oil prospectors, missionaries, health workers, researchers and volunteers all have their own particular risks, requirements, stresses and support mechanisms.

Summary

➜ With a little effort, expatriates can usually improve their home and office environment to make it healthier.

➜ In warm climates, anything that collects rainwater – e.g. old tyres and discarded buckets – provides breeding and nursery accommodation for mosquitoes.

➜ Blocked surface drains are favoured by Elephantiasis-carrying mosquitoes.

➜ Fitting mosquito-screens keeps out malarious mosquitoes and also nuisance-flies.

➜ Discarded or spilled grain, rodent food and other debris attract snakes.

➜ Psychological problems, alcoholism and even nervous breakdowns are common amongst expatriates, especially unemployed spouses. Take plenty of breaks from work and get away regularly.

➜ Spirits-drinkers seem to be more likely to get into trouble with drinking too much that those that take their alcohol more dilute.

➜ Set up good communication links with friends at home and elsewhere.

HEALTH AND HYGIENE

Malaria

Expatriates are consistently bad at protecting themselves from malaria and insect bites. Try to find out exactly what the local situation is. Many Latin American and Southeast and East Asian cities are free from the disease, so if you are city-bound it may be safe not to take any prophylaxis, but you may well need it for weekend jaunts. Even if malaria is not a local problem, take precautions against being bitten so as to avoid other insect-borne diseases (*see* pp.150–51) and do not be paranoid about the side effects of antimalarials; they are generally safe and tested medicines. I urge expatriates to follow the advice on pp.144–9. A few expatriates take their tablets carefully and then say, 'Since I am taking my malaria tablets, it's safe to sit outside at dusk [getting bitten] while I sip my gin and tonic.' It is not. Nor does the quinine in tonic protect you. Avoid bites.

A good home environment

Expatriates can make their immediate environment safer than temporary travellers can ever hope to do. Homes can be screened against mosquitoes, and properly fitting screen doors with bicycle inner tube nailed along the bottom also exclude snakes and scorpions. Tiles and high doorsteps discourage scorpions too. Those who choose to keep chickens should be aware that spilled grain encourages rodents, which encourage snakes, so site the chicken house as far as possible from the family home. Compost heaps and rubbish pits encourage snakes, and they also like to lurk in piles of rubble, so clear your home environment. The immediate area around the house can be swept and cleared to discourage mosquitoes, flies and snakes; thick, scrubby vegetation, in particular, should be removed, because it makes a good hiding place for snakes and provides resting sites for mosquitoes. All standing water should be covered or drained, and any small quantities collecting in tyres and pots should be emptied; these and plants that trap water where stems join the trunk (such as bromeliads and travellers' palms) make excellent mosquito breeding grounds.

Rural areas may have no electricity, water supply nor sanitation. You may need to dig a pit latrine or arrange to sink a tube well. Consider whether a generator is going to be useful. Fans and air conditioners help cut down mosquito bites indoors, confuse sand-flies and help you avoid prickly heat. Keep an eye on people you employ: you are responsible for their welfare. If they cough up blood, this suggests TB (*see* p.277). Advice on latrine-building and domestic arrangements is found in the Ross Institute's *Preservation of Personal Health in Warm Climates* (*see* **Bibliography**, p.333).

Filth-to-mouth pathogens and other health problems

While in their homes expatriates should be at little risk of filth-to-mouth diseases. Ensure a ready supply of boiled and filtered water, teach employees about basic hygiene and make sure they are healthy. Take care when travelling anywhere else in the country: then you become a traveller, with a traveller's increased health risks.

While I was living in Kathmandu I did a survey of my expatriate friends and neighbours. The levels of respiratory disease (which expatriates all talk and worry about a great deal because of the air pollution in the city) were no higher than at home, in spite of all the pollution, but diarrhoea and more serious illnesses were even more common than I had expected.

I was surprised by how many of us had needed to seek medical treatment outside Nepal: there were a few medical evacuations, but most trips were for operations or investigations organized at a few weeks' or months' notice; there were also some unpleasant conditions which would not clear up with local treatment. Considering the high proportion of people requiring treatment in Bangkok or at home, making sure that you have good medical insurance, covering medical evacuation, would seem crucial. Keeping a summary of any previous complicated medical details or hospital treatment is also useful on occasions.

PSYCHOLOGICAL PROBLEMS

The life of an expatriate appears romantic and attractive. The reality is that many work six- and sometimes seven-day weeks, because they are under huge pressure to achieve and are often away from their families. Pressure of work rarely leaves time to learn a local language, and this restricts the social circle to other expatriates and a select number of highly educated locals. The community is small, introverted and often obsessed by trivia. Life can seem terribly isolated. Many expatriates also move rapidly from contract to contract and from country to country, so that it is doubly hard for them to adjust to local culture and make friends. Even the expatriate community itself is constantly shifting, so friendships often remain at a very superficial level.

Volunteers are at times even worse off. Geography and lower income may isolate them from other expatriates. Local people may not value their contribution as it seems to come so cheap. Some may feel very undermined by local conditions: they are often involved in work where success or failure is immediately very obvious to them. Some volunteers may communicate better with locals than most business expats, but however well integrated they are, it can be difficult to relax properly.

Aid work, specifically, can throw people into shocking, stressful situations that are very hard to cope with. The **International Committee of the Red Cross** publishes an excellent booklet, *Coping with Stress* (*see* **Bibliography**, p.333) aimed at those working in conflict situations. It offers a self-assessment scheme. Among the symptoms of severe stress identified are: having difficulty sleeping, feeling tense and irritable, being 'jumpy', feeling distant from others, feeling physically lethargic and reliving traumatic events. Some people have attacks of dizziness, sweating, tightness in the chest and breathlessness.

Pressures at work and distance from familiar supports create tensions, and many expatriates unwind with a drink. Alcoholism is a common problem. Workaholism is too, so that when other members of the family do arrive they may feel excluded. It is healthiest to try to work sensible hours, and then relax properly doing something that allows you to switch off from work completely, though this advice is hard to keep to. If deadlines mean you must work long hours at times, compensate with the occasional long weekend away.

Understanding your stresses

Those who live abroad long-term face special problems, which can be a shock for new expatriates. The biggest are probably not tropical diseases but psychological symptoms. This is not to say that people go crazy, but that, due to a combination of 'culture shock', stress, isolation, insomnia, depression, feelings of horror at the injustices they are trying to work to correct and maybe alcoholism, they no longer feel able to cope. Isolation is often a big issue: you are on show and surrounded by people, yet you may not share a common sense of humour and, because ways of being polite differ in different cultures, people can seem rude or intrusive. Some of your actions, too, may be misinterpreted as insulting. Holding up five fingers to indicate that you'd like to buy five oranges in Pakistan, for example, is actually telling the stall-holder that he is the fifth son of the fifth wife; as Muslims are only permitted to have four wives, this means you are calling him a bastard.

Why do people work overseas? All expatriates fitted into one of three categories: mercenary, misfit or missionary. Within 'missionaries', my friend classified non-religious evangelists like myself; I am a health evangelist, preaching good hygiene and preventative medicine. We in the 'missionary' group might seem best suited to thrive under difficult conditions, but in fact we are very likely to have motivation problems. We are fired with a cause we know is right, but because our mission is so important it can throw us into conflicts. Our very passion to do good can make us intolerant or impatient, or aspire to ridiculously unreachable goals. Why don't local staff understand the importance of the work? Why is local bureaucracy slowing me down? Why don't expatriate colleagues support me? Depression and disillusionment easily grow. It is important to realize that it's not possible to change the world, so we must be satisfied with small contributions. We must not fall into the trap of blaming employers, local bureaucrats or colleagues for difficulties (local staff may also have problems adjusting to you). Try to keep problems in perspective. Even tight deadlines are more likely to be met with a relaxed approach. Keep an eye on your physical health too; you won't be efficient if you are unwell, so take time to go and see a doctor if you have symptoms or if you are worried about your health.

Those most likely to experience problems of motivation, and even clinical depression, are high achievers, people running away from problems at home, or those who have had previous psychological problems. Spouses who have given up a rewarding occupation to follow their partner, or who are worried about children's health and education, are also under great psychological pressure. Do not mislead yourself with romantic ideals. Be rational and analyse your motivation, temperament and the kind of work you will be involved in before you commit yourself. Only you can judge.

InterHealth (*see* **Useful Addresses**, p.326) have a lot of experience in medical support for Christian missionaries and other expatriates. Many companies that send employees abroad now recognize the value of counselling services, although others still provide little or no support.

Contact information: expatriates

International Committee of the Red Cross, *www.icrc.org*.
InterHealth, Partnership House, 157 Waterloo Road, London SE1 8UU, **UK t** (020) 7902 9000, **f** (020) 7928 0927, *InterHealth@compuserve.com*.

Sex and the single expat

Expatriates are very visible in the communities in which they work, and there will be a lot of interest in your activities. If you have a local lover, even a platonic friend of the opposite sex, everyone will know about it. In some cultures this will cause problems for female expatriates. You may be seen as available to all comers, and receive uninvited nocturnal visitors, or you may simply lose the status at work so important in getting things done. There may be worse problems for a local woman who is known to be liaising with a man to whom she is not married. Asian communities, in particular, are prudish about such things, and a woman in this situation can become an outcast in the community – in which she will continue to live after you have gone home. The more obvious risks of AIDS and sexually transmitted infections are covered on pp.227–40.

Sad spouses

Spouses can suffer enormously in adjusting to expatriate life. Often, they have given up an excellent job to travel, so not only do they lose a key role, they seem to lose all worth, too. It can seem as if they are just trailing along with no job, no status, no interests, and perhaps they are even assumed to be short on grey matter too. Their partner's colleagues

Sensible drinking: a few guidelines

→ Never drink spirits, and preferably no alcohol, before sundown.
→ Do not rehydrate with beer or other alcoholic drinks; quench your thirst with water or fruit juices before moving on to alcohol.
→ Avoid the habit of unwinding with a drink or two at the end of every day.
→ If you consistently drink over 21 units of alcohol a week you are drinking too much. Women should drink less than 14 units (one unit is half a pint of beer, one glass of wine or a small measure of spirits; a bottle of wine is six units).
→ Spirits drinkers seem to be more likely to get into trouble with alcohol than those who take their alcohol in more dilute forms.
→ Abstain from alcohol in the first three months of pregnancy, as it increases the chance of miscarriage; current recommendations are to take no more than one unit of alcohol per week throughout pregnancy.

may seem stand-offish, being unskilled in making small talk to homemakers. The situation can be worse for accompanying male partners, since locals may be mystified about how any man can stoop to being kept by a woman, and the status of so many is judged by job.

Even when unemployed spouses have a useful skill, they may not be allowed to work, even as volunteers. Some even feel ousted by domestic servants from the role of cook and housekeeper. Unemployed, childless, professional women have a tough time. Wives of their partner's local colleagues will be educated, but will probably be puzzled by a childless wife who has had a career but has little interest in children, cooking, make-up and clothes, and one who doesn't know how to manage servants. Situations vary, though. Remote rural postings can be hard socially, but rewarding professionally, culturally and linguistically; in big cities with their bureaucracy, it can be more difficult to find work, but there may be social advantages. Finally, expatriate communities are often very fluid, with people coming and going sometimes at very short notice and with little time for goodbyes. Making and losing friends so frequently can make life a bit sad.

The ideal expatriate

The ideally adjusted expatriate, who enjoys his/her time abroad, keeps a balanced approach to work by spending at least a whole day each week thinking about something completely different. They will have a long-term assignment (two years or more), and will take time out to go sightseeing and learn about the culture in which they are living. They will often have an interest they can follow in different countries – a sport, birdwatching, playing a musical instrument – and take some regular exercise. They appreciate a few beers, but never drink alone and seldom touch spirits.

Unemployed spouses will take lessons in the local language. This involves learning about social customs and enriches the experience of a different culture, making it possible to enquire about what things are for, why people do what they do and how novel foods might be prepared. If her role is primarily that of housewife, a spouse should do a lot of her own shopping (rather than just sending out the cook), as this forces her into contact with locals, improves her language skills and enables her to find out what is going on locally.

BABIES AND CHILDREN

Many expatriates return home in the late stages of pregnancy to have their babies. The deadline for long-haul flights on most airlines is before the 32nd week of pregancy but this varies according to the airline and the length of flight. Sometimes a pre-flight medical examination is required. After delivery, new mothers understandably want to rush back to their families. It is surprisingly hard to diagnose any diseases in early infancy, so there is a lot of sense in staying home for four to six weeks before returning abroad. Try to breast- rather than bottle-feed your baby, and make sure that this is already well established and that there are no feeding problems before leaving. The safest age to travel with small children is while they are exclusively breast-fed.

Travelling with children is a joy as they provide ready introductions to people who would otherwise not approach you. They can cause a great deal of worry when they become ill and you are far from adequate medical facilities, but as long as they are protected from insect bites, eat safe food and have had the right immunizations, they should thrive.

If infants are bottle-fed or drink from training beakers, be meticulous about sterilizing them frequently. Sterilization tablets are often hard to come by, but boiling bottles, teats and cups in water for 15 minutes is effective and can be organized anywhere. You can also use liquid bleach. Getting rid of disposable nappies (diapers) is difficult, and if put into an ordinary rubbish system they will probably be scattered far and wide. Burn them, or use terry-towel nappies with liners and plastic over-pants. Nappy liners are indestructible and block up toilets, but washing them will make a box last ages.

It is wise to contact other expatriate parents for a briefing on **local child-rearing** practices. Attitudes on what is important can be very different, and if this is not understood problems may arise. Some

Five precautions for parents

→ Travelling children must have all the usual childhood immunizations, as well as any special travel vaccines.

→ Protect children from the sun (*see* pp.164–7); they should wear a shirt, hat and sun cream even when bathing in the sea or open-air pools.

→ Children should wear long, loose clothes and cover up or come inside at dusk to avoid mosquito bites.

→ The family must become safety-conscious; children have a poor sense of danger, and buildings and equipment may not be made to the standards you are used to.

→ Ensure that children drink plenty of fluids if they get diarrhoea (preferably ORS; *see* pp.109–111).

expatriate parents assume that, because their children lack a local language, they cannot play with the neighbours, but – if allowed to – younger children usually integrate readily with other children. They have a remarkable aptitude for languages, are skilled in non-verbal communication and many games do not require words to be fun.

Adolescents arriving in a new country may not be so adaptable, as they are often going through difficult processes of self-identification. This period of turmoil can start as early as the age of eleven, and such confused youngsters can have big problems, particularly if their stay in a new country is for less than a year. They may need a great deal of time and patience; like the well-adjusted adult expatriate, they will cope better if they have a transferable hobby. They will also be more unsettled if the rest of the family is unhappy too.

Contact information: educational packs

World-wide Education, 17 Blagrave Street, Reading, Berks RG1 1QA, **UK t** (0118) 958 9993, **f** (0118) 958 9994, *www.weshome.demon.co.uk*. Sells home school packages.

Swallowing things accidentally

In my experience as acting GP to small expatriate communities, it was common for small children to swallow noxious or worrying substances and some doctors advise keeping some *ipecacuanha emetic mixture* in case of trouble. I shall also debunk some common myths about what is and is not dangerous. While most multivitamin preparations are safe, **vitamin A** and **iron**, if swallowed in overdose, can be very toxic: medical help must be sought and *ipecacuanha* should probably given to induce vomiting. On deciding to visit a doctor, try first to work out how many tablets might have been taken and show the doctor the packet/bottle. If a dangerous quantity has been consumed, a child of 6–18 months takes 10ml of *ipecacuanha*, older children 15ml and adults 30ml; dosing is repeated after 20 minutes, if necessary. **Essential oils** can cause severe toxicity if swallowed and observation in hospital after such an accident would be a wise precaution. 'Mild' **antidepressants** and **sleeping pills** can be very dangerous, even if a child only takes a few tablets, accidentally; treatment with *ipecacuanha* would again be wise in such a case. Silica gel, the desiccant found in electrical and photographic products and shoeboxes, often carries a warning: 'toxic if swallowed'. It is not dangerous if taken in small quantities. Most antibiotics and also the contraceptive pill are not toxic. An overdose of **antibiotics** is likely to cause diarrhoea, and the **contraceptive pill** may cause nausea and, rarely, even some vaginal bleeding in pre-pubertal girls, but it is not dangerous. Finally, **pencil 'lead'** is not lead at all, but inert graphite; chewing pencils should not cause health problems.

When You Get Home

Return

21

The most important thing to remember when you get home is to continue taking your antimalarial tablets for the prescribed interval: this is at least four weeks for most tablets, or a week for Malarone. And if you fall ill (especially if this happens within three months of returning), remind your GP that you have been abroad and that you may have been exposed to malaria. If ill on returning to Australia, present yourself to a hospital which specializes in infectious diseases (*see* p.328).

Summary

→ Remember the risk of serious malaria and seek medical help urgently (within 24 hours) if you fall ill within three months of returning from the tropics – even if you have taken your antimalarial tablets.

→ Antimalarial tablets should be continued for at least four weeks after leaving a malarious region; tablets do not absolutely guarantee that you will avoid malaria, but if you are unlucky enough to get it, you are less likely to die of it.

→ Other diseases imported from the tropics are unlikely to be serious, but seek a medical opinion if you notice a rash, new lumps or bumps, or are unwell. Remind your doctor that you have been abroad.

→ Don't worry about your health on your return; if you feel well, you almost certainly are well.

→ Few diseases lurk unknown without symptoms to warn you that something is wrong: those that commonly cause no symptoms in the incubation period are HIV and sometimes Schistosomiasis.

A POST-TRIP CHECK-UP?

'Should I have a medical check-up when I return from a tropical trip?' Many travellers and expatriates ask this question, and many wish to have a formal post-trip check-up by a specialist in tropical diseases. Generally, though, if a returning traveller feels well, there is no need to have a medical examination. The main exception to this guideline is Bilharzia; however, if you have an ulcer which will not heal, or if you are worried you may have malaria, HIV, or Chagas' Disease, you should also see your doctor.

Malaria

Falciparum malaria is the only common, life-threatening disease imported from warm countries. Any fever or 'flu-like illness within a year (but especially within three months) of return from a malarious region should be assumed to be malaria, and medical help should be sought urgently. Most malaria deaths are in travellers returning from Africa (Kenya is especially notorious) or Melanesia (PNG, the Solomons and Vanuatu). There is no screening test that will diagnose it before the symptoms manifest themselves, so travellers and doctors must be aware of it as a possible diagnosis. The safety net is not a clever laboratory test, but alert travellers and doctors who act quickly if symptoms of possible malaria begin. For all other aspects of malaria, *see* **Malaria**, pp.127–40. There are much rarer, but serious, causes of fever in returning travellers, but these will cause problems within a month of return (e.g. **Lassa Fever**, *see* p.285).

HIV/AIDS and sexually transmitted diseases

Our inhibitions may be on hold when we travel and casual sex is especially enticing, but it puts us at risk of contracting HIV and 25 other sexually transmitted diseases. Returning travellers should consider screening if they have put themselves at risk. Counselling about HIV testing can be arranged through your doctor or a special genito-urinary clinic. *See also* **Sex**, pp.227–40.

What do stool checks reveal?

Some doctors advocate screening faeces for parasite eggs or cysts. This may reveal an infestation, but generally they only need treating if they are causing symptoms or squeamishness. If you do experience symptoms that someone thinks may be due to worms or *Giardia* (*see* p.116), it is important that three stool samples are sent and that they are taken on different days. Only if three samples are negative is it likely that the traveller is free from parasites. Both *Giardia* and worms produce eggs and cysts intermittently, so one clear sample does not necessarily mean that you are free from parasites.

Lingering intestinal problems are common after a trip to the tropics, particularly among travellers returning from South Asia. Often no cause is found, and the symptoms settle down with time.

Stowaways

Diseases and parasites are often imported from the tropics and subtropics, especially by people who have been abroad for relatively long periods. With the exception of **Bilharzia** (*see* below), most of them pose little threat either to the infested individuals or to the general public in contact with them. Passing an earthworm-sized *Ascaris* worm is revolting, but she will have done you no harm and will probably have been alone. Most infestations will die out given time or, if they do start causing problems (as may happen on rare occasions), they can be treated easily.

Amoebae frequently infest travellers, and often cause no symptoms at all. However, in a minority amoebae can cause a liver abscess, and more commonly they cause dysentery, although you will know if you have this and will no doubt seek treatment. Unfortunately, screening will be most unlikely to detect these problems before they cause symptoms of brain or liver invasion. Travellers should think about this and realize the benefits of avoiding infestations by eating safe, properly cooked food.

Bilharzia (Schistosomiasis)

This little worm is acquired most often by travellers who have been wading or swimming in African lakes, although it is also a problem in the tropical Americas. A blood test is available to test for the parasite and, since there may be no initial symptoms, you should request one if you have put yourself at risk. Your doctor will often be able to organize it. It should be done at least six weeks (but ideally less than 12 weeks) after leaving the Bilharzia area. The Rift Valley lakes of Africa are common sites for catching Bilharzia, and a study at the Hospital for Tropical Diseases, London, found that about one third of the 344 cases treated in 1991–4 got their disease from Lake Malawi. For further details on Bilharzia, *see* **Water**, pp.185–7.

Some rarities

Chagas' Disease

This is a disease of tropical and subtropical Central and South America, transmitted by bug bites (*see* **Biters**, p.155). It is very rarely contracted by travellers, but if you have been exposed to bug bites while sleeping in a wattle and daub village hut, a blood test may help to determine if you have been infected. Screening will be justified in only a very few people.

Leishmaniasis (or Kala-azar Fever)

This can emerge months or even years after a bite by an infected Old World sand-fly, and bronchopneumonia is the most common way it manifests itself. The Mediterranean coast is a source of infection, but it is generally acquired from much further afield (*see* **Biters**, pp.154–5). If you become ill, remind your doctor about your travels. Those returning from tropical South America must seek medical help if they have a skin wound that does not heal within a couple of months.

Other troubles with worms

A blood test (ELISA) can detect filarial worms. These cause Elephantiasis, Loa-loa or River Blindness in west and central Africa, Southeast Asia and South America (*see* **Biters**, p.152; **Water**, p.188). If you have no symptoms, do not request screening unless you have been home for more than six weeks. If you have symptoms, seek medical help promptly. In a minority of those they infest, **tapeworms** can end up in the brain (*see* **Worms, Guts and Nutrition**, p.121).

YOUR MOOD AND PSYCHOLOGICAL WELFARE

Travelling is stressful, and coming home usually plunges you into reverse culture shock (*see also* **Culture shock**, pp.24–6); this can be hard to handle, especially if you are worried about finding a new job or setting up home again. Many people say that 'reverse culture shock', experienced on coming home, is worse than the difficulty of coping with new cultures; this seems to be especially true on coming home after a long trip to the developing world. Pace yourself and, if everything seems to be going to pieces, find a kindred spirit to talk to. One of the worst things about returning is being isolated by your travelling experiences. Even close friends may be unable to understand the life-changing things you have seen, so that you are distanced from them. Some employers run debriefings to help with this; if you can't find a sympathetic fellow traveller, see your doctor – and, personally, I'd recommend staying out of big supermarkets for a few months.

Reference

USEFUL ADDRESSES

Travel clinics and health information

In the UK

AMREF (African Medical and Research Foundation), 4 Grosvenor Place, London SW1X 7HJ, **t** (020) 7201 6070, **f** (020) 7201 6170. The AMREF websites, *www.amref.org* and *www.passporteastafrica.com*, provide information for travellers to each East African country. Membership: £15 for one month covers one free evacuation within a 500-mile radius from Nairobi; cover for a year (£30) or life (£100) allows one evacuation a year within a 1,000-mile radius. Money spent funds work for community hospitals throughout East Africa.

The Blood Care Foundation, PO Box 7, Sevenoaks, Kent TN13 2SZ, **t** (01732) 742 427, **f** (01732) 451 199; *www.bloodcare.org.uk*; for the Swiss office *see* Switzerland, below. Membership can also be arranged through MASTA (*see* below).

British Allergy Foundation, Deepdene House, 30 Bellegrove Rd, Welling, Kent DA16 3PY, **t** (020) 8303 8525, **t (helpline)** (020) 8303 8583, **f** (020) 8303 8792, *allergybaf@compuserve.com*, *www.allergyfoundation.com*.

British Epilepsy Association, New Anstey House, Gate Way Drive, Yeadon, Leeds LS19 7XY, **t** (0113) 210 8800; **f** (0113) 391 0300, **t (helpline)** 0808 800 5050, *epilepsy@epilepsy.org.uk*. The helpline issues an 'epilepsy passport' (50p) containing first aid information about epilepsy, in six European languages.

British Heart Foundation, 14 Fitzhardinge St, London W1H 4DH, **t** (020) 7935 0185. Has information on insurance for people with heart problems including angina and high blood pressure.

British Mountaineering Council, 177–9 Burton Road, West Didsbury, Manchester M20 2BB, **t** 0870 010 4878, **f** (0161) 445 4500, *office@thebmc.co.uk*, *www.thebmc.co.uk*. Runs mountaineering courses and advises on other courses and insurance. *See also* Union International des Associations d'Alpinisme, below.

British Society for Allergy and Clinical Immunology, 66 Weston Park, Thames Ditton, Surrey KT7 0HL, **t** (020) 8398 9240, **f** (020) 8398 2766.

Department of Health (UK), **t** 0800 555 777, *www.doh.gov.uk/hat*. Publishes *Health Advice for Travellers* (free), explaining how to get medical treatment inside and outside the EC. Pick up a copy at a UK Post Office or doctor's surgery.

Diabetes UK, 10 Queen Anne St, London W1G 9HL, **t** (020) 7636 6112, *www.diabetes.org.uk*. Issues fact sheets about individual countries, including which insulins are available; they also offer travel insurance, but compare their rates to other deals.

Divers' 24-hr emergency helpline: **t** 07831 151 523. Run by the British Institute of Naval Medicine.

Epilepsy Research Foundation, PO Box 3004, London W4 1XT, **t** (020) 8995 4781, *www.erf.org.uk*. Publishes a helpful leaflet entitled *Epilepsy and Antimalarial Medication*.

Expedition Advisory Centre, Royal Geographical Society, 1 Kensington Gore, London SW7 2AR, **t** (020) 7581 2057, **f** (020) 758 4447.

Foreign and Commonwealth Office, **t** (020) 7008 0232/3, *www.fco.gov.uk/travel*.

Holiday Care Service, 2nd Floor, Imperial Buildings, Victoria Road, Horley, Surrey RH6 7PZ, **t** (01293) 774 535, **f** (01293) 784 647, *holiday.care@virgin.net*, **t** (01293) 774 536. Offers information on holidays for those with health problems and a list of sympathetic travel insurance companies.

Hospital for Tropical Diseases, Mortimer Market, Capper St, London WC1E 6AU, **t** (020) 7387 4411, **f** (020) 7388 7645, *www.thehtd.org*. Their Health Line, **t** 0839 337 733, gives advice (by fax if required) on specific destinations. The clinic provides a comprehensive pre-departure service and post-trip consultations are also possible.

InterHealth, Partnership House, 157 Waterloo Rd, London SE1 8UU, **t** (020) 7902 9000, **f** (020) 7928 0927, *InterHealth@compuserve.com*. Travel service providing comprehensive care for aid workers, missionaries and volunteers: clinical consultations, advice, immunizations and health equipment.

Malaria Reference Centre, at London School of Hygiene & Tropical Medicine, Keppel St, London WC1E 7HT, **t** 0891 600 350 (premium rate). Details on risk levels/precautions necessary by country.

MASTA (Medical Advisory Services for Travellers), at London School of Hygiene & Tropical Medicine, Keppel St, London WC1E 7HT, **t** 0906 822 4100, *www.masta.org*. Call for a personalized health brief. Offers immunization information, arranges membership of the Blood Care Foundation and sells AIDS kits and items such as anti-mosquito anklets.

MASTA Travel Clinics, **t** (01276) 685 040. Call for the nearest; there are currently 30 in Britain. They sell malaria prophylaxis memory cards, treatment kits, bednets, net treatment kits. They do not offer post-tropical screening.

MEDEX Assistance Corporation, Victoria House, 5th Floor, 125 Queens Rd, Brighton, E. Sussex BN1 3WB, **t** (01273) 223 002, *medexasst@aol.com*. UK branch of MEDEX, offering medical cover worldwide. For US headquarters *see* 'In the USA', below.

National Asthma Campaign, Providence House, Providence Place, London N1 0NT, **t** (020) 7226 2260; **t** (**helpline**) 08457 010 203, *www.asthma.org.uk*. Has information on travel insurance for asthmatics.

Nomad Travellers' Store and Medical Centre, 3–4 Wellington Terrace, Turnpike Lane, London N8 0PX, **t** (020) 8889 7014, **f** (020) 8889 9529, *www.nomadtravel.co.uk*. Has a complete range of travel equipment and a user-friendly, on-the-spot immunization and advice service. There are several UK branches (another is soon to open in Manchester), but you can call for information (especially on immunizations) on the Nomad Travel Health Line, **t** 0891 633 414 (premium rate). Branches include:

Nomad Travellers' Store, 40 Bernard St, Russell Sq, London WC1N 1LJ, **t** (020) 7833 4114;

Nomad Traveller's Clinic, in the STA shop, 43 Queen's St, Bristol, **t** (0117) 922 6567.

Online doctors, **t** (020) 7806 4028, *www.e-med.co.uk*, *doctor@e-med.co.uk*. For a £30 membership you can arrange online consultations with a British GP from anywhere.

Royal Free Travel Health Centre, Pond St, London NW3 2QG, **t** (020) 7830 2885, *www.travel-health.co.uk*. Immunizations, kits, aviation psychology and returning travellers clinic. Has a specialist doctor on call as well as regular clinic staff. Also offers treatment for flight anxiety by a team of psychologists.

Royal Geographical Society (*see* Expedition Advisory Centre, above).

The Stroke Association, Stroke House, Whitecross St, London, EC1Y 8JJ, **t** (020) 7566 0300, **f** (020) 7490 2686, **t** (**helpline**) 0845 303 3100.

Thames Medical, 157 Waterloo Rd, London SE1 8US, **t** (020) 7902 9000. Competitively priced, one-stop travel health service. Profits go to InterHealth who provide healthcare for overseas workers on Christian projects.

Trailfinders Travel Clinic, 194 Kensington High St, London W8 7RG, **t** (020) 7938 3999. Usually has an expert travel doctor on site.

Travel Screening Services, 1 Harley St, London W1G 9QD, **t** (020) 7307 8756, **f** (020) 7636 8789, *www.travelscreening.co.uk*. A private service mainly aimed at business travellers.

Tropical Medicine Bureau, *www.tmb.le*. Irish organizaton with a useful website specific to tropical destinations.

Union International des Associations d'Alpinisme, Mountain Medicine Centre, British Mountaineering Council, 177–9 Burton Road, West Didsbury, Manchester M20 2BB, **t** (0161) 445 4747, **f** (0161) 445 4500, *www.the*

Useful websites

General

www.doh.gov.uk/traveladvice: UK Government site offering health advice for travellers.

www.fco.gov.uk/travel/countryadvice: official Foreign Office website for travellers. For pre-departure preparation tips, see ***www.fco.gov.uk/knowbeforeyougo***.

www.fitfortravel.scot.nhs.uk: travel health information from the NHS (Scotland).

www.gorge.net/hra: Himalayan Rescue Association.

www.icrc.com: International Committee of the Red Cross.

www.medicineplanet.com: information site.

www.travelhealth.com: offers extensive reports on risks for a fee of $25.

www.tripprep.com: the Travel Health Online website.

www.who.int: background information on tropical diseases and treatments.

Disabled access

www.justmobility.co.uk: good for links to other helpful sites.

www.dmoz.org/Society/Disabled/Travel: good for US travellers.

www.everybody.co.uk/airline: directory of access arrangements on major airlines.

Herbal remedies

www.24DrTravel.com: supplies some forms of echinacea and other supplements and remedies by mail order.

www.herbmed.org: herbal medicines information.

www.herbs.org: information on herbal remedies, etc.

In-flight issues

www.aviation-health.org: independent institute offering advice on in-flight health issues.

www.doh.gov.uk/dvt: has specific information about deep vein thrombosis.

www.who.int/ncd/cvd/dvt.htm: specific information on DVT.

Immunosuppression

www.aidsnet.ch: information for travellers with HIV infection, including entry restrictions for particular countries.

www.infoweb (click on Travel-Related): information for travellers with immunosuppression.

www.thebody.com: Information for travellers with immunosuppression.

bmc.co.uk. Publishes information sheets on the medical aspects of mountaineering. Most are aimed at climbers; a few are for doctors.

In North America

The **Centers for Disease Control** based in Atlanta, Georgia, are the central source of travel health information in North America, with a phone and fax-back information service. Contact: **CDC** (Attention Health Information), Center for Prevention Services, Division of Quarantine, Atlanta, GA 30333, **t** (404) 332 4559, *www.cdc.gov/travel*. Publishes the invaluable *Health Information for International Travel* and has an excellent – if scary – website. Local (county and state) public health clinics and special travellers' medicine clinics exist in most large cities in North America; most universities have medical centres too.

Travel reports in **Canada** (Ottawa) are available via **Canada t** (613) 944 6788, or **t** 1 800 267 6788; fax-call system, **f** 1 800 575 2500.

American Diabetes Association, *Icann@diabetes.org*.

Canadian Department of Trade and Foreign Affairs, *www.dfait-maeci.gc.ca*. Provides travel information.

Connaught Laboratories, PO Box 187, Swiftwater, PA 18370, USA, **t** 1 800 822 2463. Sends a free list of specialist tropical physicians in your state.

International Association for Medical Assistance to Travellers (IAMAT), 736 Center St, Lewiston, NY 14092, **t** (716) 754 4883. Non-profit foundation providing lists of English-speaking doctors abroad, and foreign health information.

MEDEX Assistance Corporation (central office), PO Box 5375, Timonium, MD 21094-5375, USA, **t** (toll-free) 1 800 537 2029, **t** (410) 453 6300, **f** (410) 453 6301, *medexasst@aol.com*. Offers medical cover worldwide for travelling individuals/families and longer-term expatriates. Provides medical evacuation assistance and help in locating appropriate medical care, and sells safe medical kits. There are branches in the UK (*see* above) and China (*see* below).

The Society for Accessible Travel and Hospitality, 347 Fifth Ave, Suite 610, New York NY 10016, USA, **t** (212) 447 7284. Some useful resources.

South American Explorers Club, 126 Indian Creek Rd, Ithaca, NY 14850, USA, **t** (607) 277 0488.

US State Department, **t** (202) 647 4000, *www.state.gov*. Alternatively, for travel emergencies, call the Overseas Citizens Services 24-hr hotline **US t** (202) 647 5225.

In other countries

Australia

The Travel Doctor – TMVC have a network of clinics in Australia, New Zealand and Thailand; they are all members of IAMAT. Call **t** 1 300 658 844 or **t** 1 300 658 844, which forwards the call to the nearest, or check *www.traveldoctor.com.au*. These clinics might be the best first port of call if taken ill in Australia with travel-related symptoms. Otherwise, the following hospitals specialize in treating infectious/tropical diseases: **Adelaide**: Queen Elizabeth; **Darwin**: Royal Darwin; **Hobart**: Royal Hobart; **Melbourne**: Fairfield (also has a travel health section); **Perth**: Royal Perth; **Sydney**: Westmead.

China

MEDEX Assistance Corporation, Regus Office 19, Beijing Lufthansa Center, No. 50 Liangmaqiao Road, Beijing, 100016, China *medexasst@aol.com*. Chinese branch of MEDEX, offering medical cover worldwide. For the US headquarters *see* above.

Nepal

CIWEC Travel Medicine Clinic, near Yak and Yeti Hotel, Durbar Marg, Kathmandu, Nepal, PO Box 1340, **t** (1) 228 531, **f** (1) 224 675, *advice@ciwecpc.mos.com.np*, *www.ciwec-clinic.com*.

South Africa

Johannesburg Clinic Travel Clinic, South Africa, **t** (11) 807 3132, **f** (11) 803 9562.

Switzerland

The Blood Care Foundation, Switzerland, **t** (22) 369 1904, **f** (22) 369 2814; for UK office *see* above. Alternatively, you can arrange membership through MASTA (*see* above).

International Association for Medical Assistance to Travellers (IAMAT), Gotthardstrasse 17, 6300 Zug, Switzerland; for US office *see* above. European headquarters.

Vietnam

Vietnam has two American-owned, comprehensive 24 hour healthcare facilities:

Telephone codes

All phone numbers listed in this book include area codes (in brackets) where applicable. To call an organization from outside the country in which it is based, first dial the international network access code (e.g. **00** from the UK) and then the relevant country code, before dialling the number listed in the guide.

Country dialling codes

Australia: +61
Canada: +1
China: +86
Ireland: +353
Nepal: +977
South Africa: +27
Switzerland: +41
UK: +44
USA: +1
Vietnam: +84

Columbia Asia Gia Dinh Clinic, 01 No Trang Long, Binh Thanh Dist, **t** (8) 803 0678, **f** (8) 803 0677.
Columbia Asia Saigon 24-hour Clinic, 08 Alexandre De Rhodes, Dist 01, HCMC, **t** (8) 823 8888, **f** (8) 823 8454, *medevacca@columbiaasia.com*, *www.columbiaasia.com*.

Courses

Britannia Airways, UK t (01582) 424 155. Courses to combat flight anxiety (one-day £130).
British Airways, UK t (0161) 832 7972. Courses to combat flight anxiety (£169 in Manchester, £189 in London).
British Mountaineering Council (*see* above). Runs mountaineering courses and advises on other courses.
Life Support, UK t (01229) 772 708. First-aid courses.
Outward Bound, Watermillock, Penrith, Cumbria CA11 0JL, UK, *www.outwardbound-uk.org*. Survival skills and expedition courses.
St John Ambulance, UK t (01438) 740 044. First-aid courses.
Wilderness Medical Training, UK t (01926) 882 763. First-aid courses.

Equipment and supplies

Equipment and information to protect travellers are available from **Interhealth**, **MASTA** clinics, **Nomad** (*see* individual entries above) and many outdoor suppliers. Some sources are listed below.

General travel supplies

BCB, Freepost, Cardiff CF1 1YS, UK, **t** 0808 100 2867. Travel supplies, including marine safety/adventure equipment.
Cotswold, Broadway Lane, South Cerney, Cirencester, Gloucestershire GL7 5UQ, UK, **t** (01285) 860 612. Shops in London, Reading, Mancester, Southampton and Bewts-y-Coed. Good range of filters, bednets, blister relief kits, etc.
Craghoppers Ltd, Risol House, Mercury Way, Urmston, Manchester M41 7RR, UK, or: PO Box 1944, Leigh-on-Sea, Essex, SS9 1TR, UK, **t (for a brochure)** (0161) 749 1364, **t (helpline)** (0161) 749 1310, *www.craghoppers.com*. Sells tightly woven clothes that make it difficult for mosquitoes to bite through; there is also some protection from the sun and they are treated with pyrethroid to repel biters.
Field & Trek, Langdale House, Sable Way, Laindon, Essex SS15 6SR, UK, **t** (01268) 494 444, *www.fieldandtrek.com*. Sells bednet impregnation kits and a range of outdoor equipment.
Frio Cooling Products, Freepost SWC 0667, Haverfordwest, SA62 5ZZ, UK, **t** (01437) 741 700, *www.friouk.com*. Sells a range of wallets that, after immersion in water, keep contents cool for several days.
Homeway Medical, West Amesbury, Salisbury, Wilts SP4 7BH, UK, **t** (01980) 626 361, *www.travelwithcare.co.uk*. Has a good range of travel accessories, including flight socks.
InterHealth (*see* above). Travel service which also has a range of health equipment.
MASTA (*see* above). Sells AIDS kits, anti-mosquito anklets, etc.
MASTA Travel Clinics (*see* above). Sells malaria prophylaxis memory cards, nets and net treatment kits.
Medex Assistance Corp. (*see* above). Sells safe medical kits.
Medic Alert Foundation, Freepost, 1 Bridge Warf, 156 Caledonian Road, London N1 9BR, UK, **t** 0800 581 420, or: **Medic Alert Foundation International**, Turlock, CA 95380-1009, **US t** (209) 668 3333 or **t** (toll-free) 1 800 344 3226. Supplies bracelets alerting medics to medical conditions; allow 28 days.
Mountain Equipment Co-op, (mail orders) 130 W. Broadway, Vancouver, BC Canada V5Y 1P3, **f** (in N. America) 1 800 722 1960; **f** (local/intl) (604) 876 6590; **t** (in N. America) 1 800 663 2667; **t** (local/intl) (604) 876 6221, *www.mec.ca*. Lifetime membership is $5. Good range of equipment for self-propelled wilderness activities.
New Angle Products, Box 25641, Chicago, IL 60625, **US t** (773) 293 2655; *www.whizzy4you.com*. Produces the Whizzy, a disposable, foldable device allowing you to pee while standing up.
Nomad, UK t (020) 8889 7014, **f** (020) 889 9529. Millbank bags and water filters, among other supplies (*see* above).
SafariQuip, The Stones, Castleton, Hope Valley, Derbyshire S33 8WX, UK, **t** (01433) 620 320, **f** (01433) 620 061, *www.safariquip.co.uk*. Mail-order travel accessories for water sterilization, bednets, first aid, etc.
Simpson-Lawrence, 218–28 Edmiston Drive, Glasgow G51 2YT, UK, **t** 0870 9000 0527. Adventure/survival supplies.
Young Explorers, The Minories, Stratford-upon-Avon CV37 6NF, UK, **t** (01789) 414 791, *www.youngexplorers.co.uk*.

Antivenom

Lister Institute of Preventative Medicine, Elstree, Herts WD6 3AX, UK. Stocks scorpion antivenom.

Contraception and feminine hygiene

Green Baby, 345 Upper St, London N1 3QP, UK, **t** (020) 7226 4345, *www.greenbabyco.com*.
Plush Pants, 55 Newlands Ave, Cheadle Hulme, Cheshire SK8 6NE, UK, **t** (0161) 485 4430, *www.plushpants.freeserve.co.uk/FOR_MUM.html*.
Quick and Direct, 137a Hersham Road, Walton-on-Thames, Surrey KT12 1RW, UK, **t** (01932) 232 443, *info@QuickandDirect.com*. Mail-order condoms in various sizes.

Twinkle Twinkle, Briley Cottage, Beggars Hill Rd, Lands End, Twyford RG10 0UB, UK, **t** (0118) 934 2120, *www.twinkleontheweb.co.uk*.

Yummies, 52 Holland St, Brighton BN2 9WB, UK, **t** (01273) 672 632, *www.yummiesnappies.co.uk/PROD_cloth_pads.html*. Sells washable sanitary cloth made in soft unbleached flannelette.

In-flight travel supplies

For flight-anxiety courses, *see* 'Courses', above, or contact the **Royal Free Travel Health Centre** (*see* above, p.327) which offers treatment by a team of psychologists.

Activa Healthcare Ltd, Units 26/27 Imex Business Park, Shobnall Rd, Burton-on-Trent, Staffs DE14 2AU, UK, **t** (01283) 540 957, **f** (01283) 845 361, *information@activa.uk.com*, *www.legshealth.com*. Produces flight socks.

Airogym, 10 Crystal Business Centre, Ramsgate Rd, Sandwich, Kent CT13 9QX, UK, **t** (01304) 614 650, *info@airogym.com*, *www.airogym.com*. Airogyms for £11 including postage and packing.

Aviation Health Institute, 8 King Edward St, Oxford, OX1 4HL, UK, **t** (01865) 715 999, **t (order hotline)** (01685) 202 708, **f** (01865) 726 583, *www.aviation-health.org*. Has an online shop selling travel products, e.g. masks to protect from in-flight infections.

Homeway Medical, West Amesbury, Salisbury, Wilts SP4 7BH, UK, **t** (01980) 626 361, *www.travelwithcare.co.uk*. Provides flight socks among other travel health accessories.

PharmWest, 520 Washington Blvd No. 401, Marina Del Rey, CA 90292, **US t** (310) 301 4015, **US f** (310) 577 0296; **Ireland t** 463 7317, **Ireland f** 463 7310, **UK t** (free) 800 8923 8923, *www.pharmwest.com*. Stocks melatonin for jet lag.

Pocket Gym Ltd, Corbin Way, Gore Cross Business Park, Bradpole, Bridport, Dorset DT6 3UX, UK, **t** (01308) 421 150 or **t (order hotline)** 0800 072 0898, *salespocketgym@btinternet.com*. Produces the pocket gym, priced at £17.95.

Scholl, **t** (0161) 654 3000, *www.schollflightsocks.co.uk*. Produces support stockings and flight socks.

Worldwide Health, Freepost, Alderney GY1 5SS, UK, **t** 08700 760 750. Stocks melatonin.

Teaching aids for expats

TALC (Teaching Aids at Low Cost), PO Box 49, St Albans, Herts, AL1 5TX, UK, **t** (01727) 853 869, **f** (01727) 846 852, *talc@talcuk.org*, *www.talcuk.org*. Sells oral rehydration measuring spoons, thermometers, distributes the classic book *Where there is no Doctor*, as well as *Where there is no Dentist* and other titles.

World-wide Education, 17 Blagrave St, Reading, Berks RG1 1QA, UK, **t** (0118) 958 9993, **f** (0118) 958 9994, *www.weshome.demon.co.uk*. Sells home school packages.

Travel insurance

Age Concern Insurance Services, Lowthian House, Market St, Preston PR1 2ET, **t** 0845 601 2234 (*lines open Mon–Fri 8am–8pm, Sat 9–5*). Covers almost anyone with very few exclusions; they have no age limits.

British Heart Foundation (*see* above). Has information on insurance for people with heart problems, including high blood pressure.

British Mountaineering Council (*see* above). Advises on insurance for mountaineers.

Club Direct Travel Insurance, Dominican House, St John St, Chichester, PO19 1TU, UK, **t** 0800 074 4558, *www.clubdirect.co.uk*. Cover up to age 74.

Columbus, 17 Devonshire Sq, London EC2M 4SQ, **t** 0845 330 7076, *www.columbusdirect.com*.

Coventry Travel Insurance, PO Box 163, Chichester, W. Sussex PO19 1BE, UK, **t** (01243) 621 010. Cover up to age 75.

Diabetes UK (*see* above). Offers travel insurance (but compare their rates).

Independent Travellers Insurance Services (ITIS), 363A Kenton Rd, Harrow HA3 0XS, UK, **t** 0870 241 0370, **f** 0870 241 1683 , *itis@dircon.co.uk*, *www.itis.dircon.co.uk*.

MEDEX Assistance Corporation (*see* above). Offers medical cover worldwide.

National Asthma Campaign (*see* above). Has information on insurance for asthmatics.

Options Insurance Services Ltd, Lumbry Park, Selborne Rd, Alton, Hampshire GU34 3HF, UK, **t** 0870 848 0870, *www.optionsinsurance.co.uk*. Cover up to the age of 84.

Perry Gamble, Broadway House, 112–34 The Broadway, London SW19 1RL, UK, **t** (020) 8542 1122. Cover up to age 79.

Saga Services, Saga Building, Middleburg Sq, Folkestone, Kent CT20 1AZ, **t** 0800 056 5464, *www.saga.co.uk*. Offers travel services, insurance and health information.

Travel Insurance Club Ltd, PO Box 67, Westcliff-on-Sea, Essex SS0 7LT, UK, **t** 0800 163 518, *www.ticdirect.co.uk*. Covers dangerous activities.

Travel Protection, 2nd Floor, Westgate House, 2–4 Queen St, Belfast, BT1 1EB, UK, **t** (02890) 320 797, *www.thetravelprotectiongroup.co.uk*. Cover up to age 75.

Tyser UK Ltd, Acorn House, Great Oaks, Basildon, Essex SS14 1AL, UK, **t** (01268) 284 361, *www.tyseruk.co.uk*. Insurers who are sympathetic to epileptics; they often offer cover with no extra loading.

Worldwide Travel Insurance Services Ltd, The Business Centre, 1–7 Commercial Rd, Paddock Wood, Tonbridge TN12 6YT, UK, **t** (01892) 833 338, *www.worldwideinsure.com*.

BIBLIOGRAPHY

I have drawn on standard medical texts and journals which are not listed here, so this is not a comprehensive reading list. It includes literature that supports some of the comments I have made (particularly when they have been controversial), or provides fuller descriptions of particular problems. I also write as J.M.Wilson.

General medical

Centers for Disease Control, *Health Information for International Travel.* The best English-language publication for up-to-date international disease risk information. Single copies available from CDC (*see* above, p.328); multiple copies are sold by the Superintendent of Documents, US Government Printing Office, Washington DC 20402; *see also www.cdc.gov/travel.*

Dawood, R. (ed.), *Travellers' Health* (2002; OUP). Each section is written by an expert, so a good text for professionals, but many lay readers find it intimidating.

Department of Health (UK), *Health Advice for Travellers: Anywhere in the World* (leaflet T5; Central Office of Information, HMSO). For lay readers. Includes forms **CM1** and **E111**, which enable holders (if British residents) to obtain emergency treatment in the EU. Available online at *www.doh.gov.uk/hat* or free via freephone **t** 0800 555 777, or from BAPS, Health Publications Unit, Heywood Stores, Manchester Rd, Heywood, Lancashire OL10 2PZ, UK; often available at UK Post Offices and clinics.

Department of Health (UK), *Health Information for Overseas Travel.* Text for medical professionals can be looked up at: *www.the-stationery-office.co.uk/doh/hinfo/index.htm.*

Lockie, C. et al., *Travel Medicine and Migrant Health* (2000; Churchill Livingstone, UK).

Ross Institute of Tropical Hygiene, *Preservation of Personal Health in Warm Climates* (1978). Advice aimed especially at long-term, remote stays.

Scurr, J.H. et al., 'Frequency and prevention of symptomless deep-vein thrombosis on long-haul flights: randomised trial', *Lancet* 12 May 2001 **357** 1485–9 (2001).

Warrell, D. & Anderson, S., *Expedition Medicine* (1998; Royal Geographical Society, London; Profile Books, London). Good for large expeditions. Call **UK t** (020) 8324 5530.

WHO, *International Travel and Health* (2002; WHO Publications, Geneva, Switzerland; HMSO, UK). Comprehensive and authoritive. View at *www.who.int/ith.*

Wilson-Howarth, J. & Ellis, M., *Your Child's Health Abroad* (1998; Bradt Publications, UK; Globe Pequot, USA). A manual for travelling parents; still – I feel – the only comprehensive medical guide for families. See *www.bradt-travelguides.com.*

'Features', 'Getting Ready' and 'Immunizations by Region'

Anon, 'Typhoid vaccination: weighing the options', *Lancet* **340** 341–2 (1992).

Barnett, E.D. & Chen, R., 'Children and international travel: immunizations', *The Pediatric Infectious Disease Journal* **14** (11) 982–992 (1995).

Hoke C.H., Nisalak, A., Sangawhips, N. et al, 'Protection against Japanese encephalitis by inactivated vaccines', *New England Journal of Medicine* **319** 608–14 (1988).

Ruff, T.A., Eisen, D., Fuller, A. & Kass, R., 'Adverse reactions to Japanese encephalitis vaccine', *Lancet* **338** 881–2 (1991).

Rowlands, E., *Weather to Travel* (2001; Tomorrows Guides, Hungerford).

Tucker, S., *Have Toddler Will Travel: the complete survival guide for holidays at home and abroad* (2002; Hodder). A 448-page tome stuffed full of useful information.

'Special Travellers'

Royal College of Obstetricians, *Travelling in Pregnancy*. Copies available from RCOG, 27 Sussex Place, Regents Park, London NW1 4RG, **UK t** (020) 7262 5425.

Sinclair, J., 'Travelling with diabetes', *Journal British Travel Health Association*, **1** 27–31 (2000).

'Medicines'

Anon, '"Mexican aspirin" – a "stronger" variety of aspirin', *Southern Medical Journal* **89** 612–14 (1996).

Illingworth, R. (ed. Warrell, D. & Anderson, S.), 'Expedition Medical Kits', *Expedition Medicine* (1998).

Melchart, D., Linde, K. and Kaesmayr, J., 'Echinacea for preventing and treating the common cold' (Cochrane Review), *The Cochrane Library* **issue 4** 2001 (2001; Oxford: Update Software).

'Flight'

Bor, R., Josse, J. & Palmer, S., *Stress-free Flying* (2000; Quay Books, Wiltshire).
Spitzer R.L., et al, 'Jet lag: clinical features, validation of a new syndrome-specific scale, and a lack of response to melatonin in a randomised, double-blind trial', *American J Psychiatry* **156** 1392–6 (1999).

'Bowels' and 'Worms, Guts and Nutrition'

Chiodini, P.L., 'A "new parasite": human infection with *Cyclospora*', *Transactions Royal Society of Tropical Medicine & Hygiene* **88** 369–371 (1994).
Eastaugh, J. & Shepherd, S., 'Infectious and toxic syndromes from fish and shellfish consumption', *Archives of Internal Medicine* **149** 1735–40 (1989).
Khan, L.K., Li, R., Gootnnick, D., et al, 'Thyroid abnormalities related to iodine excess from water purification units', *Lancet* **352** (9139) 7 Nov 1998 (1998).
Rosenberg, M.L., Hazlet, Schaefer, K.K., J., Wells, J.G. & Pruneda, R.C., 'Shigellosis from swimming', *Journal American Medical Association* **236** 1849–52 (1976).
Steffan R., 'Rifaximin: a non-absorbed antimicrobial as a new tool for treatment of travelers' diarrhea', *Journal of Travel Medicine* **8, supplement 2** S34–9 (2001).
Wilson, J.M. & Chandler, G.N., 'Sustained improvements in hygiene behaviour amongst village women in Lombok, Indonesia', *Transactions Royal Society of Tropical Medicine & Hygiene* **87** 615–16 (1993).

'Malaria' and 'Biters and Insect-borne Diseases'

Barrett, P.J., Emmins, P.D., Clarke, P.D. & Bradley, D.J., 'Comparison of adverse events associated with use of *mefloquine* and combination of *chloroquine* and *proguanil* as antimalarial prophylaxis: a postal and telephone survey of travellers', *British Medical Journal* **313** 525–8 (1996).
Bradley, D.J. & Warhurst, D.C., 'Malaria prophylaxis: guidelines for travellers from Britain', *British Medical Journal* **310** 709–714 (1995).
Harrison, G., *Mosquitoes, Malaria and Man: a History of Hostilities Since 1880* (1978; John Murray).
Jelinek, T., Amsler, L., Grobusch, M.P. & Nothdurft, H.D., 'Self-use of rapid tests for malaria diagnosis by tourists', *Lancet* **354** 9190 (1999).
Layton, A.M. & Cunliffe, W.J., 'Phototoxic eruptions due to doxycyline: a dose related phenomenon', *Journal of Clinical and Experimental Dermatology* **18** 425–7 (1993).

'Hot Places' and 'Water'

Gowen, P., *Good Beach Guide* (1996, 1998; Norwich & Broadland Friends of the Earth, 38–40 Exchange St, Norwich NR2 1AX, **UK t** (01603) 625 394). Mainly covers Norfolk and Suffolk.
Tomchik, R.S., Russell, M.T., Szmant, A.M. & BlackN.A., 'Clinical perspectives on seabathers eruption, also known as "sea lice"', Journal *American Medical Association* **269** (13) 1669–72 (1993).

'High, Cold and Dark'

Bartsch P., Merki, B., Hofsteeter, D., Maggiorini, M., Kayser, B. & Oelz, O., 'Treatment of acute mountain sickness by stimulated descent', *British Medical Journal* **306** 1098–1101 (1993).
Bezruchka, S., *Altitude illness, prevention and treatment* (1994; The Mountaineers, 1011 SW Klickitat Way, Seattle, WA 98134, USA; Douglas & MacIntyre, Vancouver V5L 2H1, Canada; Cordee, Leicester LE1 7HD, UK, *www.cordee.co.uk*).
Deegan, P., *The Mountain Traveller's Handbook* (2002; The British Mountaineering Council, *www.thebmc.co.uk*; distributed by Cordee, Leicester LE1 7HD, *www.cordee.co.uk*).
Howarth, J.W., Hazards of trekking in Nepal, *Travel Medicine International* **15** 82–7 (1997).
Keller, H.-R., Maggiorini, M., Bartsch, P., & Oelz, O., 'Stimulated descent v *dexamethasone* in treatment of acute mountain sickness: a randomised trial', *British Medical Journal* **310** 1232–5 (1995).
Ng, J.D., White, L.J., Parmley, V.C., Hibickey, W., Carter, J. & Mather, T.H., 'Effect of simulated high altitude on patients who have had radial keratotomy', *Ophthalmology* **103** (3) 453–7 (1996).
Pollard, A.J. & Murdoch, D.R., *The High Altitude Medicine Handbook* (1997; Radcliffe Medical Press, Oxford).

Pollard, A.J. & Murdoch, D.R., 'Children in the mountains', *British Medical Journal* **316** 874 (1998).
Shlim, D. et al, 'Helicopter rescues and deaths among trekkers in Nepal', *Journal of the American Medical Association* **261** 1017–19 (1989).
White, A.J., 'Cognitive impairment of acute mountain sickness and *acetazolamide*', Aviation, *Space & Environmental Medicine* **July 1984**, 598–603 (1984).
Wilkerson J.A. (ed.), *Medicine for Mountaineering* (1985; The Mountaineers, 306 Second Ave. West, Seattle, WA 98119).

'Skin' and 'Sex'

Hardy, D.B., 'Cashew nut dermatitis: traveller beware', *Travel Medicine International* **11** (1) 9–11 (1993).
McCrae, A.W.R. & Visser, S.A., '*Paederus* in Uganda: outbreaks, clinical effects, extraction and bioassay of the vesicating toxin', *Annals of Tropical Medicine & Parasitology* **69** 109–20 (1975). Excellent paper on rove beetle blistering.
Sinclair, J., Cohen, J. & Hinton, E., 'Use of the oral contraceptive pill on treks and expeditions', *British Journal of Family Planning* **22** 123–6 (1996).

'Animals'

Bewes, P.C., 'Management of wounds', *Journal of Wound Care* **June**, 205–7 (1994).
Burford, T., *Backpacking in Central America* (1996; Bradt Publications, UK; Globe Pequot, USA).
Caras, R., *Dangerous to Man* (1975; Penguin).
Visscher, P.K., Vetter, R.S. & Camazine, S., 'Removing bee stings', *Lancet* August 1996, **348** 301–2 (1996).
Warrell, D.A. (ed. Weatherall, D.J., Ledingham, J.G.G. & Warrell, D.A.), *Venoms and Toxins of Animals and Plants in The Oxford Textbook of Medicine* (1987; OUP). Best review of the consequences of venomous bites, etc., but frightening clinical descriptions unmitigated by data on actual risks; it also lists antivenom sources.
Wilson, J.M., 'The scorpion story', *British Medical Journal* **295** 1642–4 (1987).
Wilson, J.M., 'A sting in the tail', *Lemurs of the Lost World: exploring the forests and crocodile caves of Madagascar* (1995; Impact Books, London). What a scorpion sting feels like. Also available from 33 Hartington Grove, Cambridge CB1 7UA.

'Ailments' and 'Accidents'

Dickson, M., *Where there is no Dentist* (1983; The Hesperian Foundation, California).
Werner, D., *Where there is no Doctor* (1977; The Hesperian Foundation, California).
Yin J.-P., 'CS gas injury to the eye: blowing dry air on to the eye is preferable to irrigation', *British Medical Journal* **311** 276 (1995).

'Expatriates' and 'Return'

Brouwer, M.L., Tolboom, J.J.M. & Hardeman J.H.J., 'Routine screening of children returning home from the tropics: retrospective study', *British Medical Journal* **318** 568–9, with comments in volume **319** 121 (1999).
Conlon C.J., Peto, T. & Ellis, C.J., 'Post-tropical screening is of little value unless the traveller feels unwell', *British Medical Journal* **307** 1108 (1993).
Day, J.H., Grant, A.D., Doherty, J.F., Chiodini, P.L. & Wright, S.G., 'Schistosomiasis in travellers returning from Africa', *British Medical Journal* **313** 268–9 (1996).
International Committee of the Red Cross, *Coping with Stress* (1997; ICRC, Geneva).
Ross Institute of Tropical Hygiene, *Preservation of Personal Health in Warm Climates* (1978). Advice aimed especially at long-term, remote stays.
Schouten, E.J., & Borgdorff, M., 'Increased mortaility among Dutch development workers', *British Medical Journal* **311** 1343–4 (1995).
Wilson-Howarth J. & Ellis, M., *Your Child's Health Abroad: a manual for travelling parents* (1998; Bradt Publications, UK; Globe Pequot, USA).
Wilson-Howarth J. & M Ellis, M., 'Illness in expatriate families in Kathmandu, Nepal', *Travel Medicine International* **15** 150–55 (1997).

INDEX

Generic names of drugs are in *italics*.